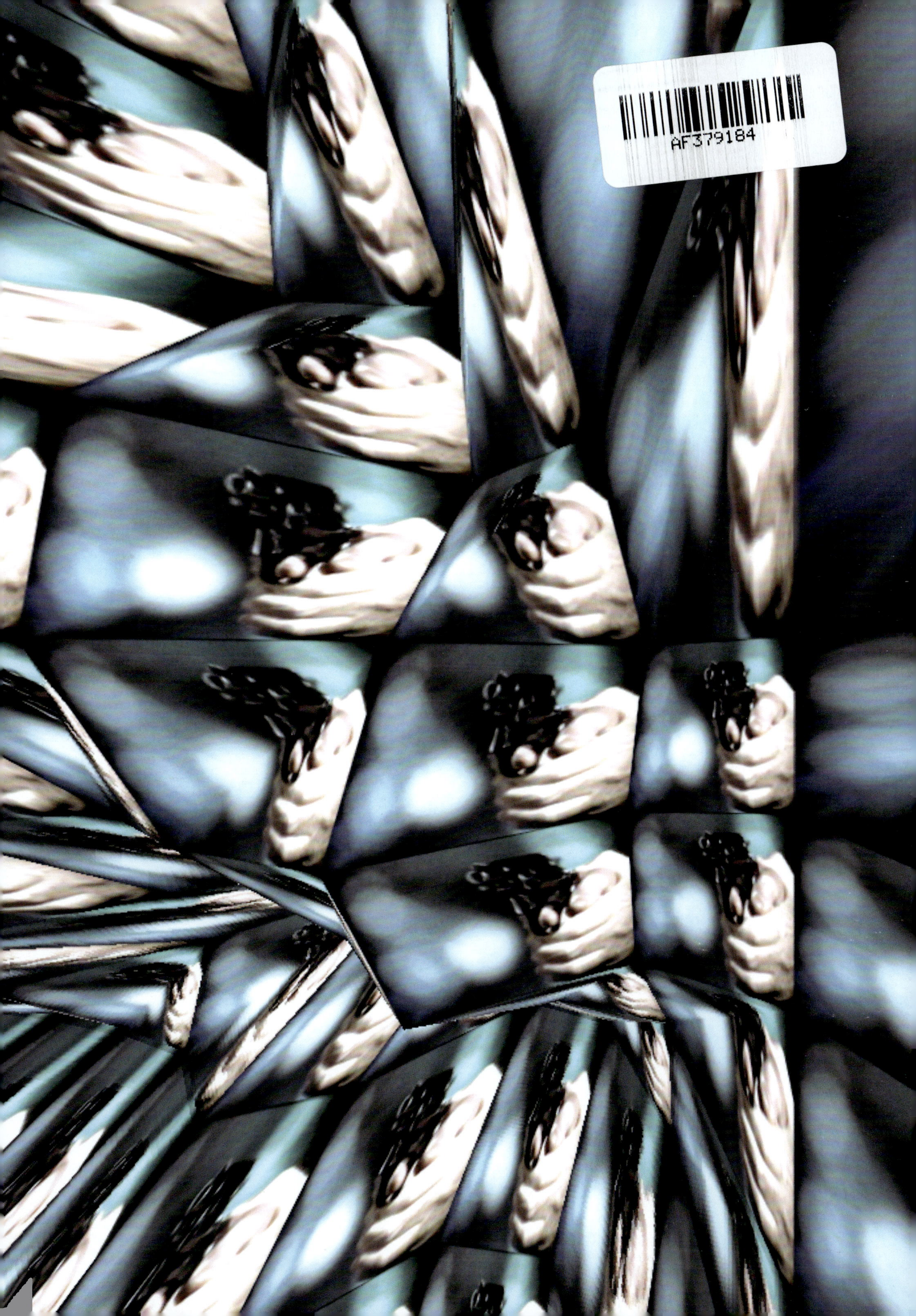
AF379184

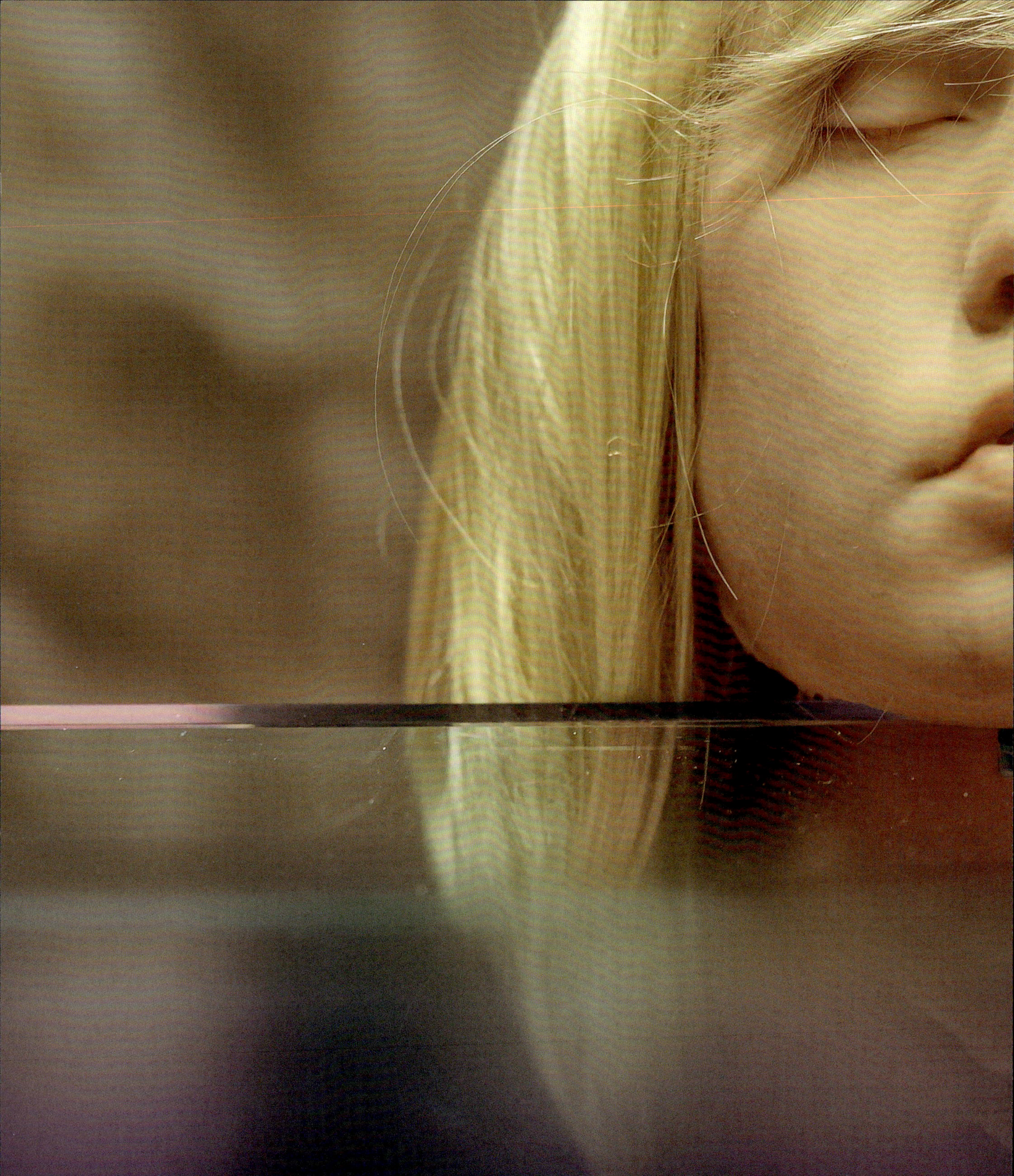

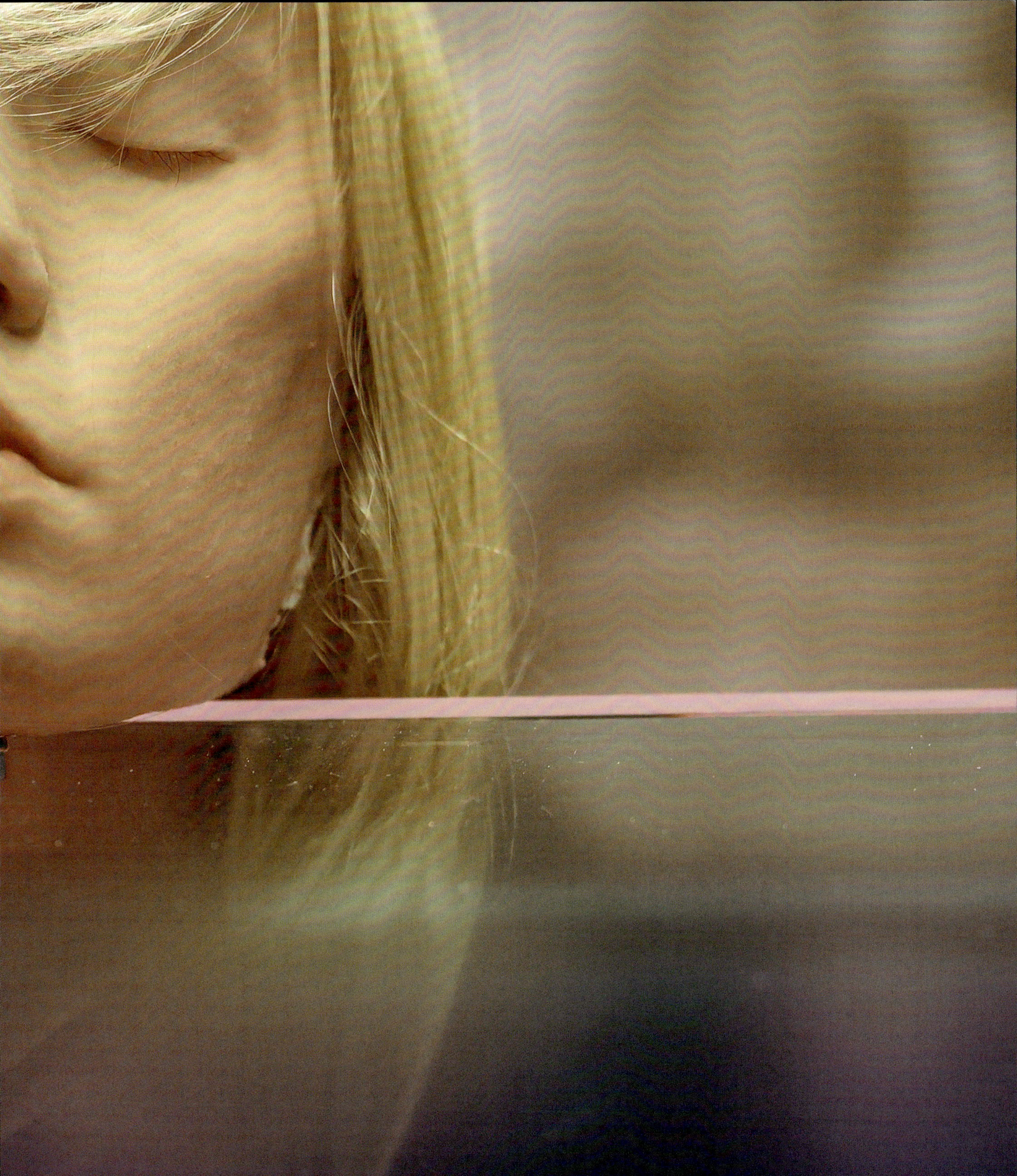

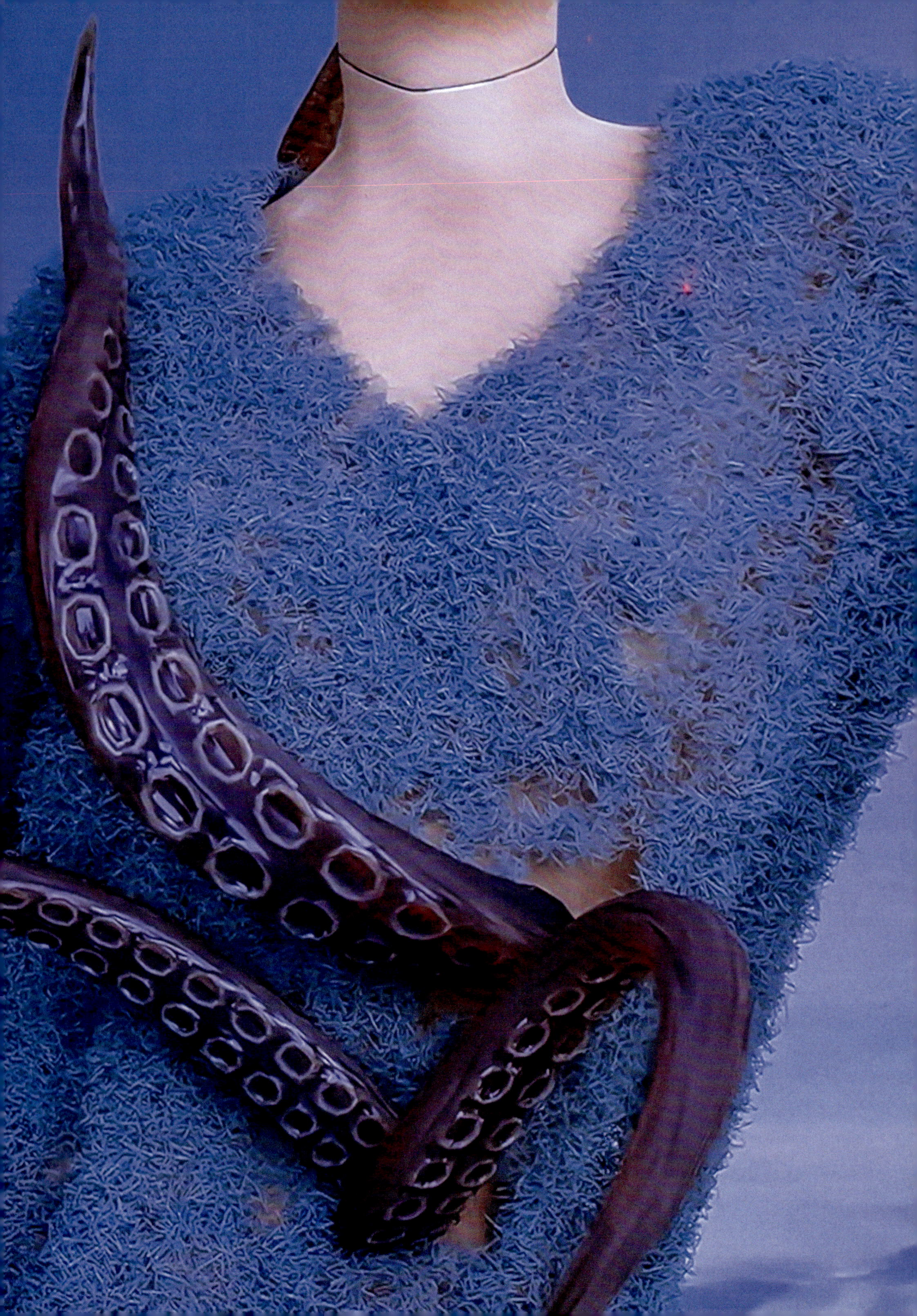

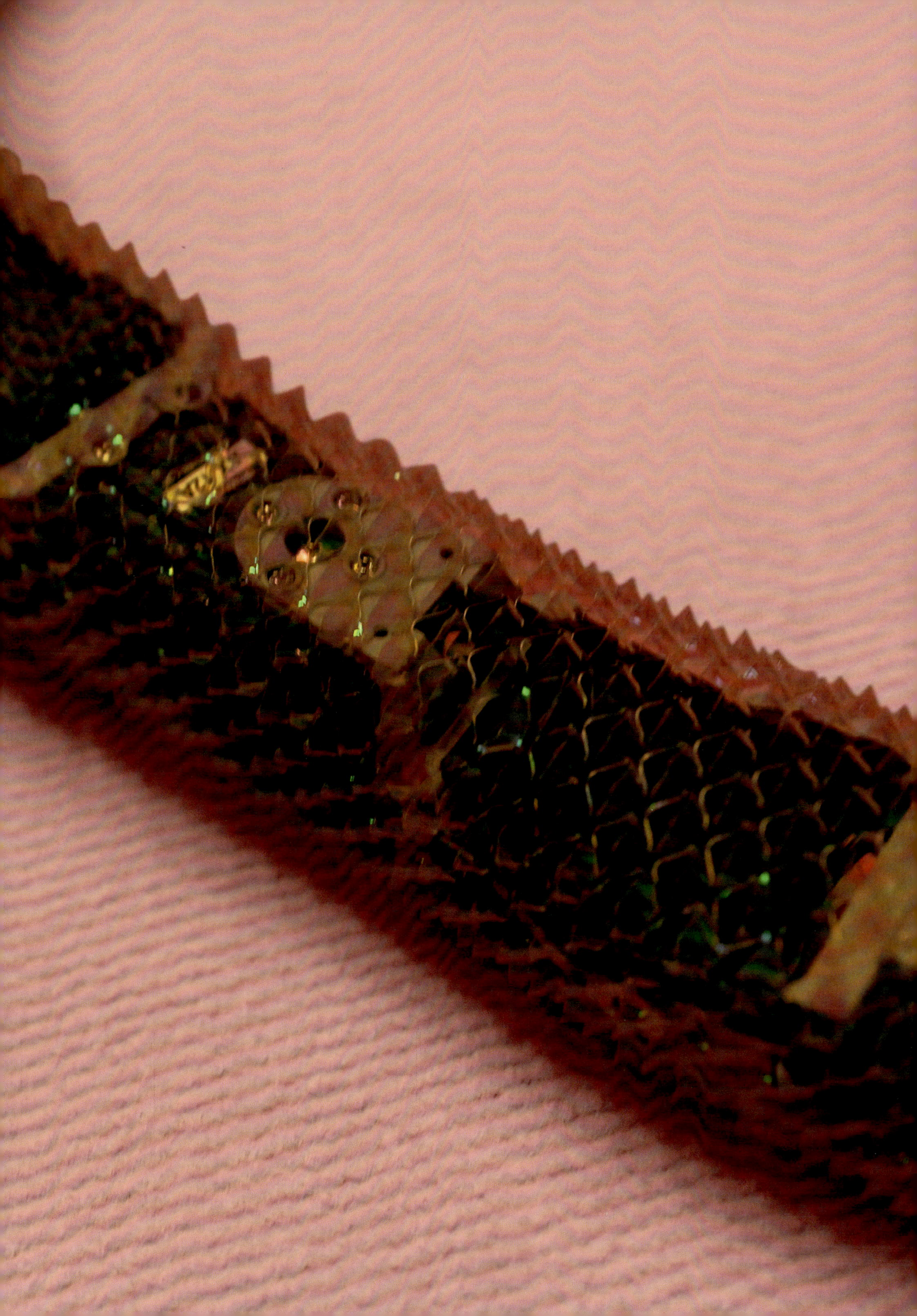

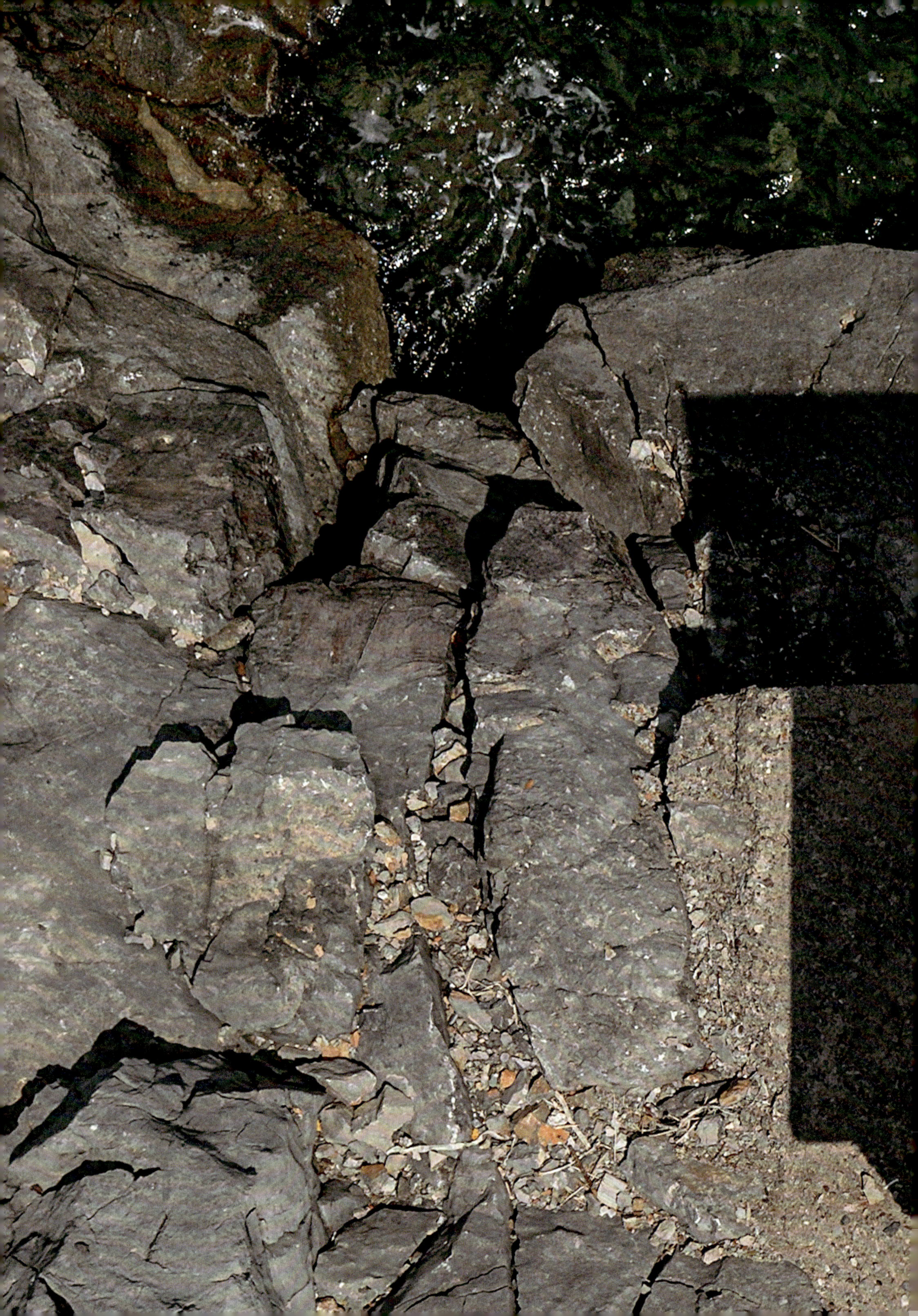

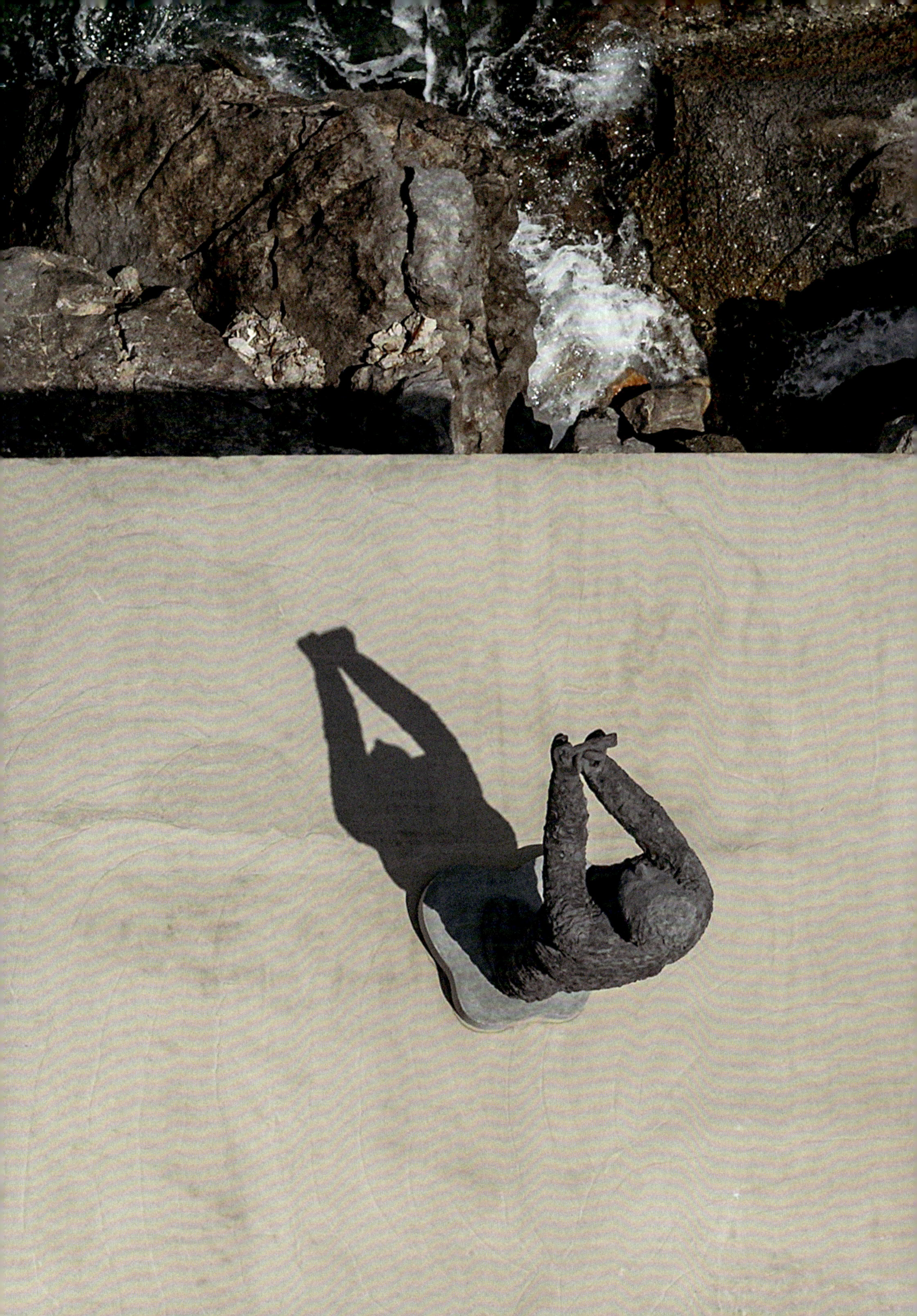

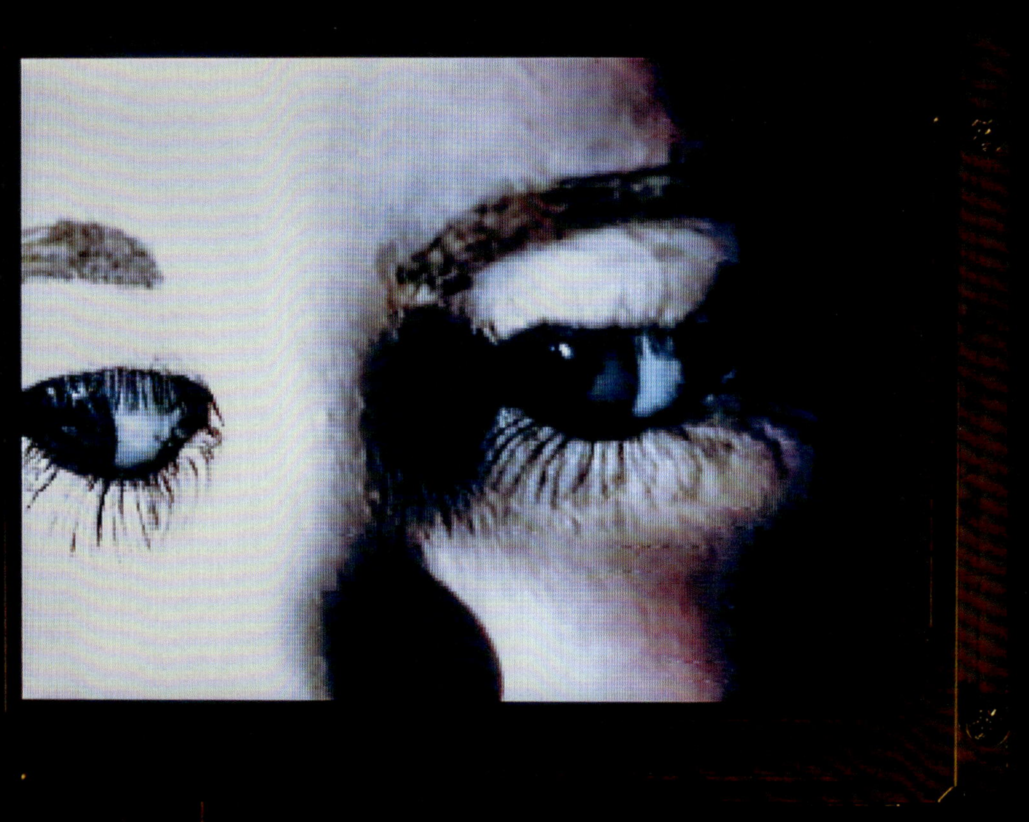

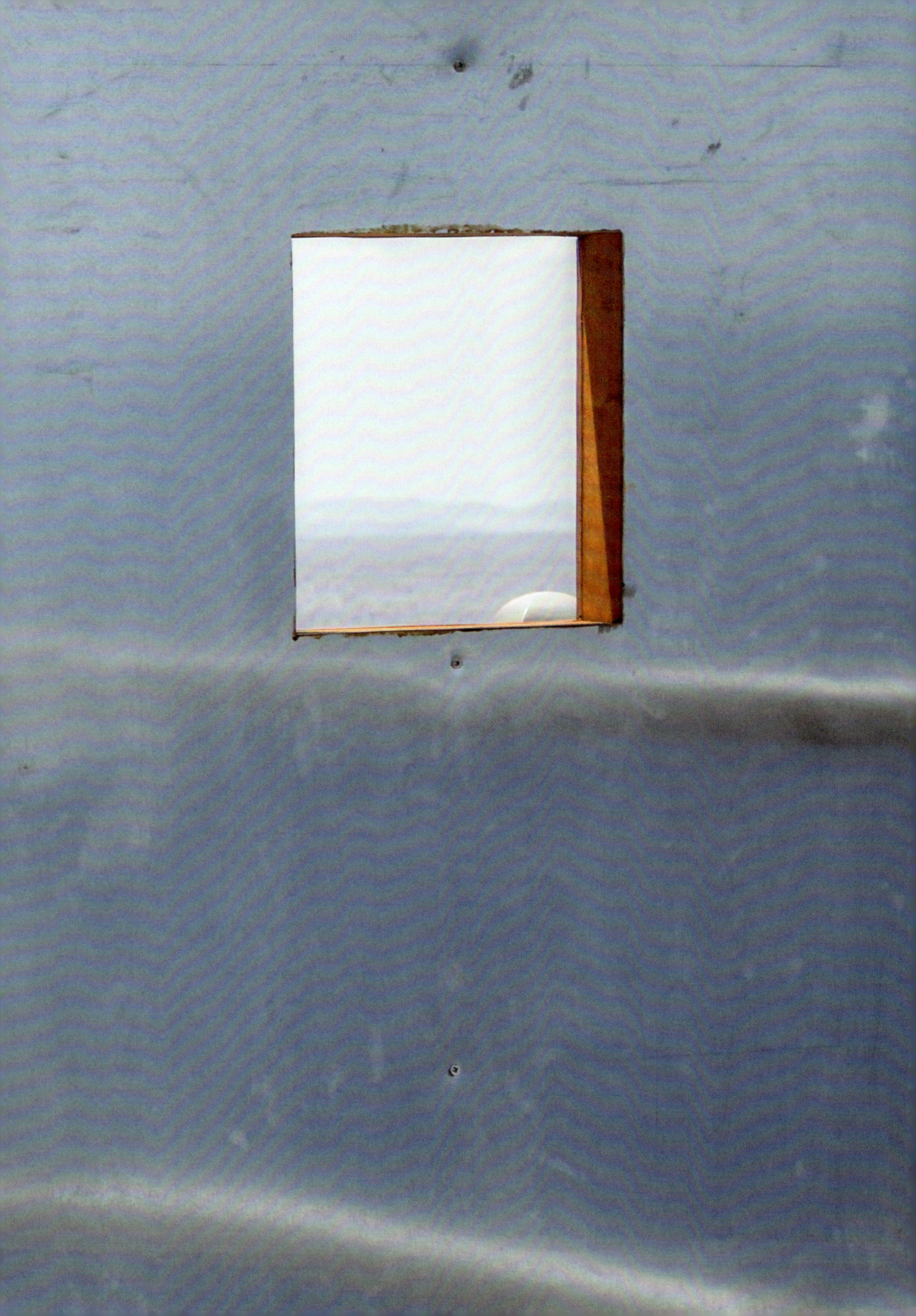

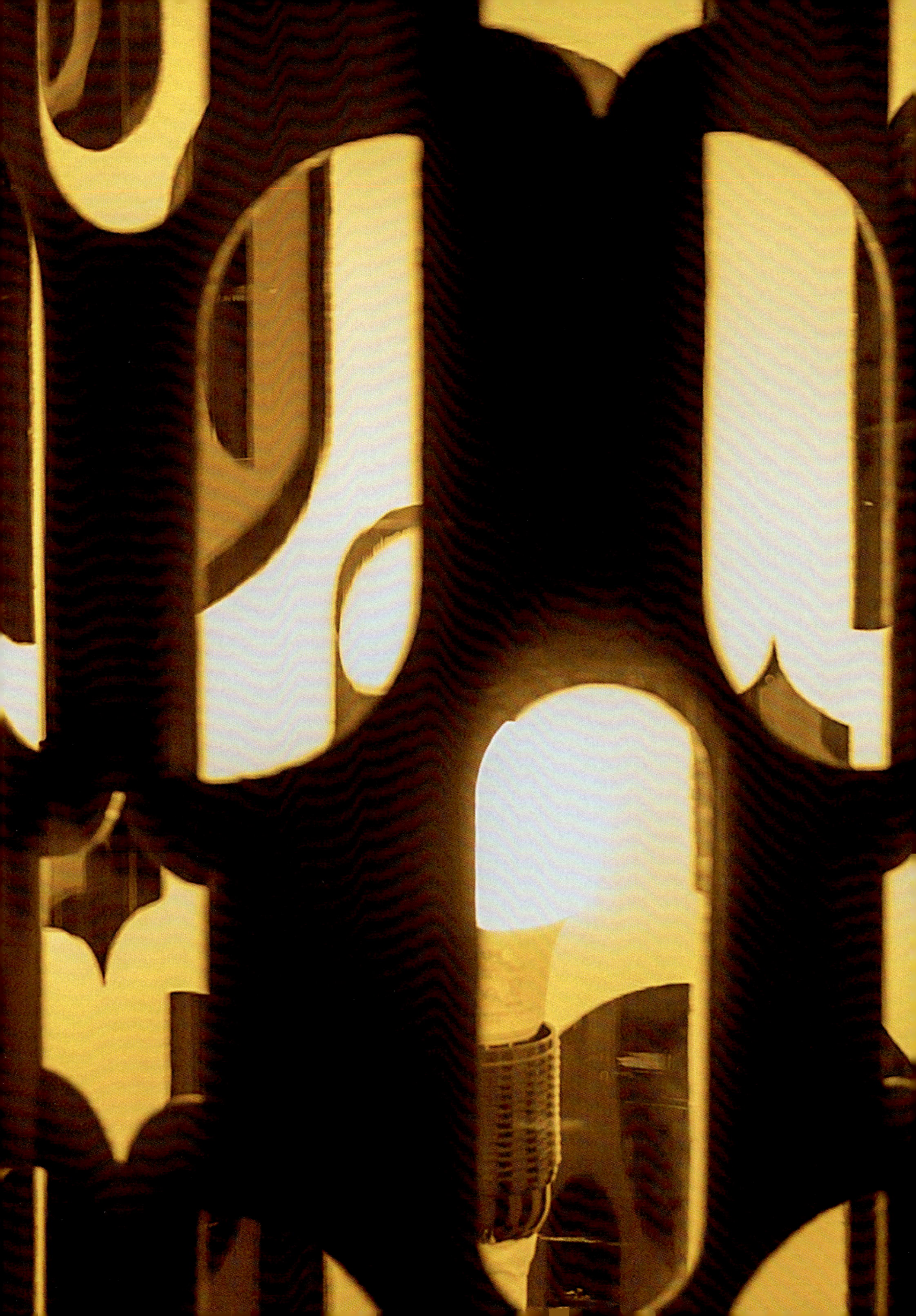

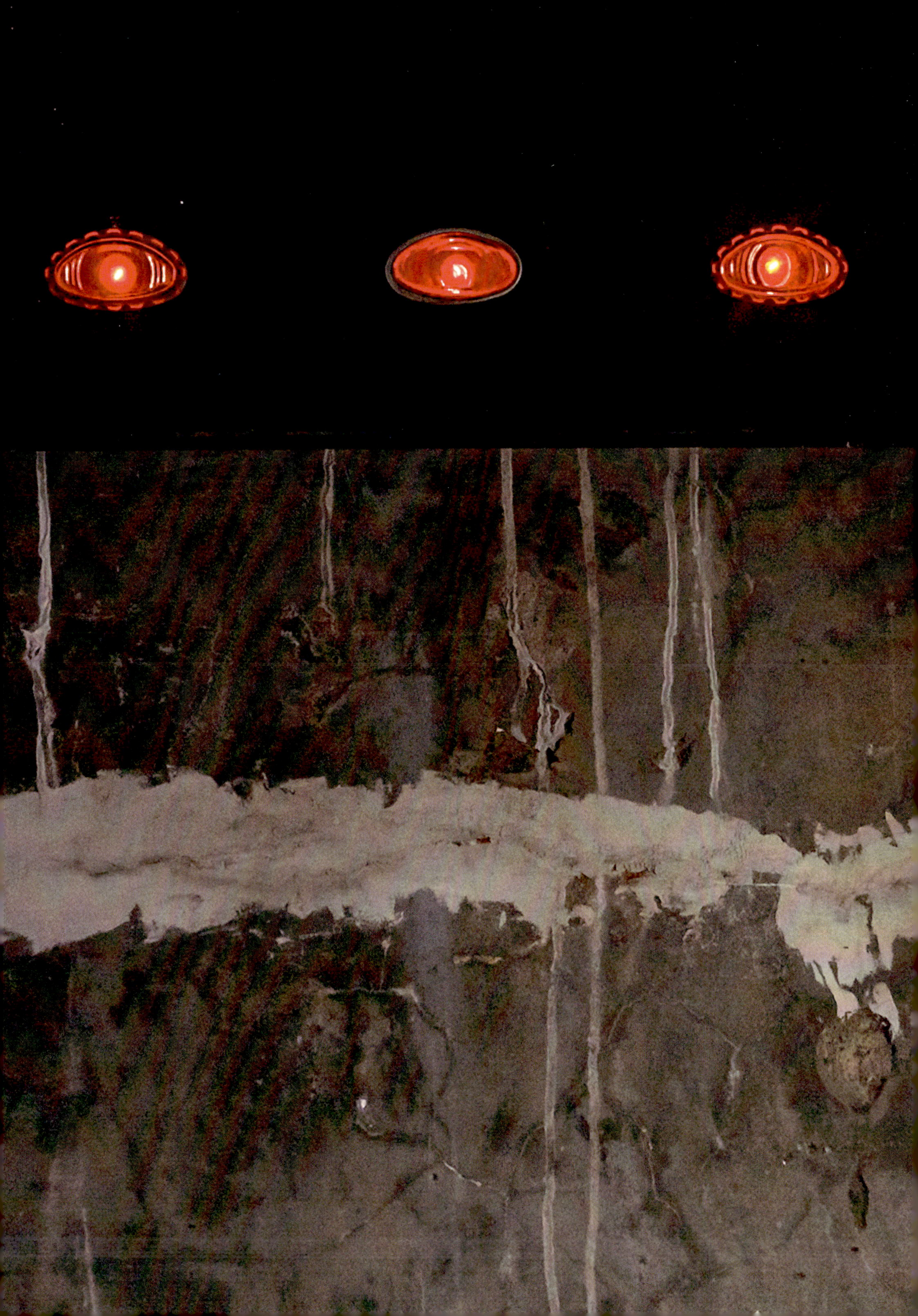

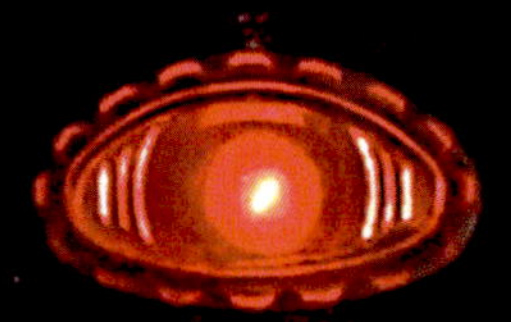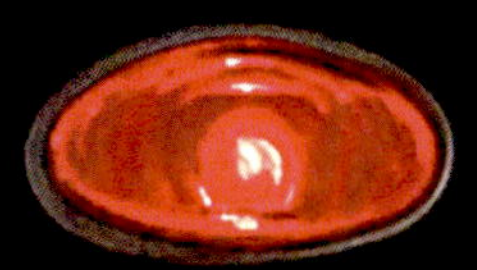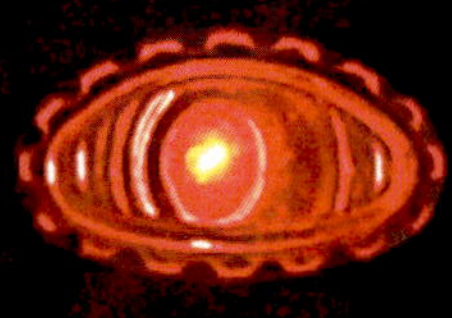

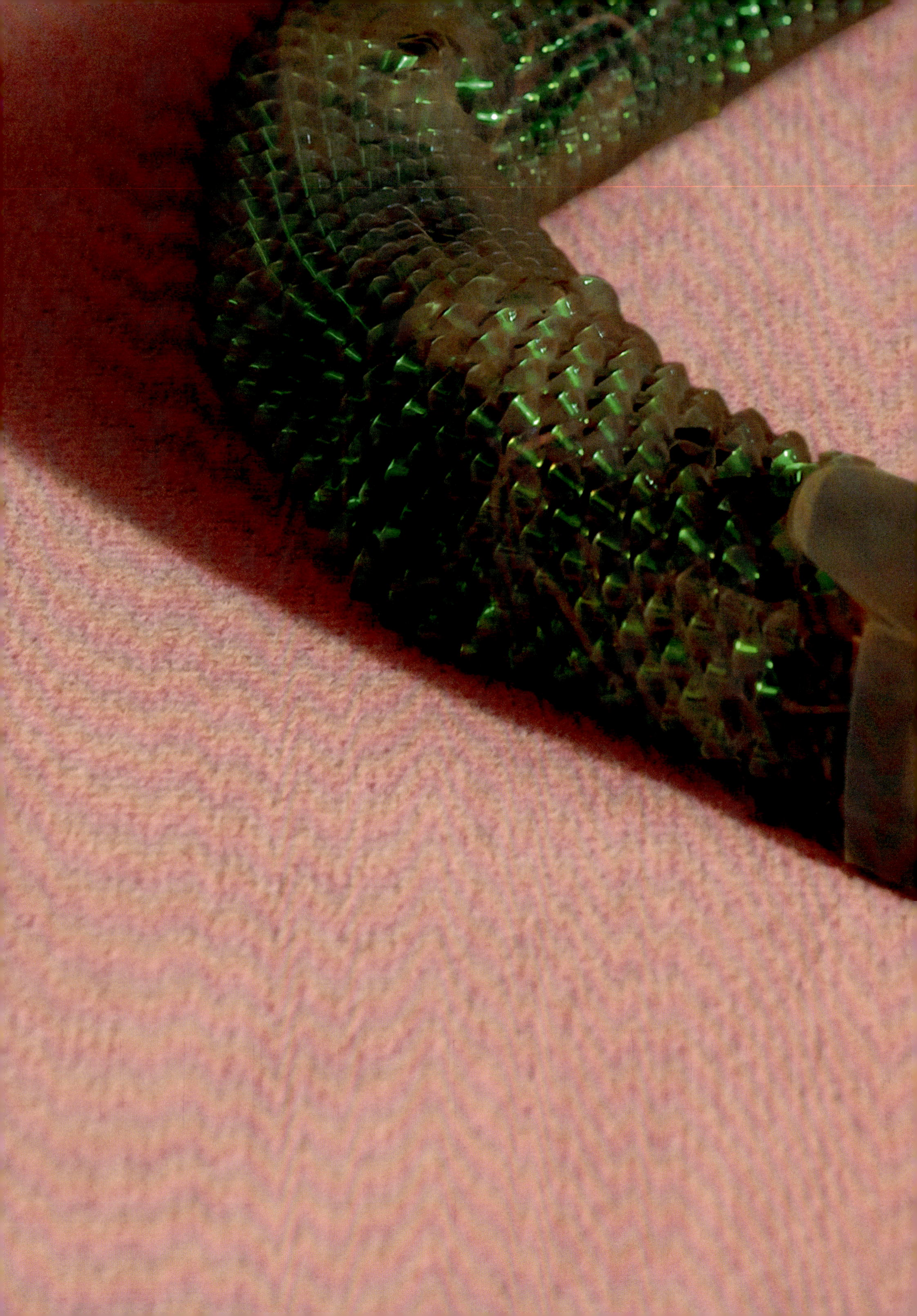

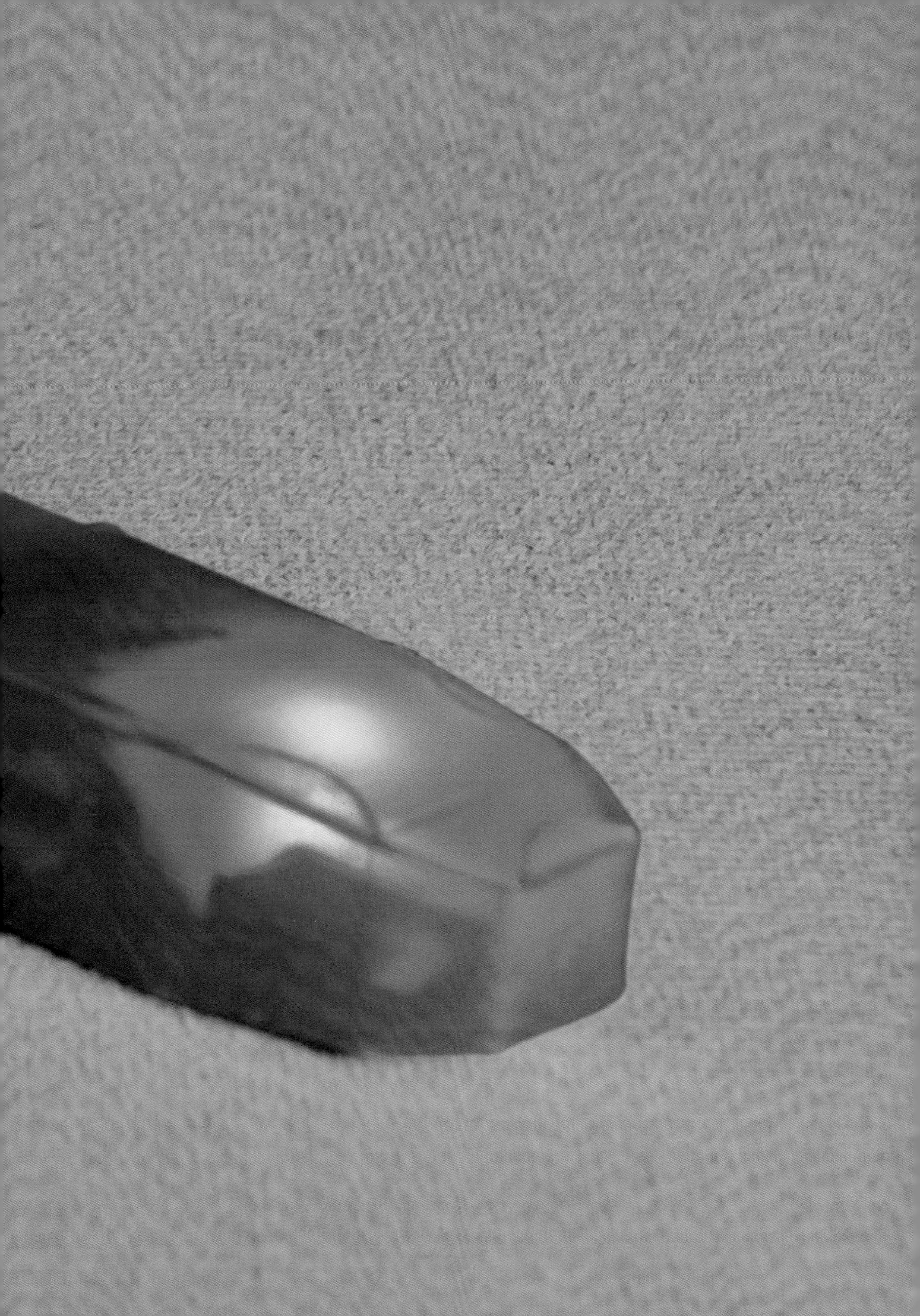

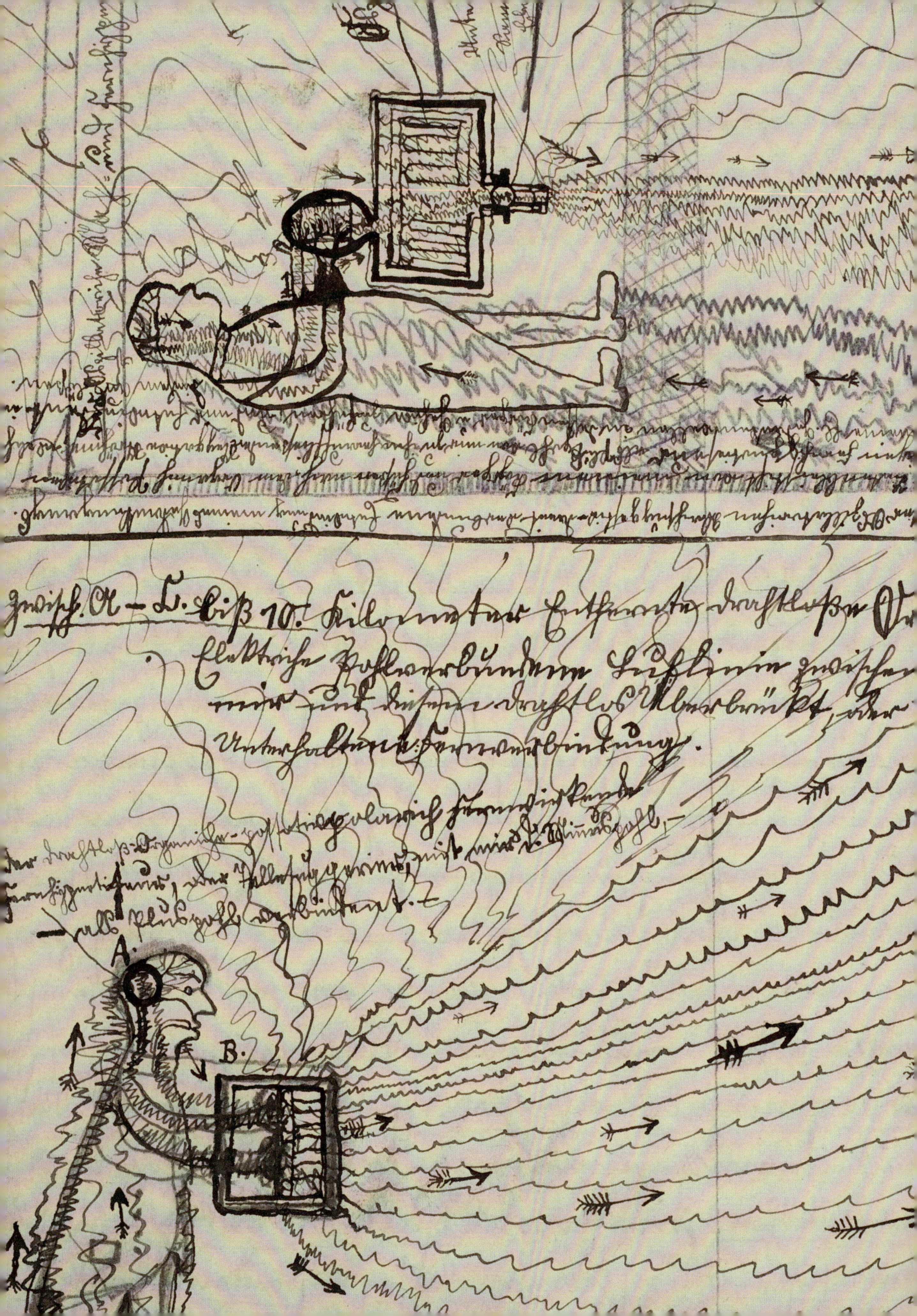

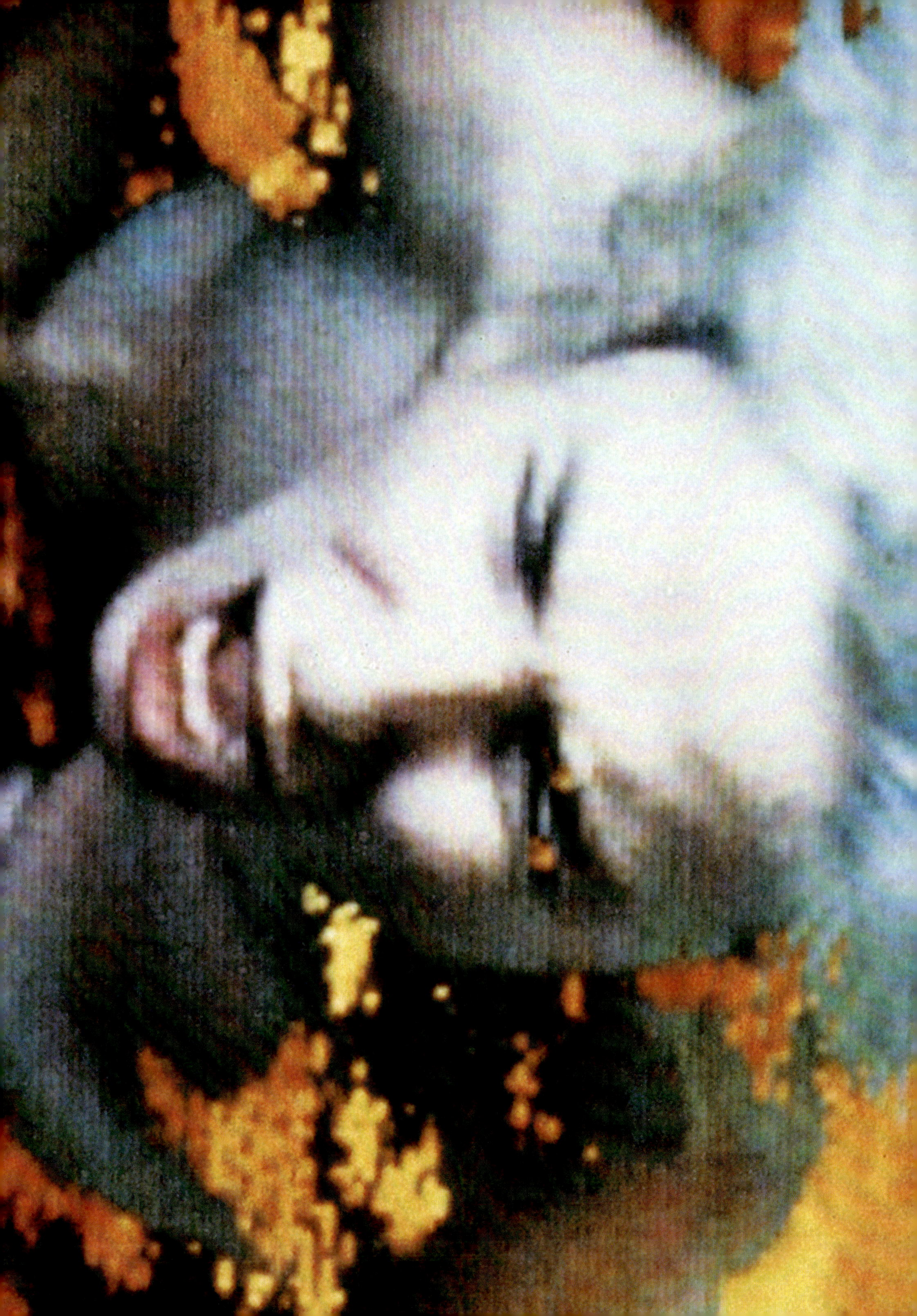

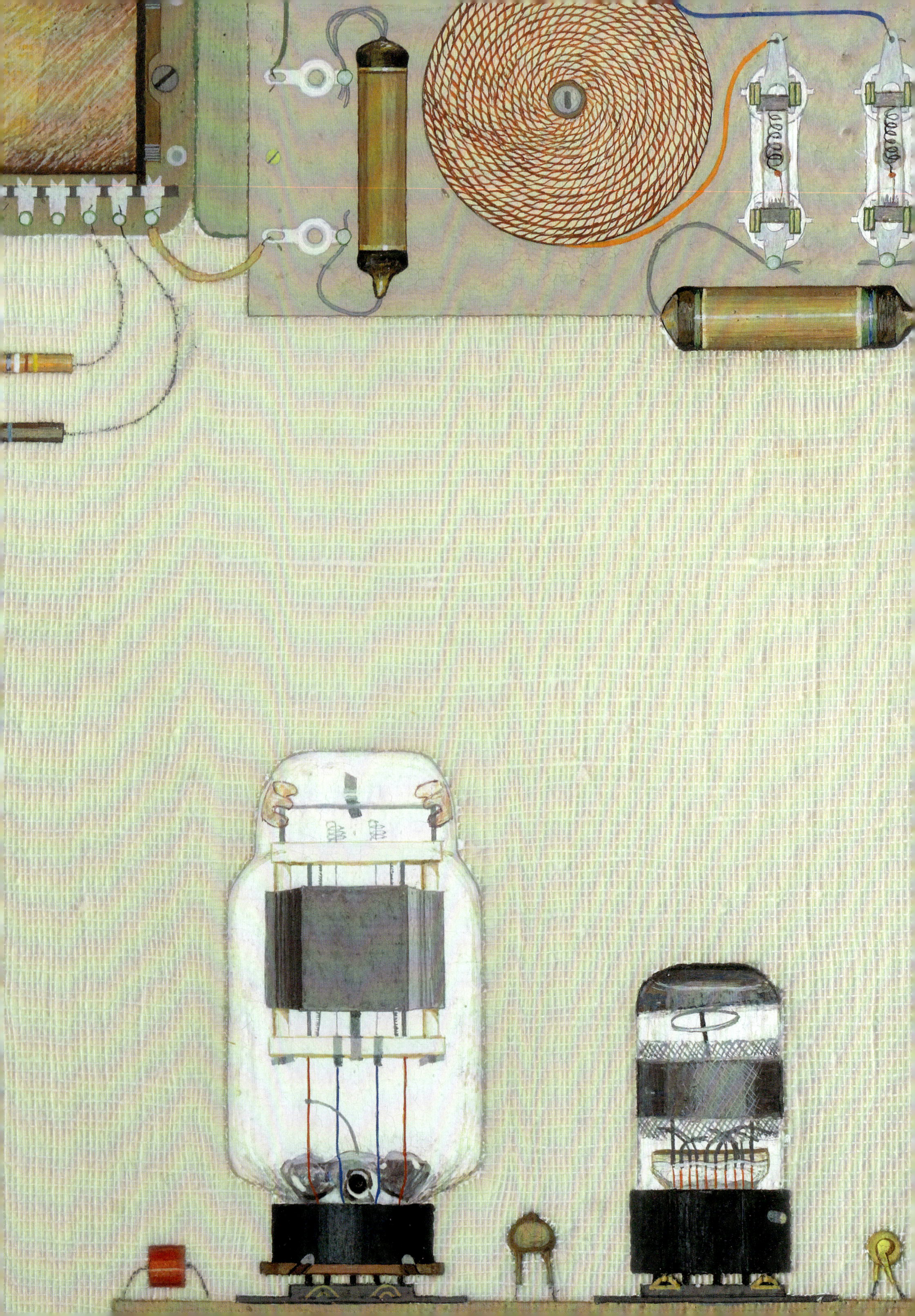

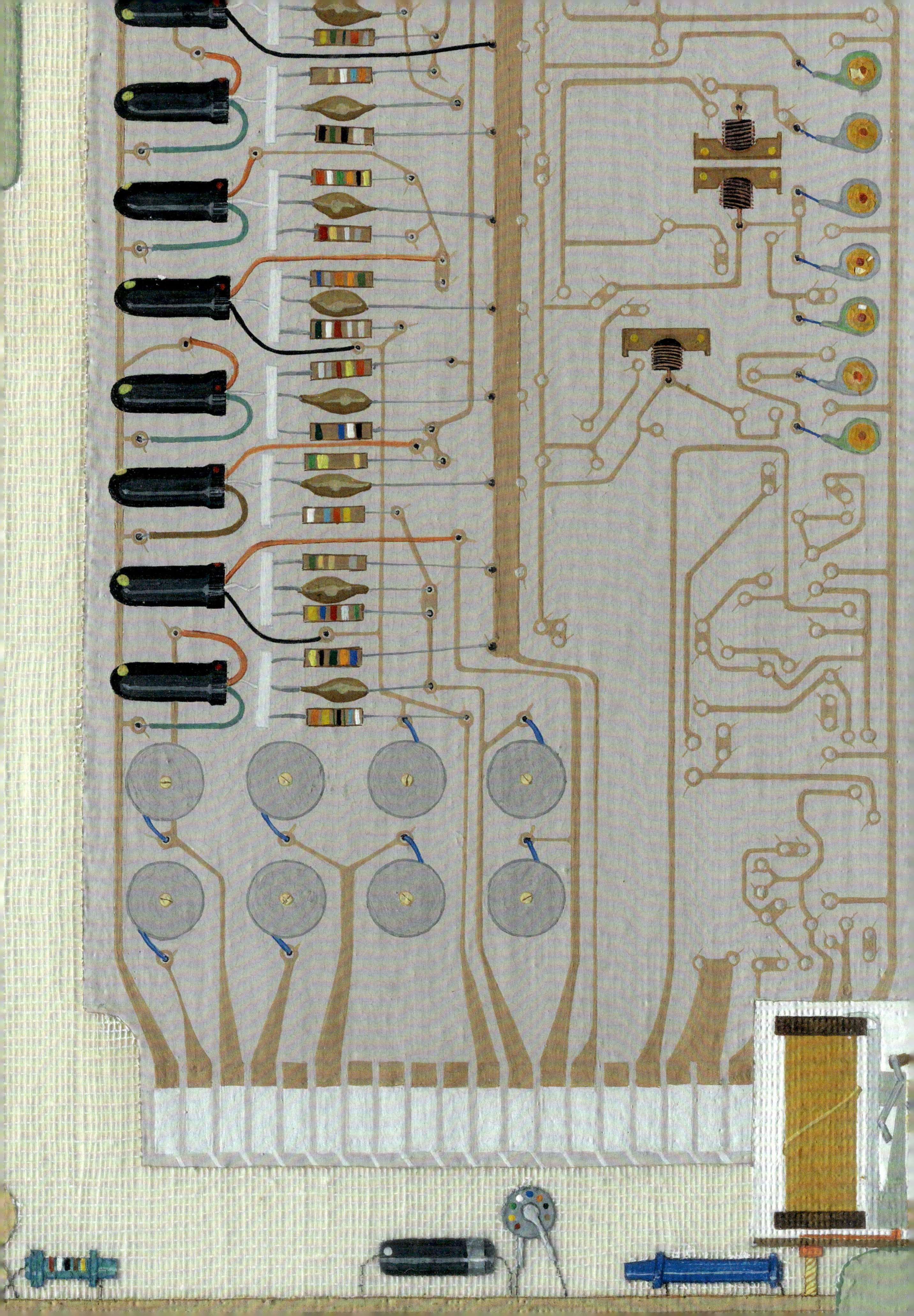

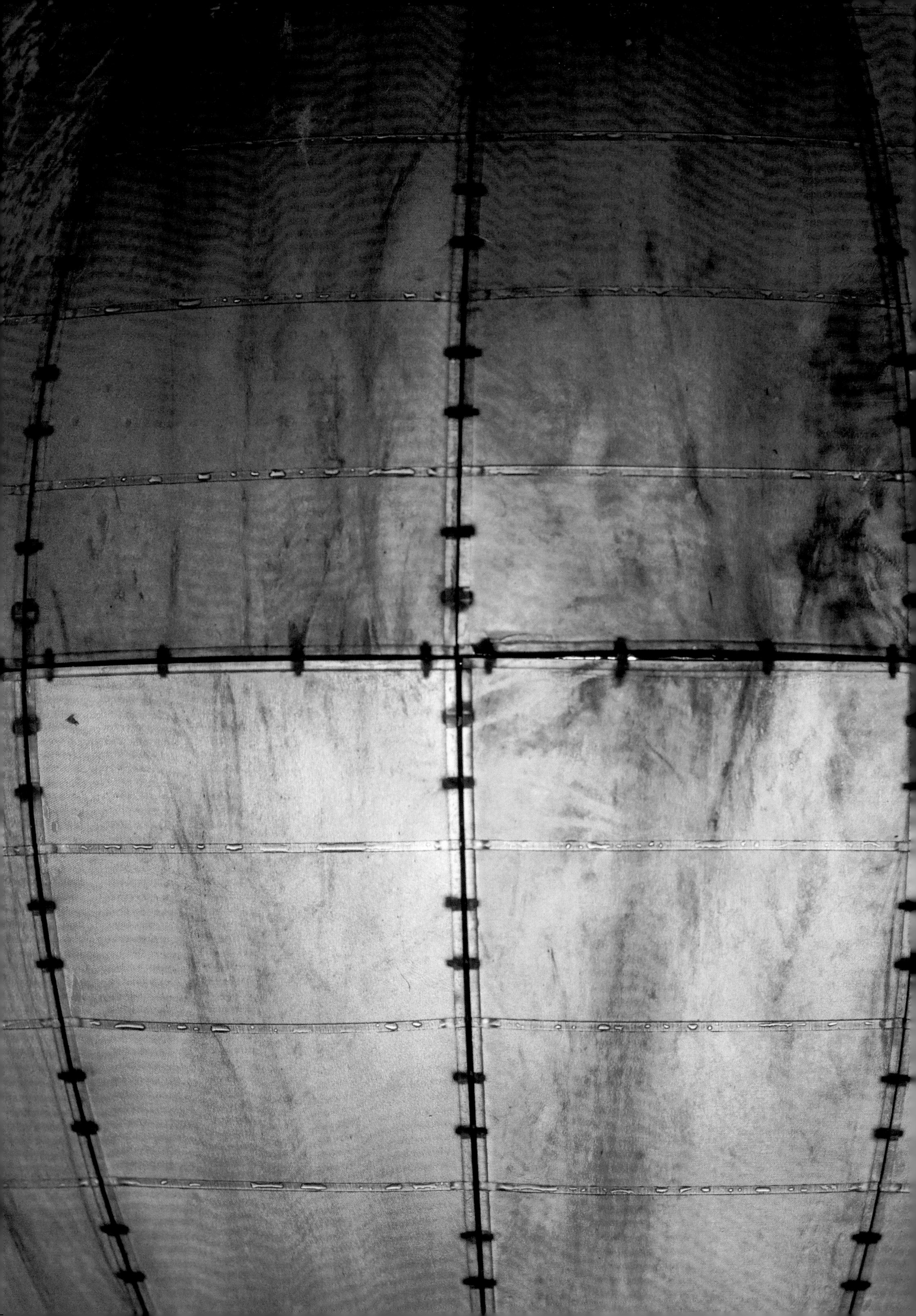

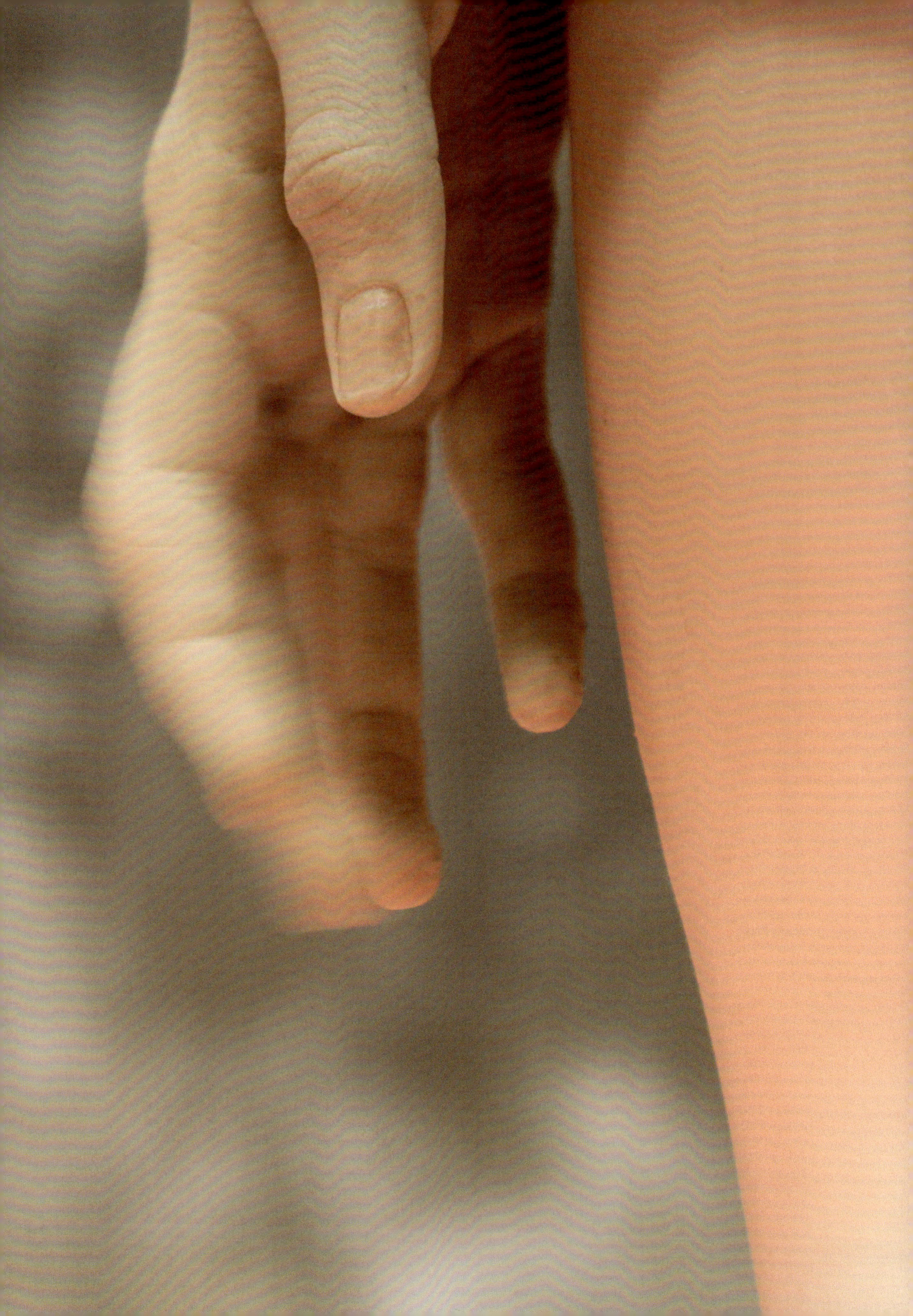

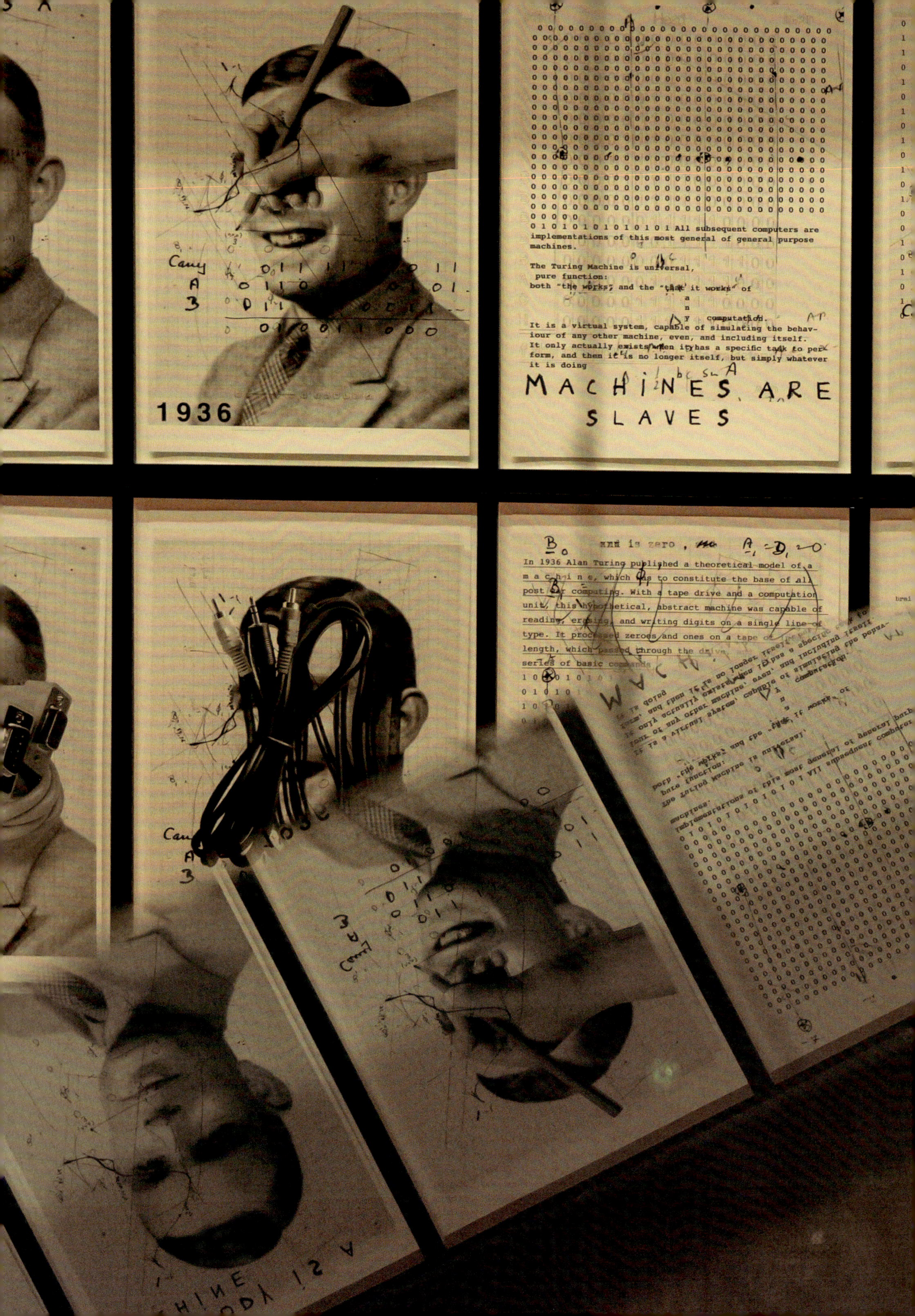
1936

0 1 0 1 0 1 0 1 0 1 0 1 All subsequent computers are
implementations of this most general of general purpose
machines.

The Turing Machine is universal,
pure function:
both "the works" and the "that it works" of
computation.
It is a virtual system, capable of simulating the behav-
iour of any other machine, even, and including itself.
It only actually exists when it has a specific task to per-
form, and then it is no longer itself, but simply whatever
it is doing

MACHINES ARE
SLAVES

In 1936 Alan Turing published a theoretical model of a
m a c h i n e, which was to constitute the base of all
post-war computing. With a tape drive and a computation
unit, this hypothetical, abstract machine was capable of
reading, erasing, and writing digits on a single line of
type. It processed zeroes and ones on a tape of
length, which passed through the drive
series of basic commands.

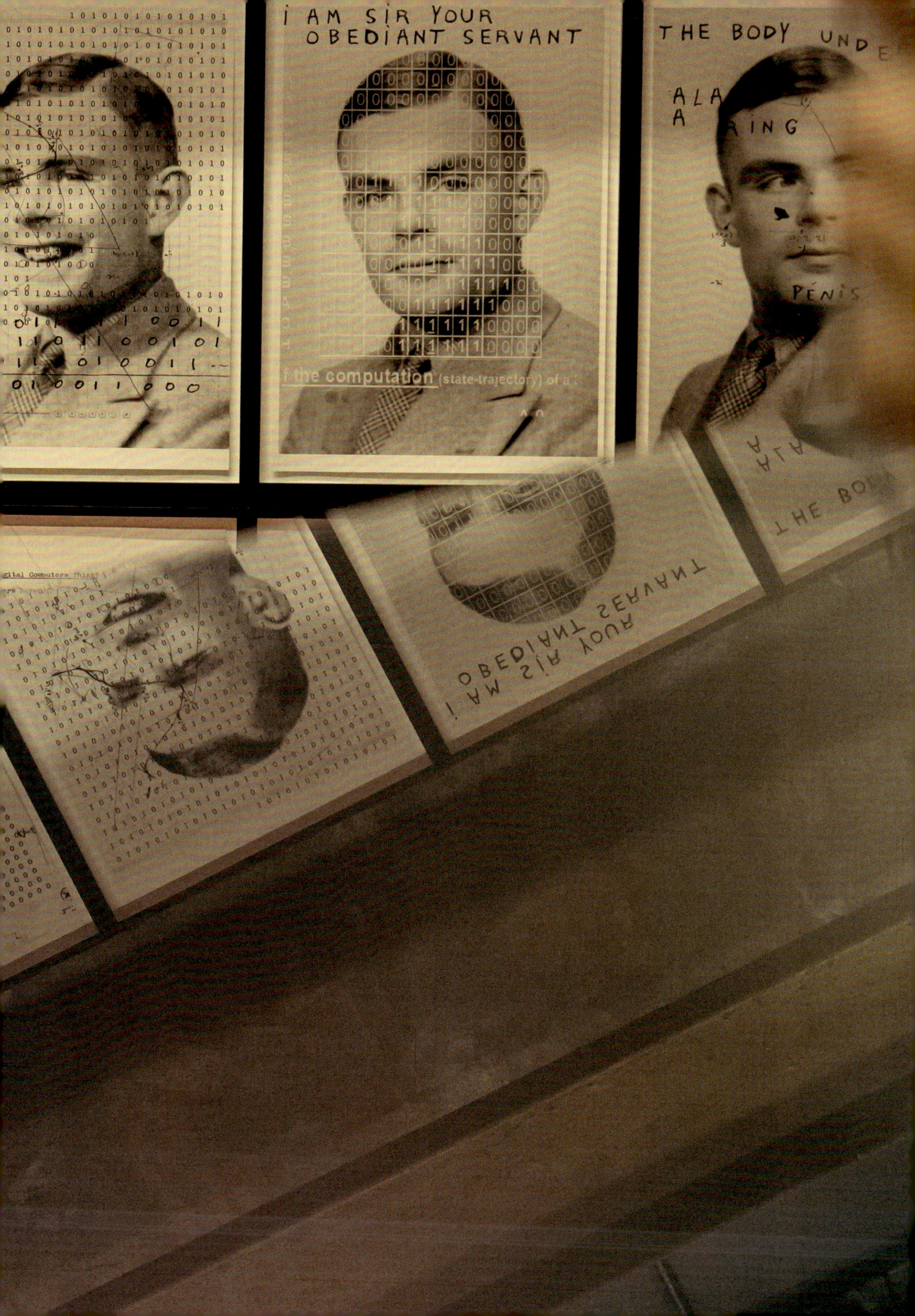

i AM SiR YOUR
OBEDIANT SERVANT
THE BODY UNDE
ALA
A   RING
PÉNIS
i the computation (state-trajectory) of a
gital Computers Think?

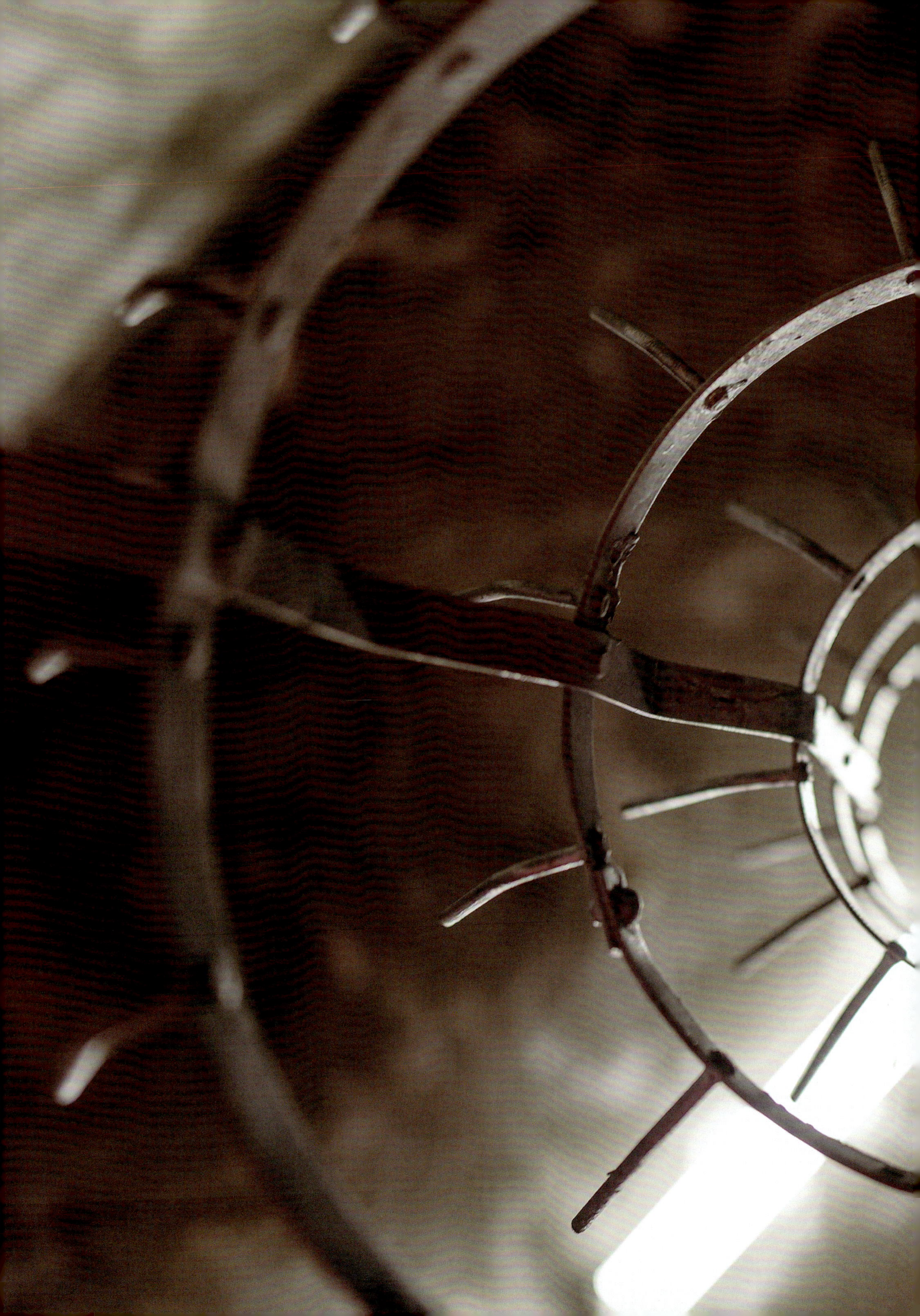

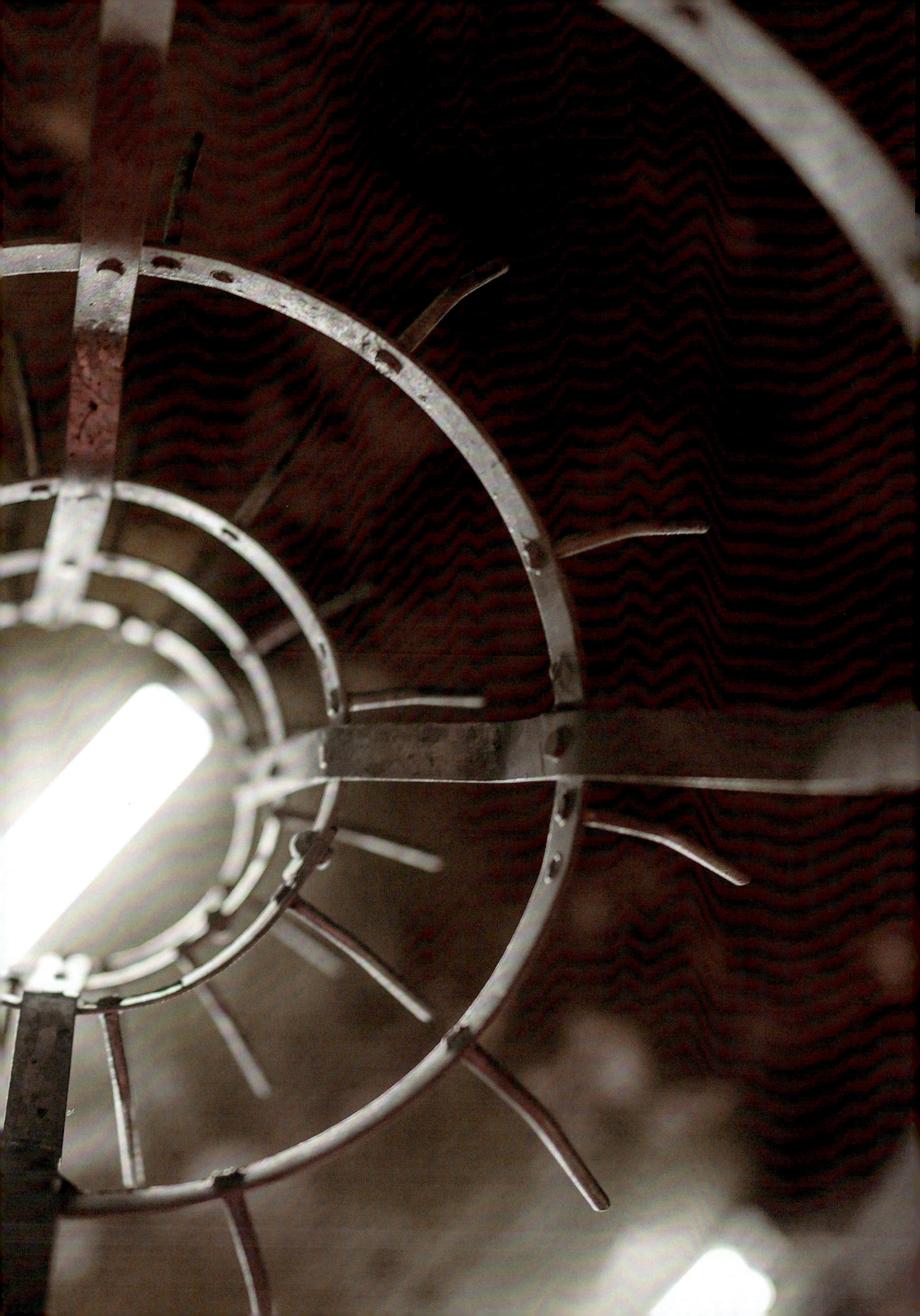

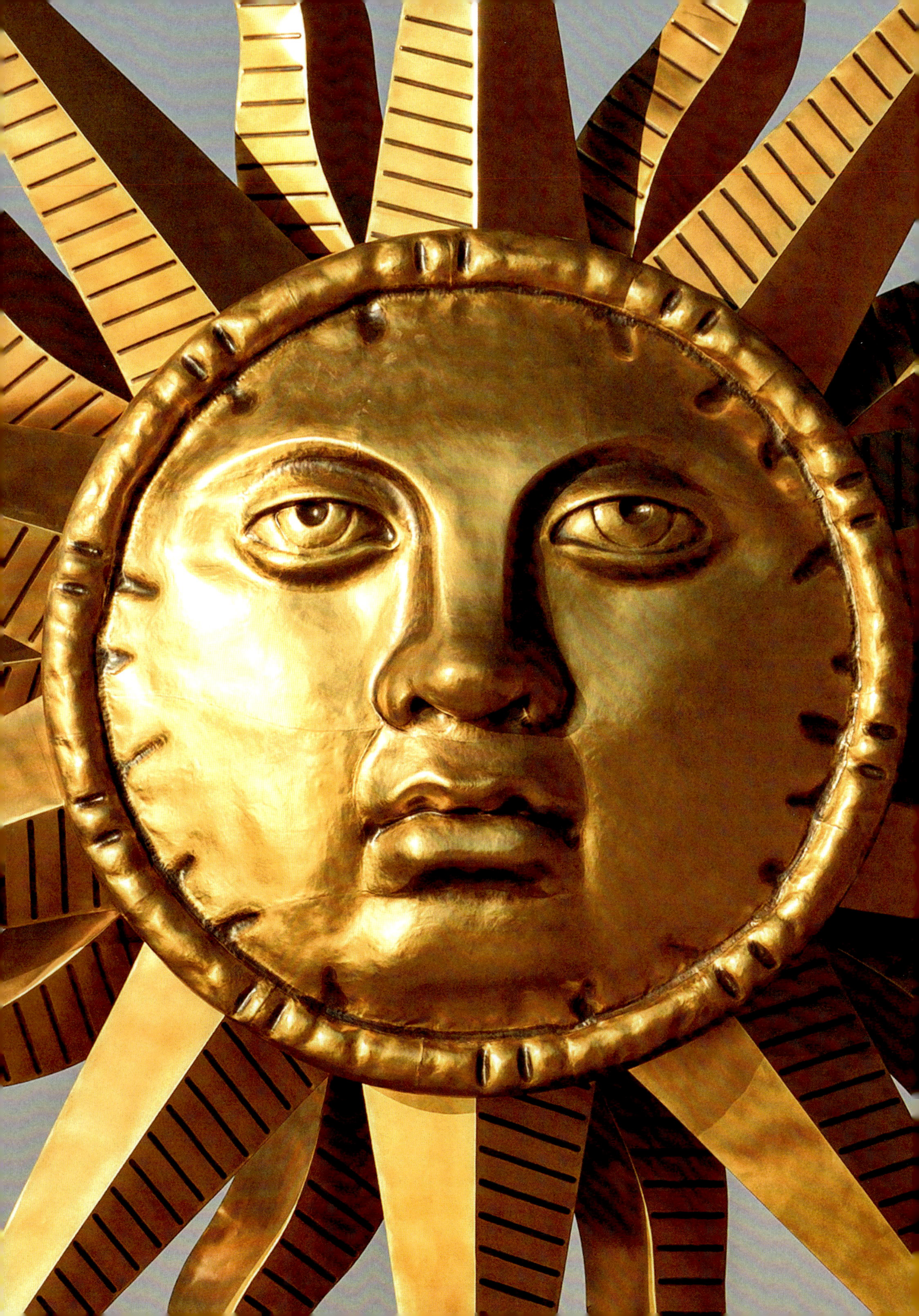

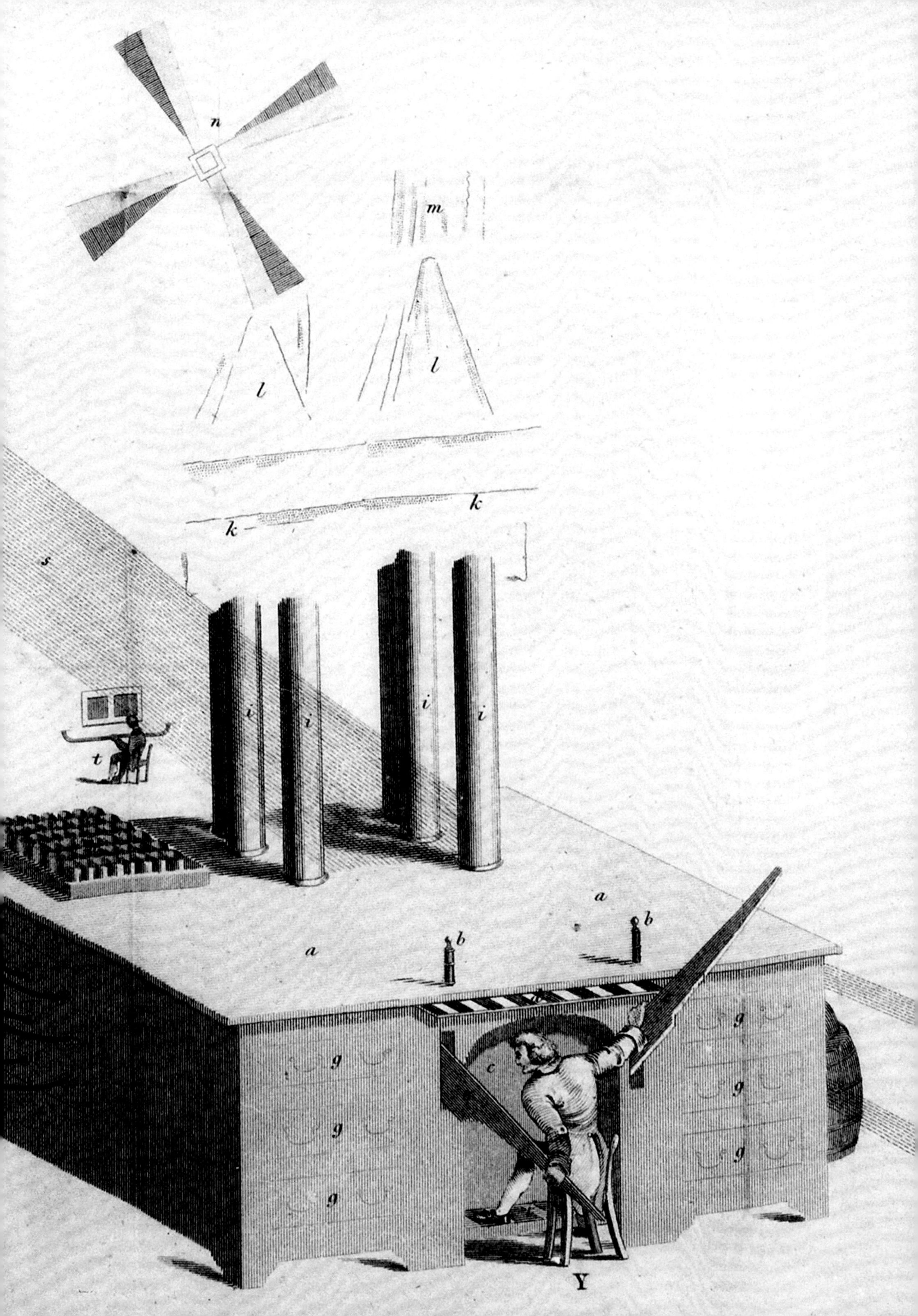

n
m
l
l
k
k
s
i
i
i
i
t
a
a
b
b
g
g
g
g
g
c
Y

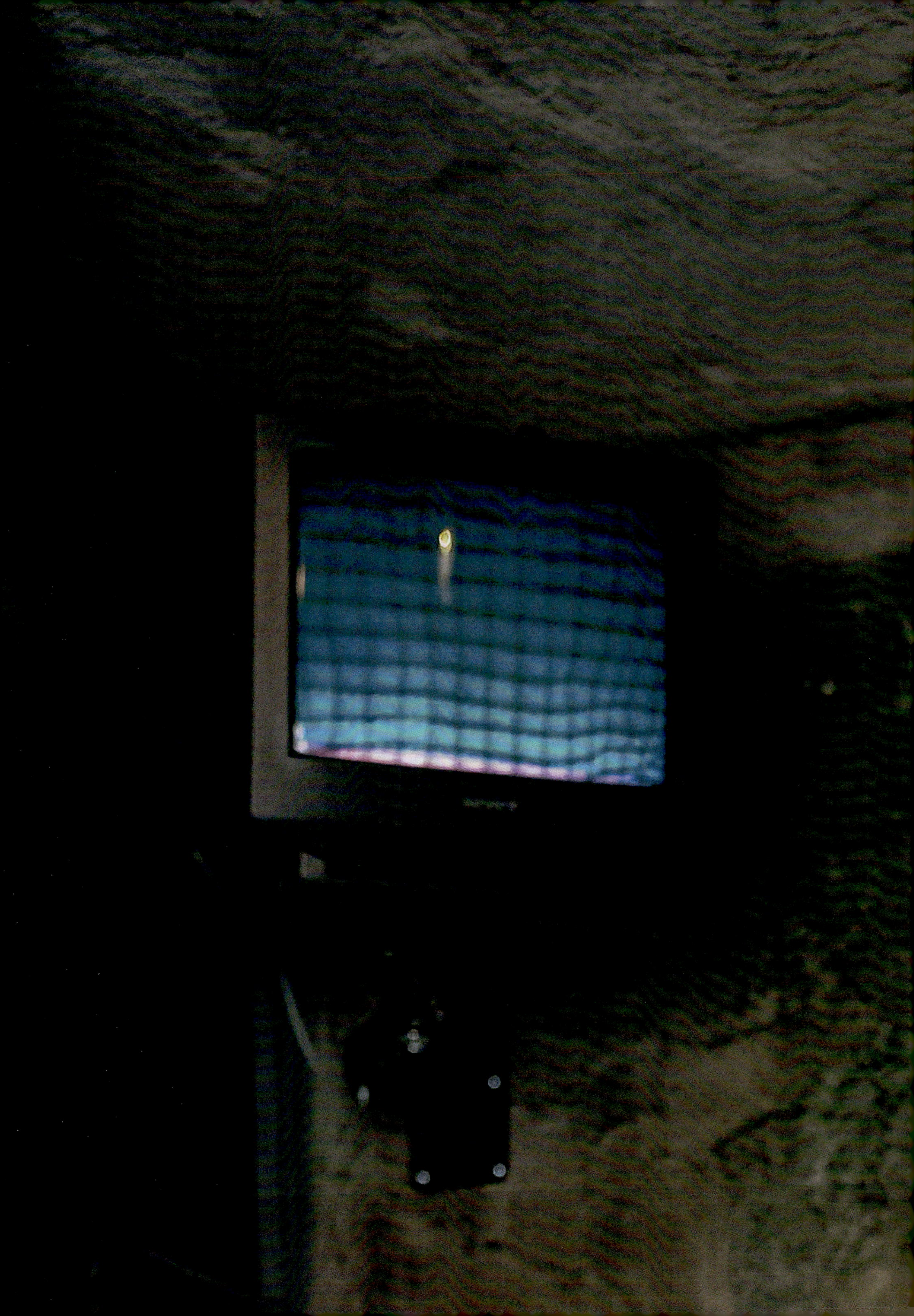

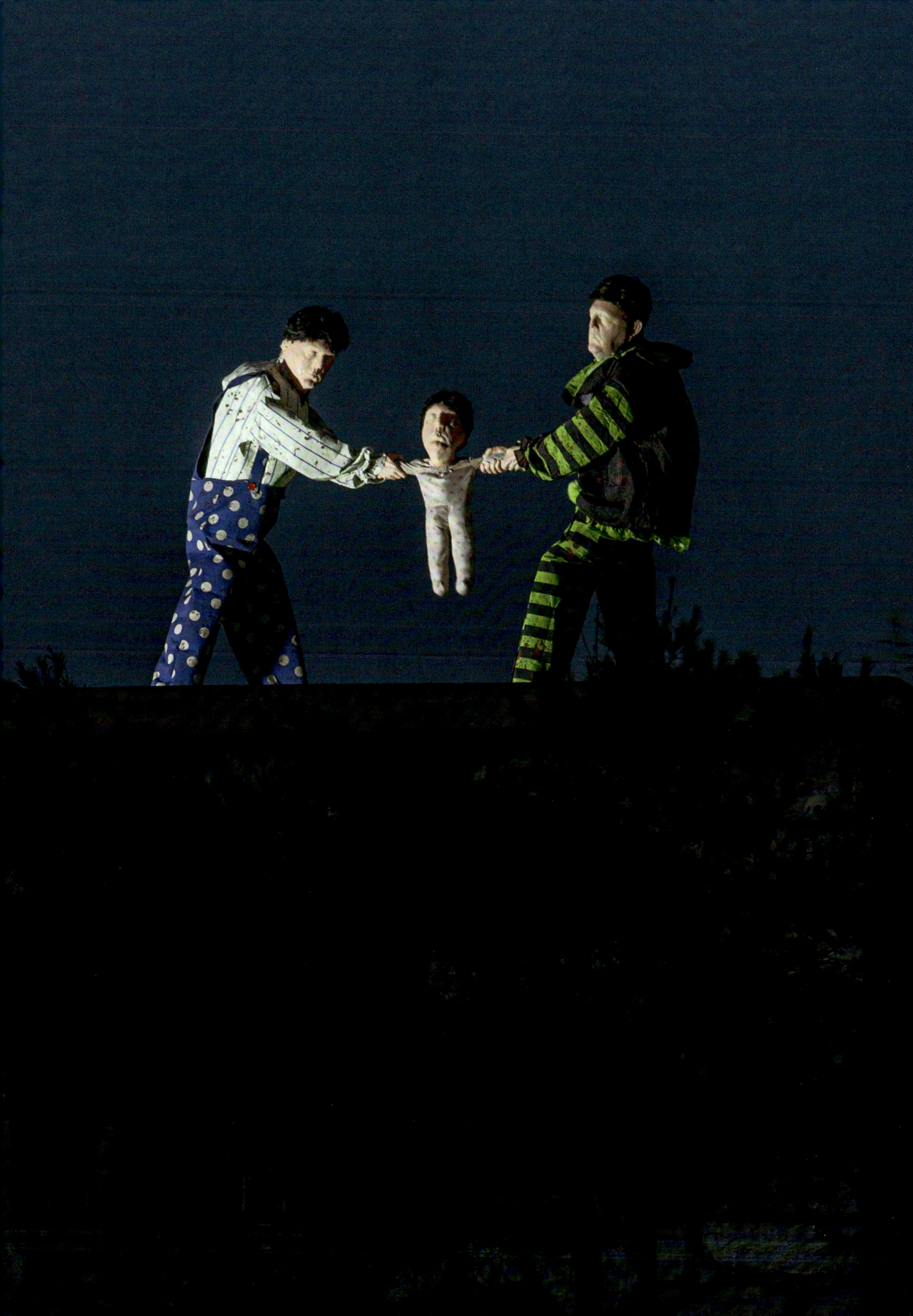

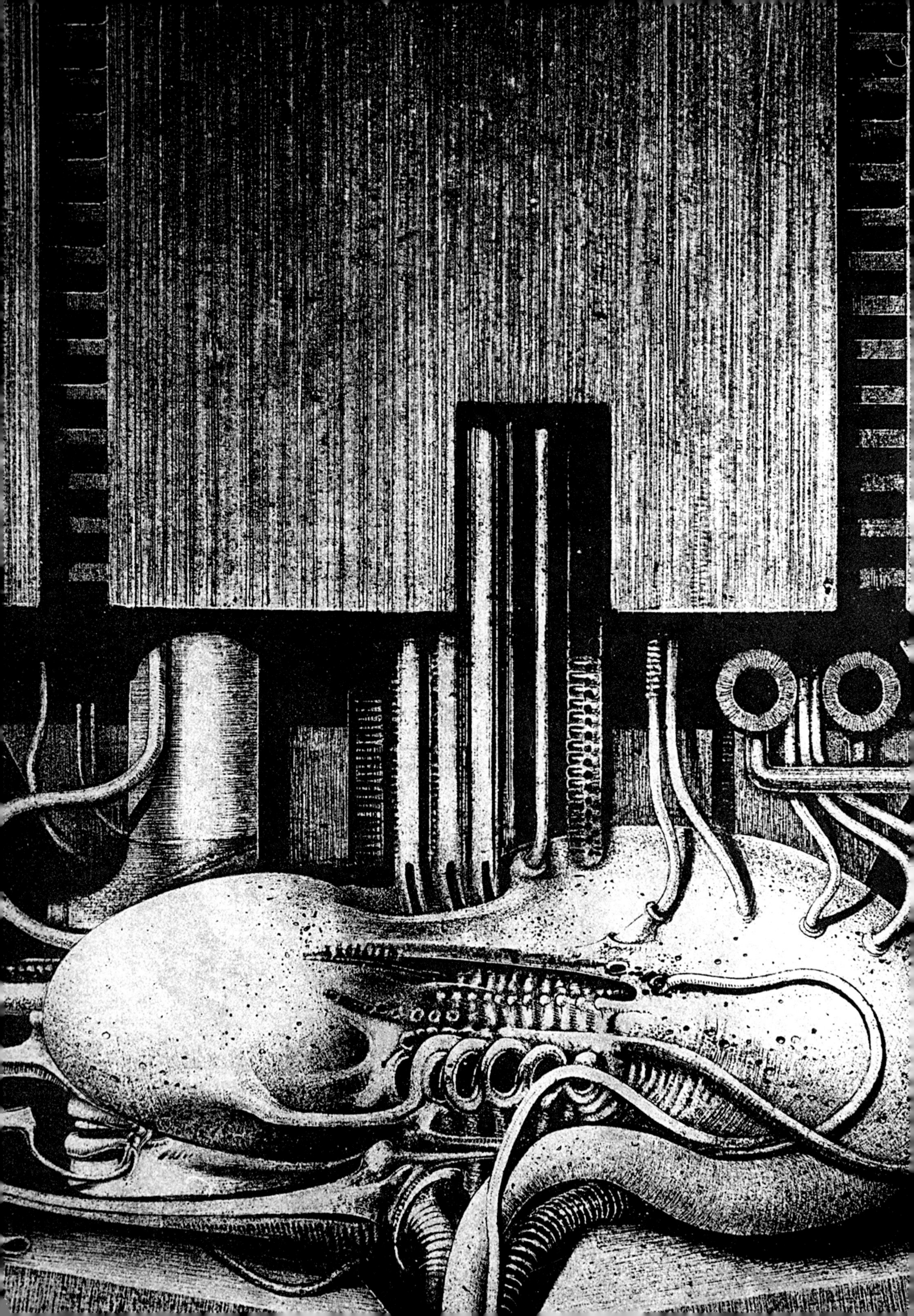

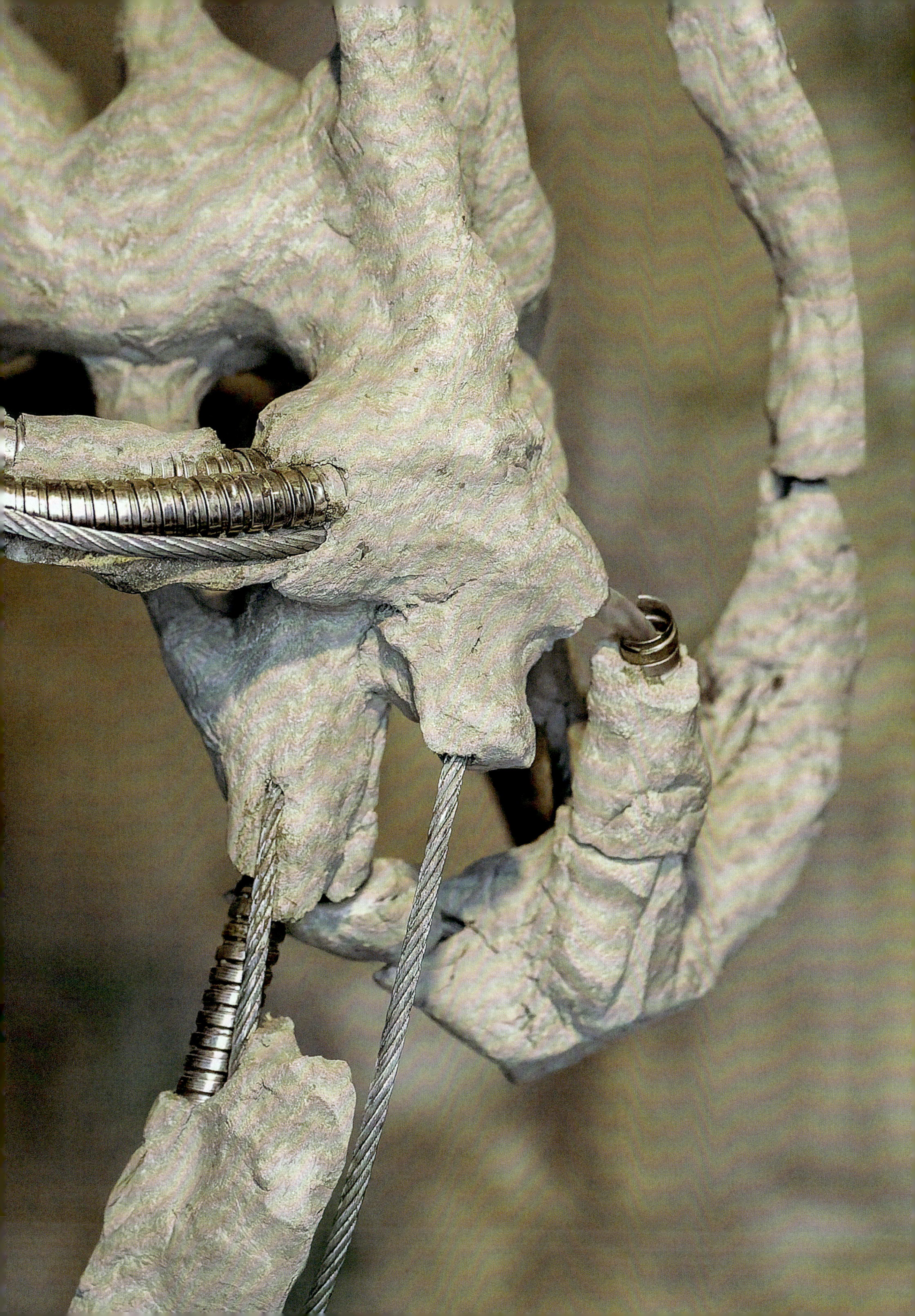

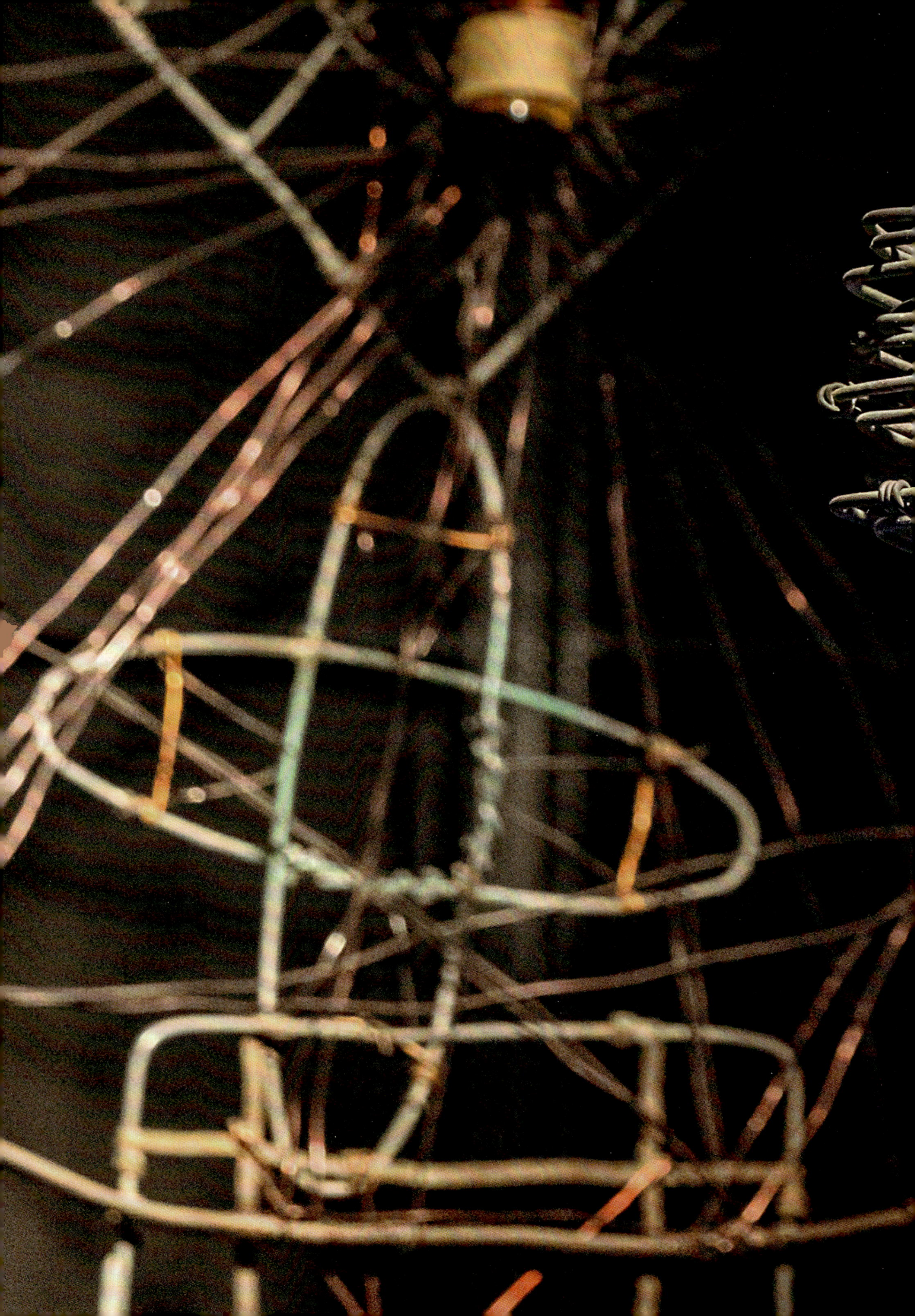

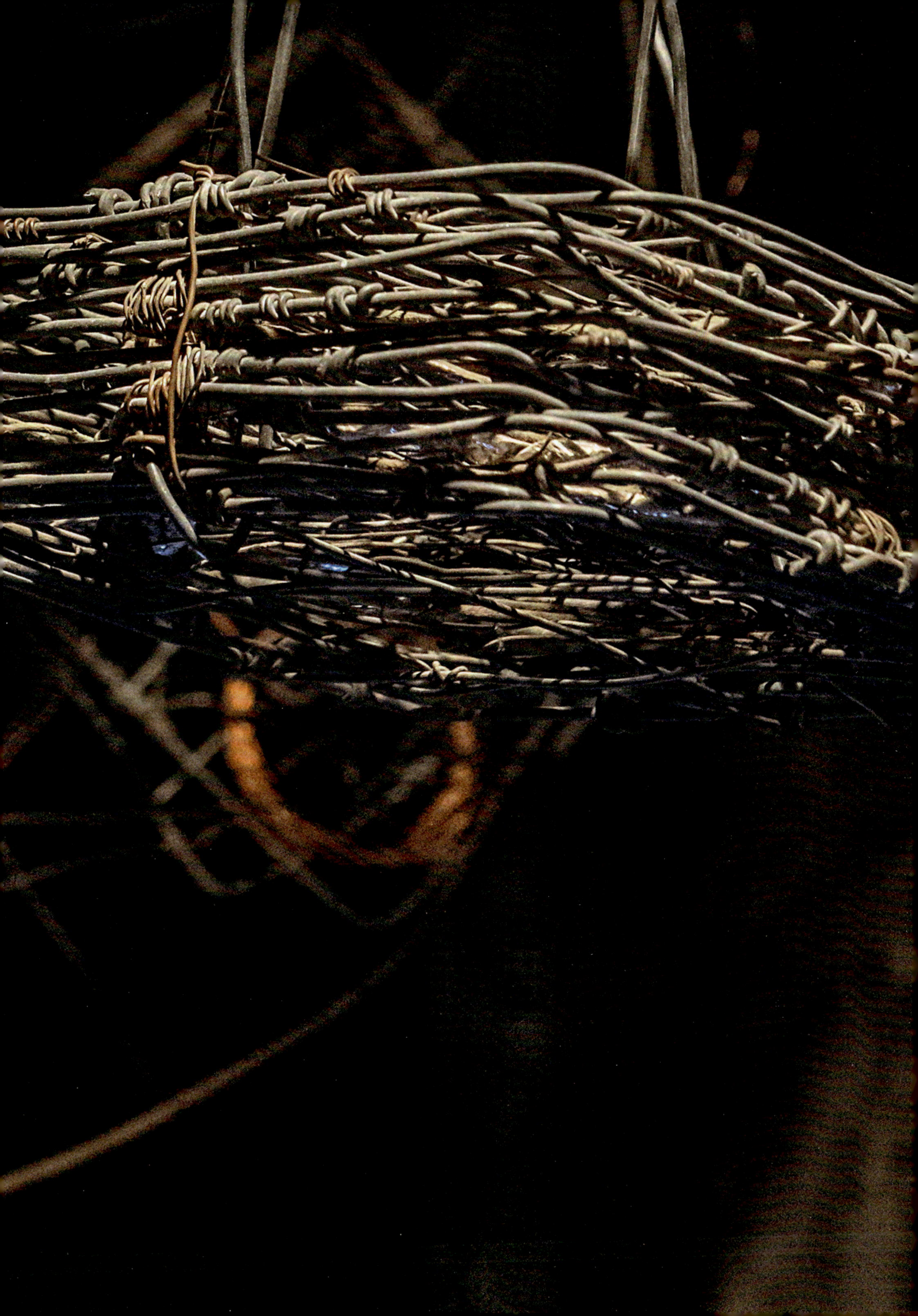

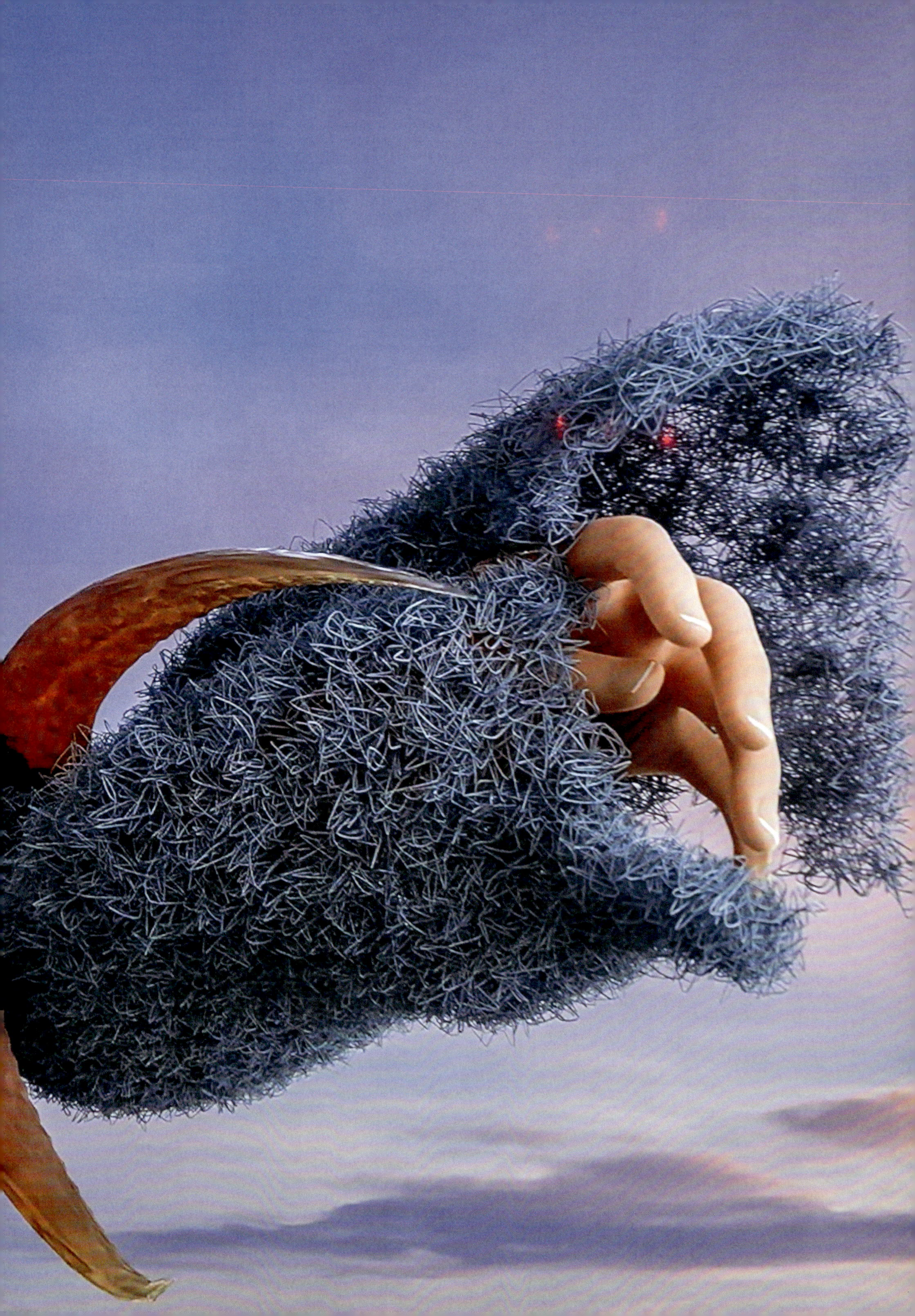

DREAM MACHINES

ΔΕΣΤΕ

Dream Machines

Daniel Birnbaum and Massimiliano Gioni

Dream Machines is an exhibition that explores the impact of technology on the human imagination. Combining works from the celebrated Dakis Joannou Collection, new commissions, and loans from major museums and collectors, it presents historically significant works alongside a selection of curious objects — such as drawings by patients in psychiatric hospitals or controversial psychiatrist Wilhelm Reich's orgone energy accumulator. New experiments with virtual and augmented reality are on display alongside interventions by influential artists such as Peter Fischli and David Weiss, Philippe Parreno, Pipilotti Rist, Ulla Wiggen, and Sturtevant, as well as a number of younger practitioners, including Cao Fei, Mire Lee, Henrik Olesen, Pamela Rosenkranz, Mika Rottenberg, Andro Wekua, and Anicka Yi.

Approaching the Slaughterhouse in Hydra, the site of the exhibition, the viewer comes across an unexpected scene: on the roof of an unremarkable structure next to the footpath, a strange tug-of-war involving two not entirely benign-looking characters pulling a baby back and forth. It is a slightly alarming and never-ending to-and-fro that is going nowhere. The baby's body, hanging in midair, is swaying gently, its head surprisingly large. On closer inspection one notices that the three figures, the two clown-like grown-ups and the baby, have the same facial features. All three of them are clearly manifestations of the same individual, the sculpture's easily recognizable creator: Swiss artist Urs Fischer, a regular visitor to the island.

Fischer's *Chalk and Cheese* (2022) is not the only work that has escaped the interior of the Slaughterhouse. Installed in and around the cave-like space, this *boîte-en-valise* of an exhibition itself becomes a "bachelor machine" (to use Marcel Duchamp's term), its artworks caught in an endless mechanical ballet that breaks out of the physical architecture, creating thematic connections between inside and outside. A case in point: above the Slaughterhouse, Jeff Koons's solar *Apollo Wind Spinner* (2020–22), visible from afar, summons the viewers to a show in which rotation is a recurring theme, perhaps most evident in Maurizio Cattelan's *Dynamo Secession* (1997/2023), a bicycle rigged to an electricity generator that powers a light bulb in the exhibition space (creating a frenetic rhythm), and Ulf Linde's reinterpretation of Marcel Duchamp's *Coffee Mill* (1911), described by André Breton as an infernal machine. The upper part of the little painting is a diagrammatic rendering of the mill's handle seen simultaneously in several positions as it revolves. Like Koons's golden disc above the roof, it appears to reference the Vergina Sun, the rayed solar emblem that appeared in ancient Greek art.

On top of a small house below the Slaughterhouse, closer to the ocean, Judith Hopf's *Phone User 5* (2021–22) is stretching out her arm holding a smartphone. Is she documenting something in the sky? Thematically, Hopf's concrete sculpture is connected to works inside the gallery as well as in the virtual sphere, like Rist's *Selbstlos im Lavabad (Selfless in the Bath of Lava) (Bastard Version)* (1994), a single-channel video and sound installation visible on a mobile phone lying on the carpeted floor. The artist herself appears on the screen, gesticulating, trying hard to get the visitor's attention. Pointing her phone toward the sky above the water, Hopf's concrete phone user also alludes to dimensions invisible to the naked eye. Lee Bul's AR sculpture, *Willing to Be Vulnerable – Metalized Balloon VER.AR22* (2022), accessed through the Acute Art app, is a geolocated virtual object visible through the phone. Anchored in the blockchain, it lives in many worlds at once.

Perception, reality, existence…concepts that have always been intertwined with psychology, physiology, and technology in the widest sense of the terms, beginning already with the Greek notions of *physis* (that which springs forth of itself) and *techne* (that which depends on human actions in order to come into being). Reality seems increasingly to be dependent on techniques that make entities available and inscribe them in our field of experience — something that Gaston Bachelard emphasized when he suggested to think less in terms of phenomenology, or how phenomena are given to us, and more in terms of a *phenomenotechnique*, how phenomena are generated. [01]

01 —— Hans-Jörg Rheinberger, "Gaston Bachelard and the Notion of 'Phenomenotechnique,'" *Perspectives on Science* 13, no. 3 (Fall 2005): 313–28.

The works in *Dream Machines* move and come to life: Wekua's automaton moves its fingers, while Rosenkranz's robot snake crawls on the floor, and Yi's artificial insects fly, trapped in a lamp. A disc plays the poems of Duchamp, while Parreno resurrects an ancient baroque robot continuously rewriting a letter. Physically modest in size, the exhibition presents a number of momentous works that branch out not only into the surrounding landscape, but also into virtual space. The gallery is thus the entry to a labyrinth—a node in a network that connects dimensions, virtual and real. Nathalie Djurberg and Hans Berg's *It Will End in Stars* (2018) presents a fairy-tale-like story visible through VR headsets. Jacqui Davies's speculative film-catalogue, screened at an open-air cinema during the opening, was also sent out as an invitation to the exhibition and made available online; in the exhibition it reappears on a tablet installed on one of the Slaughterhouse's small terraces. Ever since Sigmund Freud's essay "The Uncanny," which includes his legendary analysis of German Romantic writer E.T.A. (Experiments in Art and Technology) Hoffmann's terrifying story "The Sandman" (1816)—who was said to steal the eyes of children—a physical attack on the eyes has been a recurring theme in art and literature, from Surrealism to science fiction. The obsession with the eyeball has been at the center of innumerable explorations of the uncanny—visions that explore all the traumas associated with losing one's sight, with Georges Bataille and Luis Buñuel being the modernist virtuosos of violent ocular fixations. These motifs appear in Davies's collage: she excerpts from Ridley Scott's *Blade Runner* (1982), which revisits all the themes from Hoffmann's dark tale and takes eyeball anxiety to a new level. We are told that replicants—human as well as animal—are equipped with synthetic eyes that give off an orange glow. Eyes also play a key role in the film's so-called Voight-Kampff test, where fluctuation of the pupil and involuntary dilation of the iris indicate the capability of empathy—and thus humanness. The optical instruments, artificial eyes, and desirable automatons of dark romanticism return in the film's recent sequel. Set twenty-five years in the future, the world of Denis Villeneuve's *Blade Runner*

2049 (2017) is inhabited by holograms and mixed-reality creatures. The virtual and the real have merged into a sinister amalgamation.

Technology creates utopian dreams. It also creates paranoia. The twentieth century is pervaded by this conflict between "apocalyptic and integrated" intellectuals and artists, as Umberto Eco would have described them: technophobes versus ecstatic mystics of technology. Taking its name from Brion Gysin's legendary 1961 Dreamachine — an invention that, in spite of its modesty, was believed by many of its users, such as William S. Burroughs and Allen Ginsberg, to revolutionize human consciousness — the show revisits moments of both anticipation and distress.

In 1919, the year of Freud's essay with its analysis of "The Sandman," Victor Tausk, one of his disciples, committed suicide. His "On the Origin of the 'Influencing Machine' in Schizophrenia," also published that year, has since become a classic in psychiatric literature. It describes, in the words of writer Christopher Turner, the extravagant mechanical devices that paranoid schizophrenics invent in their imaginations to explain away their mental disintegration: "As the boundaries between the schizophrenic's mind and the world break down, they often feel themselves persecuted by 'machines of a mystical nature,' which supposedly work by means of radio-waves, telepathy, x-rays, invisible wires, or other mysterious forces. The machines are believed to be operated by enemies as instruments of torture and mind-control, and the operators are thought to be able to implant and remove ideas and feelings, and inflict pain, from a distance."[02] Influencing machines are, according to Tausk, regularly described by their troubled creators as complex structures. They are constructed of wheels, wires, batteries, and the like. Sometimes these fantastical devices are as visually appealing as the creations of celebrated artists. Jakob Mohr, who suffered from paranoid schizophrenia and rendered the machines that controlled him in spectacularly detailed drawings, is a case in point. "Waves are pulled out of me through the positive electrical fluorescent attraction of the organic positive pole as the remote hypnotizer through the earth,"[03] he explained, claiming his machine to be a magnet as well as a gun.

02 —— Christopher Turner, "The
Influencing Machine,"
Cabinet, no. 14, Summer 2004,
https://www.cabinetmagazine.
org/issues/14/turner.php.
03 —— Ibid.

Artists have always embraced new visual media. And yet one cannot say that the art world's dominant attitude toward modern technology has been one of sheer enthusiasm, even if the last century saw moments of techno-optimism, from Italian Futurism and Russian Constructivism to E.A.T., a global project of the 1960s discussed in this book by Michelle Kuo. Key voices of philosophy and critical theory, such as the Frankfurt School's most somber representatives, including Walter Benjamin and Theodor Adorno, established an attitude of techno-skepticism so fundamental that any form of playful affirmation, let alone enthusiasm, appeared naive at best. The essence of technological reason, they claimed, lies in hegemonic control and totalitarian exploitation of nature. Its distancing effects make it an enemy of more authentic forms of experience, such as that of great art.

And yet, at a moment when we can no longer imagine a world without technology, it is vital to ask how we (the inhabitants of this planet) imagine the world and its machines. These machines and their products are all present in the exhibition: photography, film, radio, television, video, the computer, virtual reality, blockchain technology…The introduction of new machineries continuously changes the possibilities of artistic expression. It was Benjamin who observed a prophetic capacity in certain works of art that allude to technologies that have not yet been developed. What could be examples of such prophetic power? It has been claimed, for instance, that certain nineteenth-century novels anticipated cinema — that they are written for a medium that did not yet exist. Emily Brontë's *Wuthering Heights* (1847), one could claim, is written like a screenplay. Similarly, the branching narratives of Jorge Luis Borges's short stories seem in certain ways to anticipate hypertext fiction. Duchamp's *The Bride Stripped Bare by Her Bachelors, Even (The Large Glass)* (1915–23) has been said to predict the emergence of virtual space. In the late 1960s, John Cage explored how electronic media had extended the human mind beyond the individual and made it social: through technology we have produced an extension of our brains into the world formerly outside of us. The human nervous system is no longer inside but "out there," where electronic media let us join our friends (and perhaps enemies) in virtual environments.

Half a century later, popular culture and art overflow with fantasies of simulated worlds and virtual spheres, while the corporate tech avant-garde launches optical instruments that promise no less futuristic electric dreams. One of today's most vociferous techno-optimists, Ray Kurzweil, believes that, a few years from now, virtual reality will be totally realistic and compelling and that we will spend most of our time in virtual environments. The ever-accelerating progress of technology will, according to Kurzweil, culminate in the Singularity, the almost vertical phase of exponential growth when technology seems to be expanding at infinite speed — a disruptive moment of total transformation, in which machines will theoretically become sentient and more intelligent than humans.

Against this messianic anticipation of the entire planet becoming an intelligent machine, critics of cognitive capitalism scrutinize how today's digital technologies form the foundation of a surveillance economy that makes possible the expropriation of critical human rights. Should artists in the future celebrate emerging technologies, or should they be part of a new resistance?

Clearly technology itself does not have the answer. Asked this question, ChatGPT's Open AI responds in a characteristically pointless way:

> Ultimately, it's up to each individual artist to decide whether they want to celebrate emerging technologies or resist them. Both approaches can be valid and can lead to interesting and thought-provoking art.

Among the works on display in *Dream Machines* are the fragile machines of Emery Blagdon, a self-taught artist from Nebraska who believed his copper and metal assemblages had curative properties and could heal the world. Perhaps it is this relationship to technology — the mythic, the prophetic — that we need today more than ever.

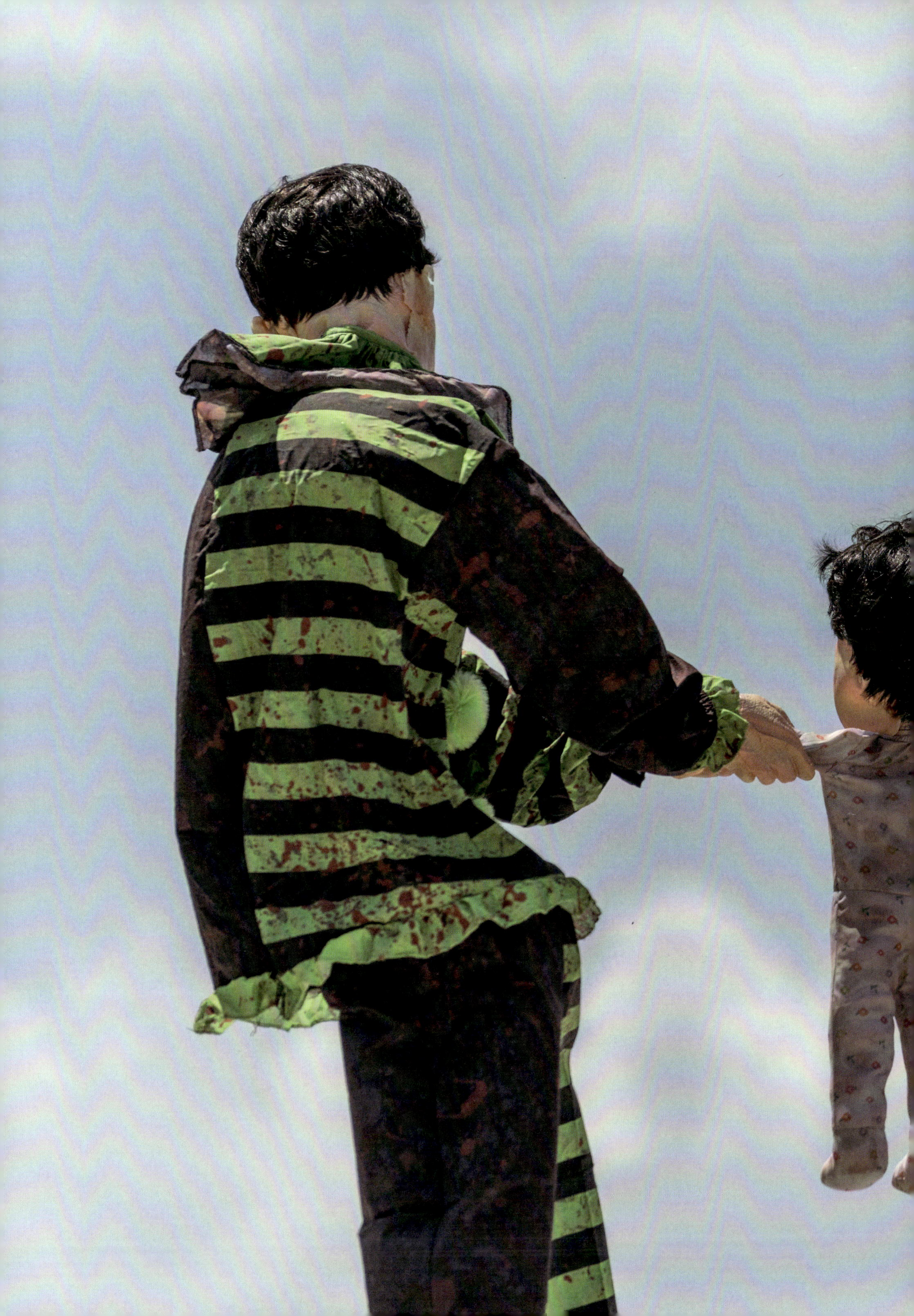

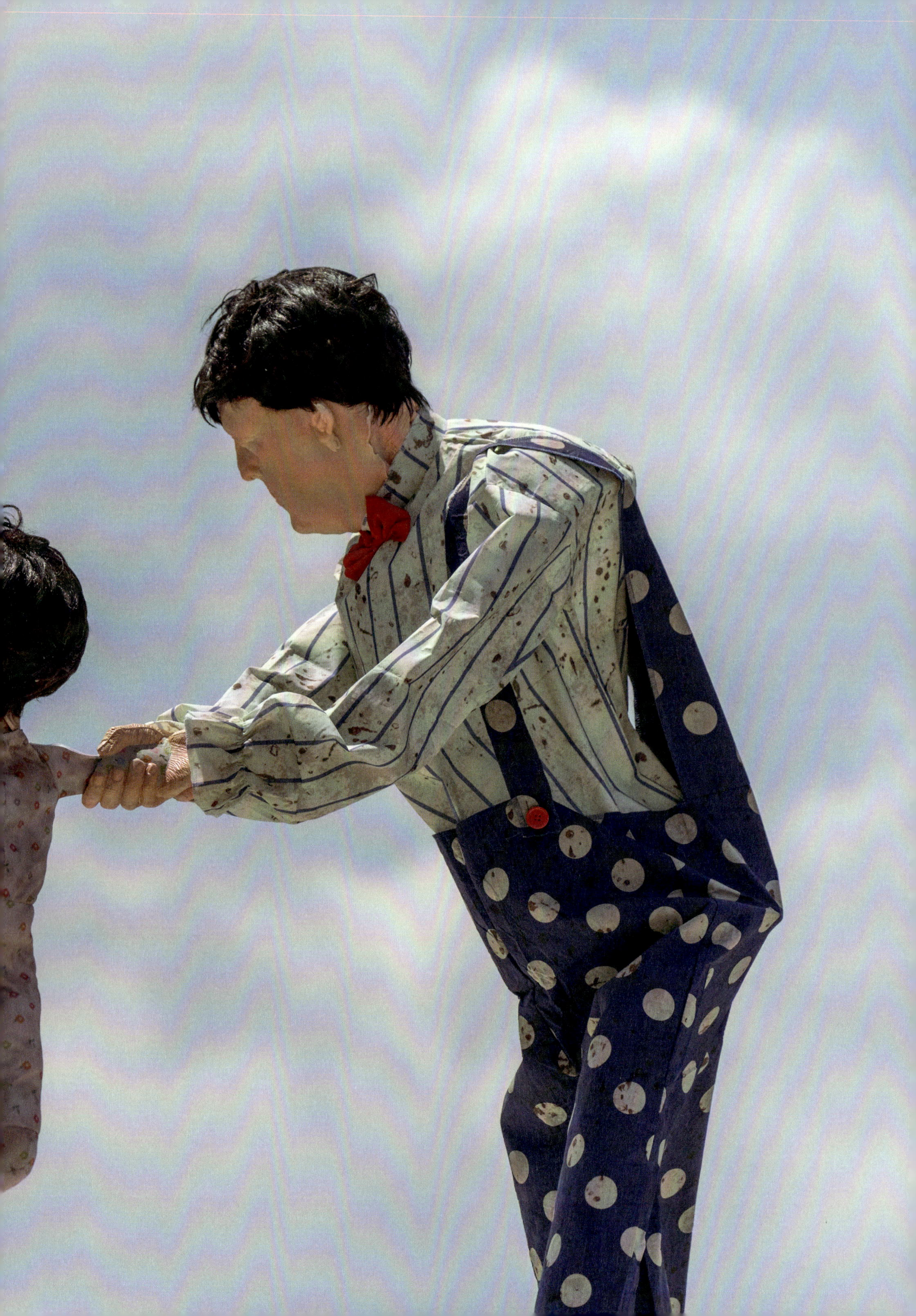

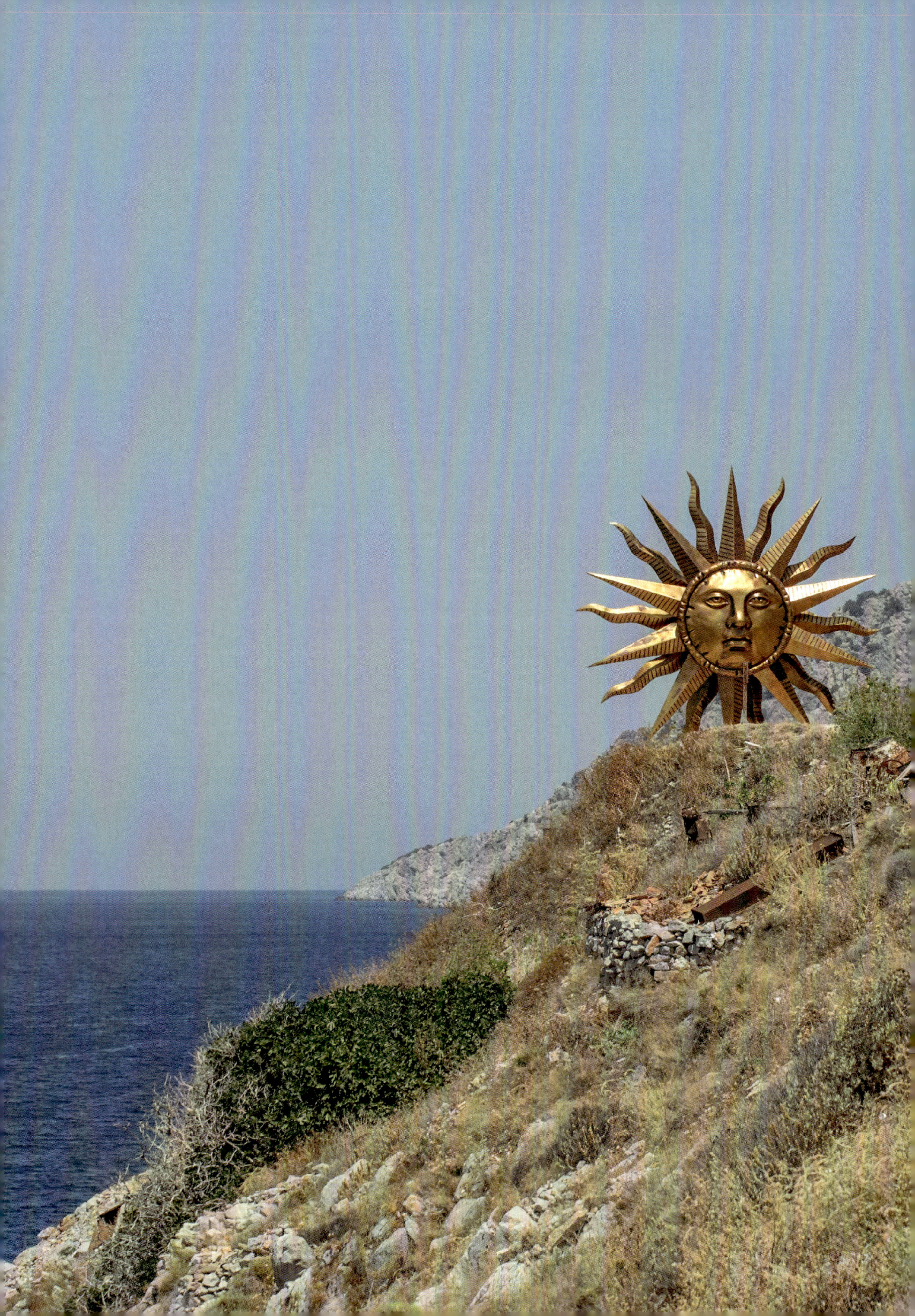

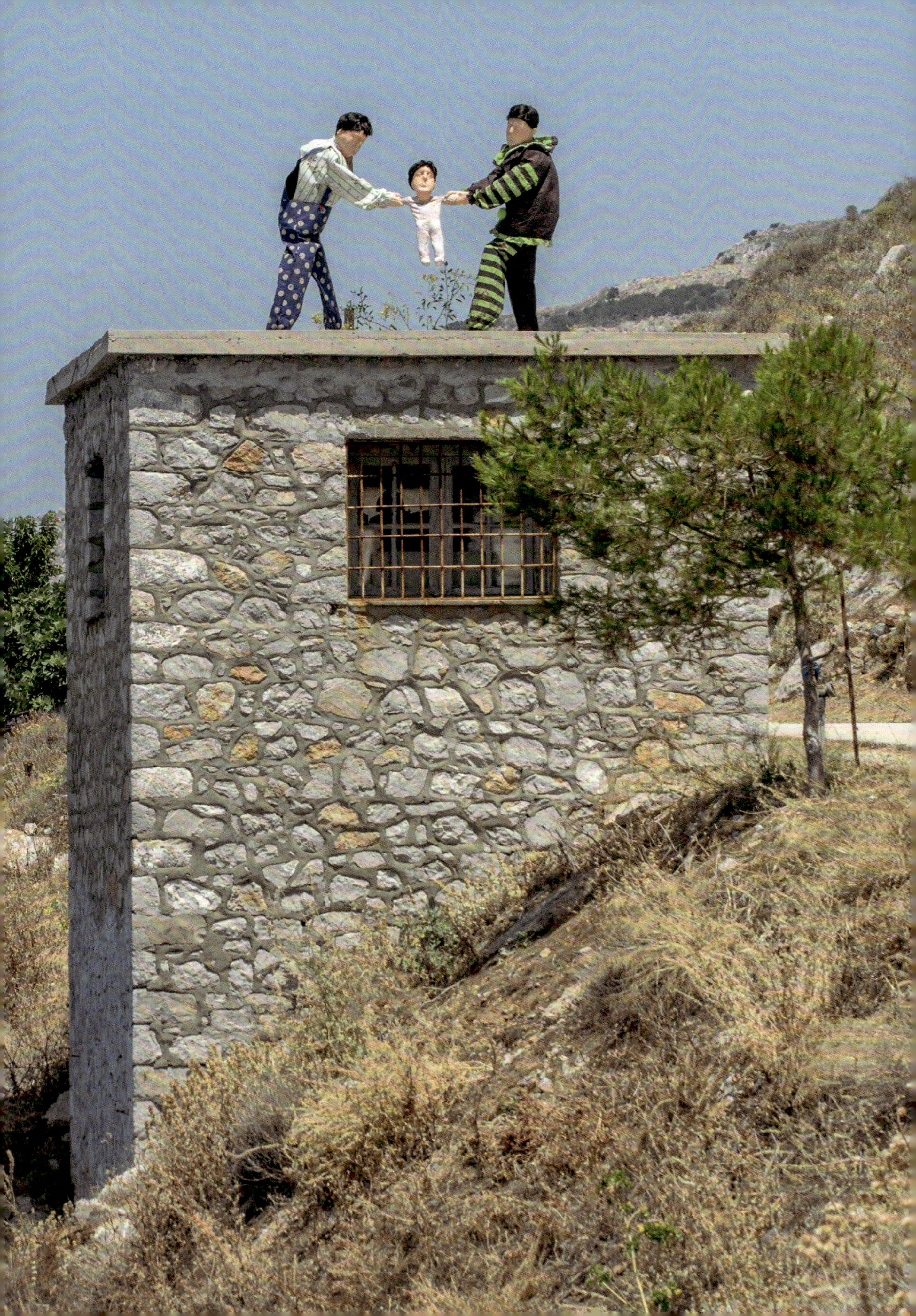

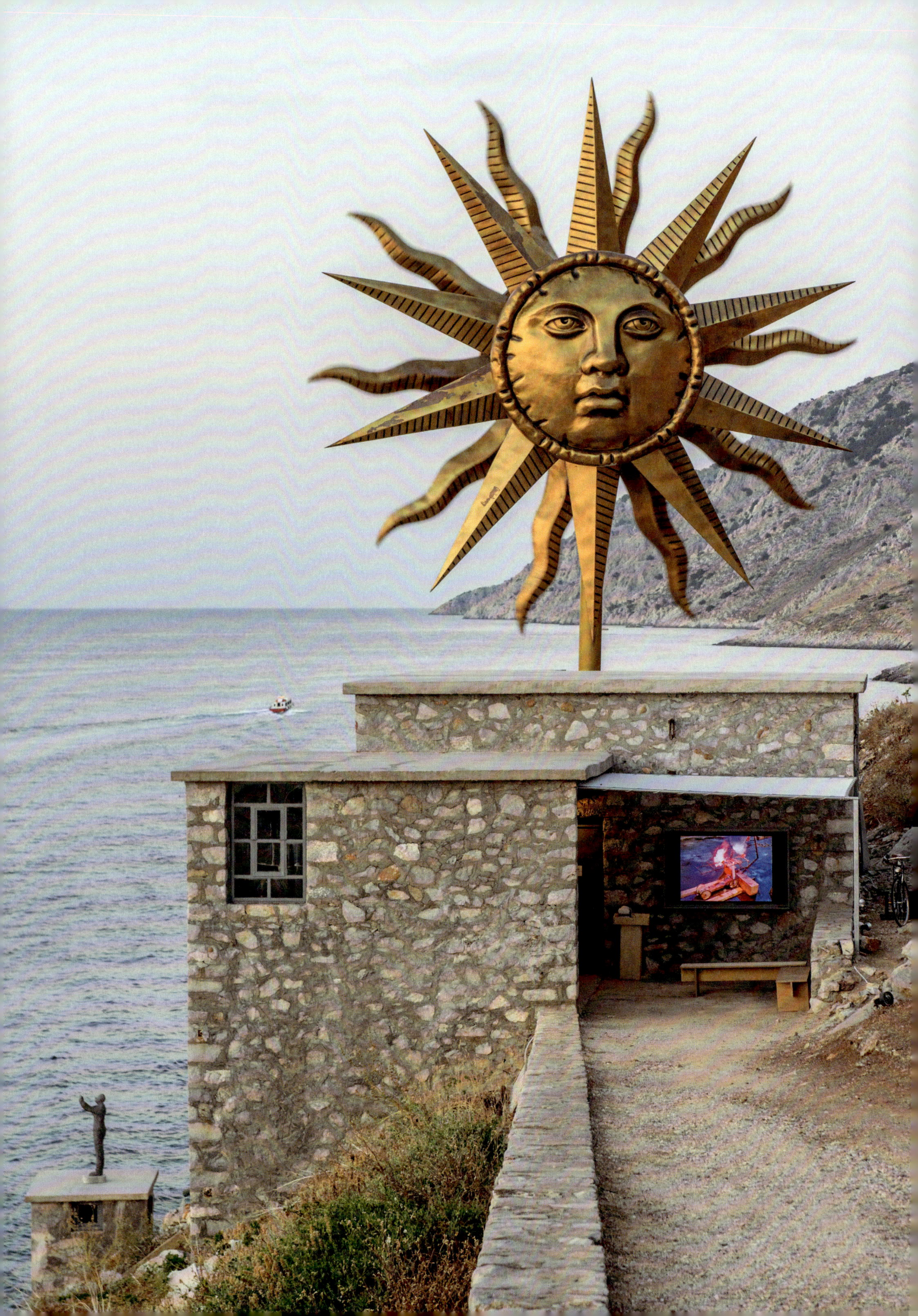

INSTALLATION VIEW (T–B)

Jeff Koons
Apollo Wind Spinner,
2020–22

Peter Fischli and
David Weiss
*Der Lauf der Dinge
(The Way
Things Go)*, 1987

Maurizio Cattelan
Dynamo Secession,
1997/2023

Judith Hopf
Phone User 5,
2021–22

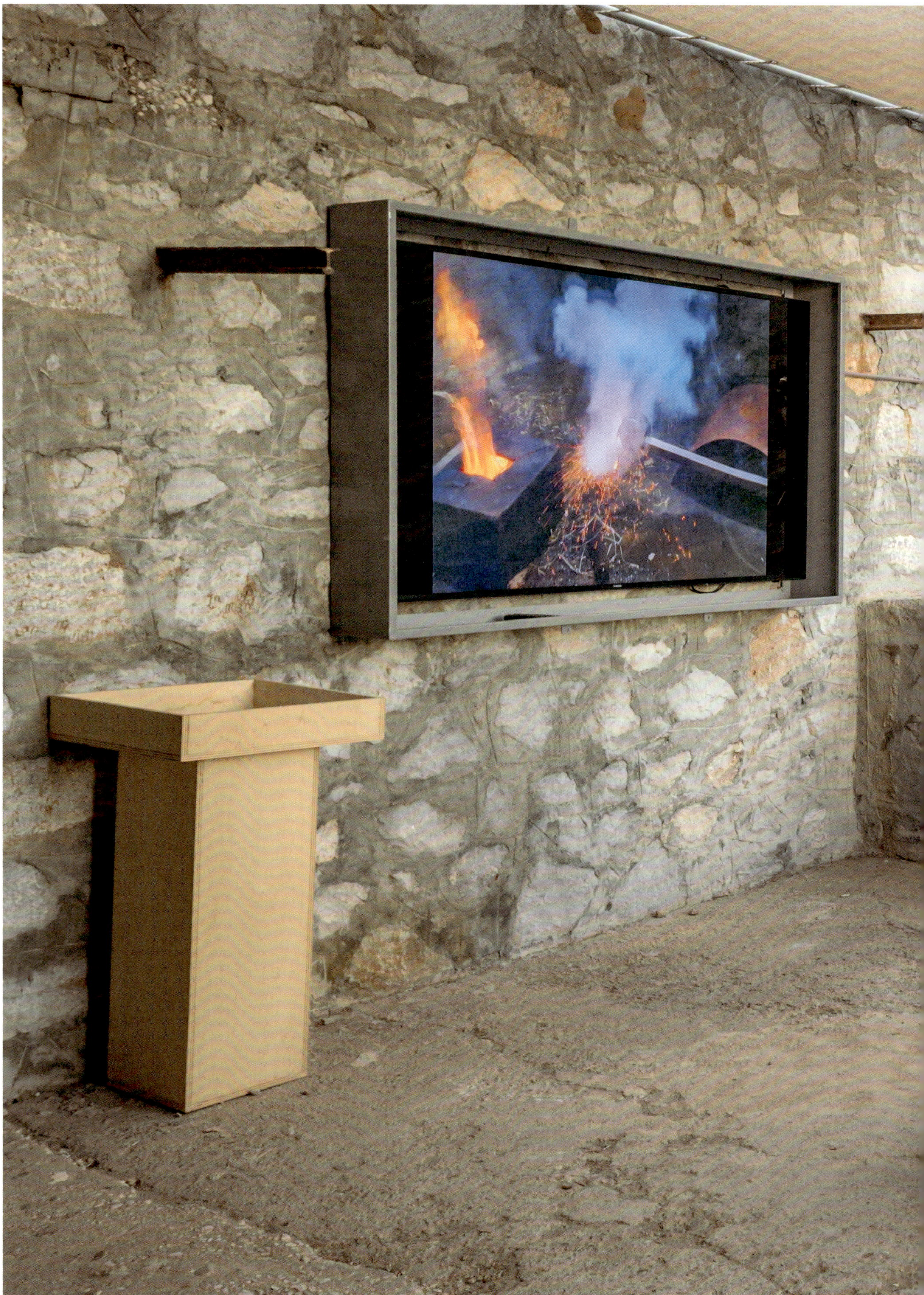

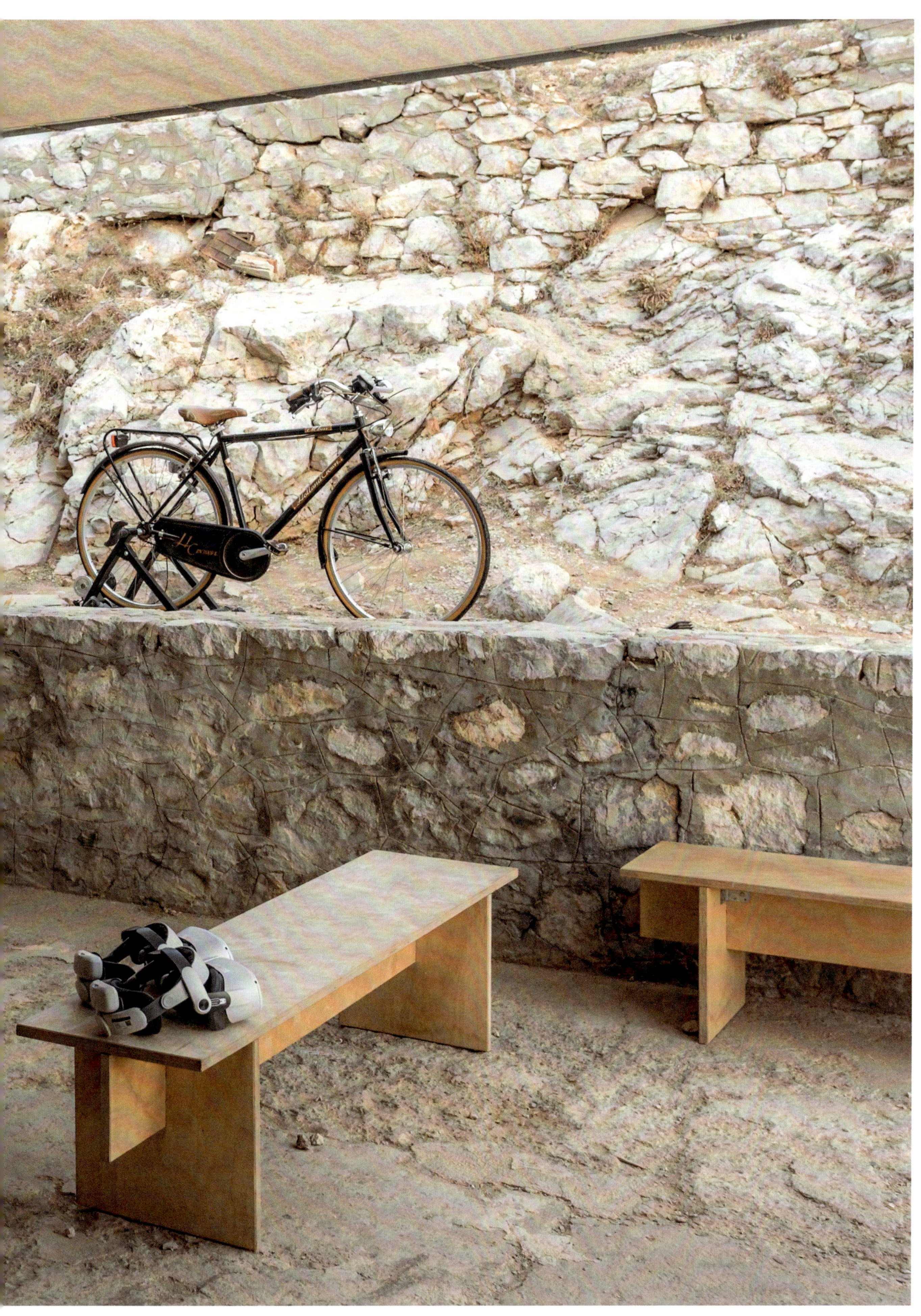

PP.050–051   INSTALLATION VIEW (L–R)

Peter Fischli and
David Weiss
*Der Lauf der Dinge
(The Way
Things Go)*, 1987

Nathalie Djurberg
and Hans Berg
It Will End in Stars, 2018

Maurizio Cattelan
Dynamo Secession,
1997/2023

P.053   INSTALLATION VIEW (L–R)

Nathalie Djurberg
and Hans Berg
It Will End in Stars, 2018

Camille Henrot
Dawg Shaming, 2017

H. R. Giger
*Biomechanoid
(Biomechanoid Portfolio,
4)*, 1969

James Tilly Matthews
The Air Loom, 1810

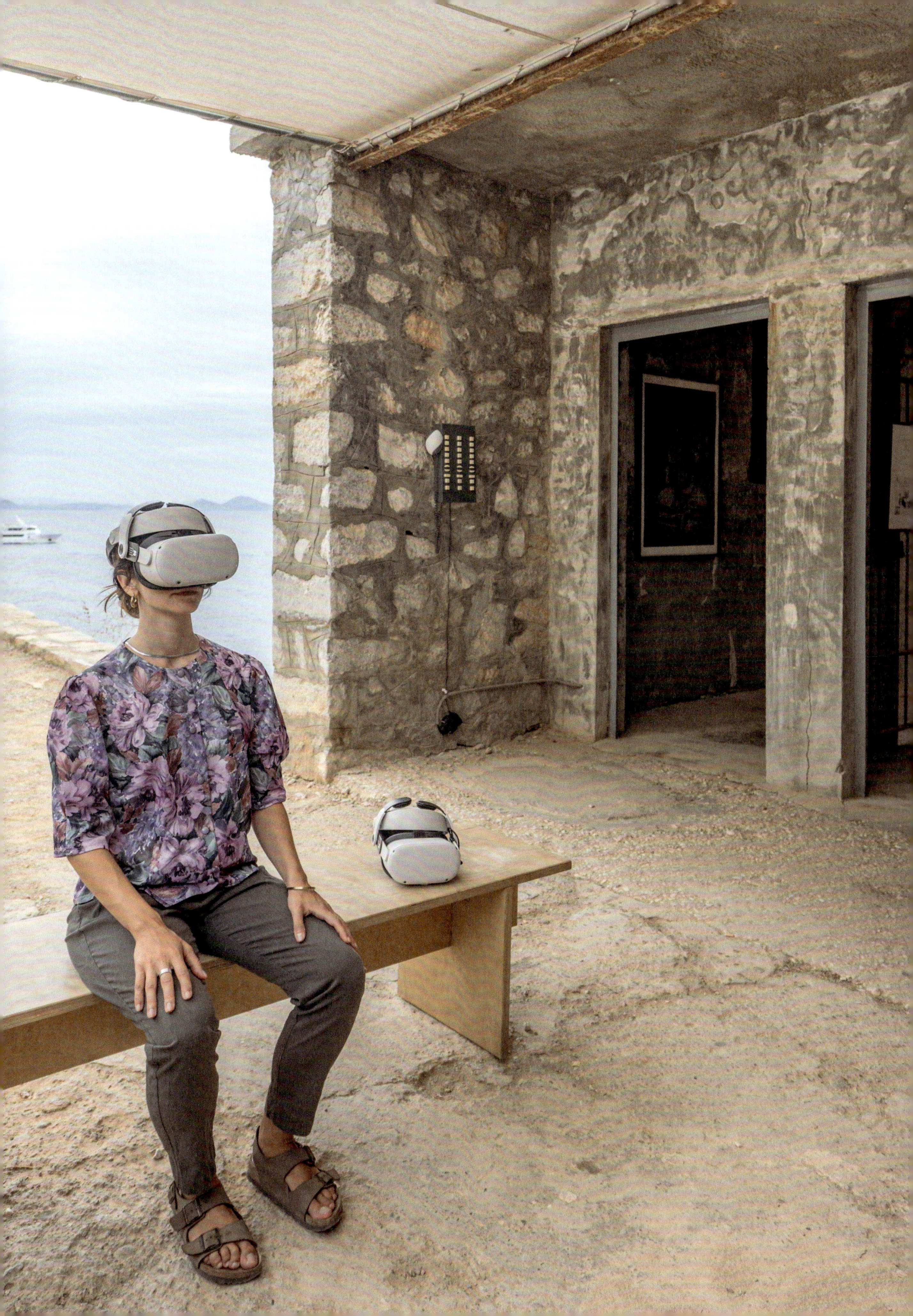

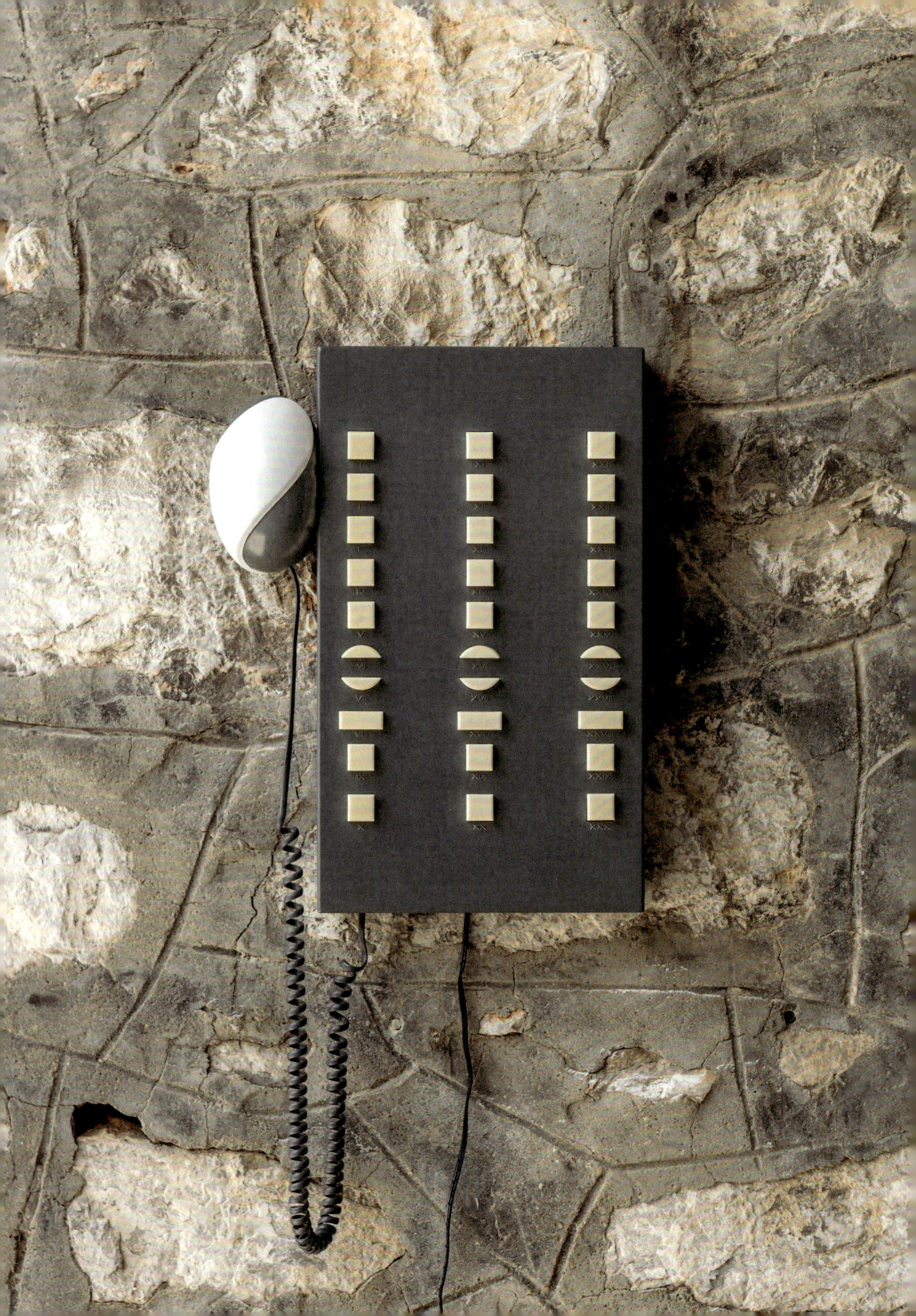

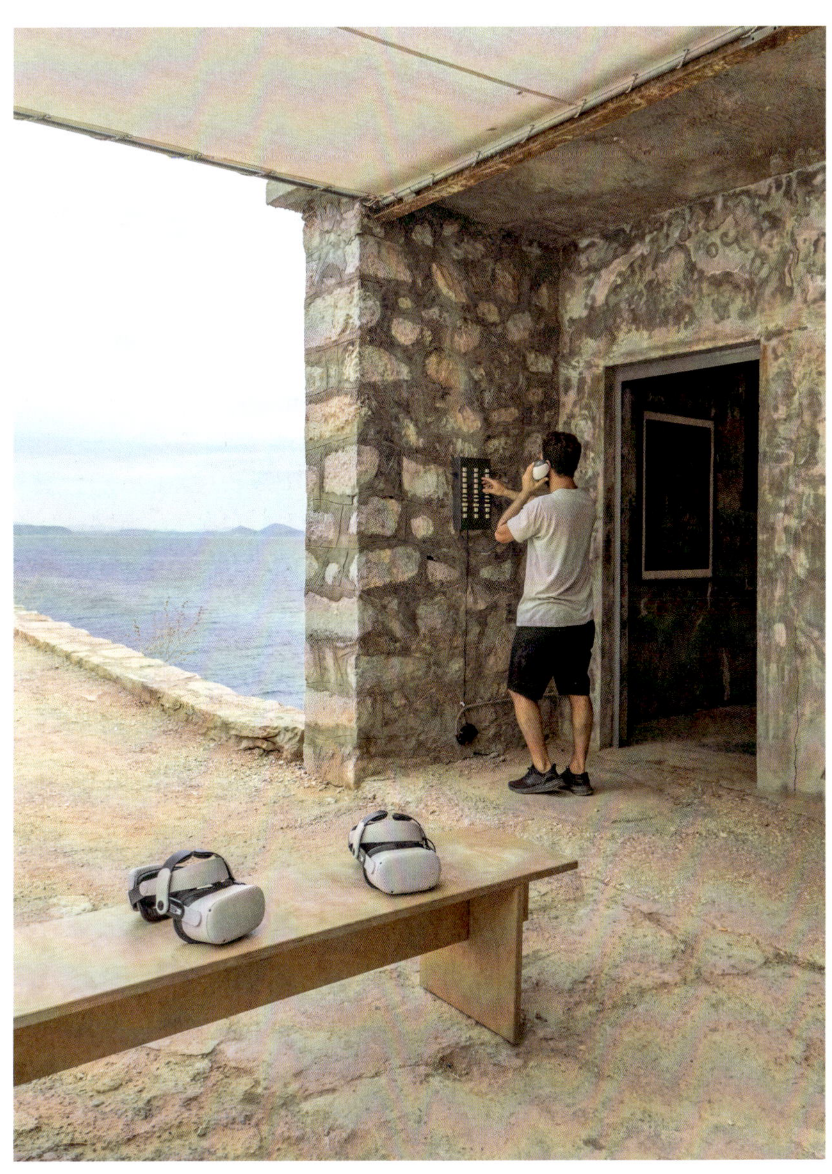

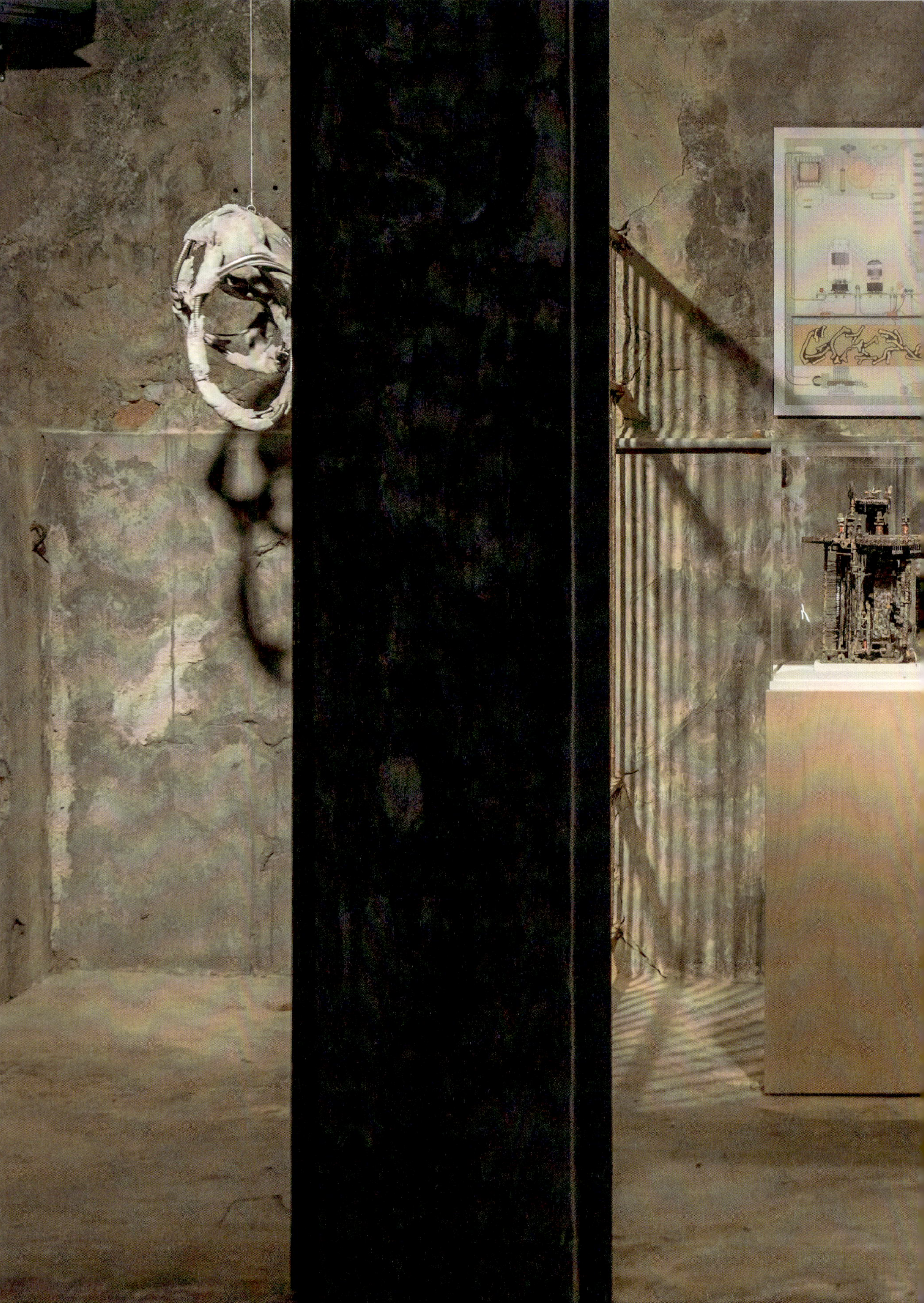

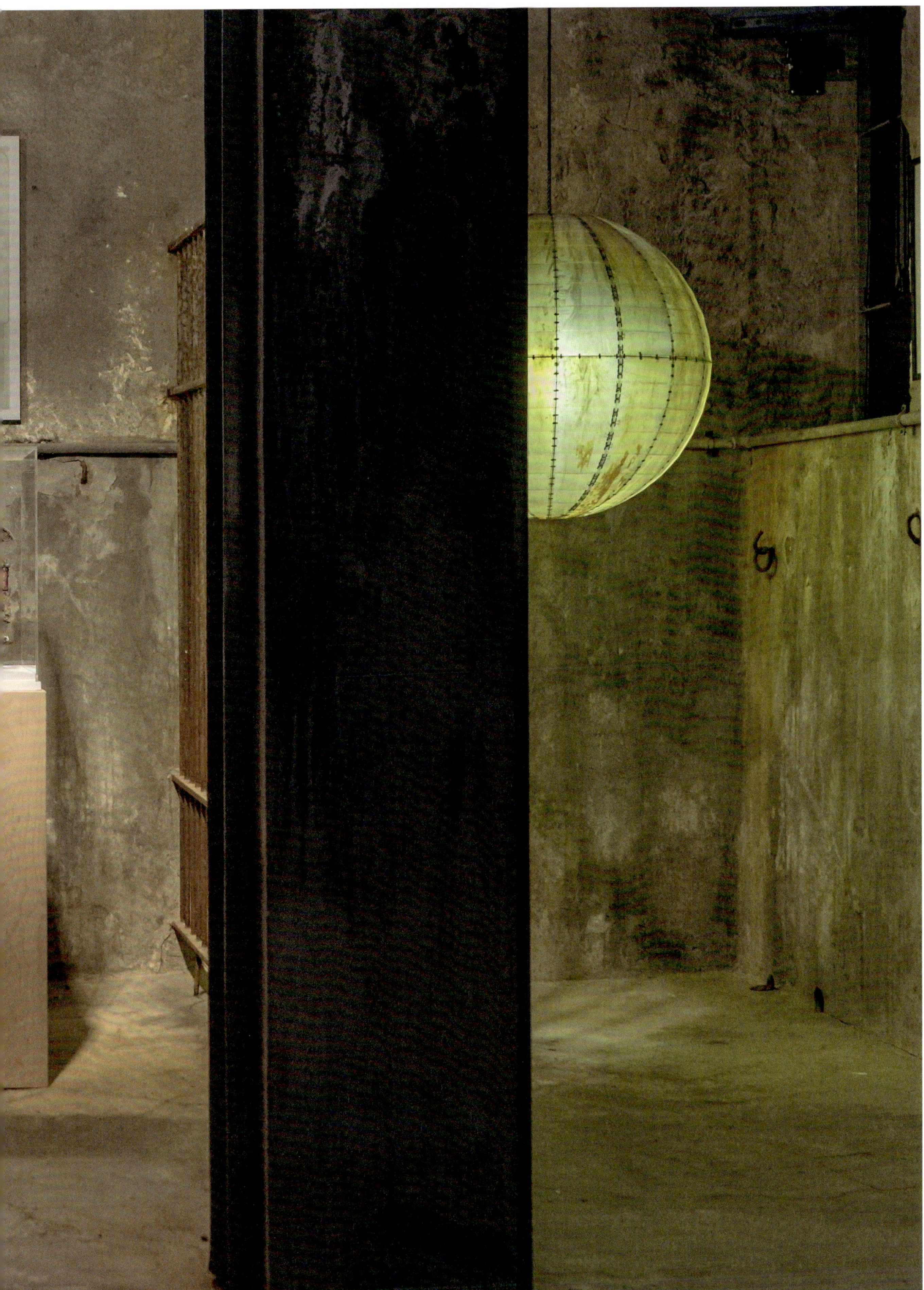

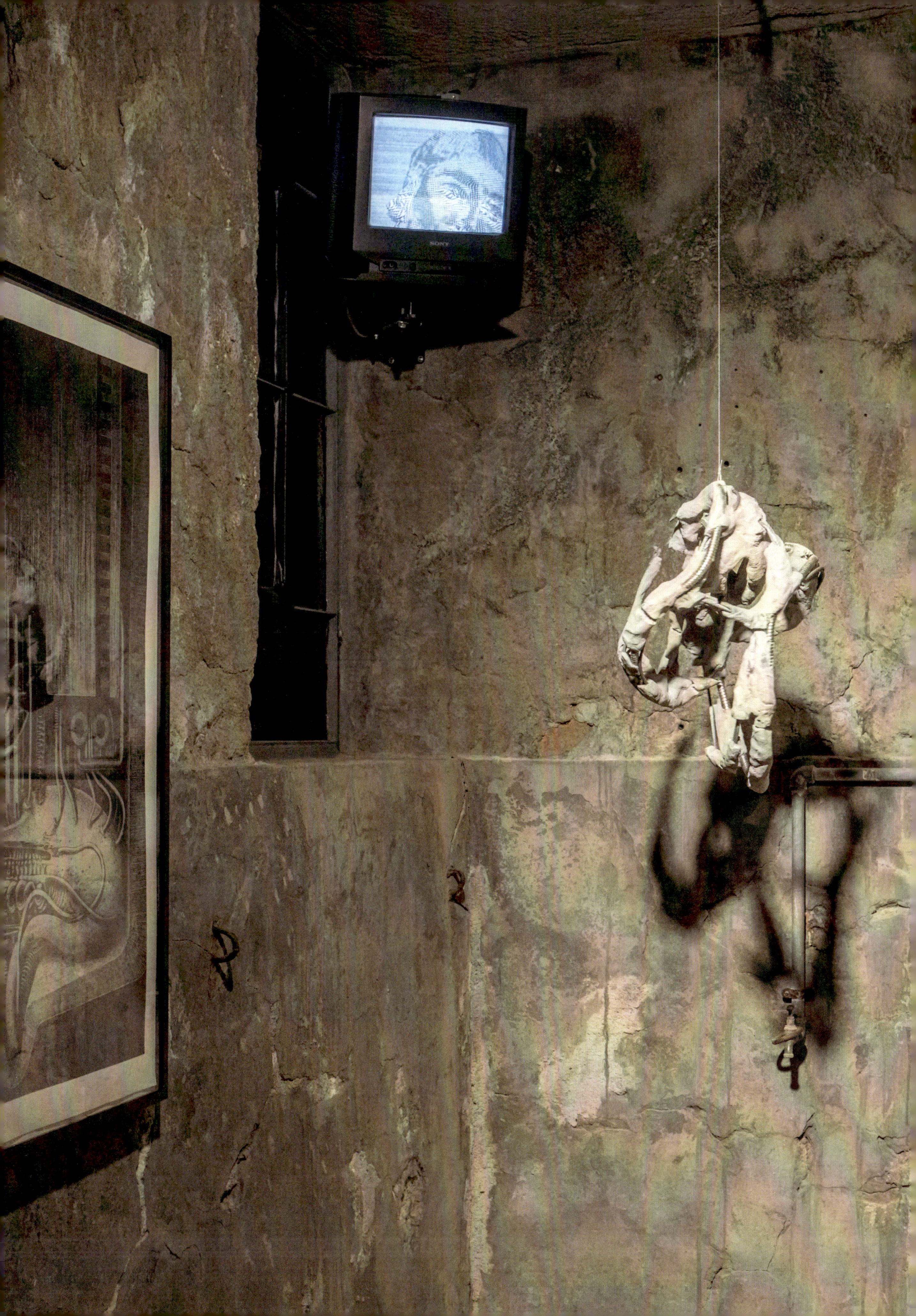

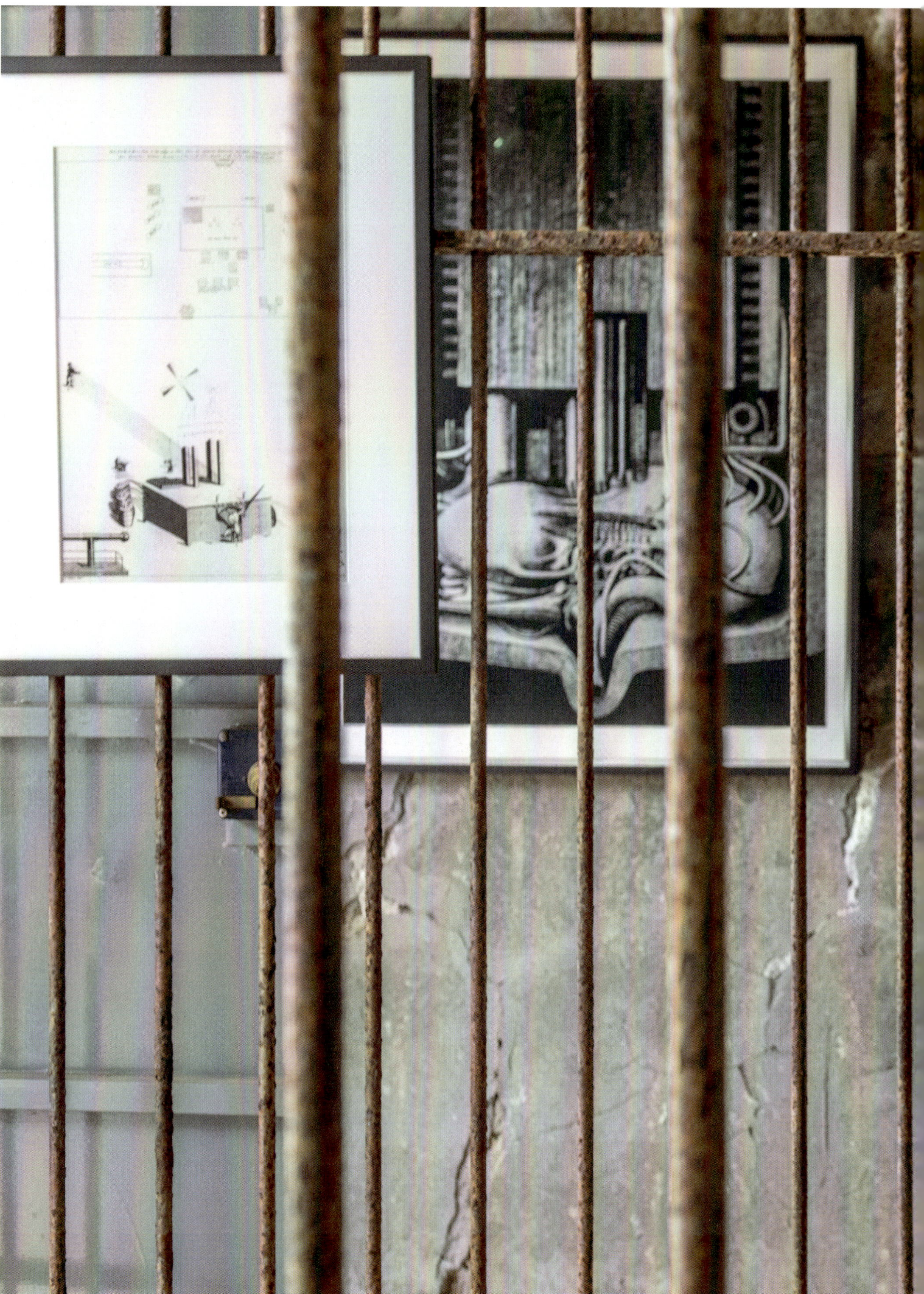

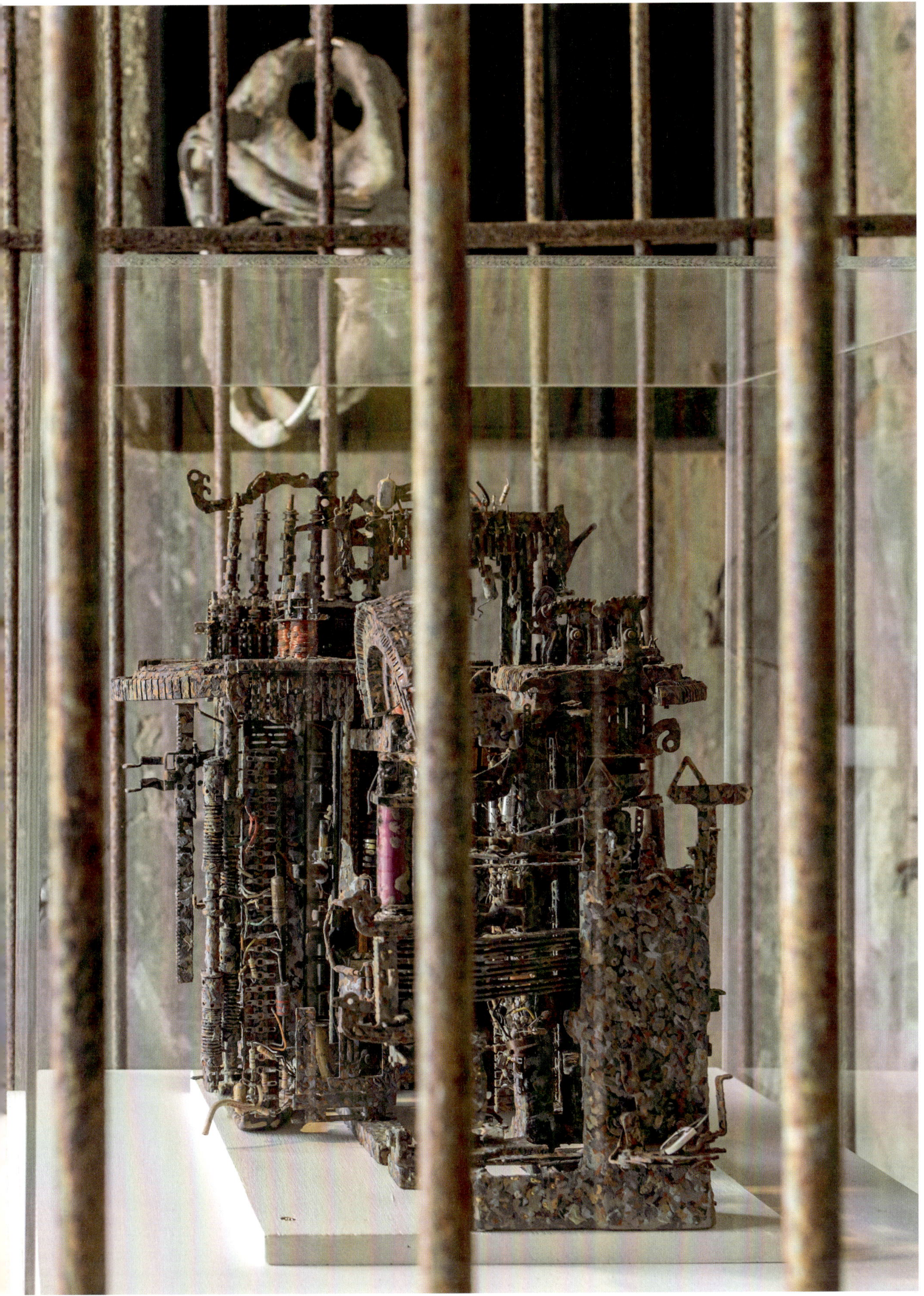

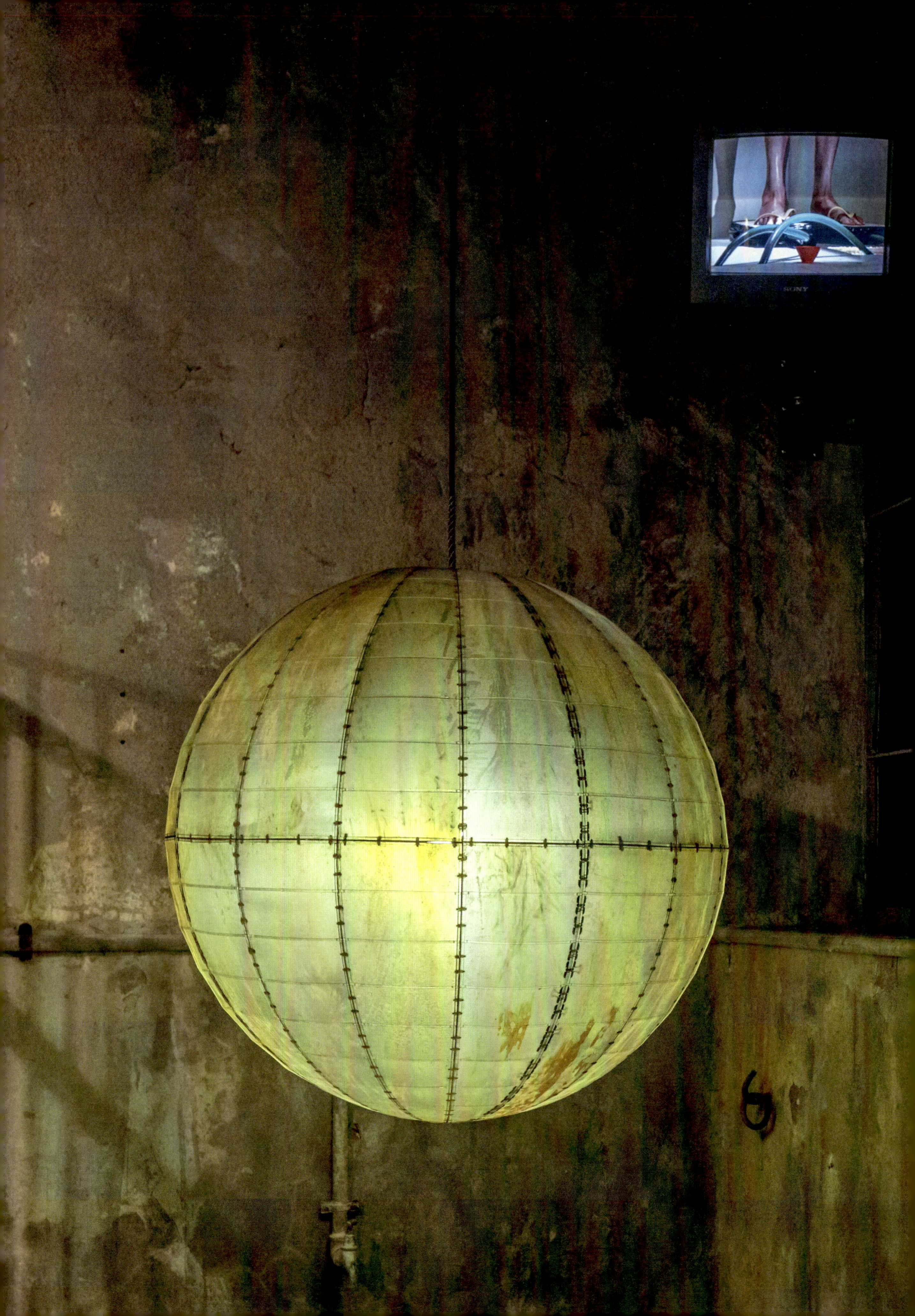
SONY

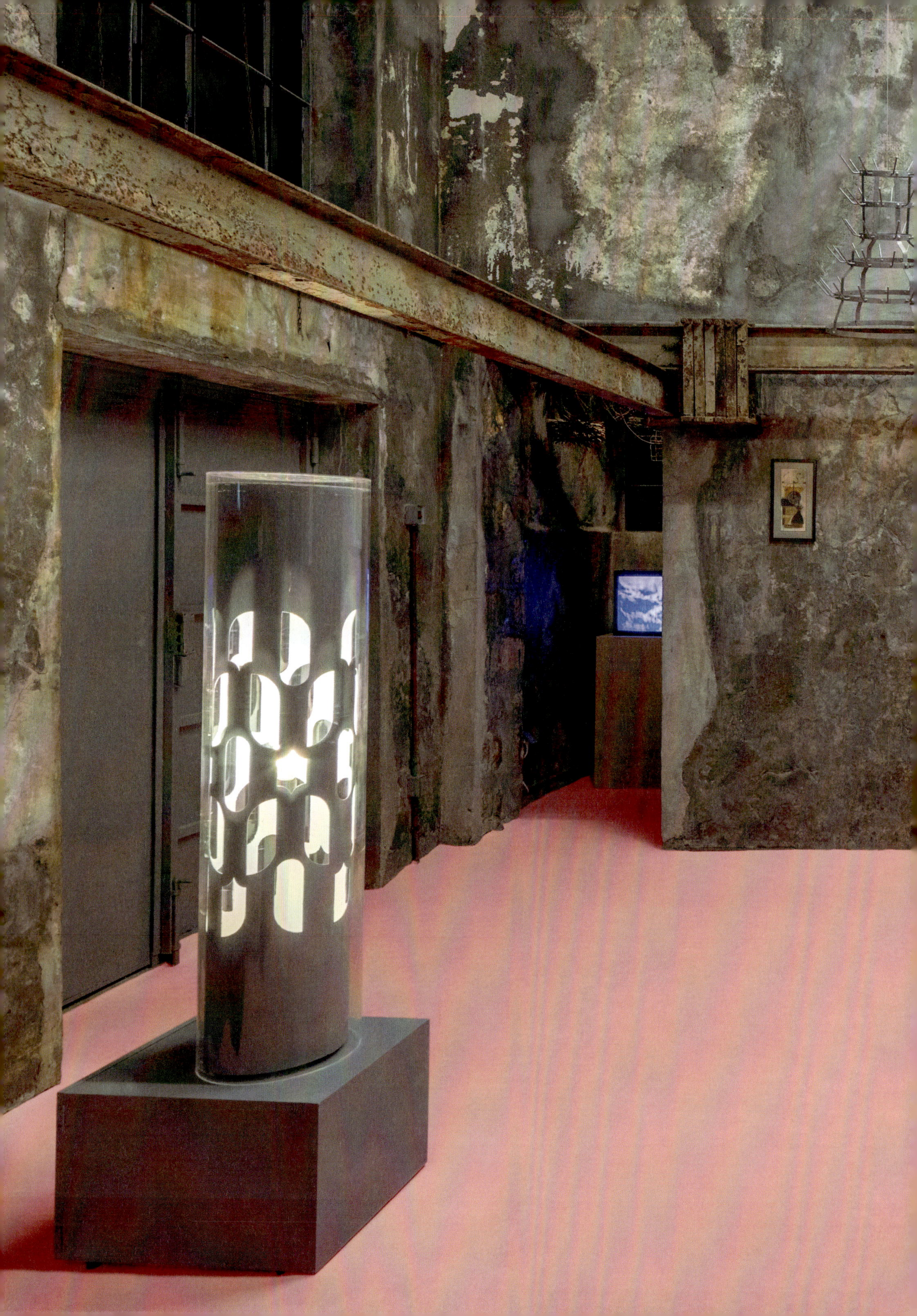

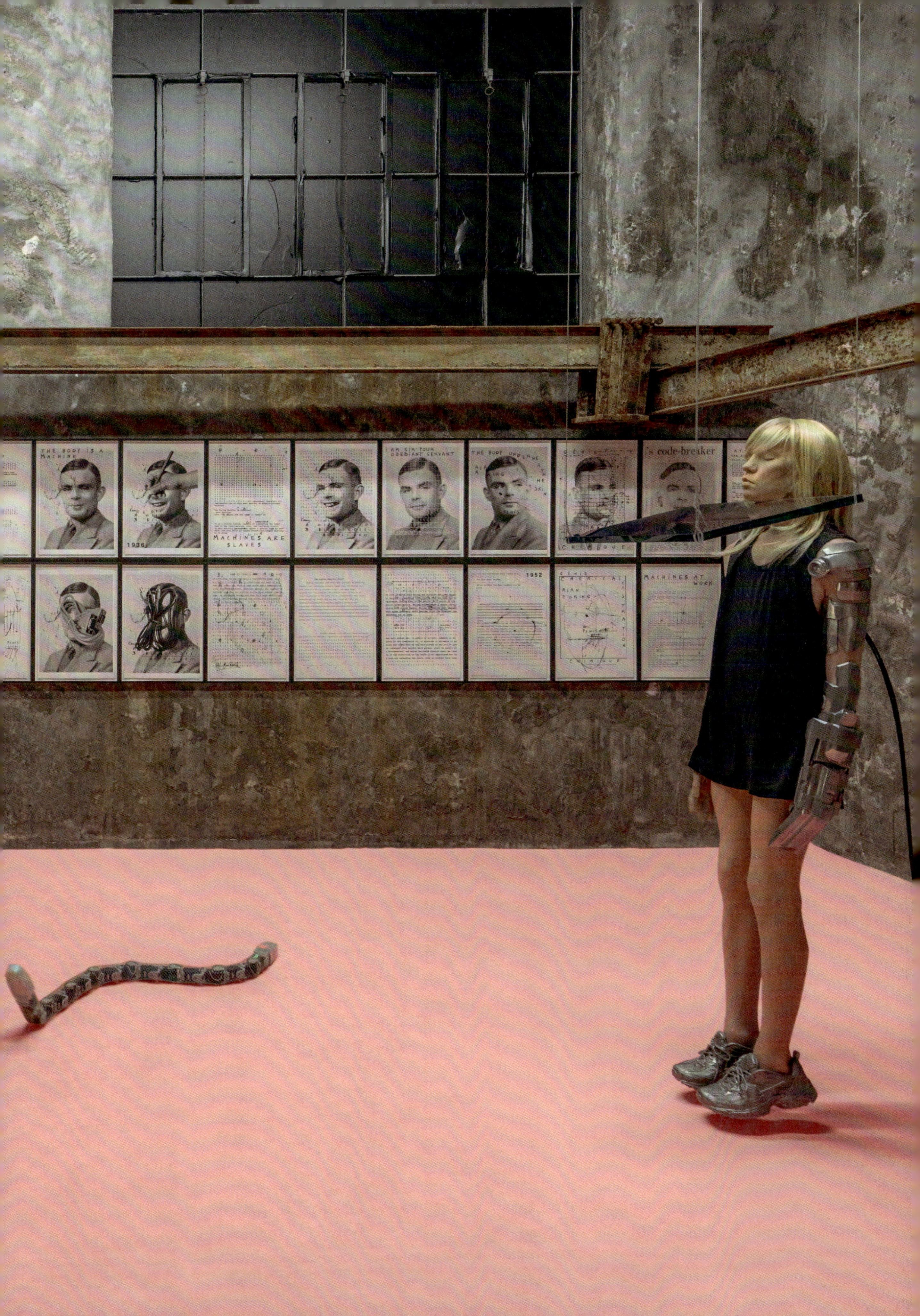

THE BODY IS A MACHINE
1936
MACHINES ARE SLAVES
I AM SIR, YOUR OBEDIANT SERVANT
THE BODY UNDERNEATH THE SKIN
ALAN TURING
's code-breaker
1952
CHEMICAL CASTRATION
ALAN TURING
CRITIQUE
MACHINES AT WORK

Brion Gysin
Dreamachine, 1961

Seth Price
Untitled Film/Right,
2006

Ulf Linde
*Replica of Marcel
Duchamp's Moulin à
Café*, 1911/1960

Sturtevant
Duchamp Porte-bouteilles,
1992

Henrik Olesen
A.T., 2012

Pamela Rosenkranz
Healer (Waters), 2019

Andro Wekua
Untitled, 2014

Andro Wekua
Untitled, 2014

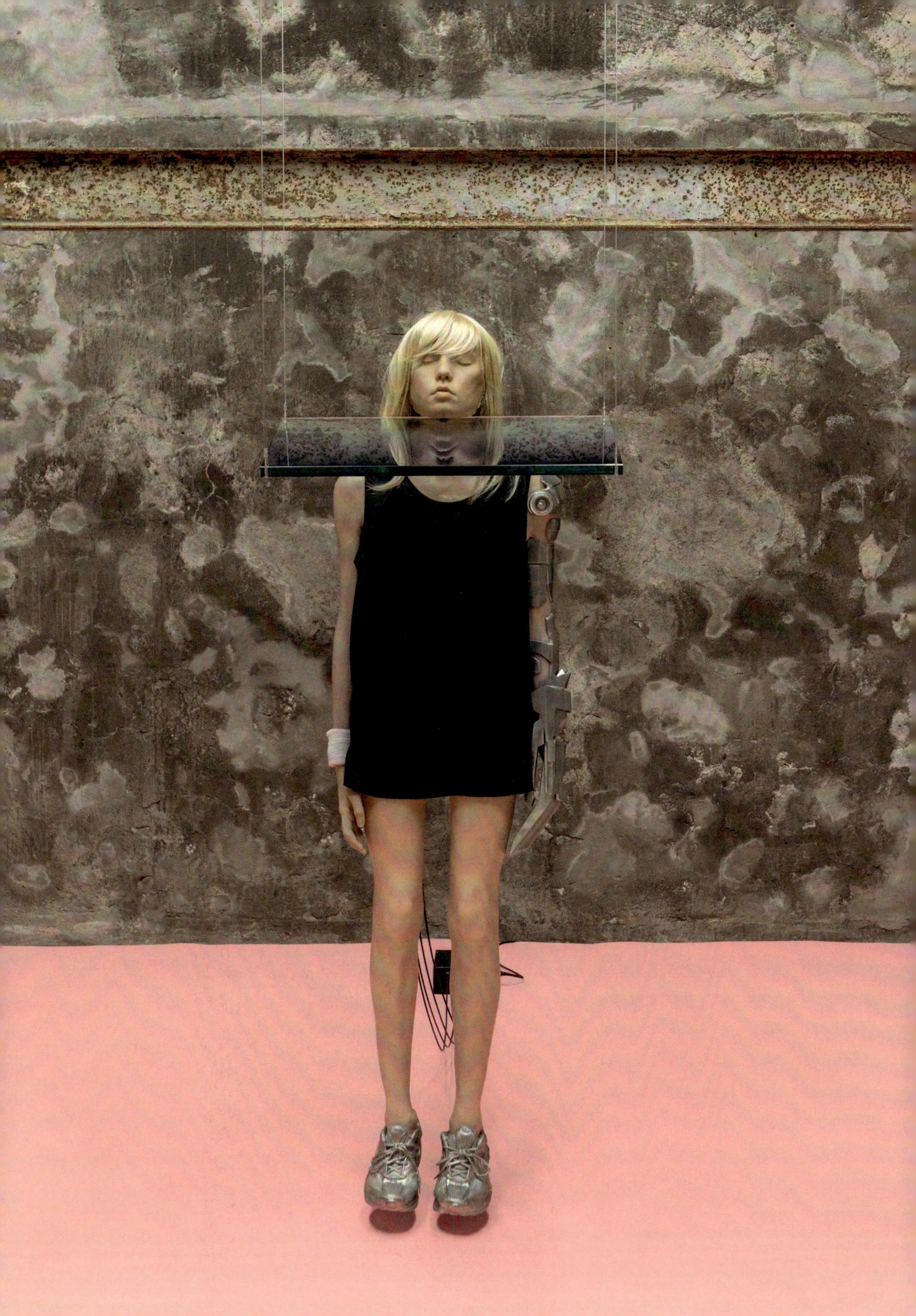

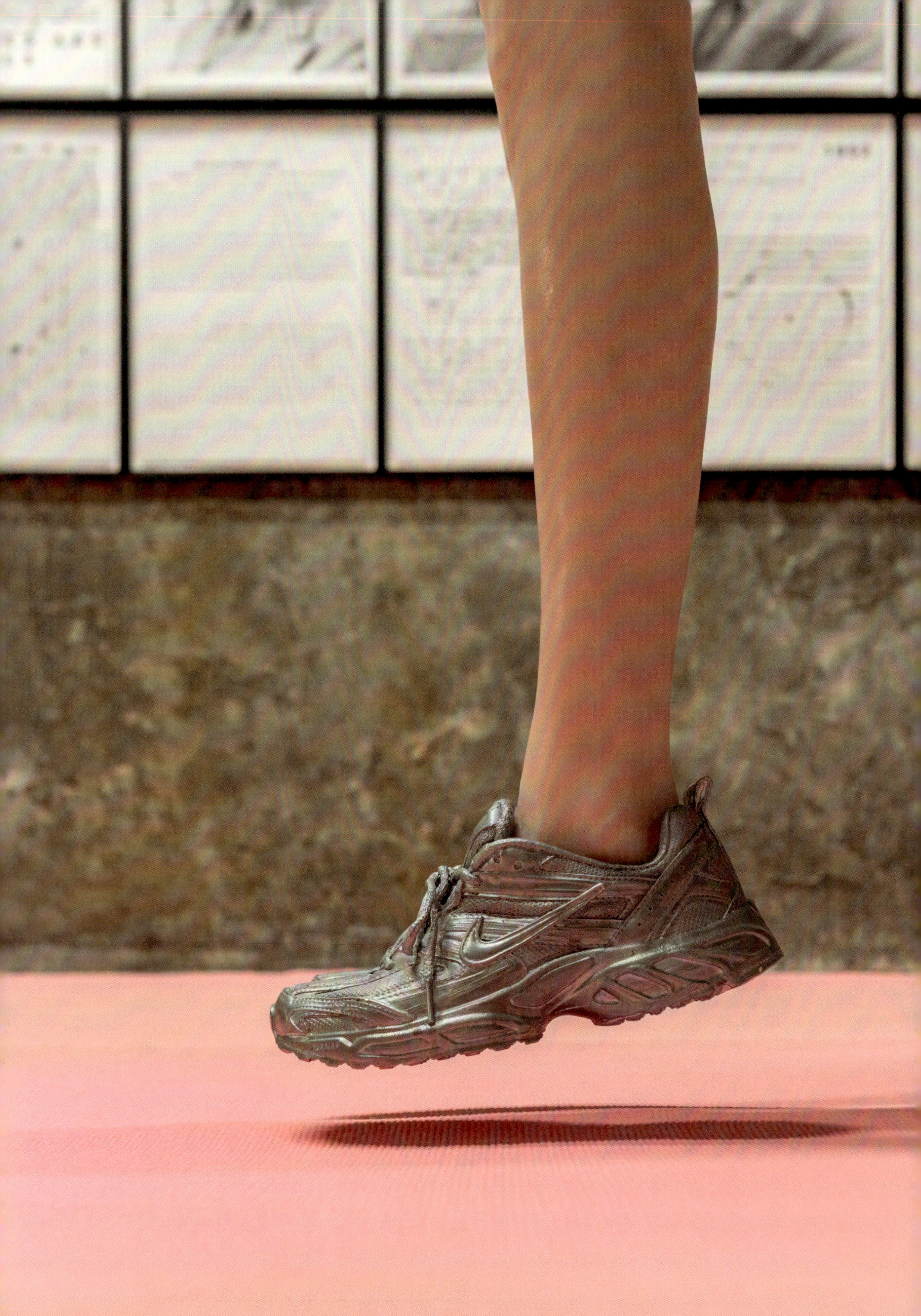

P.068 INSTALLATION VIEW (L–R) P.069

Henrik Olesen
A.T., 2012

Andro Wekua
Untitled, 2014

Pipilotti Rist
*Selbstlos im Lavabad
(Selfless in the Bath
of Lava) (Bastard Version)*,
1994

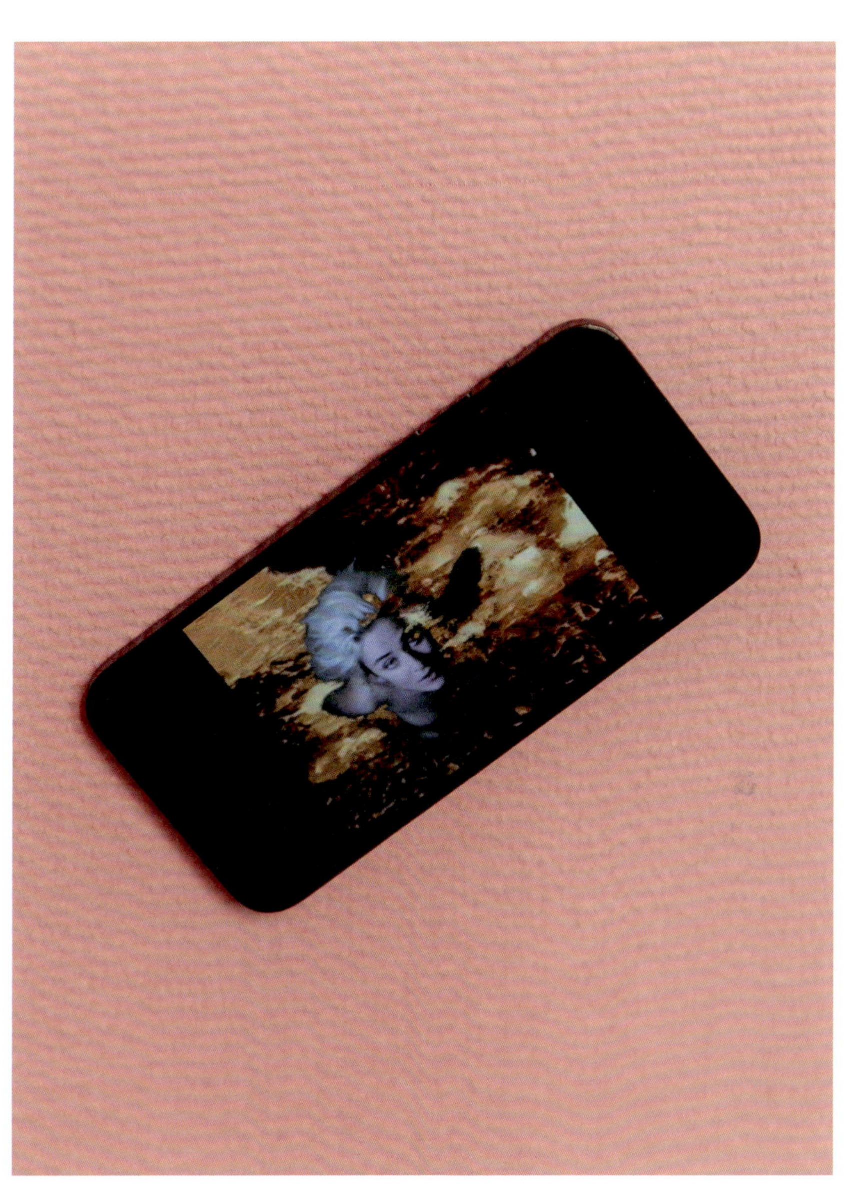

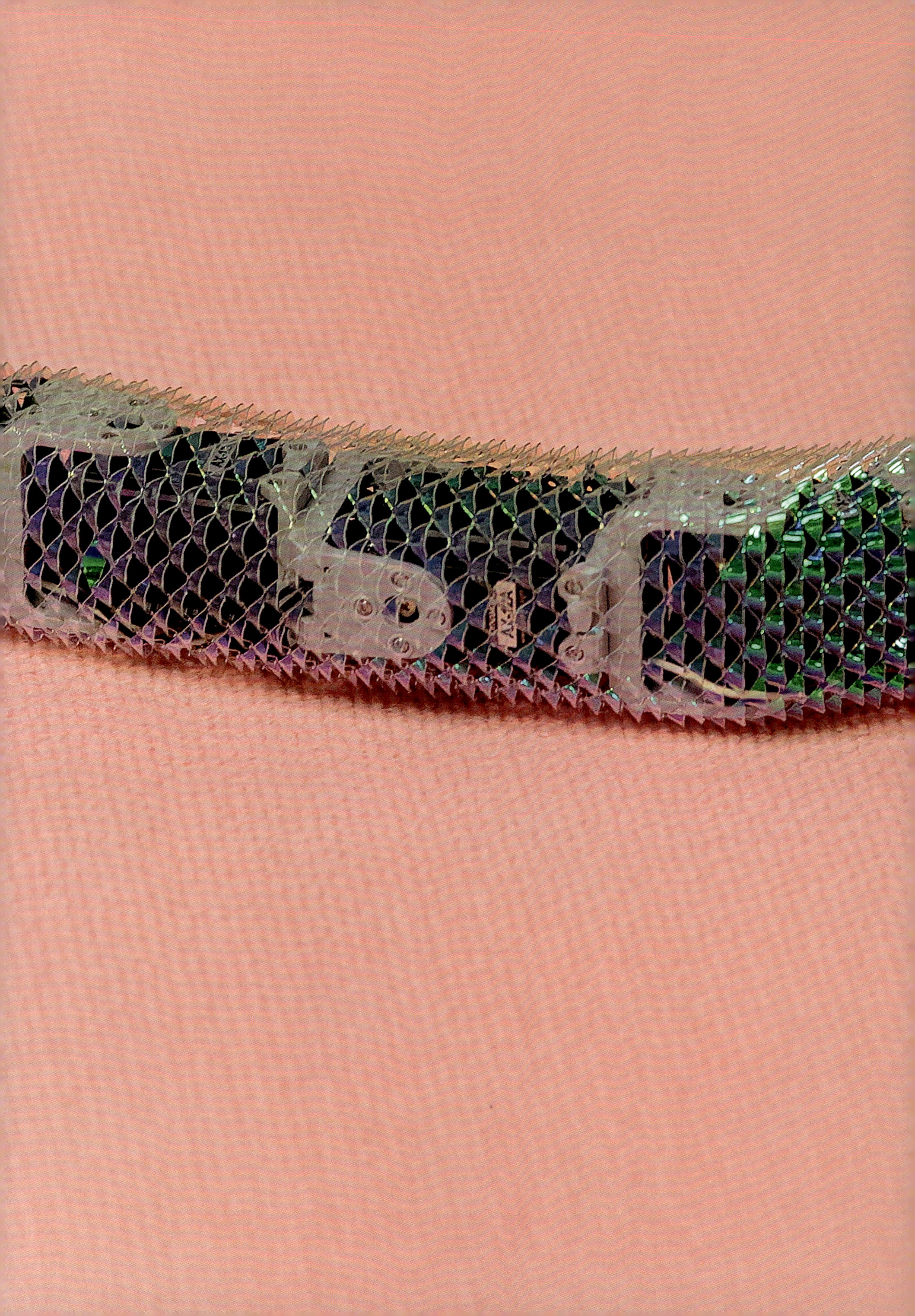

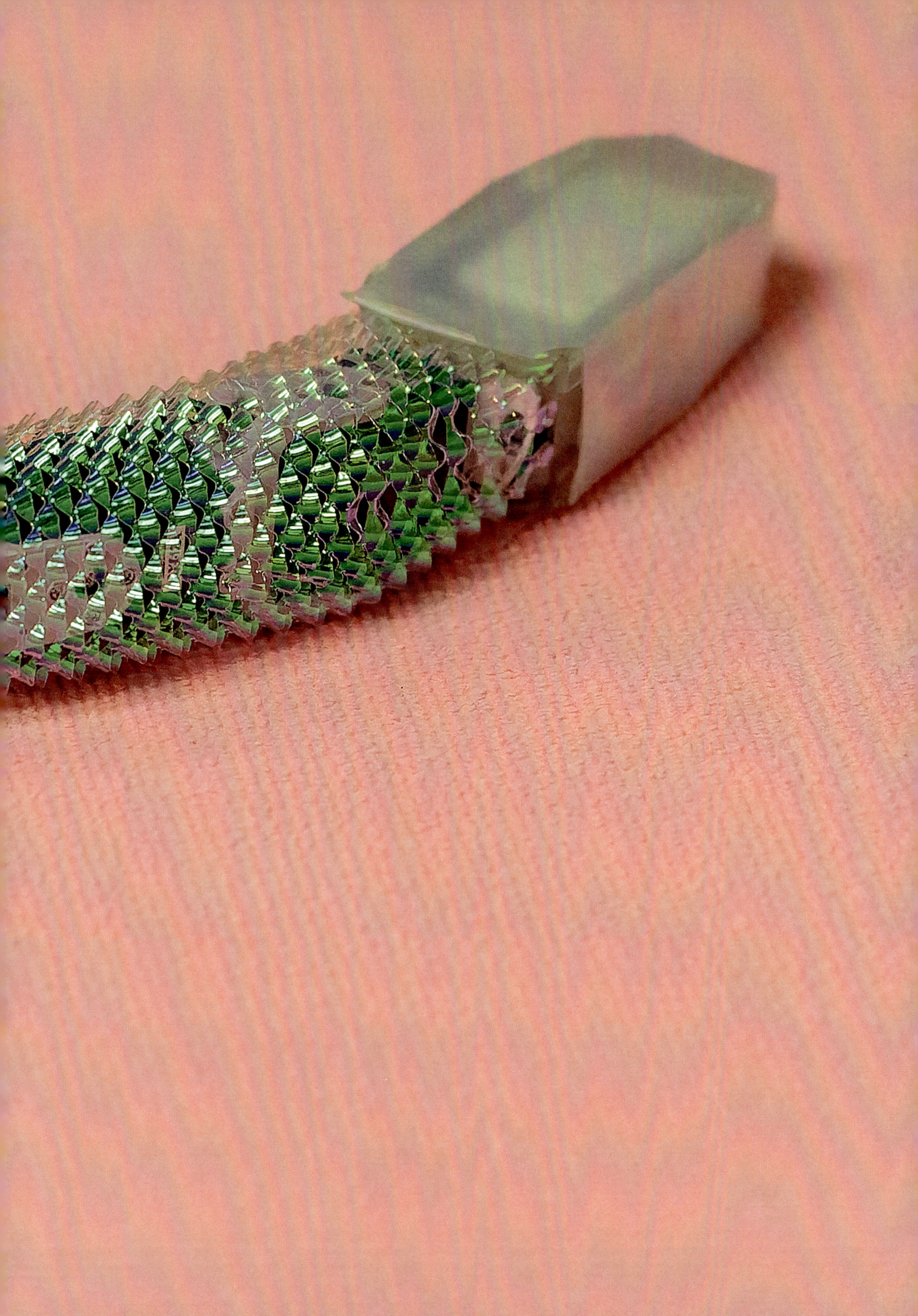

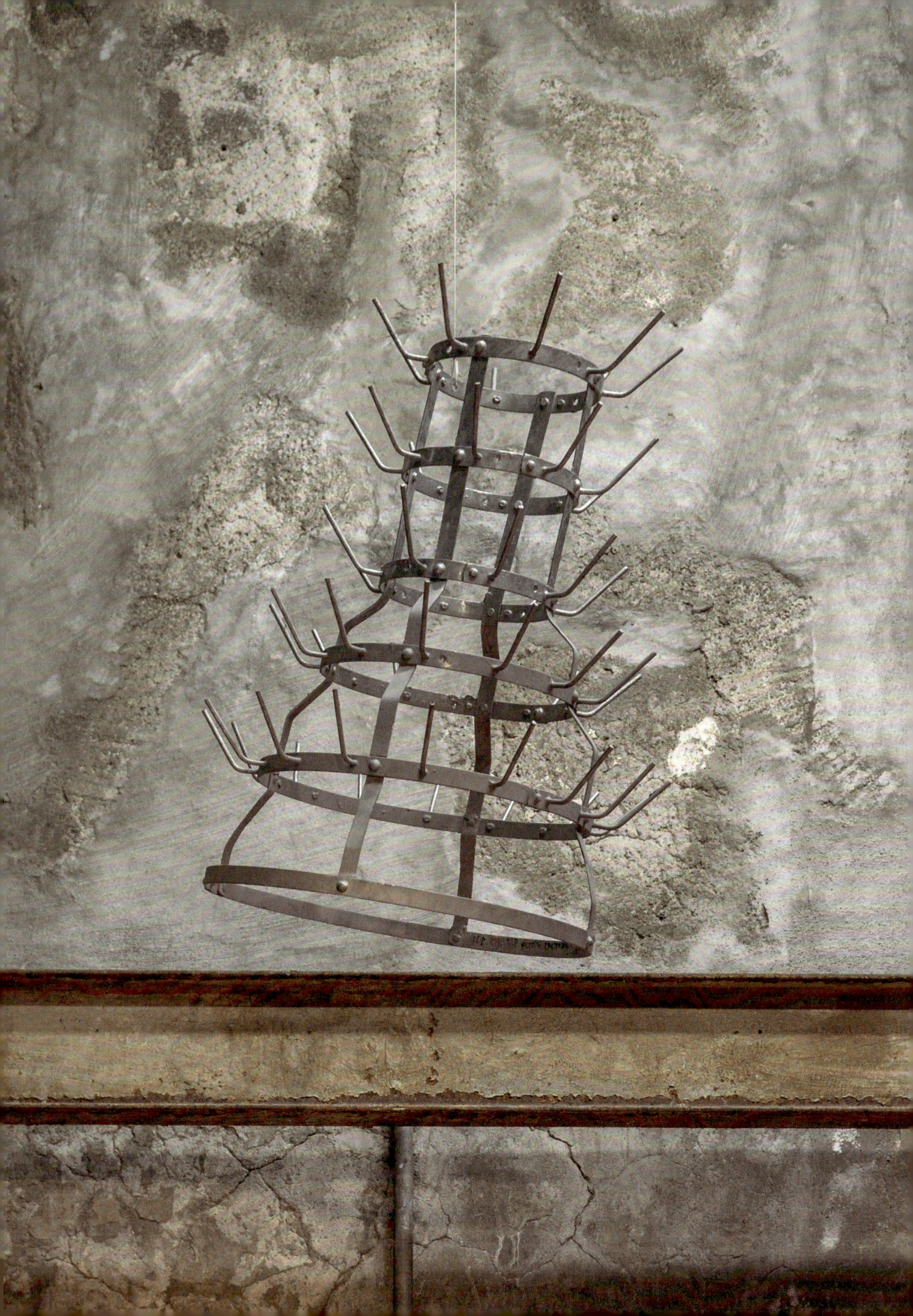

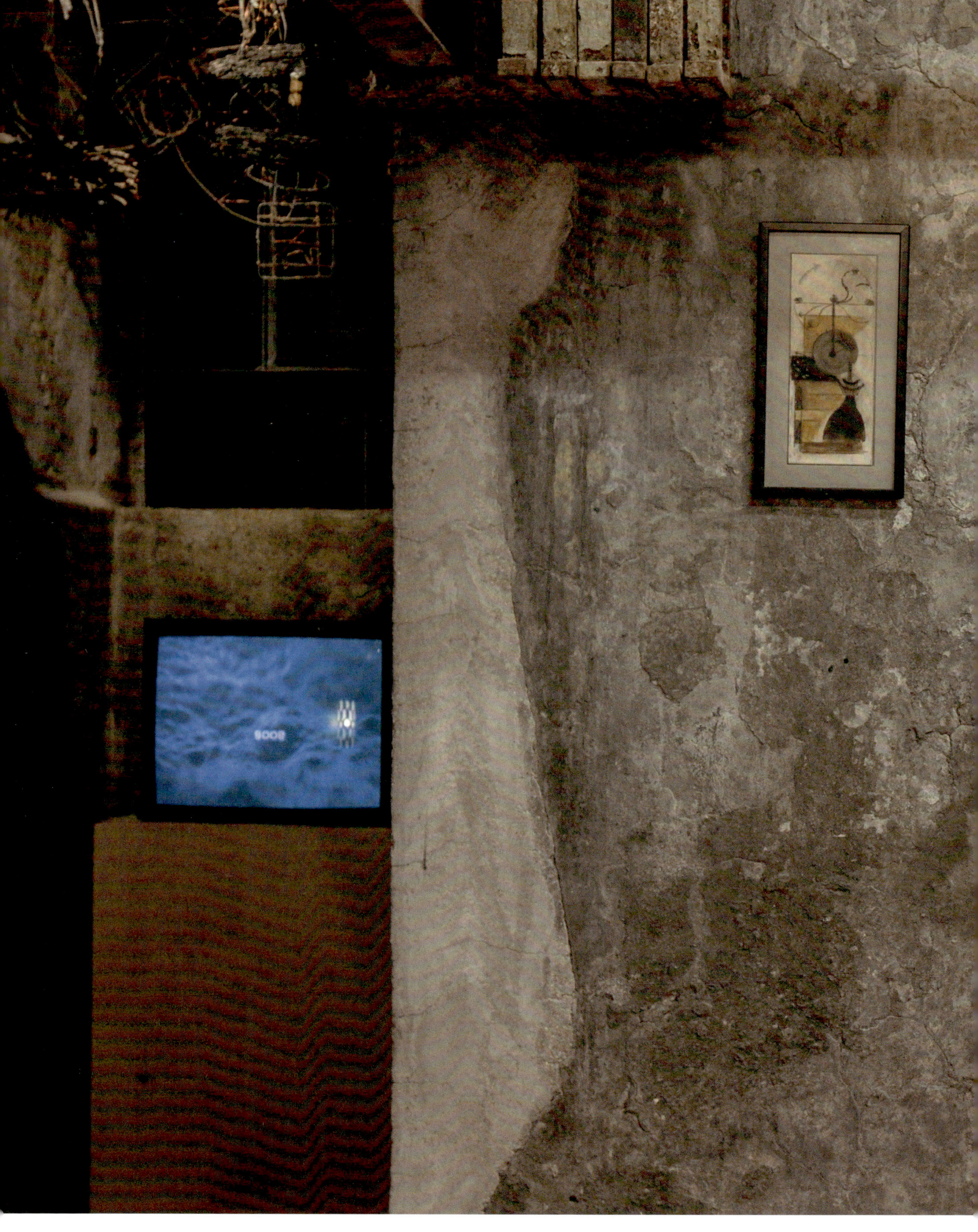

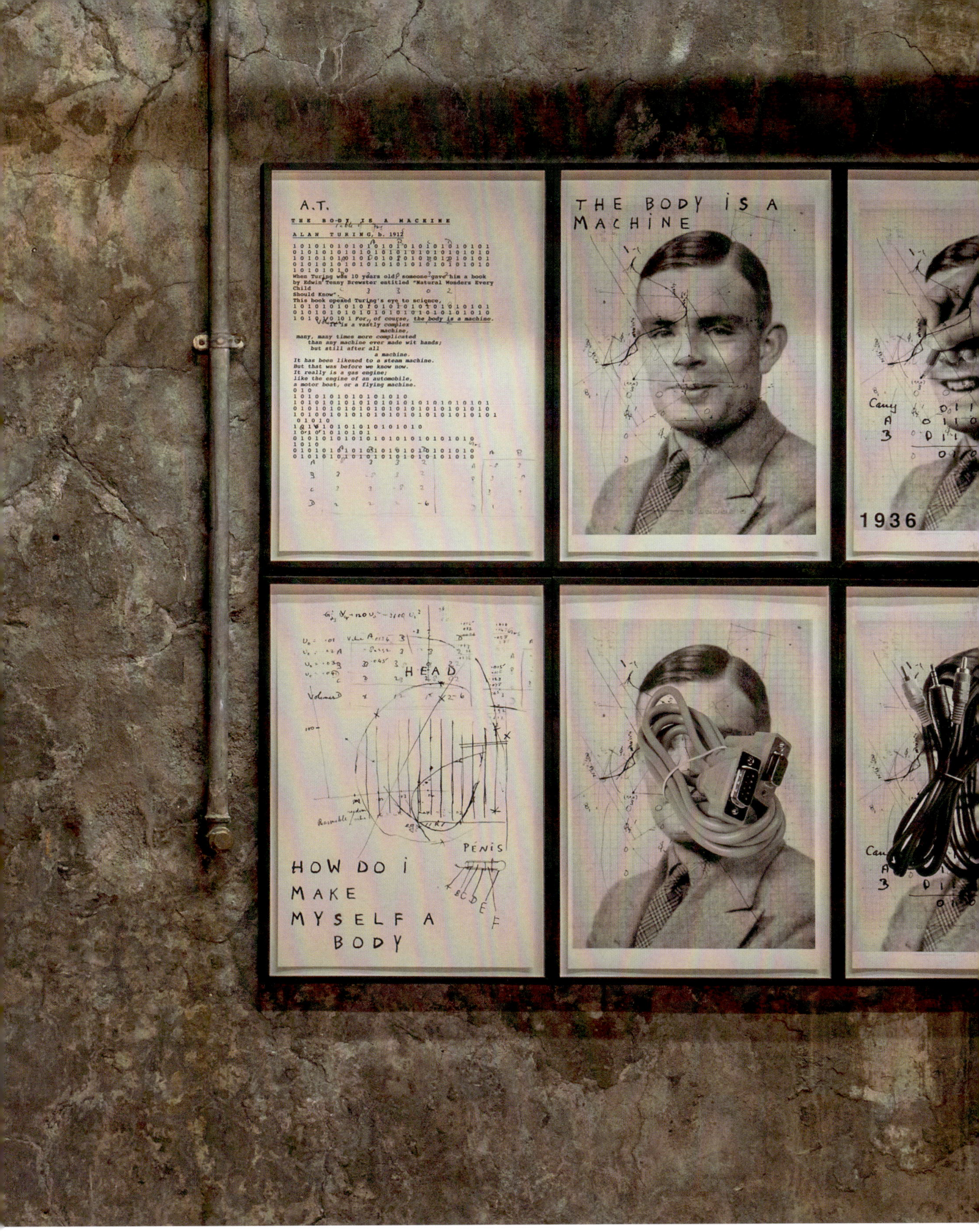

A.T.
THE BODY IS A MACHINE
ALAN TURING, b. 1912
1 0 1 0 1 0 1 0 1 0 1 0 1 0 1 0 1 0 1 0 1 0 1 0 1 0 1
0 1 0 1 0 1 0 1 0 1 0 1 0 1 0 1 0 1 0 1 0 1 0 1 0 1 0
1 0 1 0 1 0 1 0 0 1 0 0 1 0 1 0 1 0 1 0 0 1 0 1 0 1 0 1
0 1 0 1 0 1 0 1 0 1 0 1 0 1 0 1 0 1 0 1 0 1 0 1 0 1 0
1 0 1 0 1 0 1 0
When Turing was 10 years old someone gave him a book
by Edwin Tenny Brewster entitled "Natural Wonders Every
Child
Should Know".
This book opened Turing's eye to science,
1 0 1 0 1 0 1 0 1 0 1 0 1 0 1 0 1 0 1 0 1 0 1 0 1 0 1
0 1 0 1 0 1 0 1 0 1 0 1 0 1 0 1 0 1 0 1 0 1 0 1 0 1 0
1 0 1 0 1 0 10 1 For, of course, the body is a machine.
It is a vastly complex
machine,
many, many times more complicated
than any machine ever made wit hands;
but still after all
a machine.
It has been likened to a steam machine.
But that was before we know now.
It really is a gas engine;
like the engine of an automobile,
a motor boat, or a flying machine.
0 1 0
1 0 1 0 1 0 1 0 1 0 1 0 1 0 1 0
1 0 1 0 1 0 1 0 1 0 1 0 1 0 1 0 1 0 1 0 1 0 1 0 1 0 1
0 1 0 1 0 1 0 1 0 1 0 1 0 1 0 1 0 1 0 1 0 1 0 1 0 1 0
1 0 1 0 0 1 0 1 0 1 0 1 0 1 0 1 0 1 0 1 0 1 0 1 0 1 0 1
0 1 0 1 0
1 0 1 0 1 0 1 0 1 0 1 0 1 0 1 0
1 0 1 0 1 0 1 0 1 0 1
0 1 0 1 0 1 0 1 0 1 0 1 0 1 0 1 0 1 0 1 0 1 0 1 0 1 0
1 0 1 0
0 1 0 1 0 1 0 1 0 1 0 1 0 1 0 1 0 1 0 1 0 1 0 1 0 1 0
0 1 0 1 0 1 0 1 0 1 0 1 0 1 0 1 0 1 0 1 0 1 0 1 0 1 0
THE BODY IS A MACHINE
1936
HOW DO I
MAKE
MYSELF A
BODY
HEAD
PENIS

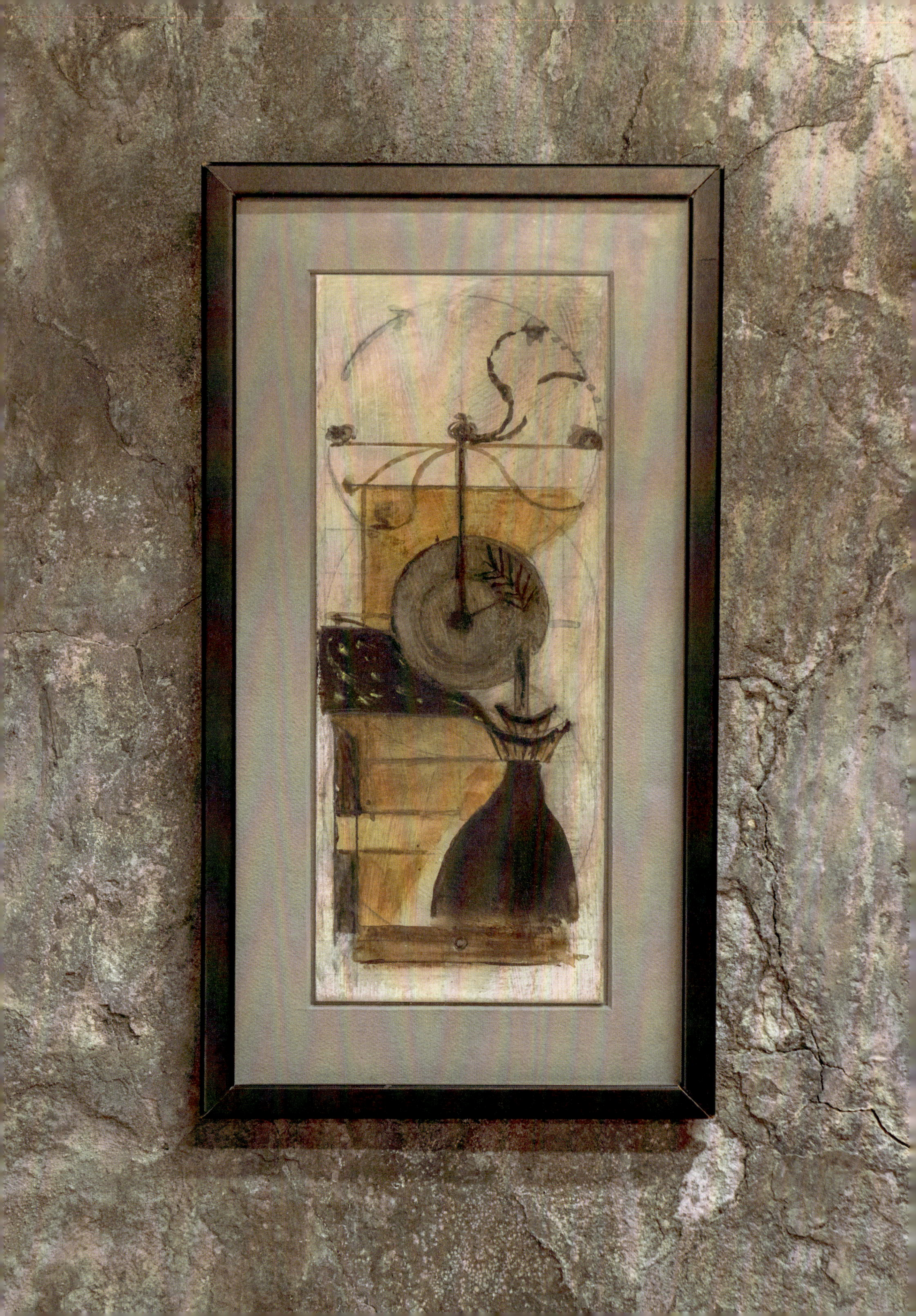

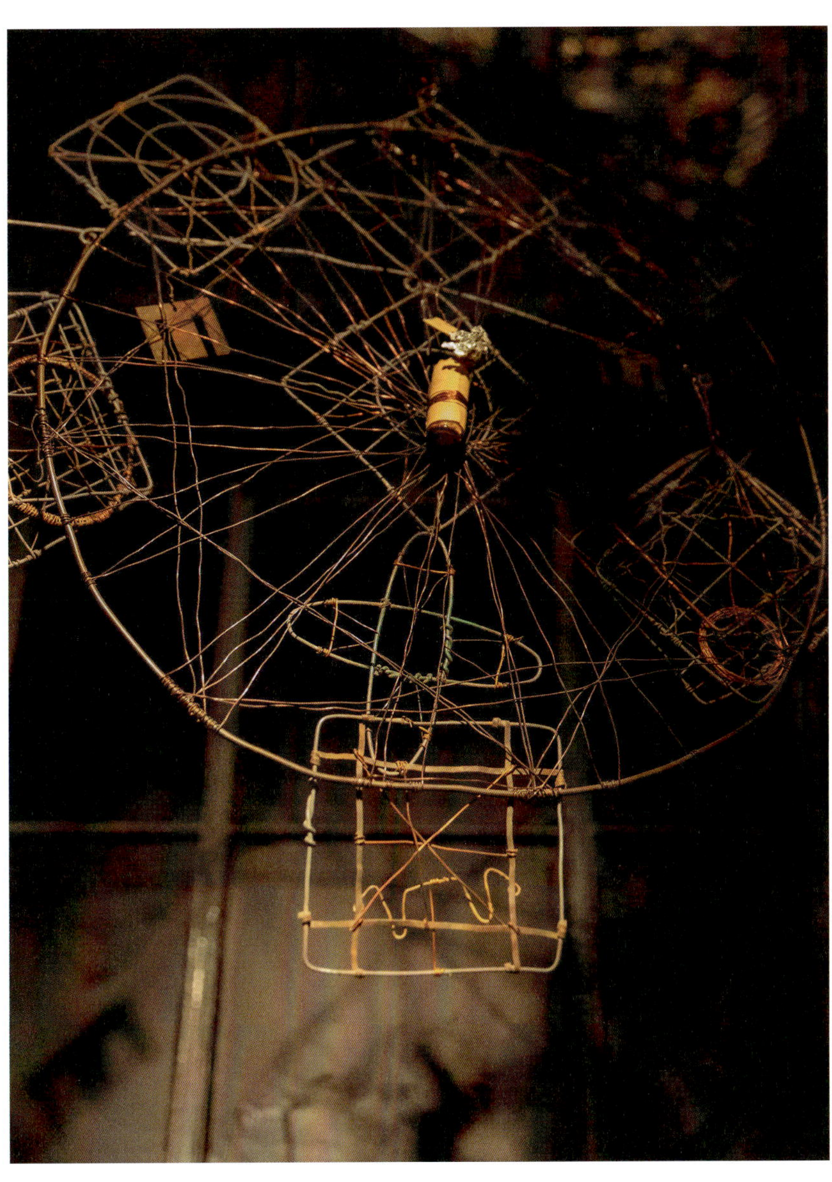

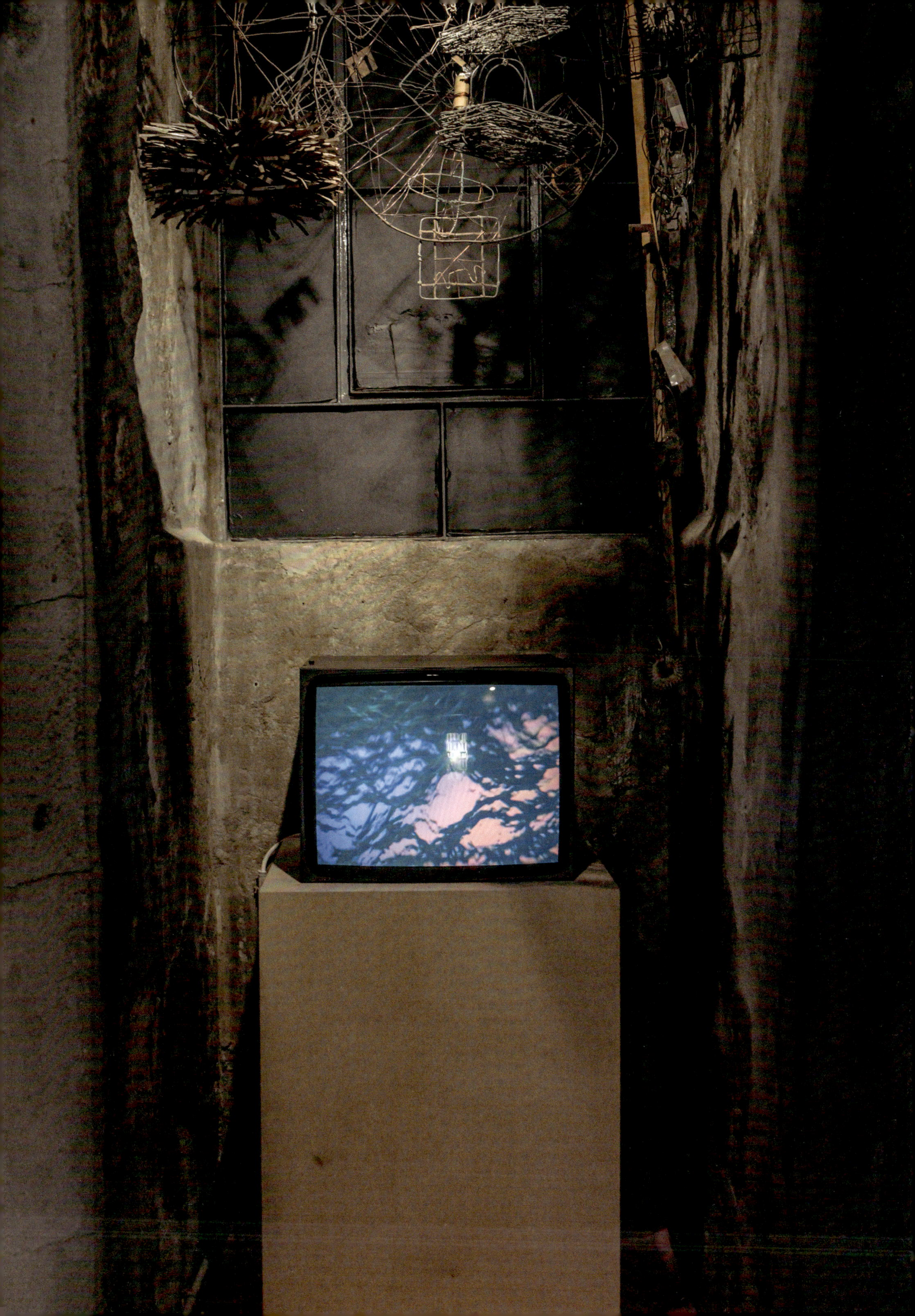

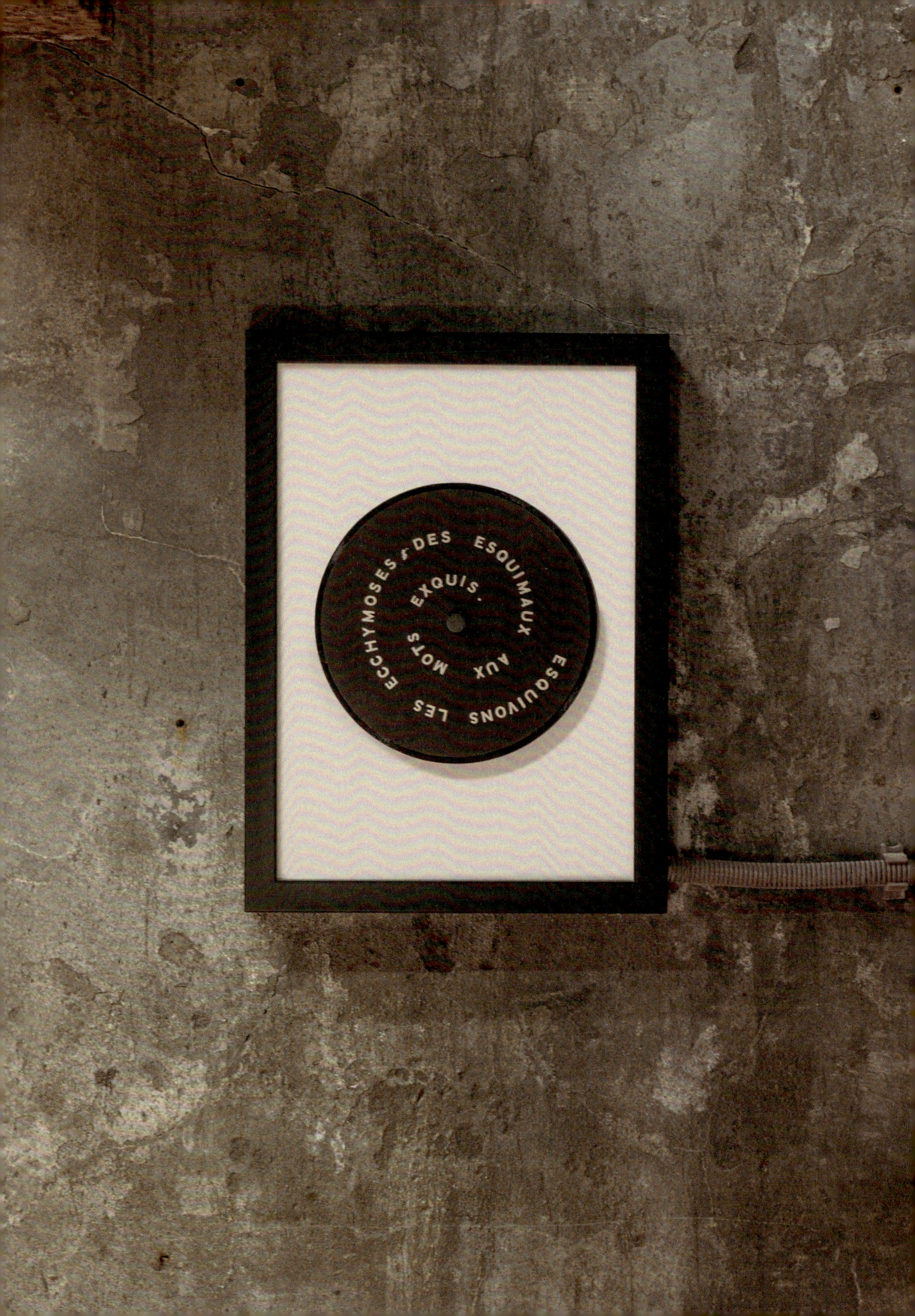
ECCHYMOSES DES ESQUIMAUX
ESQUIVONS LES MOTS AUX
EXQUIS.

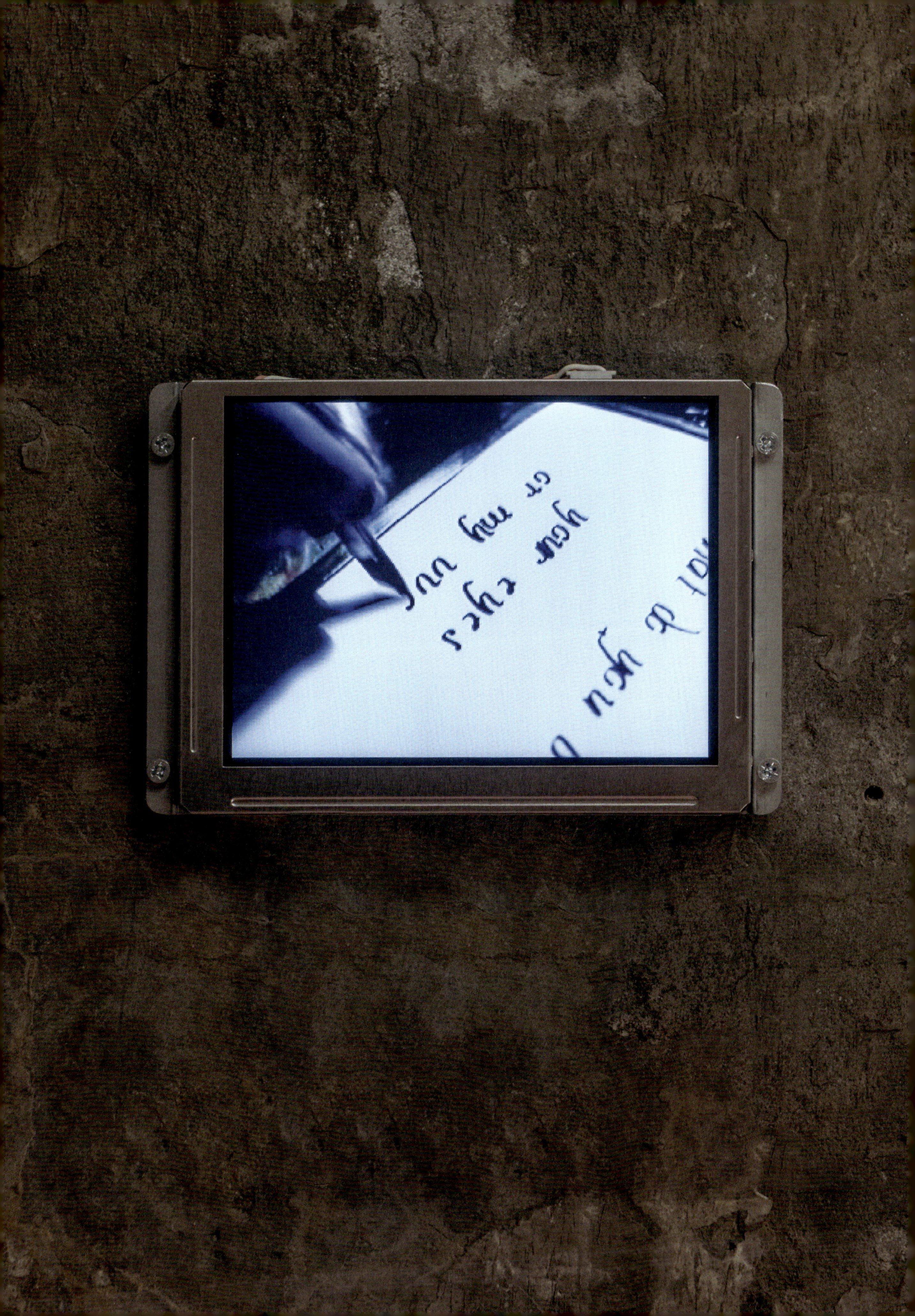

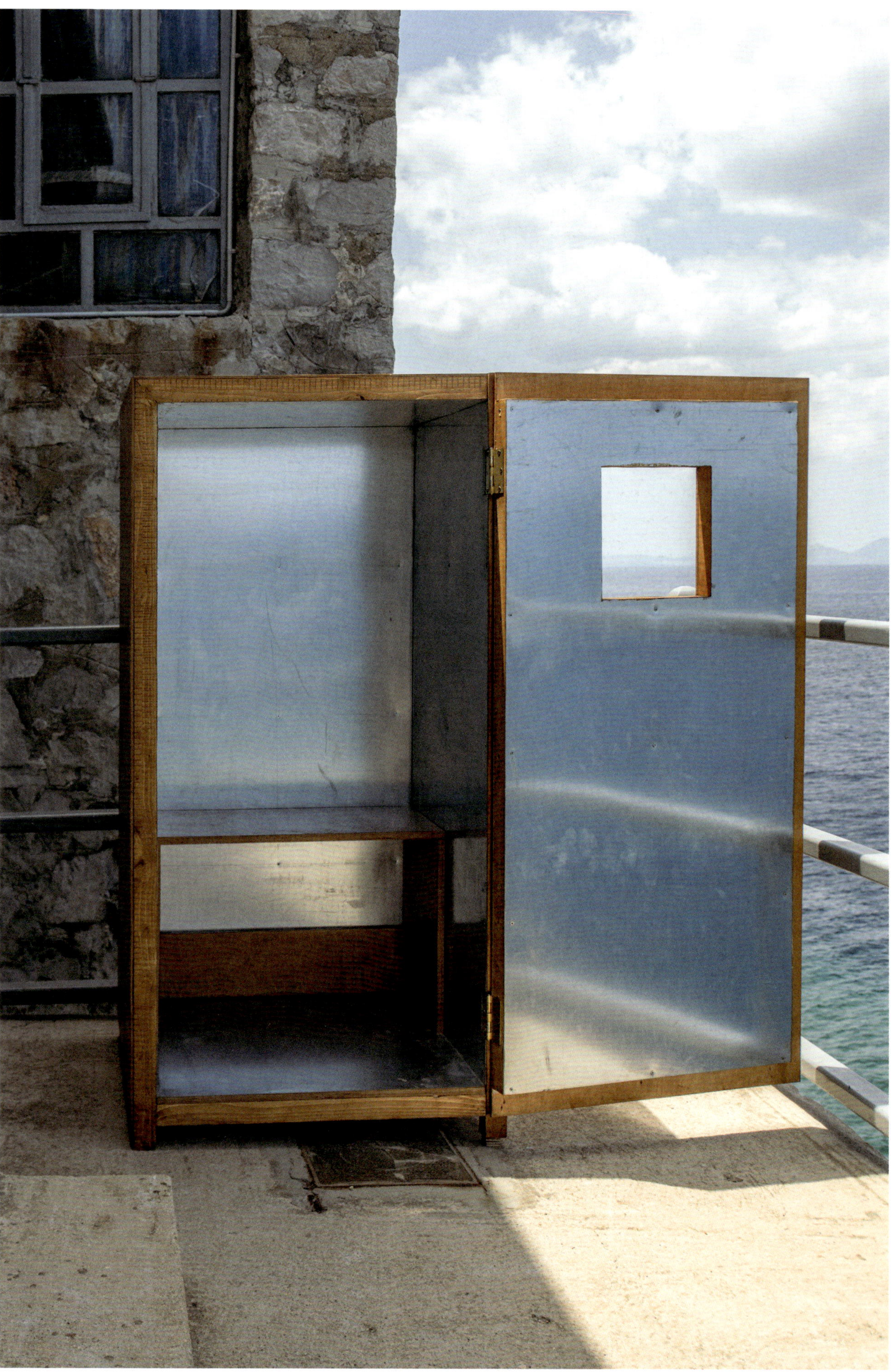

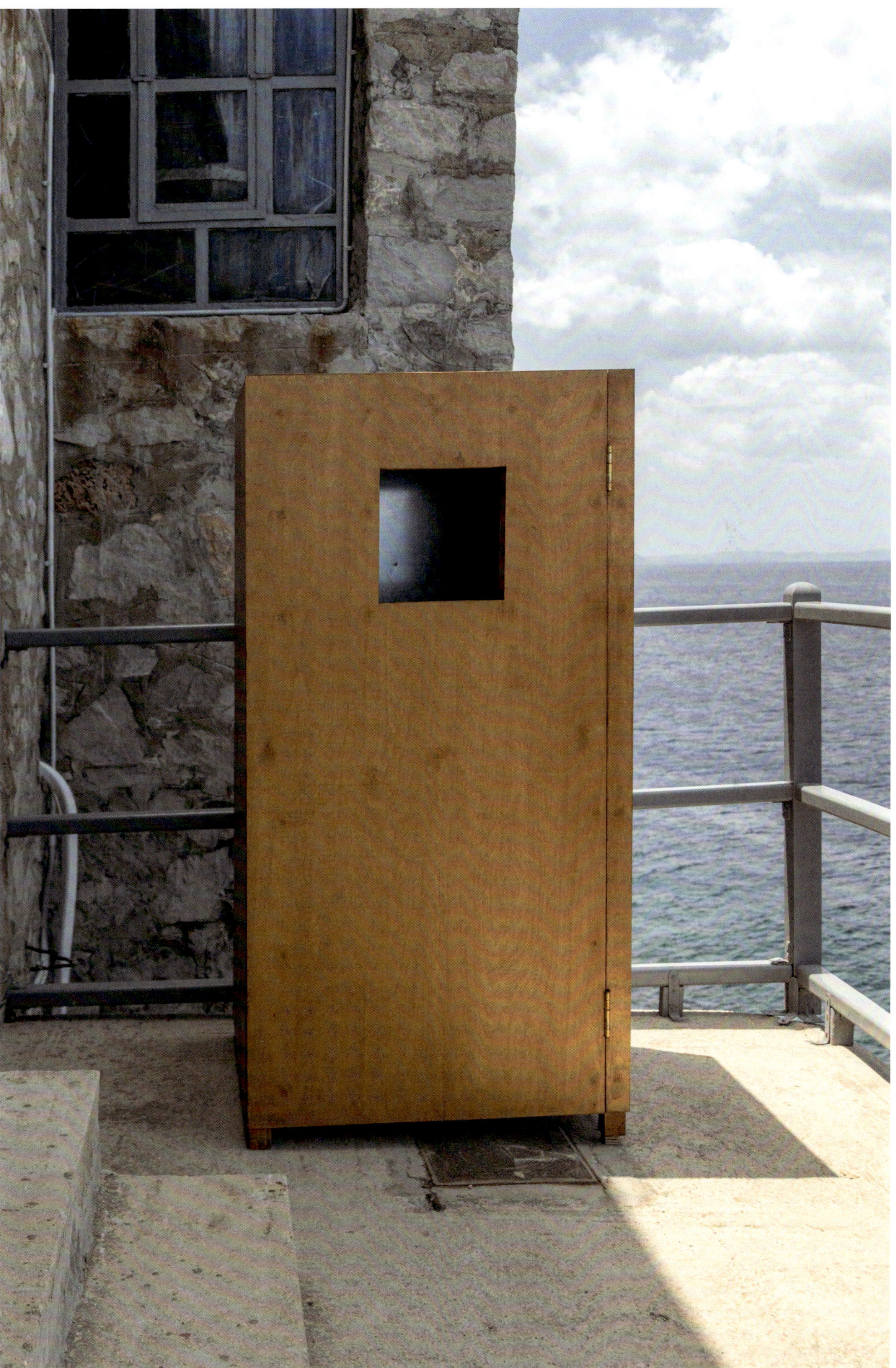

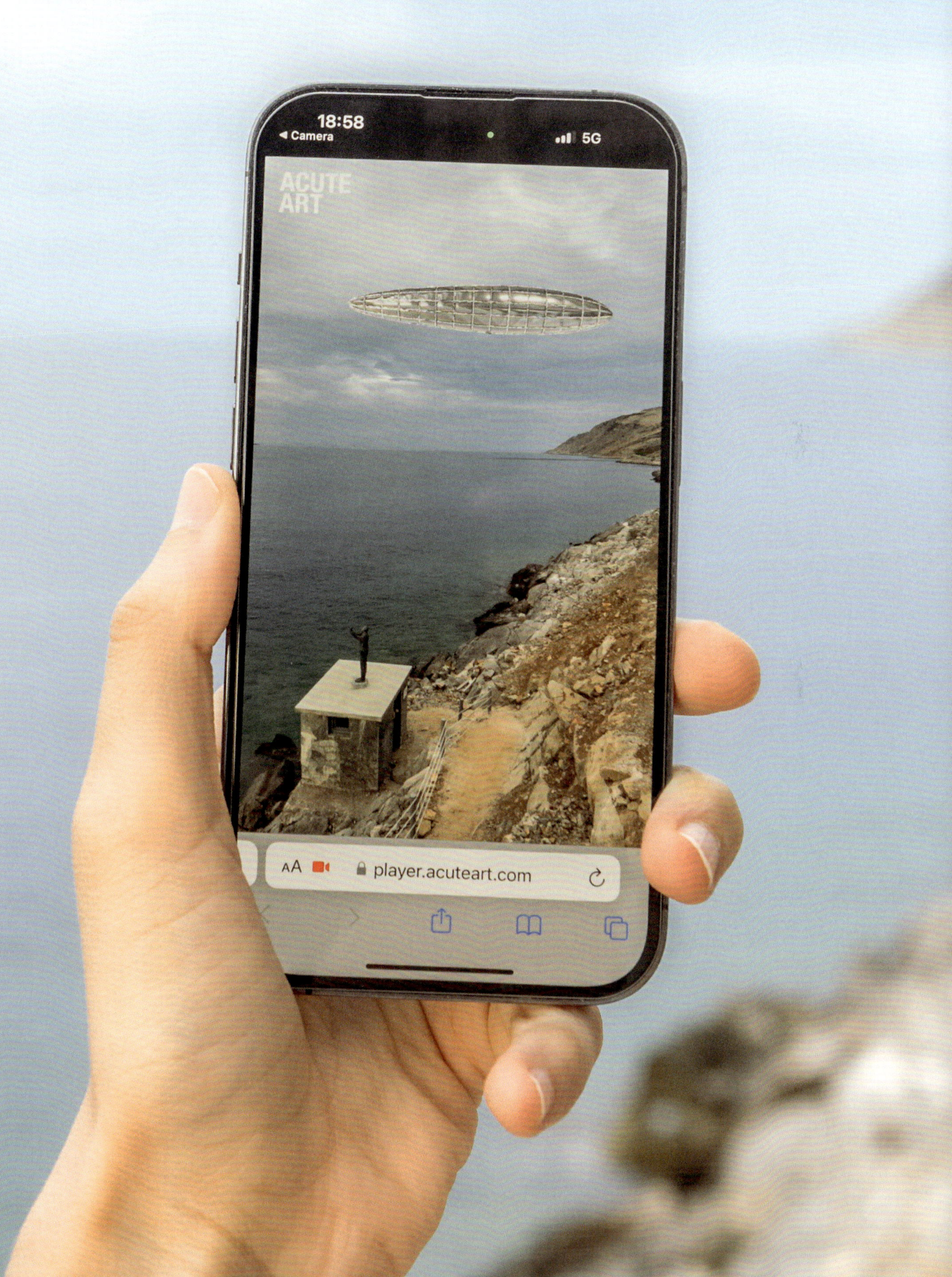
18:58
Camera
5G
ACUTE
ART
AA
player.acuteart.com

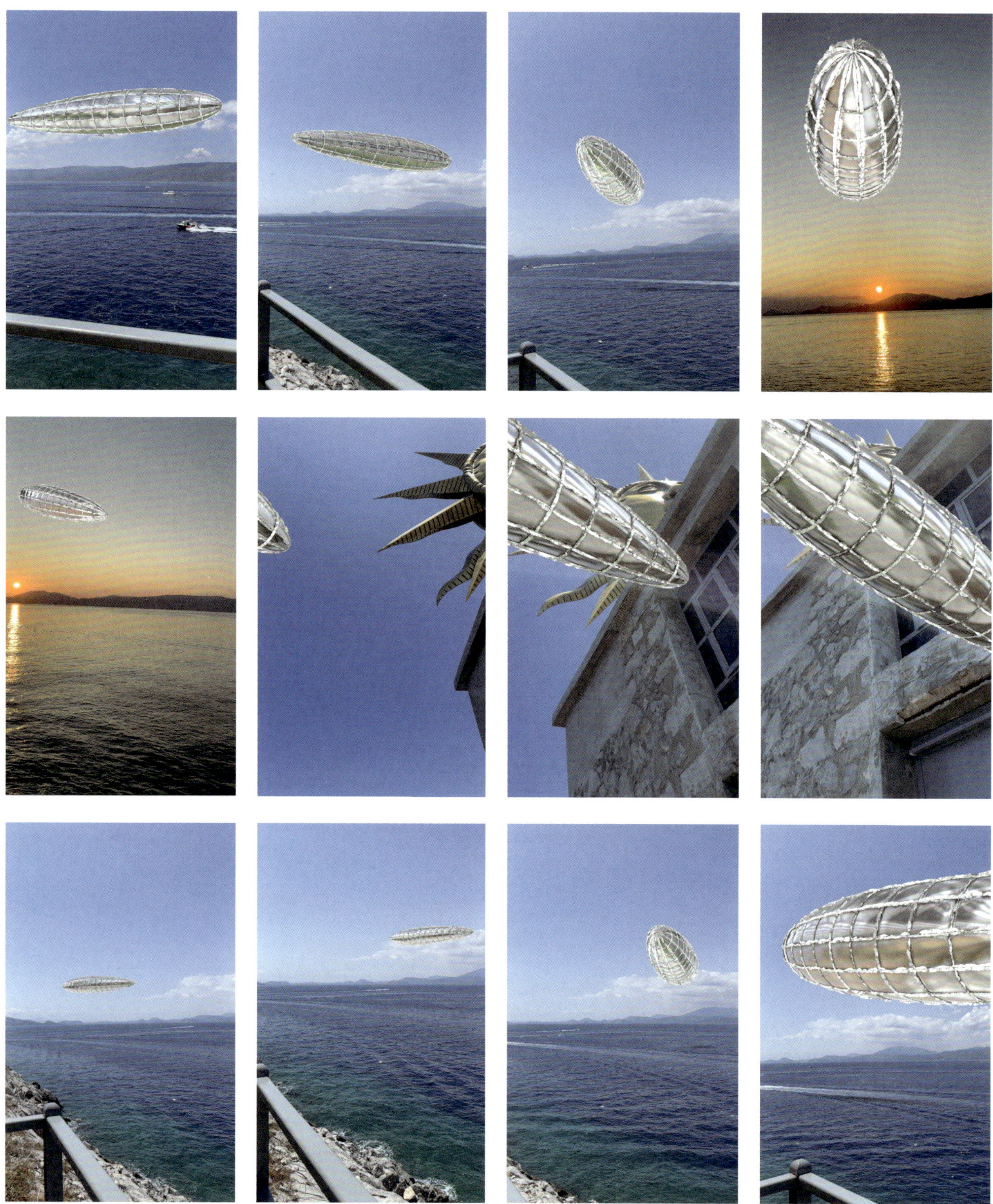

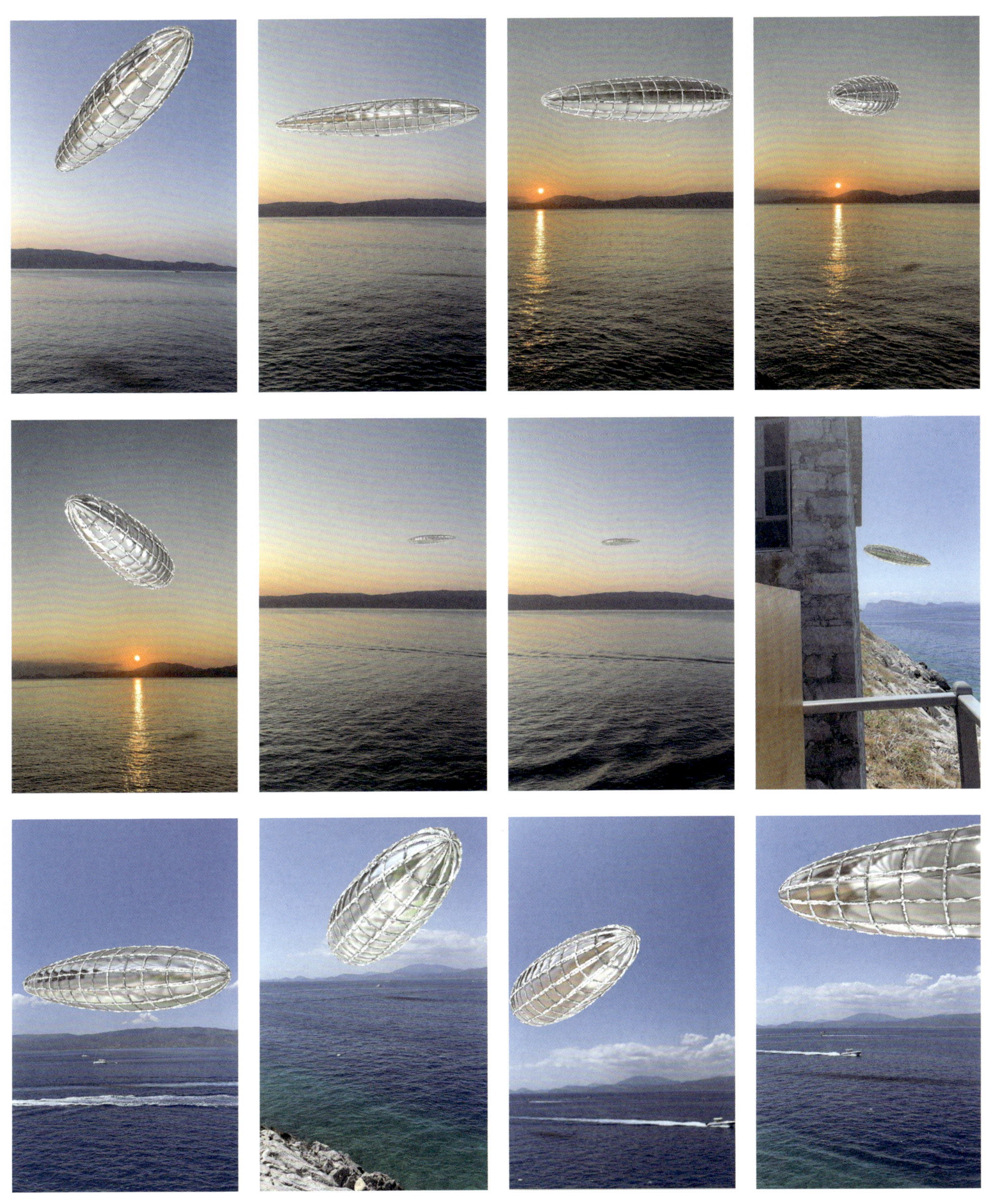

PP.086–087 Lee Bul
Willing to Be Vulnerable –
Metalized Balloon
VER.AR22, 2022

PP.088–089 INSTALLATION VIEW (L–R)
Jeff Koons
Apollo Wind Spinner,
2020–22

Judith Hopf
Phone User 5, 2021–22

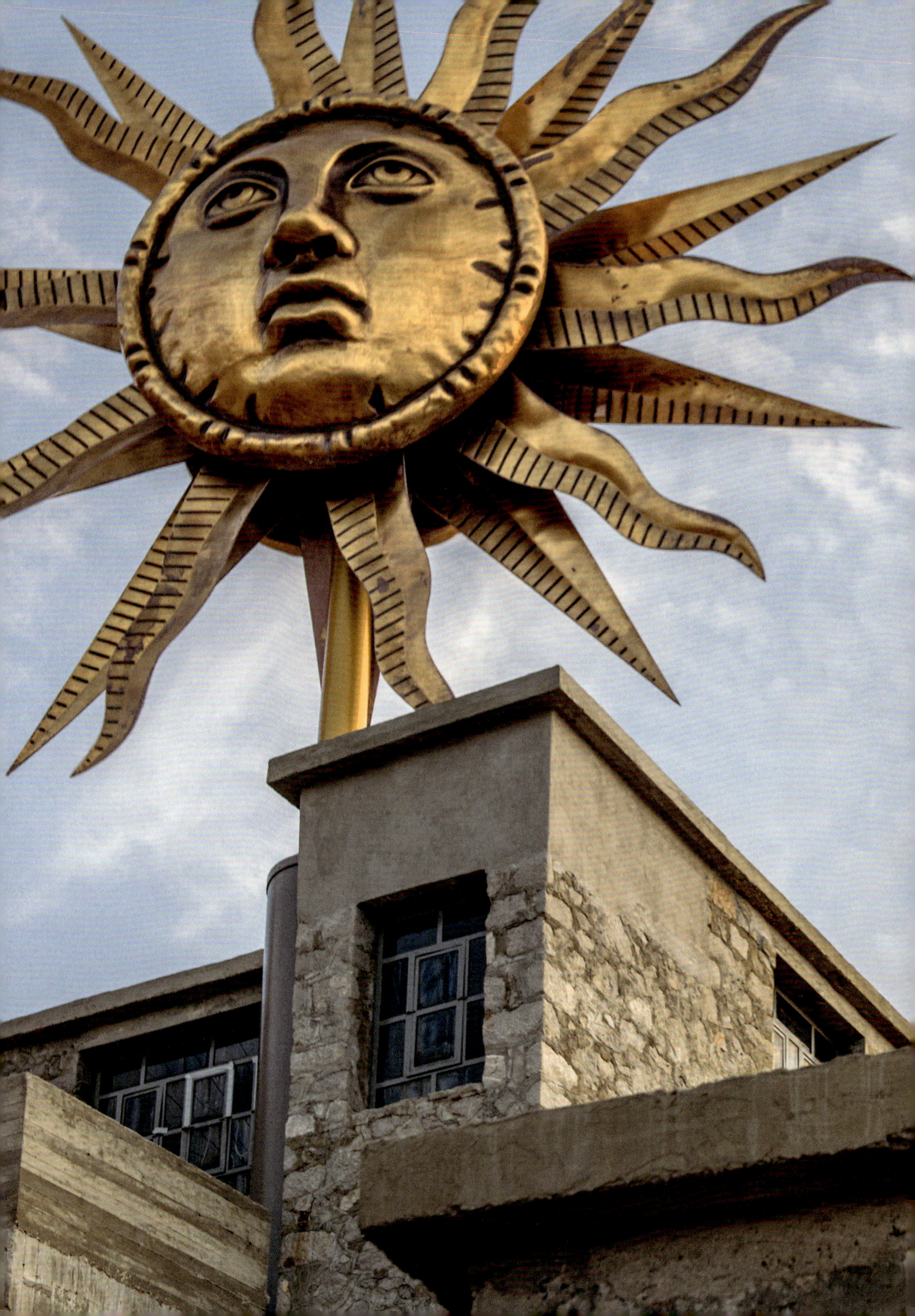

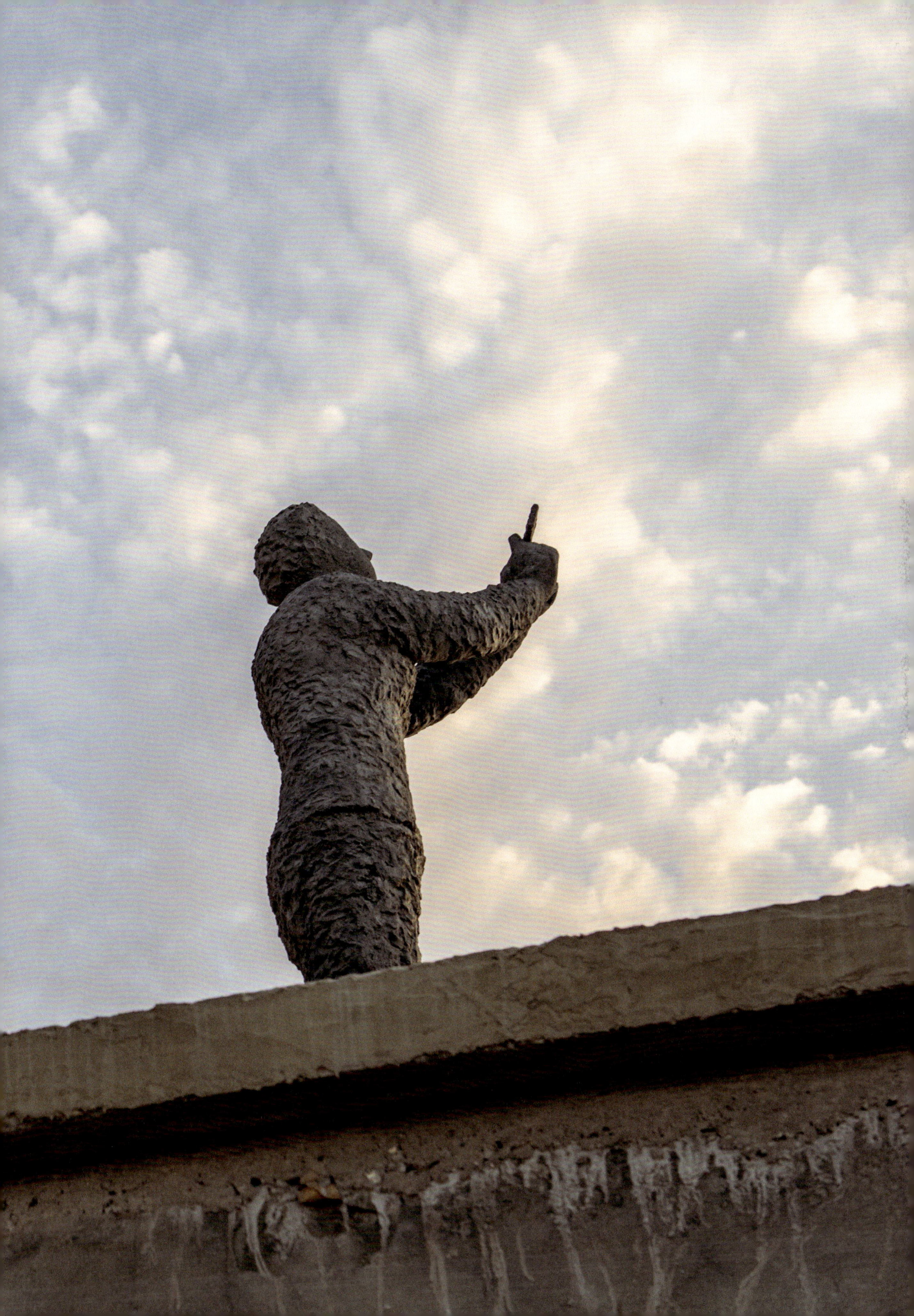

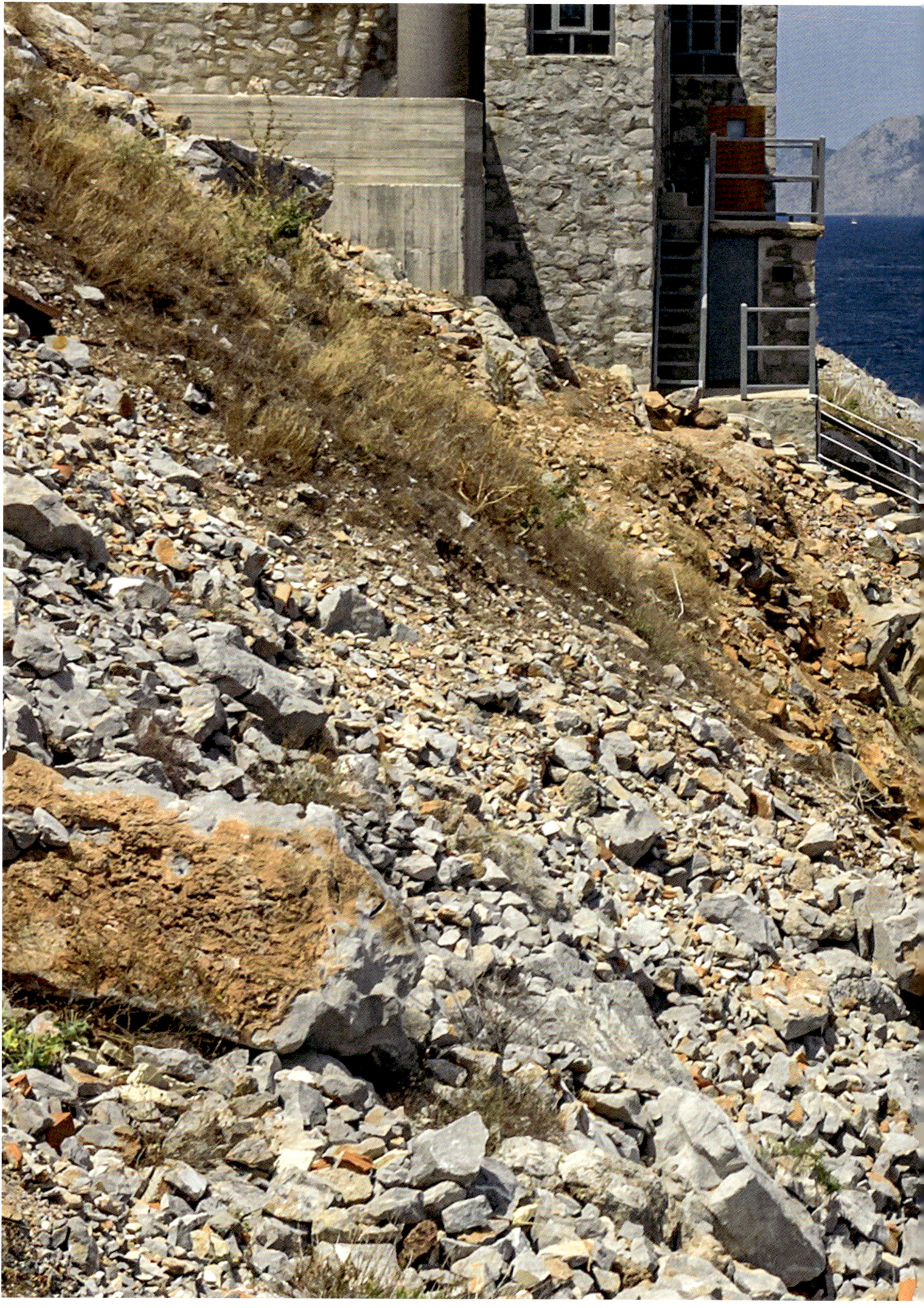

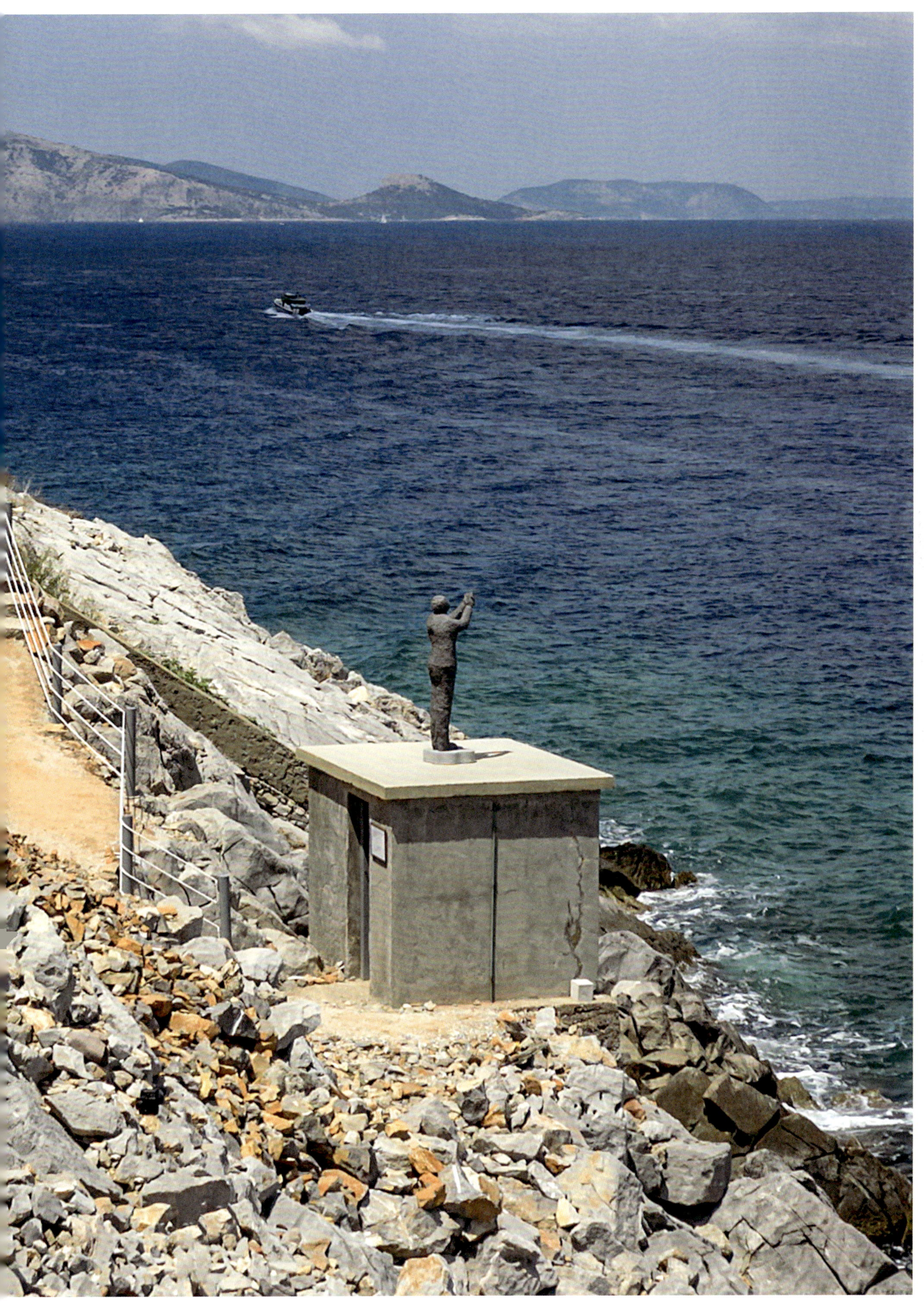

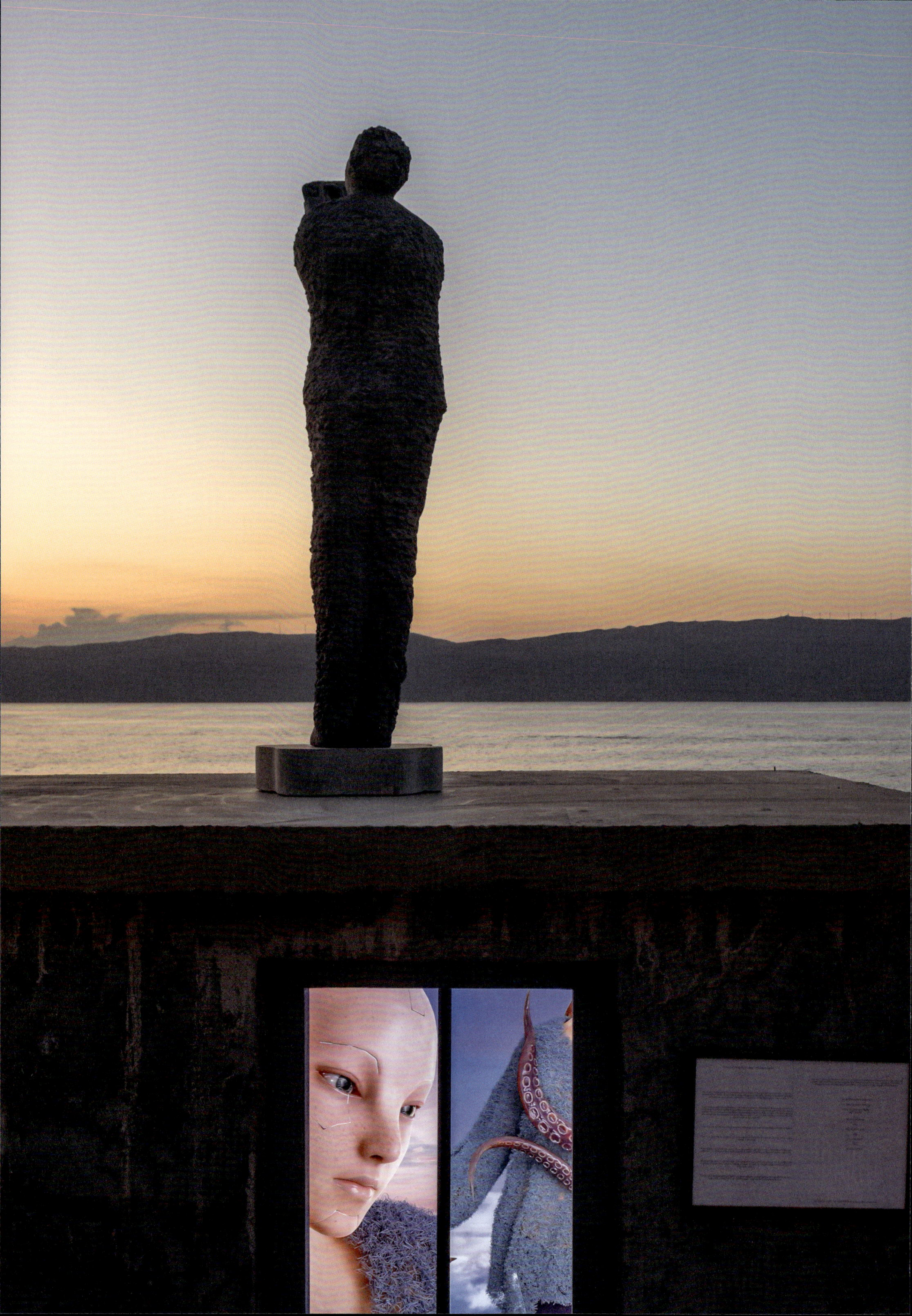

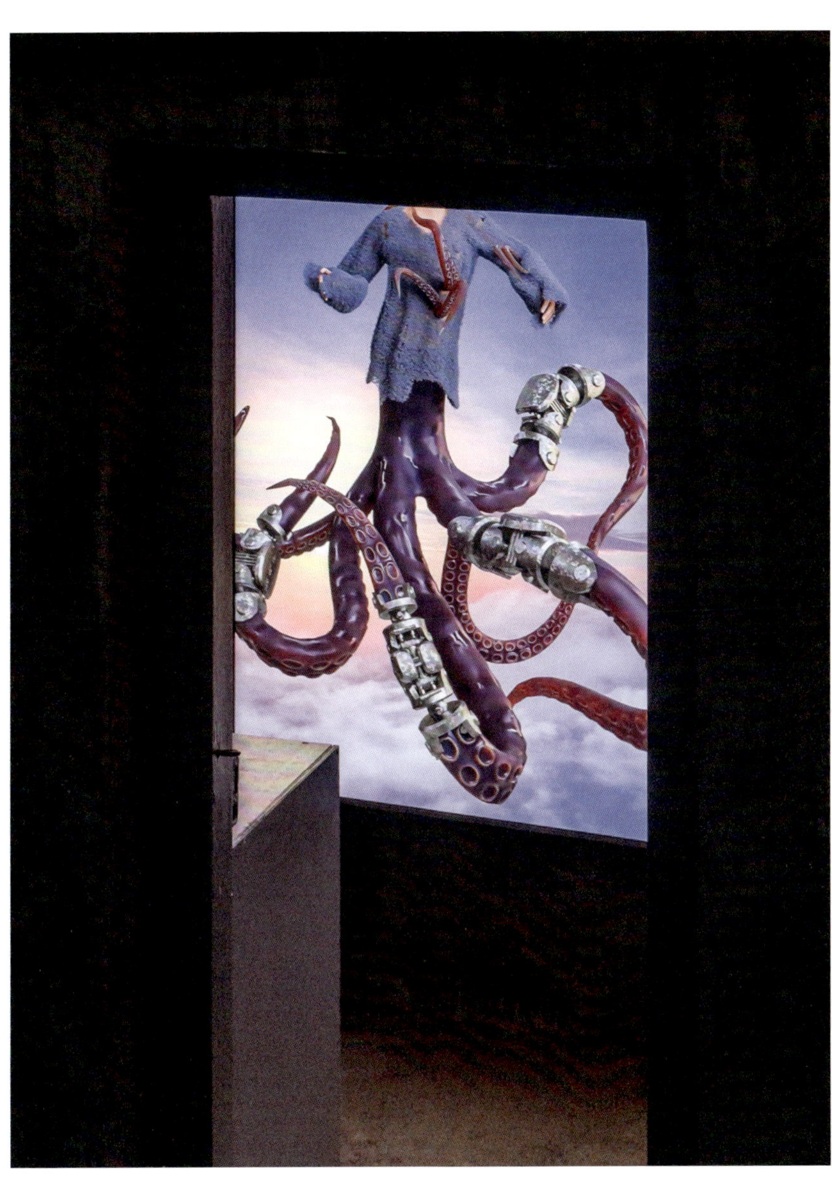

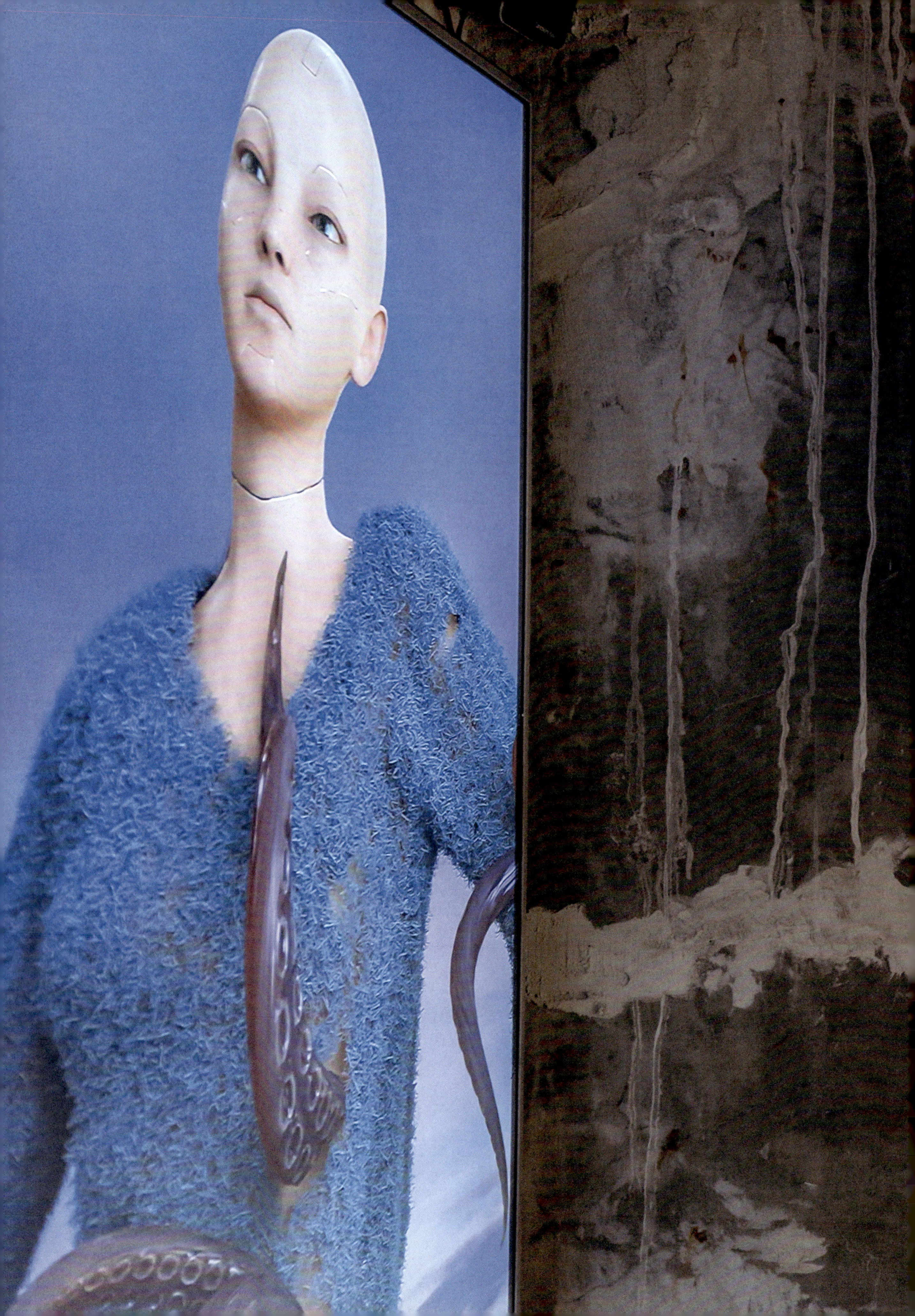

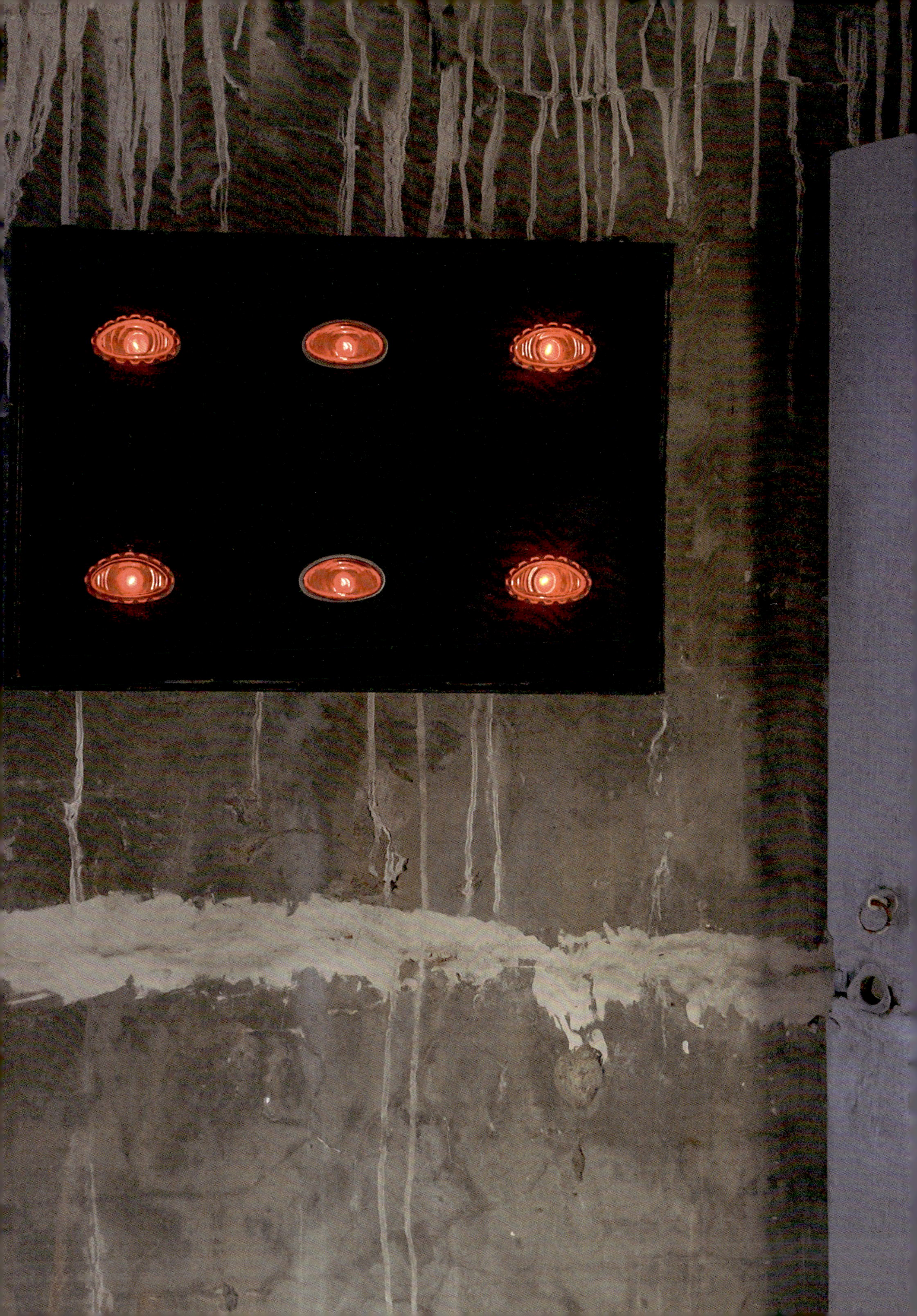

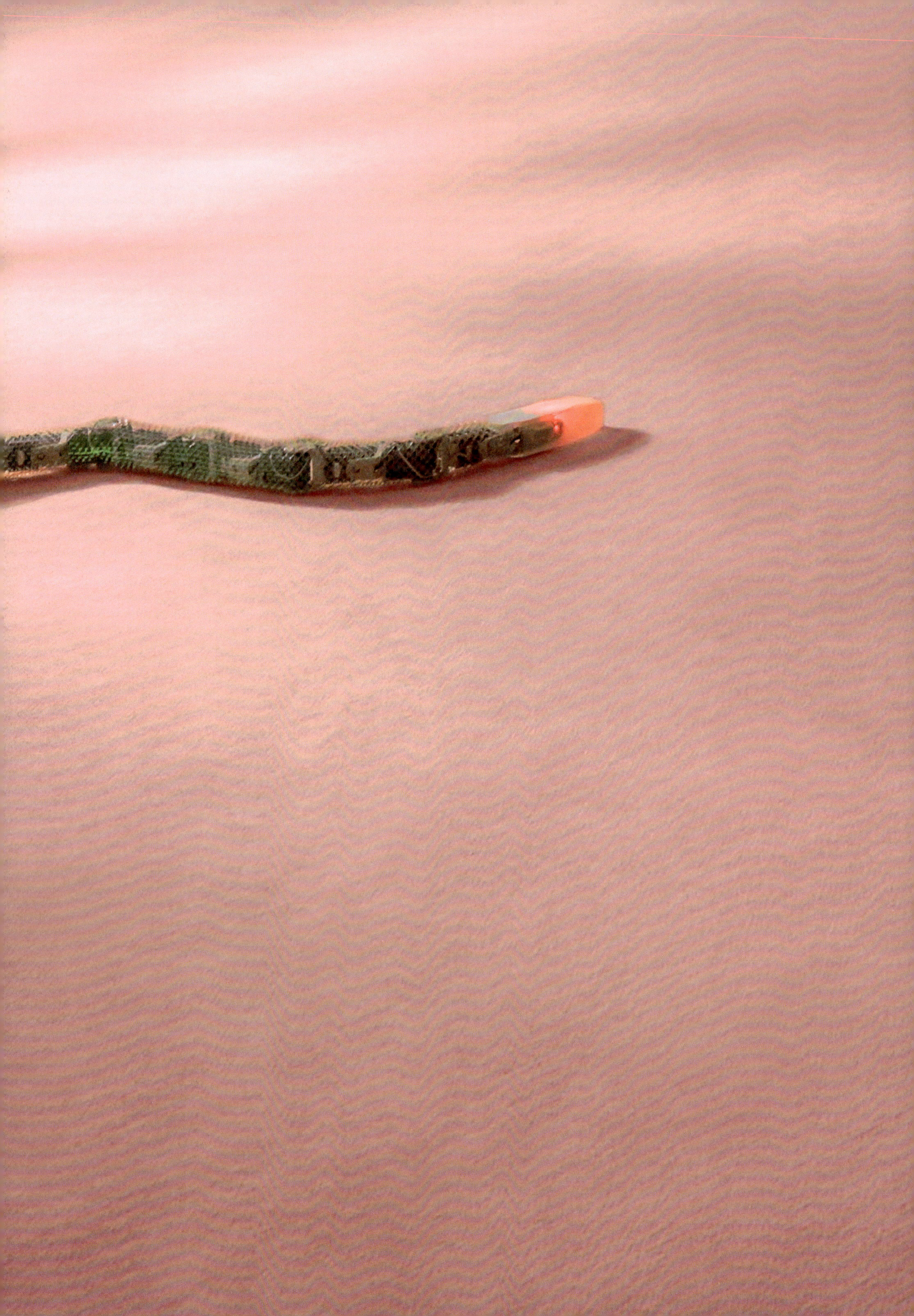

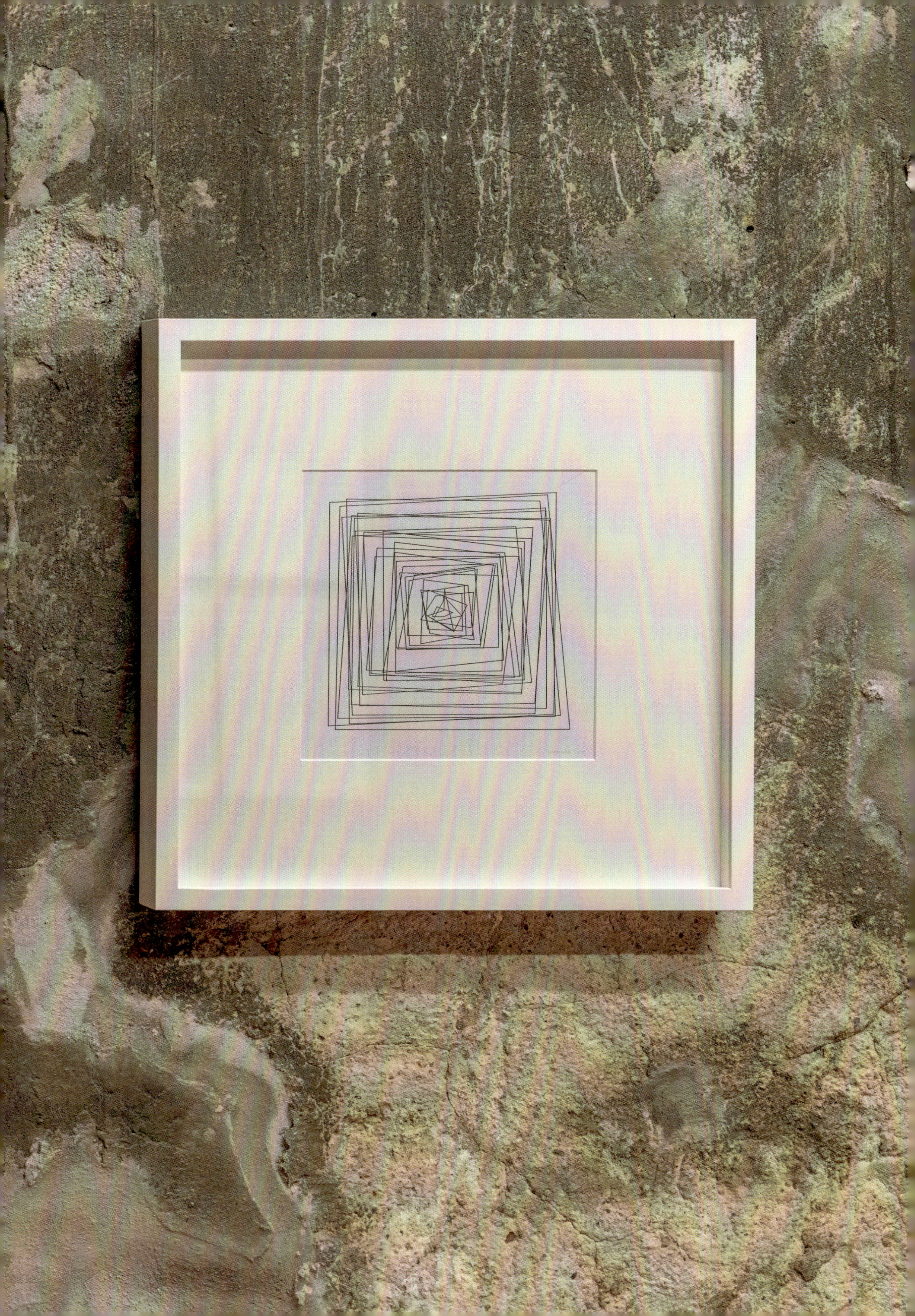

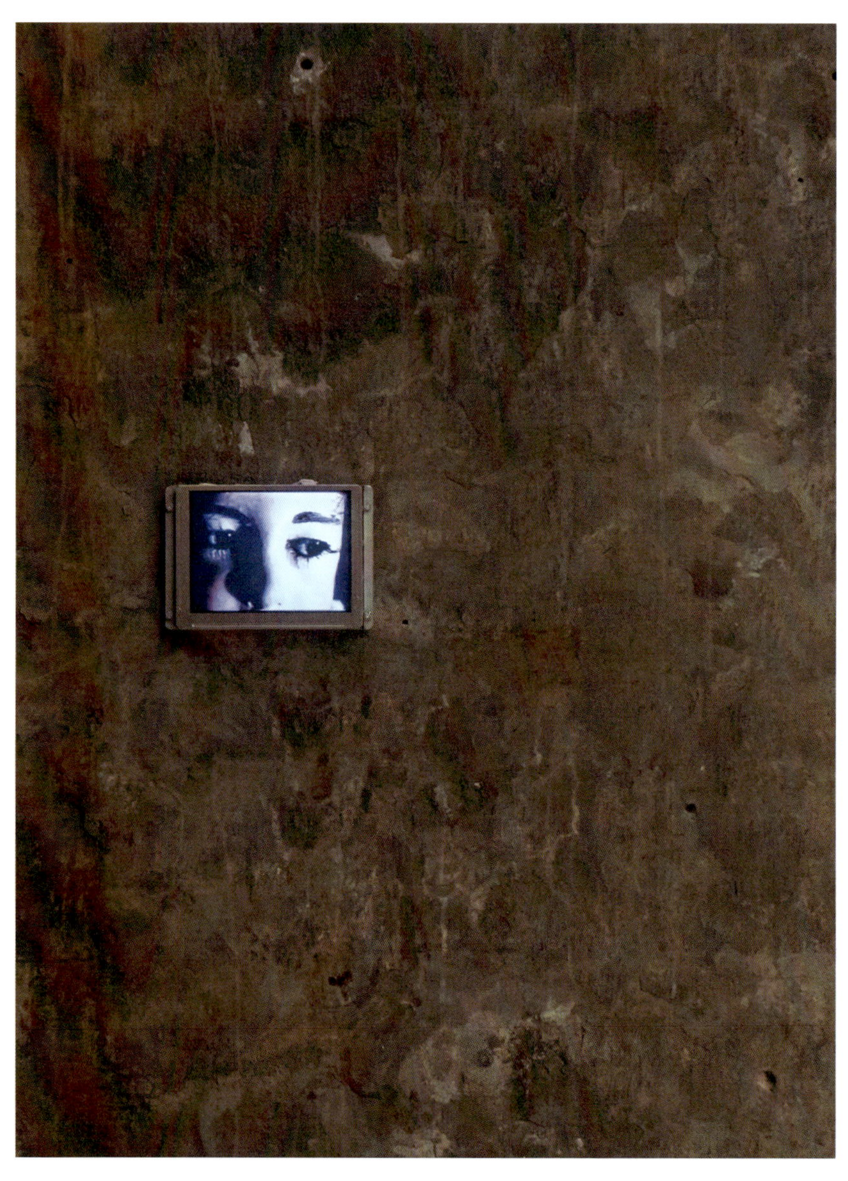

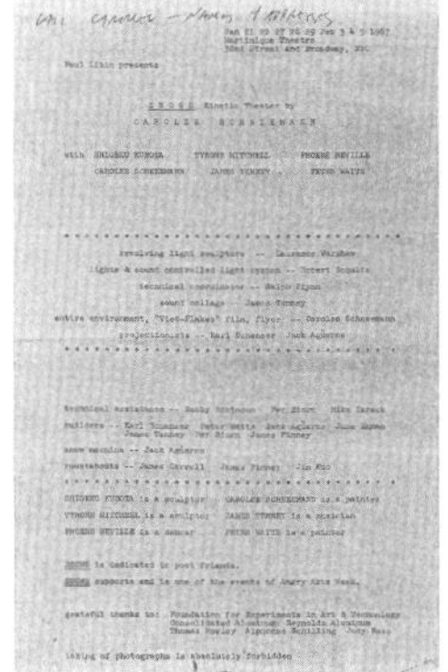

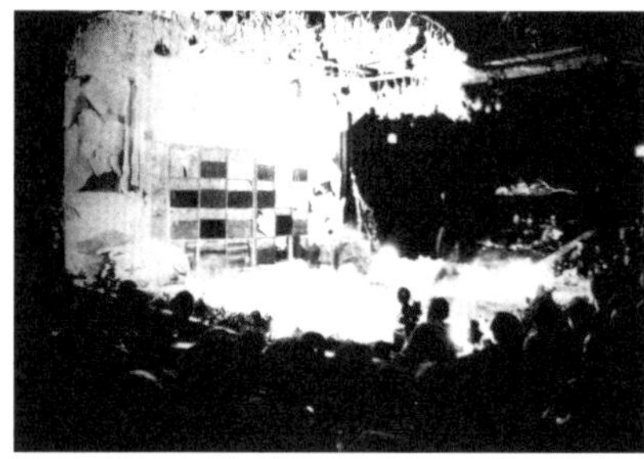

FIG.01 Program for Carolee Schneemann, *Snows*, January 1967, Martinique Theater, New York

FIG.02 Carolee Schneemann, *Snows*, January 1967, Martinique Theater, New York

One of these possibilities was to repurpose models of scientific labor and technological invention. Could you take the existing method of technical innovation and change it, then make it produce something else? Such a route might circumvent the teleologies of modernist formalism and scientific progress alike. It might also, surprisingly, provide an alternative to neo-avant-garde strategies based on negation, ludic participation, and indeterminacy. Art historians have overwhelmingly evaluated the neo-avant-gardes (however diverse) as defensive postures (however slight or oblique) against reification and instrumental technocracy — implicitly accepting the logic of the two-culture divide, pitting art against technology once more. Yet these antagonistic positions cannot account for the activities of Experiments in Art and Technology (E.A.T.), an extraordinary organization begun in the US in 1966 with the explicit aim of facilitating collaborations between artists and engineers. Engineers Billy Klüver and Fred Waldhauer of Bell Laboratories and artists Robert Rauschenberg and Robert Whitman connected with others in their fields — eventually leading to a global, sprawling network of more than five thousand participants. This was a scale never seen before, nor since, in the history of modern art.

Over the course of several years, E.A.T. developed an increasingly sophisticated method of matching artists to engineers and vice versa. This growing web of connections was laconically dubbed the "Technical Services Program" — informally referred to as the "matching system." Through it, more and more actors became involved in the organization, and the organization's activity became increasingly distributed across geographic space as well as the realm of information, of telecommunications, of subjects and data. Artists and engineers were "matched" via a primitive database using an edge-notched card cataloguing system and then, by 1969, an IBM mainframe computer. --04

E.A.T.'s Technical Services Program entailed coordinating interests and needs: if an artist was interested in lasers, or wanted to make a floating object, or explore computer sound, how would the appropriate engineer-partner be found? How would the right artist be paired with the right engineer or scientist — someone who was willing and able to answer questions, consult on a project, or collaborate actively in its realization?

The matching techniques — the cards, files, communications media — of the Technical Services Program produced a peculiar hybrid: not quite an artist only, nor an engineer alone, but a new collaborating subject. And how, exactly, did these subjects collaborate? One of the first such endeavors was Carolee Schneemann's "kinetic performance" *Snows*, which debuted in January 1967 at the

Martinique Theater in New York [FIGS. 01–02].--05 In the months beforehand, Schneemann worked with Bell Labs engineers Robbie Robinson, Ralph Flynn, and others to develop an extraordinary range of technical effects, devices, and props for the piece, which involved live performers, an elaborate array of strobes, film, slide, and light projections, a color organ, complex sound effects and an audio collage by James Tenney, and falling "snow." An audiovisual network ran throughout the entire environment: the engineers rigged a live feedback system so that audience members' movement would trigger light and sound effects. They placed contact microphones underneath seats in the theater, which would pick up and amplify sound in the audience via speakers arrayed around the space; some of the noise was also fed into the color organ, triggering light effects via the organ; and, in addition to the microphone input, photocells would pick up bodily movement and trigger silicon-controlled rectifiers in the overhead stage lighting, controlling the dimming and raising of certain lights.--06 Finally, Flynn devised a sound system that flexibly interchanged light and sound as inputs, so that light could produce sound and vice versa: "All audio was controlled by a speaker distribution matrix which enabled us to distribute as many as 20 inputs into any of 20 audio inputs."--07

The *Snows* system was born of the basic connections made via Klüver over the past several years with Bell engineers and the systems and equipment originally produced for *9 Evenings* (October 1966), E.A.T.'s first large-scale collaborative project, during which E.A.T. was formally organized. After discussing the possibilities for collaboration at initial E.A.T. meetings in November 1966, Schneemann began working with engineer Lawrence Warshaw to build light machines incorporating an electronic color organ developed by Robert Schultz.--08 Schultz, in turn, would work on floor and overhead lighting systems with Schneemann and two of her assistants, dancer Phoebe Neville and Jack Agueros.--09 Warshaw spoke to Klüver about the use of E.A.T. equipment "even though E.A.T. is not yet set up for lending." Klüver put them in contact with Robbie Robinson, "who begins opening all possibilities for us."

As Schneemann writes:

Early in the morning, Schultz, Warshaw, Tenney and I drive station wagon out to Bell Labs. Lightly snowing. Robbie takes us to old house in Berkeley Heights which serves as storage for EAT materials and is in itself a complex environment which I would like to use. Bitterly cold. Picking and choosing like crazy in Woolworth's: these transistors, those cables, these SCR's…the stuff all looks very junky, mute and utterly unrelated to the images it will go to realize. (They tell me we've picked $4,000 worth. Libin has set entire "Snows" budget

04 -- For an extensive discussion of E.A.T.'s Technical Services Program and matching systems, see Kuo, "To Avoid the Waste of a Cultural Revolution," 149–64. See also "Matching of Engineers and Artists," *E.A.T. News* 1, no. 2 (June 1, 1967), 6; "E.A.T. Technical Services: Description of Programs or Services," grant proposal submitted to New York State Council on the Arts, July 15, 1970. Fondation Daniel Langlois, Collection E.A.T., E.A.T. C10-10; 186; 2.

05 -- The performances of *Snows* took place on January 21–29 and February 3–5, 1967. Program for "SNOWS: Kinetic Theater by Carolee Schneemann," 1967. E.A.T./GRI Box 41, Folder 1.

06 -- "Snows … involved primarily audio and visual techniques. A color organ was used to trigger lights on Laurence Warshaw's color machine. This color organ was activated either manually or by sounds produced by the actors on stage. Silicon controlled rectifiers (SCR's) were used on most of the overhead stage lighting, and some were triggered by photo cells picking up various light changes. Several of the audience seats were wired with contact mikes which picked up random noises from the audience movement and were fed to speakers placed around the theater. Some of the noises were also fed to the color organ and SCR units. Strobes and movie projectors were used throughout the piece." Ralph Flynn, Technical Coordinator, "Technical Description, *Snows*." E.A.T./GRI Box 41, Folder 1.

07 -- Ibid.

08 -- Warshaw would go on to found the Intermedia Workshop at the NYU School of Continuing Education. See Laurence Warshaw, "Intermedia Workshop," in "The Arts of Activism," ed. Edward Kamarck, *Arts in Society* 6, no. 3 (Fall/Winter 1969): 448–51.

09 -- Flynn, "Technical Description, *Snows*."

at $400…which we exceed as it turns out.) Station wagon jammed with plastic boxes, cable, wire, power amplifiers, transceivers, photoresistors, tone controls, preamps, mikes, contact mikes, speaker matrix, huge speakers, motors, string! We can barely squeeze ourselves back in. The guys happy as monkeys surrounded by bananas; I'm brooding. [10]

The stuff — the media itself — was all "unrelated to the images it will go to realize." In other words, Schneemann noted the *opacity* of these diverse things and tools, their dumbness and mystery. Rather than a hermeneutically laden set of signifiers, of vessels of content, she described this assemblage as a set of black boxes. Moreover, because of their obdurate, closed quality, they were very different from the malleable materials of traditional sculpture, the "truth to materials" transparency of Constructivism or Minimalism, or even of the process-based work of the time:

> The mechanical materials have a buried character; working parts all covered — the boxing doesn't indicate the interesting things inside. These objects have a sub-visual domination over immediate time and space. All mysterious promise. Not malleable. (Unlike taking of hunk of plastic in my hands, some living arms and legs, a cranky projector with a fine shape. A preposterous journey about to unfold and where was controlling center after all?) [11]

As the engineer Per Biorn described it, Schneemann wanted "large colored lenses" through which to project the lights, onto two big walls. "Well, how do we do that?" Actual magnifying lenses at that scale would be an "impossible expense," as Schneemann put it. [12] So Biorn thought back to a kinetically collapsing grid for Yvonne Rainer's performance in 9 *Evenings*, and they decided to make a frame of two-by-fours with chicken wire on the front and back. They would then use plastic bags filled with colored water to act as the lenses, lit from behind. Hanging them would prove problematic, however. Schneemann detailed the thought process:

> Discover [the bags'] size, weight of water, prohibit hanging. Spend a week learning about industrial plastic bags. We'll have to build a structure, floor to ceiling cage to support bags.…No longer possible to keep "water lens" in center of performing area — three sided stage exacts compromise; lens set toward back of stage, leave several sections without bags so that we can crawl in and out. [13]

Schneemann then began working with Flynn, who, as she put it, was "a master":

> [Flynn] came to the Martinique shortly after we had sorted EAT's equipment [from 9 *Evenings*] and found much of it damaged. Watching him handle a broken pre-amp I saw we had a "master" ("and I'm so young," he said). As Robbie had

promised, "Flynn will take care of everything" and he worked with us continuously. The "everything" had to encompass an enormous range of details — mechanical, aesthetic, practical, visionary. His help was especially invaluable to me because of his own experience with theater while a student. At this point we had only two weeks until performance…the technical possibilities of the equipment we now had [were] generating ideas which could take months to realize. I had to insist that we concentrate on what was immediate and possible, to give up many past and new ideas. Ralph assisted me in this crucial sorting. (Light and sound systems, special machines, strobes, films, environment and action were in the relationship I wanted before performance and everyone had time to feel free, clear and aware of the over-all rhythm of "Snows.") *Fortunately my own metaphoric, collage process with all materials — which meant many changes and variations — was a matter of course to Flynn."* [14]

Flynn enabled Schneemann to "sort" — to compose the "collage process" of actions, events, and techniques that would make up *Snows*. And this was ultimately a formal decision: "It was finally, always necessary for me to see a thing to know if it was really what was needed; since each element transformed any other once it was visible or audible, entire relationships would be shifted." Schneemann declared, to this end, that she wanted technicians to become more like performers, to make analogous decisions based on spontaneity, observations, "discoveries." "Technicians keep disappearing into their material, while we are emerging," she wrote; the process of their mutual realization would transform the "generative material." And she wanted to expose the technological components — but the apparatus proved resistant:

> For "Snows" I wanted to get all the mechanical parts sort of naked, edging the stage out of their protective boxes, jackets, casings. Not only did I discover they were unlikely to function so exposed but on the low, three sided stage they would be in continual danger from performers falling onto them, kicking them over…and they could injure performers. I wanted the piles of cable we used to line the aisles, to be walked over and around; fire laws made this prohibitive. Machines which finally did function as performer-objects were the light sculpture, the snow machine, hand held beams, two noisy hand-directed 16mm projectors, an 8mm projector, two strobe lights, and floor mikes nested in silver foil. [15]

In this way, Flynn, Biorn, Warshaw, and the devices and machines themselves were decisive: they altered and shaped Schneemann's work, and they continued to do so even during the duration of the performance. For Schneemann:

10 -- Carolee Schneemann, "Aspects of E.A.T. in the Making of 'Snows,'" 1967. E.A.T./GRI Box 41, Folder 1. Schneemann also made an initial plea for assistance in an E.A.T. membership form: "Work in progress 'Snows,' to be performed early January (?), uses moving lights, moving objects (in the air) and enlargement materials for which I NEED HELP!" Carolee Schneemann, artist membership form, c. 1967. E.A.T./GRI Box 6, Folder 46.
11 -- Schneemann, "Aspects of E.A.T. in the Making of 'Snows.'"
12 -- Schneemann wrote, "Magnifying lens would be impossible expense (Polymer dome!)." Ibid.
13 -- Ibid.
14 -- Ibid. Emphasis added.
15 -- Ibid.

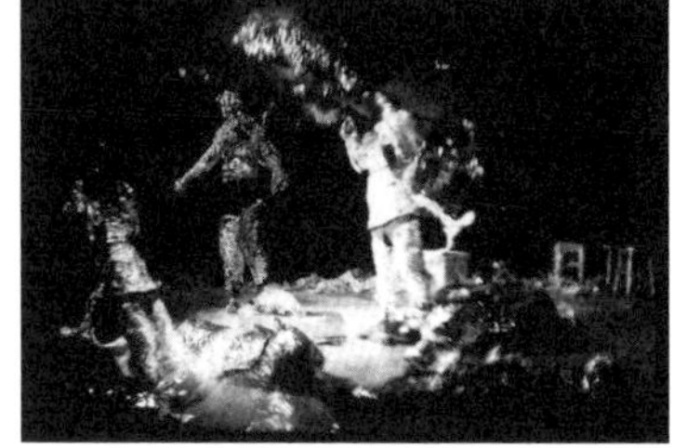

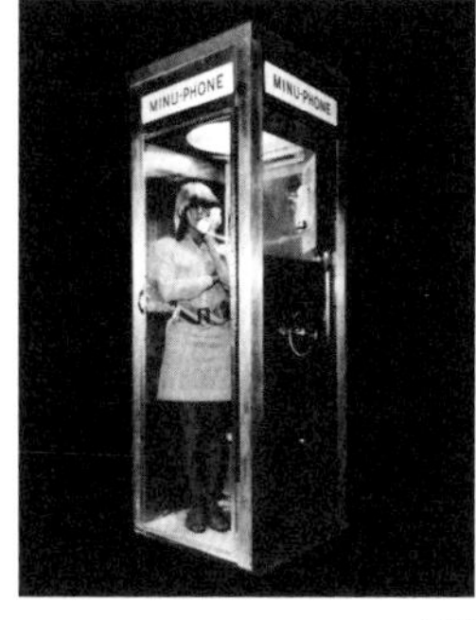

> My problems with technology are concrete, personal; my difficulties with using technicians are mechanical. *I want to work with the gestures of machines; to expose their mechanical action as part of any total environment to which it contributes its particular effect. I would like technicians to be interchangeable with performers wherever possible.* [16]

The actual performance combined six performers — three men and three women — with the color organ and "color machine" devised by Warshaw; contact mikes that picked up audience movement and sound and triggered light effects on stage; strobes and film projectors that projected the collaged footage shot by Schneemann; and the snow machine that sprayed artificial snow amid a set of sparkling foil and chunks of foam **[FIG.03]**. Toward the end of the performance, Scheemann's *Viet-Flakes* montage, comprising documentary and newspaper photography of Vietnam, was projected. The projections were immersive, the snow and strobes and lights often blinding. The choreographic movements were a barrage of near-antagonistic actions, from pushing and dragging to covering in foil and white greasepaint, augmenting the flashing visuals, staging a blizzard of media imagery and light, as if, in Schneemann's own words, staging "the hell breaking loose" in the world at the time. [17] In this way, Schneemann explicitly staged *Snows* as a protest against the Vietnam War, during a "Week of Angry Arts" across New York. [18]

Pamela M. Lee has incisively read *Snows* as an instantiation of image overtaking the body — of the political and documentary image, namely, searing footage from Vietnam, becoming an excess of material, auditory, and tactile feedback that overwhelms the performer and viewer and marks the limit of the function of visual representation. [19] Looking into the actual process and collaboration of *Snows* reveals another dimension, one that has little to do with representation (or its limits) and more to do with media — the techniques, materials, and actualities of how the work came into being. It reveals the radical transduction of subjects and objects, technicians and performers, machines and stuff, relays and systems, in *Snows* — an interplay that paralleled the horrific equation of the same entities under the mantle of war. Automatic gestures and spontaneous movements, virtual effects and obdurate sensation, the remote and the proximate, were produced, leveled, in one and the same "collage."

By the end of 1967, more than sixty E.A.T. matchings had been made. [20] And numerous artists' proposals would, like Schneemann, suggest networks and environmental systems of all kinds. Marta Minujín's *Minuphone* (1967), for instance, directly tapped into the telecommunications network, whimsically exploring its paradoxical

FIG.03 Carolee Schneemann, *Snows*, January 1967, Martinique Theater, New York

FIG.04 Marta Minujín, *Minuphone*, 1967. Telephone booth, electronic parts, dimensions variable. Engineer: Per Biorn. Installation view, Howard Wise Gallery, 1967. Inside booth: Marta Minujín

intertwining of mediated dispersion and individual physical effect [FIG.04]. Engineer Per Biorn worked with Minujín to construct a telephone booth containing a push-button telephone, which controlled nine functions in a random sequence. Only seven of the nine functions would work during any call, and the sequence would change when the phone was hung up.[21] "The circuit is activated when the phone is lifted and an audio amplifier picks up from 7 to 10 audio pulses from the push button phone and activates a stepping switch. When the first word is spoken in the phone after 7 dial tones the sequence begins."[22] A mechanically generated "wind in the face," siren sounds, live video of the caller projected on the floor of the booth (a "shadow created on a fluorescent blind TV image of the caller's face in the floor of the booth"), black and green water in the walls, a tape recording and playback of the caller's conversation; a half-second echo; and two colored lights in the ceiling, each corresponding to a pitch of voice. The TVs in the booth were continuously on, and various circuits, recorders, and tape systems produced the audiovisual effects. Minujín invoked McLuhan, but this was no seamless microcosm of the global village. Rather, the experience casually manifested both video and audio telecommunications as the heterogeneous, splintered, material and virtual, connected and isolated, all within the enclosed yet networked architecture of the telephone booth.

Between 1967 and the end of 1970, the number of received artists' matching forms grew to 2,500.[23] Surveying the raft of applications reveals an increasingly staggering array of media. Tony Conrad underlined everything from "film," "music," and "electronics" to "physics" as interests; Ornette Coleman specifically asked for Ralph Flynn as a collaborator; John Chamberlain checked "Sculpture" as his medium of interest;[24] Dan Graham cited "film, holography"; "poetry; information theory — computer speech," circling the latter and noting: "both are areas of interest in my work."[25] Deborah Hay wrote: "I need an electronic engineer familiar with amplification techniques. Concert first week April, 1968. To build a large cube (possible 7 foot square) that would have a pendulum at its center inside. The materials at the base of pendulum would be used to create different sounds upon hitting the walls of the cube. Gradually the sound will grow from normal object-contact to amplification of all the possibilities within the cube i.e., string, sides of cube, pendulum, top, bottom etc."[26] And none other than Eva Hesse circled "Chemistry" as "interested possible resources," followed by: "Sculpture…(rubber, plastic, vynil [sic], glues, (epoxy) resin, sculpmetal,) Chemistry."[27] From Hesse to Graham, then, artists with whom we associate new and unorthodox materials of the time were *not* simply emerging from some wellspring, Venus-like, with knowledge about these materials and technologies: E.A.T.

16 — Ibid. Emphasis added.

17 — Carolee Schneemann, interview by Gene Youngblood, in *Expanded Cinema* (New York: P. Dutton, 1970), 369.

18 — The Week of Angry Arts ran from January 29 to February 8, 1967. See Carolee Schneemann, "Snows," in *More Than Meat Joy: Complete Performance Works & Selected Writings*, ed. Bruce McPherson (New Paltz, NY: Documentext, 1979), 128; Rasa Gustaitis, "'Angry Arts' War Protest Opens in N.Y.: Unprecedented in Scope," *Washington Post, Times Herald*, January 30, 1967, D8.

19 — Pamela M. Lee, *Chronophobia: On Time in the Art of the 1960s* (Cambridge, MA: MIT Press, 2004), 209–14. More recently, Erica Levin has read the piece in terms of photography, systems of control and their breakdown. Levin, "Dissent and the Aesthetics of Control: On Carolee Schneemann's *Snows*," *World Picture* 8 (Summer 2013), http://worldpicturejournal.com/article/dissent-and-the-aesthetics-of-control-on-carolee-schneemanns-snows/.

20 — *E.A.T. News* 1, no. 4 (December 20, 1967); see also E.A.T. artists' matching forms, 1967. E.A.T./GRI Box 6, Folder 1.

21 — E.A.T., "Performance projects: April 1967 to present," 1968. E.A.T./GRI Box 6, Folder 11.

22 — *E.A.T. News* 1, no. 2 (June 1, 1967). See also "Partial list of Technical Assistance to Large Interactive or Environmental Pieces—1968." E.A.T./GRI Box 9, Folder 26.

23 — "Artists' matching forms," 1970. E.A.T./GRI Box 6, Folder 40.

24 — Tony Conrad, Ornette Coleman, John Chamberlain, E.A.T. artist matching forms. E.A.T./GRI Box 6, Folder 40.

25 — Dan Graham, artist membership form, c. 1968. E.A.T./GRI Box 6, Folder 41.

26 — Deborah Hay, artist membership form, c. 1968. E.A.T./GRI Box 6, Folder 42.

27 — Eva Hesse, artist membership form, c. 1968. E.A.T./GRI Box 41, Folder 2.

was a catalyst, a crucial source of information that shaped these new practices and future projects.

Forrest Myers explored even more sophisticated systems, making a technologically advanced riff on Richard Serra's verb list, presaging his xenon light project for the Pepsi Pavilion (and starring his high-priority ideas):

> To experiment with weightless chambers
> *To circuit a piece for 4 outdoor searchlights
> To experiment with aluminum extruder
> *To cast a glass rectangle 6 feet high by 2 feet square
> To illuminate a gas-filled hollow glass rectangle
> of the same dimensions
> *To find a liquid solution that can be electrically
> charged so that it can be illuminated
> To get a light ray to bend in mid-space
> To build a 16 mm sky projector powerful enough
> to project on low cloud ceilings
> To build a 20 foot walk-through Theremin
> To build a strobe light system powerful enough to
> light the top 20 stories of the Empire State Building
> To discover a practical method for coloring
> sky-writer's smoke
> To work with a glass extruding system, also glass
> casting (Pittsburgh Plate Glass, etc.)
> To build paper rockets with colored smoke trails
> To build a tracking system that throws a triangular
> reflection on the surrounding hillside or cityscape, etc.
> *To install xenon search lamps vertically on the
> Staten Island ferries as well as a lamp on the Staten
> Island and Manhattan ferry piers. [28]

Other artists were interested in computing. Jackson Mac Low, for example, had created intermedia and language work connected to Fluxus, and was well suited to newer systems of audiovisual production, language programming, and automation or random generation. He could hardly contain his enthusiasm for the new organization: "The possibilities opened by E.A.T. seem so great & so much what I've needed for so long that it is hard to stop talking about them once I begin. Maybe I've been afraid hitherto to contact you because of this." [29] In his previous work, Mac Low recounted:

> Carefully made verbal or musical structures have been swal-
> lowed up in a sea of generalized noise — often quite interesting
> in itself, perhaps, but certainly not what I had in mind when
> composing the pieces. So the first problem I'd like engineers
> to help me with is the production of clear performances of
> my various simultaneous poems & other simultaneities. For
> many of them this wd involve movable mikes, pre-amps, amps,

& loudspeakers — that is, each performer shd be able to be a moving sound source & able to regulate the volume & tone quality of the sound produced by amplification equipment attached to him without trailing wires, &c. Others need several tape recorders, each with its own amplification & speaker placed among the audience, along with either stationary or moving performers. [30]

In other words, Mac Low aimed to improve his signal-to-noise ratio. The artist also expressed interest in developing new uses of light in performances, such as strobes: "I have not done so hitherto because no such equipment was available to me." Inspired by the color organ/light machine used in *Snows*, Mac Low hoped to work with "various forms of light-to-sound & sound-to-light conversions involving photocells & the like...I'm especially interested in the possibilities for using computers in the mixing and modification of prerecorded materials & the use of computer-generated sounds along with recorded speech & sounds from the environment & the radio." Like Schneemann and others, then, this became a vision of conversion — not only between light and sound but language: "I'd like to be able to produce electronic poems incorporating sounds produced by photocells converting various kinds of light phenomena to acoustic ones & conversely to produce films or TV tapes including images produced by converting the sounds of some of my poems & musical pieces." And the artist was not only interested in real-time effects but in the incorporation of new technologies into production: "I want to learn much more about the kinds of equipment available, & whether any of it is available for use in the process of composition itself."

Finally, E.A.T. connected Mac Low with Ralph Flynn, who worked with him on an audio system for audience participation in a poetry reading at St. Mark's Church, in April 1968. [31] This would lead to a matching with Herbert Bohnert, an engineer at IBM, who collaborated with Mac Low to develop computer programs to generate poetry. Extending his investigation into chance operations and systems, Mac Low explored the use of digital algorithms in combination with compositional decisions made by the poet. The following year, in 1969, he would begin a computer poetry collaboration for the LACMA *Art and Technology* exhibition in 1970–71. The latter is more well known, but it is clear that prior to the *A&T* work, Mac Low had begun extensive research into random generation and computational languages via E.A.T. Throughout his experimentation with sound, script, and systems, Mac Low saw each sensory effect and medium as a kind of signal, leveling very different phenomena into the same kind of malleable entity. As he concluded on his E.A.T. membership form: "What is your field? Potentially, all waves in the space-time continuum." [32]

28 — Forrest Myers,
artist membership form,
April 1, 1968.
E.A.T./GRI Box 6, Folder 44.

29 — Jackson Mac Low,
artist membership form,
n.d. (c. 1967).
E.A.T./GRI Box 6, Folder 44.

30 — Ibid.

31 — Mac Low to Ralph Flynn,
February 15, 1968.
E.A.T./GRI Box 12, Folder 2.
Mac Low details the
aftermath of the show at
St. Mark's; he is grateful
for Flynn's assistance
and wants to work with him
again; he alludes to his
visit to Mount Kisco, NY,
to visit the IBM Watson
Research Center at Yorktown
Heights, NJ, with Herbert
Bohnert of IBM, organized
by E.A.T.

32 — Ibid.

33 -- See artist matching
forms, 1967–69. E.A.T./GRI
Boxes 6, 7, 8, 9.

34 -- *Four Pianos* was in fact an
early version of *Piano Phase*
(1967), which is seen as
Reich's first published live
phase shifting composition.
See Keith Potter, *Four Musical
Minimalists: La Monte Young,
Terry Riley, Steve Reich,
Philip Glass* (Cambridge:
Cambridge University Press,
2002), 182–83.

35 -- According to Potter, the
keyboard used was specifically
a clavinet, an electronically
amplified clavichord that had
just been introduced in 1964
by the German manufacturer
Hohner and was "state-of-the-
art" at the time. Ibid., 195.
No notes in Flynn's write-up
specify clavinets, but the
instrument is cited in a notice
in the *Village Voice*: "Park
Place Pianos," *Village Voice*,
March 16, 1967, 11.

36 -- Ralph Flynn, "Technical write-
up on 4 Pianos," n.d.
E.A.T./GRI Box 11, Folder 12.

37 -- This is how the work is
titled in the program for the
performance; subsequently,
Neuhaus would refer
to the work as *By-Product*.

38 -- See Flynn, "Technical write-
up on 4 Pianos," which
also discusses Neuhaus's
By-Product; Simone [Forti]
Whitman, "Interview with
Max Neuhaus and Ted Wolff,"
Techne 1, no. 1 (April 14,
1969): 4.

39 -- Theodore Strongin, "Concert
is Given by Percussionist:
Neuhaus Rubs, Tickles and Pats
Variety of Instruments,"
New York Times, June 3, 1964.

40 -- Whitman, "Interview with
Max Neuhaus and Ted Wolff," 4.
Wolff said of their working
relationship: "One of the
interesting things here is
that Max doesn't just look
for an immediate empirical
solution to a confined problem
like, 'Should #18 or #20 wire?'
He asks, 'Should I use 18
or 20 and then why. And then
why the why. And then the
theory behind the way of the
why…. And this is like
a big giant step rather than
just saying, 'Hey! Get me
out of the same bind but a
little bit different.'"

That vast continuum, it seemed, was the attraction for many artists in the E.A.T. matching system. The most popular areas of interest denoted in the matching forms support precisely this allover view of media: light, sound, electronic music, sculpture, and architecture.[33] For example, a few months after *Snows*, Steve Reich worked with Robby Robinson on *Four Pianos*, presented at the Park Place Gallery on March 17, 18, and 19, 1967, as part of a three-evening program of compositions by Reich, performed by the musician with Philip Corner, Jon Gibson, Arthur Murphy, and James Tenney at Park Place Gallery, where the January 1967 E.A.T. meeting had recently taken place **[FIG.05]**. *Four Pianos* is one of the very first pieces of live phase shifting.[34] Whereas Reich had produced phase shifting with tapes, following the work of Terry Riley, this work incorporated live performers, tape loops, and a type of early electronic keyboard, which entailed the work with Robinson.[35] As Flynn described it in his technical report:

> The "Four Pianos" concert consisted of four electronic pianos. Each pianist played the same 12 note progression but in a variable predetermined phase shift. A series of interesting and fascinating sounds resulted. Mr. Reich also presented some pre-recorded tapes using much the same technique as the live piano concert.[36]

Reich and Robinson linked the bodily experience of the performers to electronic synthesis in an exploration of both the mechanically accurate and involuntary variation, however slight, modulation of rhythm and time. The algorithmic compositional system of phasing was no longer limited to the machine. It expanded to an extraordinary combination of human subject, machine, and interface.

That same set of performances also featured Max Neuhaus's *Bi-Product* of 1966–67.[37] The artist collaborated with engineers Flynn and Ted Wolff on rigging photocells that would pick up variations in light and shadow in the performance venue; these inputs were converted into electronic signals that would trigger a printing device to generate markings on a paper tape feed, segments of which were distributed to the audience at the end of the concert.[38] Neuhaus had apparently attempted to create a similar device in a performance with Tenney and Mac Low in 1964, but it did not work; the drawings faded quickly from the paper.[39] Flynn and Wolff came up with a system that would actually function, using a newly developed thermal ink. They successfully created a series of translations between the space of the body, signal, sound, and writing — a field of conversion and notation. As Neuhaus would later muse, in a conversation with Wolff published in E.A.T.'s journal *Techne*, "The whole thing about electronics, it seems to me, is that it's the most flexible way to do anything. And it's like a super material you can do anything with. Artistically and musically."[40]

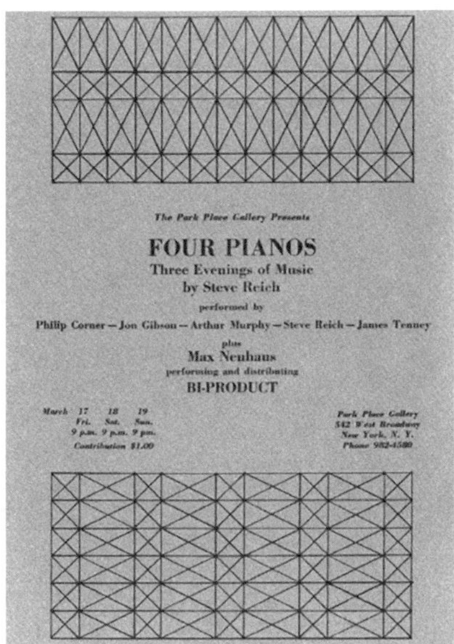

05

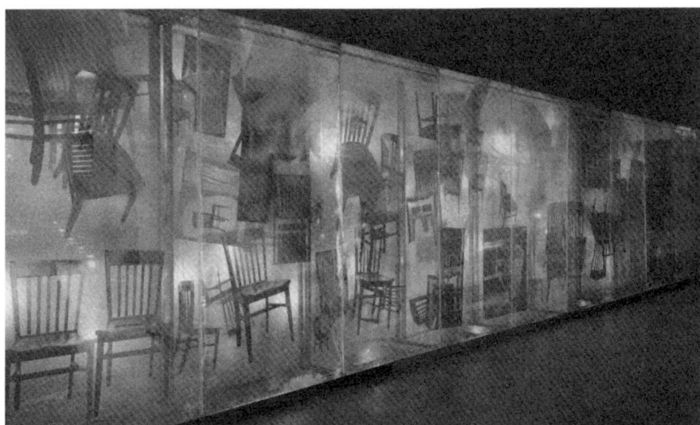

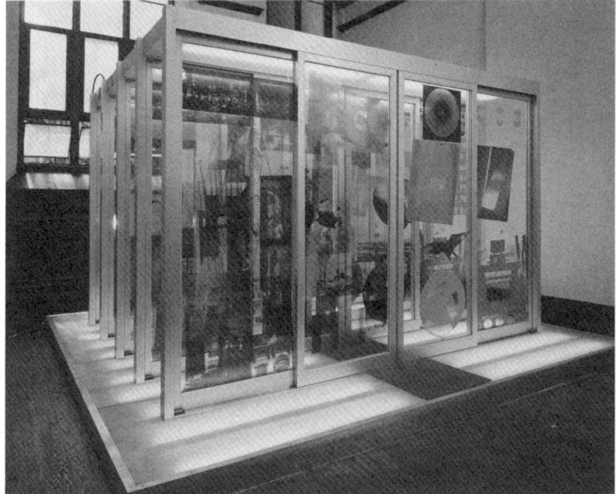

06—07

08

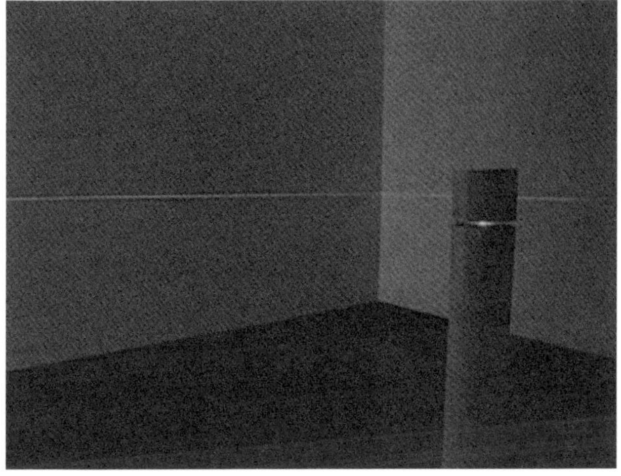

FIG.05 Program for Steve Reich, *Four Pianos*, and Max Neuhaus, *Bi-Product*, 1967

FIG.06 Robert Rauschenberg, *Soundings*, 1968. Mirrored Plexiglas and silkscreen ink on Plexiglas with concealed electric lights and electronic components, 243.8 × 1097.3 × 137.2 cm

FIG.07 Robert Rauschenberg, *Solstice*, 1968. Silkscreen ink on motorized Plexiglas doors in metal frame mounted on platform with concealed electric lights and electronic components, 304.8 × 436.9 × 436.9 cm

FIG.08 Robert Whitman, *Solid Red Line*, 1967. Machined metal, helium-neon laser, mirrors, and motor, 30.5 × 45.7 × 76.2 cm. Engineers: Larry Heilos, Eric Rawson. Dia Art Foundation

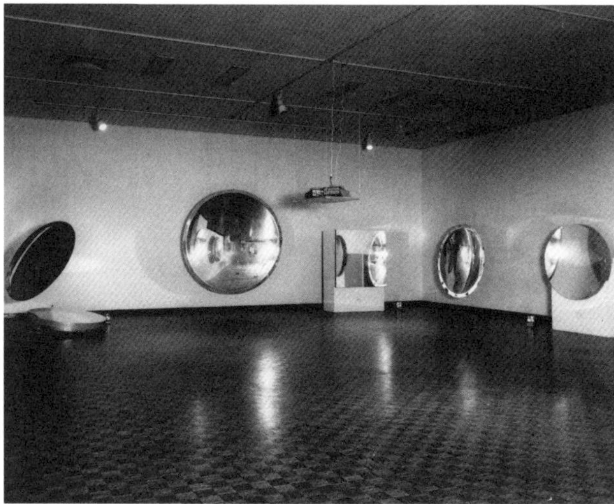

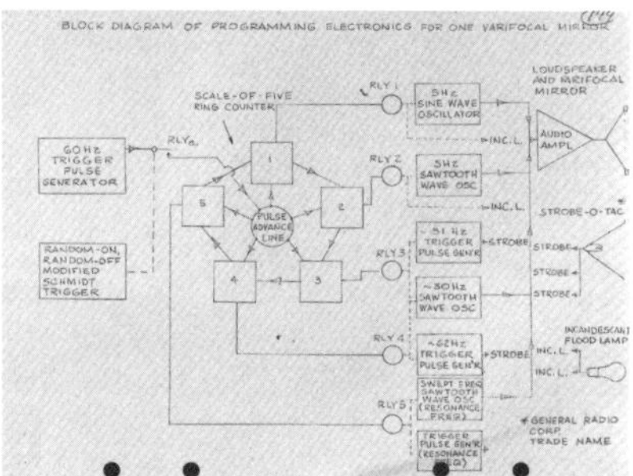

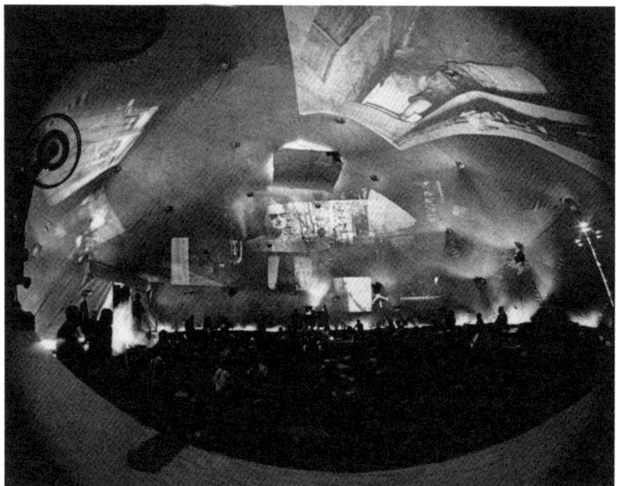

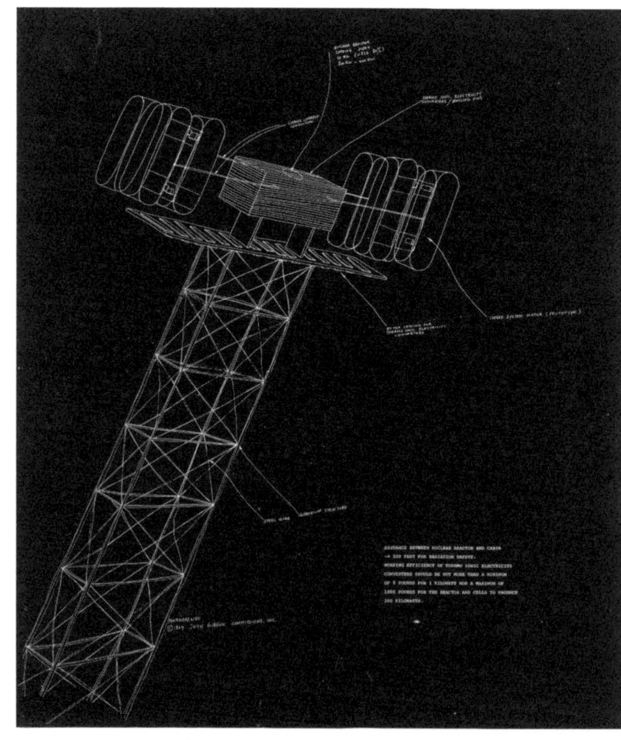

FIG.09   Robert Whitman, *Pond*, installed at the Jewish Museum, New York, 1968

FIG.10   Eric Rawson, block diagram of programming electronics for one varifocal mirror, 1968. In Eric Rawson and Robert Whitman, "Report on a Light Sculpture Using Varifocal Mirror," n.d.

FIG.11   Stan VanDerBeek's Movie Drome at Design-In, Central Park, New York, 1967

FIG.12   Panamarenko, blueprint drawing, "Closed System Power Devices for Space/Portable Air Transport/Gas Turbines, 27 East 67th St., New York, April 19–May 9, 1969"

By 1968, E.A.T. Technical Services had aided a wide array of artists, including Donald Judd, Alison Knowles, Richard Serra, Larry Rivers, Michael Snow, and Kenneth Snelson. Yet perhaps the most striking development was the gravitation toward large-scale, responsive environments. Advances in sensors and circuits — all powered by the transistor, that landmark invention at Bell — allowed artists to pursue immersive, interactive, quasi-architectural enclosures. Extensive correspondence with the London-based design group Archigram, for example, reveals the extent to which proposals sent to E.A.T. immediately skewed toward elaborate architectural and engineering construction projects. In the fall of 1967, David Greene of Archigram wrote to Klüver to inquire about collaborating, as "we all have an insatiable interest in the feedback of technology into the built environment (or built non-environment)."[41] The group had been invited to create a construction for the Milan Triennale in May 1968, "a multi-sensory assembly in which it is hoped that the visitor to the exhibit can control and choose his programme."[42] "The design of the assembly is in a very loose state at the present," Greene wrote, "but we were wondering if there was any chance of getting the EAT Program in a cooperating role in this project? As you will know from Archigram Magazine, we have many ideas, but need the technical know-how and apparatus that can make them possible."[43]

E.A.T. began to organize successfully matched projects according to type. One main category emerged as: "Technical Assistance to Large Interactive or Environmental Pieces."[44] In 1968, E.A.T. helped realize ambitious installations such as Rauschenberg's *Soundings*, with sonically triggered lights illuminating a series of panels screen-printed with the silhouettes of chairs, launched at the Stedelijk Museum in Amsterdam **[FIG.06]**; and *Solstice*, a four-panel platform with automated sliding doors, each screen-printed with a different color from the CMYK four-color printing process, so that one walked through it as if entering a color printing separation system. The work was unveiled at Documenta IV that same year **[FIG.07]**.[45]

Whitman's *Solid Red Line*, a motorized red helium-neon laser projected horizontally around a room and appearing to "erase" itself, debuted at Pace Gallery in New York **[FIG.08]**, realized with optics scientist Eric Rawson and laser specialist Larry Heilos (who had collaborated on *9 Evenings*), both of Bell Labs; a simple motor, laser, and mirror produced the effect.[46] Whitman's *Pond*, a sound-activated mirrored "environment," as the E.A.T. documents call it, opened at the Jewish Museum in New York in fall 1968, actualized in collaboration with Rawson and more than ten other engineers (including Flynn, Herbert Schneider, Witt Wittnebert, and others); an elaborate block diagram maps out the input

41 — Greene to Billy Klüver, August 28, 1967. E.A.T./GRI Box 10, Folder 1.

42 — Greene to Billy Klüver, October 25, 1967. E.A.T./GRI Box 10, Folder 1.

43 — Ibid.

44 — E.A.T., "Notes on matchings, 1968–69." E.A.T./GRI Box 9, Folder 26.

45 — On Rauschenberg's *Solstice*, *Soundings*, and *Mud Muse*, see Michelle Kuo, "'Inevitable fusing of specializations': Rauschenberg and Experiments in Art and Technology, 1966–70," in *Robert Rauschenberg*, ed. Leah Dickerman and Achim Borchardt-Hume, exh. cat. (New York: Museum of Modern Art; London: Tate Modern, 2016), 260–71.

46 — Robert Whitman, "Dark," text on laser construction for Pace Gallery exhibition, 1967. E.A.T./GRI Box 27, Folder 18.

of sound, which would activate motion in a series of vibrating mylar "varifocal" mirrors [FIGS.09-10].[47] The next year, Whitman would then begin a long collaboration with the PhilcoFord scientist John Forkner on subsequent mirrored pieces for the LACMA *Art and Technology* exhibition (1970–71), the US Pavilion at Expo 70 in Osaka, and the mirrored dome of E.A.T.'s Pepsi Pavilion at Expo 70. Stan VanDerBeek received help on electronics for his "Geodesic Dome Projection Theatre," as it was labeled in the E.A.T. records, better known as his Movie Drome, a homespun circular projection environment built in VanDerBeek's backyard in Stony Point, New York [FIG.11].[48]

One of the most ambitious and technically complex — even fantastical — proposals came from Belgian artist Panamarenko, who sent extensive blueprints and drawings for his wildly large-scale dirigible designs. One proposed a continuously accelerating spaceship powered by a nuclear reactor [FIG.12]: "[T]he ship would ultimately achieve millions of miles an hour.…A thing like this can not only change the world but also time."[49] Peter Poole of E.A.T. sent letters on Panamarenko's behalf to engineers from various aerospace and defense corporations on June 17, 1969, focusing on one design in particular, a radically lightweight helicopter design that could be operated by one person:[50]

> In a box of 16×16×18" are two motors of 200 cc, 13,000 rpm, and 18 hp. Eight knife-like propellers carefully placed and surrounded by a reservoir for fuel and oil. There is also a seat. That is about all you need to fly around. Just start the motor, sit in it, and fly for half an hour or two hours. With fuel and motors, everything, it weighs 20 lbs. *If this thing is not going to change the world, then the next proposal will.* Every detail of these projects is carefully studied and has nothing to do with science-fiction. They are open for study and, after agreement with me, for production.[51]

The responses ranged from dismissive to supportive — evincing a surprising gulf of opinion. Niels O. Young, who ran a small firm, Block Engineering, in Cambridge, MA, and who would go on to participate in the E.A.T./MoMA competition,[52] wrote in support — but then observed the complete lack of interest in this kind of project from the aircraft industry:

> I am in total sympathy with Panamarenko's motives (or so I think). But I have myself dredged very far and wide searching for an engineering solution and not found one. In this search one is encouraged by the fact that practically no aircraft company (and I have canvassed Hiller, Sikorsky, Gyrodyne and Fairey) has the same motive. They spend their money to maximize profits and build better military or transport machines.[53]

Young's response reveals the utter chasm between mainstream industrial application and Panamarenko's quixotic concept. And yet Chester Sandberg, of the electrical and mechanical engineering corporation Raychem, argued, "[I]f what [Panamarenko] described were at all feasible under the present state of the art they would be on the market. I know of no acceptable motor with the proper power to weight ratio described. At the moment most of what Panamarenko states is just science fiction."[54] In another twist, for Donna Wilson of the defense/aerospace giant McDonnell Douglas, the proposal was not "science fiction" enough:

> The proposal is a misuse of the concept of imagination. In today's technological milieu that threatens to destroy human life and values, we desparetly [*sic*] need imaginative alternatives, but flying machines have existed in our collective storehouse of fantasy for centuries (e.g., see the recent exhibit *The Machine* by the New York Museum of Modern Art). If engineers and technicians need new grist for their mills (and I seriously believe they do) then why do artists continue to be obsessed with symbols or metaphors that are well known and explored? Their chief value to the human race has always been in their function to be the precursors of consciousness. I suggest that a proper use of imagination would be to turn to what we can hope to receive from the future — not to what we already know of the past.[55]

Finally, according to John Pruner of the major aerospace think tank Lawrence Livermore Laboratories:

> Mr. Panamarenko's design concept is basically feasible and is not without precedent. A similar device called the Bensen B-12 Sky-Mat was built and flown by the Bensen Aircraft Corporation. It had 10 5-ft. dia rotors, each driven by a 10 hp West Bend engine. Maximum take-off weight was 800 lbs.
>
> I believe one could construct a scaled down version of the Bensen B-12 helicopter using 8 rotors driven by two 18 hp engines to lift one man…Mr. Panamarenko's helicopter design concept is an exciting challenge not only from the stand point of design and construction but also of performance, stability, and control. To Mr. Panamarenko, I would like to express an earnest and sincere "Good luck and many happy lift-offs."[56]

Pruner's flatly pragmatic acknowledgment, Wilson's disappointment, Sandberg's dismissal, Young's enthusiasm: the engineers' responses are all clearly at odds with one another. And so their critical and epistemological divides become clear: on the one hand, openness and experimental possibility; on the other, a pessimistic resignation to the utter instrumentalization of technology, consignment to a world in which the technological resources and

47 — Eric Rawson and Robert Whitman, "Report on a *Light Sculpture Using Varifocal Mirror*," n.d. E.A.T./GRI Box 27, Folder 18. See also Eric Rawson, "Pond," *Techne* 1, no. 1 (April 14, 1969): 10. Rawson writes, "Pond is a light and sound environment that occupied a 70-foot by 40-foot gallery at the Jewish Museum in New York City. Arranged around the perimeter of the room were a variety of large electronic vibrating mirrors and rigid spherical mirrors. Automatic slide projectors, suspended above the observers' heads near the room center, projected images intermittently onto (and reflected images from above) the vibrating and rigid mirrors. A recorded voice spoke occasional words or phrases from loudspeakers distributed about the room." Loudspeakers were additionally installed in each varifocal mirror; when the speakers were activated with sound, "the effect [was] both acoustical and visual; the observer hears (or feels) the sound waves and observes his reflected image moving back and forth behind the mylar mirror as the mylar film changes curvature due to the pressure of the sound waves."

48 — VanDerBeek to Sue Hartnett (E.A.T.), January 30, 1967. E.A.T./GRI Box 6, Folder 47.

49 — Panamarenko, "Closed System Power Devices for Space/ Portable Air Transport/Gas Turbines, 27 East 67th St., New York, April 19–May 9, 1969," proposal and statement for exhibition at John Gibson Communications, New York. E.A.T./GRI Box 6, Folder 26.

50 — Panamarenko, E.A.T. matching card, 1968. E.A.T./GRI Box 13.

51 — Panamarenko, "Closed System Power Devices for Space." Emphasis added. For a different reading of the Panamarenko proposal and response, focusing on the Pruner and Wilson letters, see Matthew Wisnioski, *Engineers for Change: Competing Visions of Technology in 1960s America* (Cambridge, MA: MIT Press, 2012), 299.

52 — For further information regarding the E.A.T./MoMA competition, see Kuo, "To Avoid the Waste of a Cultural Revolution," 213–23.

53 — Young to Peter Poole, June 18, 1969. E.A.T./GRI Box 6, Folder 26.

54 — Sandberg to Peter Poole, June 26, 1969. E.A.T./GRI Box 6, Folder 26.

55 — Wilson to Libby Joyce, editor of *Techne*, July 15, 1969. E.A.T./GRI Box 6, Folder 26.

56 — Pruner to Peter Poole, July 21, 1969. E.A.T./GRI Box 6, Folder 26.

57 —— Panamarenko to John Gibson, August 1, 1969. E.A.T./GRI Box 6, Folder 26.

58 —— For a succinct reading of Fuller's utopianism, see Sean Keller, "Navigating Systems," *Artforum International* 47, no. 3 (November 2008): 282–94.

sophistication needed to engineer a project such as Panamarenko's was hopelessly out of reach. For Panamarenko, who had turned from proto-Conceptual assemblages in the 1960s to the dirigibles that would consume the rest of his career, the design problem of the personal flying vehicle was in and of itself an ongoing investigation that need not be fulfilled, or work. After correspondence with Poole and these engineers, Panamarenko would go on to attempt to implement some aspects of Pruner's recommendations, producing highly complex blueprints and designs; but he would never successfully produce a personal, wingless flying device of this scale.[57] His interaction with E.A.T. attested to the endlessness of his project — an openness and infinitude that could not have been more different from the scientistic positivism of Buckminster Fuller's breathlessly optimistic schemes.[58] If Fuller made engineering utopian, Panamarenko made it weird.

E.A.T. created a weird science, indeed. Their matchings and collaborations defied any conventional hierarchy between art and engineering: the artists did not simply follow engineers' instructions, nor did the engineers take a back seat to the artists. Far from it — they created and changed the very form of the work. People, things, tools, and networks all became part of the collaboration.

The Technical Services Program led to the vast proliferation of these collaborations — via "Local Groups" from Stockholm to Ahmedabad to Tokyo. E.A.T. would irrevocably change art and its cherished notions of a singular creator laboring alone. It changed technology, too, with echoes of the organization's breakthrough inventiveness, its rejection of orthodoxy, in today's Silicon Valley-speak "disruption." And E.A.T. also changed what art and technology could be *together*, beyond simplistic binaries of utopia or dystopia, auguring possibilities still to come.

Utopian Optimism & Fearful Paranoia

Daniel Birnbaum, Massimiliano Gioni, and Ben Lévne Weitzman

BLW *Dream Machines* is an extensive show about a massive topic in a tiny space at the periphery of an island seemingly untouched by the surges of technological progress. How did this contradictory exhibition come to be?

MG From the beginning, Dakis and Lietta Joannou's vision of transforming a former slaughterhouse near Hydra's port into a project space opted for repurposing a small existing structure rather than constructing a new one. A readymade, in a way. While the space typically hosts annual solo exhibitions, exceptions were made for *Dream Machines* and a small group show I curated in 2021, titled *The Greek Gift*. This year, the *Apollo Wind Spinner* (2020–22) — the centerpiece of Jeff Koons's exhibition *Apollo*, at the Slaughterhouse in 2022 — was gifted to Hydra and will remain permanently displayed, so we thought it would be interesting to use this work and the slaughterhouse itself, a killing machine, as a starting point for an exhibition. I had invited Daniel to contribute an essay to the Koons exhibition catalogue and he drew very interesting connections between Koons's work and Duchamp's, which paved the way for this rather small philosophical show about machines. The paradox of staging a show about such a complex theme in this remote location and with limited exhibition space is undeniably evident. However, perhaps like a butterfly effect, this humble origin has the potential to reach and impact a wide audience.

DB In *Apollo*, Koons positioned his art in relation to the readymade. When I was asked to write the essay for the catalogue, I wanted to connect it to Duchamp's *Coffee Mill* (1911), which is often treated as the secret key to his other works. In general, I think we're often formed by the places where we work. At the Moderna Museet, where I spent almost a decade, one of the key threads running through the collection is art and technology. There's an extensive collection dedicated to Duchamp, filled with authorized replicas, and the museum is connected to Experiments in Art and Technology, an initiative that aimed to bridge the gap between artists and technologists. Nowadays at Acute Art, we're driven by a similar vision. We want to see what happens when artists are given access to tools they wouldn't typically have. We conducted a little experiment with Koons, which we showcased in Stockholm. Initially, we were focused on big names like Olafur Eliasson and Marina Abramović, but now we're more interested in working with up-and-coming artists.

BLW Locomotion seems to be a key element in the show, as well as reproduction. For example, you don't show Duchamp's original *Coffee Mill*, understandably, but Ulf Linde's 1960 replica of Duchamp's work.

MG Of course, we simply wouldn't be able to show the originals in the Slaughterhouse, which is a place with no climate control and with some of its rooms basically outdoors. However, a show centered on machines is inevitably a show about reproduction, where the notion of an original loses its significance and copies take center stage. That's why we have an actual Duchamp, and then Ulf Linde's copy and Elaine Sturtevant's replica (*Duchamp Porte-bouteilles*, 1992). As the mysterious secret key to Duchamp, *Coffee Mill* is also an erotic metaphor. It's very sensual, which is one of the subthemes in the show, relating to the Surrealist and Dadaist idea of the machine as carnal, as flesh. In this sense, Duchamp's famous *The Bride Stripped Bare by Her Bachelors, Even* (1915–23), often referred to as *The Large Glass*, was also described by its author as a "bachelor machine," a peculiar combination of sexuality and fatality — a machine that engages in self-pleasure but doesn't produce anything tangible. This explains why many elements in our show are designed to rotate and move. They are caught in a kind of masturbatory mechanical ballet: they are unproductive machines. The exhibition is also filled with works — like Brion Gysin's *Dreamachine* (1961) and Wilhelm Reich's *Orgone Accumulator* (1940) — that are built from instructions one can find online or in books. These pieces suggest that art, when freed from sentimental projections, can be easily built and reconstructed. Duchamp explored this idea, through his notes for *The Green Box* (1934), for example.

DB As compact and small as the show is, we began thinking about it as a show about a century of art and technology. Over this period, several paradigmatic shifts occurred with the advent of various technologies: photography, cinema, video cameras, television, the internet, and now emerging technologies like AR and VR, which you, Ben, and I are currently grappling with and trying to understand. These transformative changes are all present within the exhibition.

MG This is also evident in the displays we have: a Barco monitor from the 1970s, an iPhone showing Pipilotti Rist's *Selbstlos im Lavabad (Selfless in the Bath of Lava) (Bastard Version)* (1994), and a VR headset for Nathalie Djurberg and Hans Berg's *It Will End in Stars* (2018).

BLW The show does feel like an ode to a century driven by technological advancements.

MG You can also think of it as a requiem, filled as it is with obsolescent machines. There's an undercurrent of fear and angst in the exhibition.

We present a diagram from an 1810 medical book (*Illustrations of Madness* by John Haslam) depicting a case study of James Tilly Matthews, a London tea broker afflicted with schizophrenia and haunted by the paranoia of being controlled by an Air Loom — a fearsome machine that used mesmeric rays and enigmatic gases to manipulate minds from afar. This fear of being dominated by a machine is the same as our contemporary unease surrounding the potential dominance of artificial intelligence in our lives. It echoes the historical fear that the Luddites, members of a nineteenth-century textile workers movement in England, harbored toward the advancement of looms, as they believed this technology threatened their livelihoods.

BLW   In a way, it did. As did many of these machines. Their fear was not unjust.

MG   The title of the exhibition, inspired by Gysin's *Dreamachine*, tries to encompass this dual nature of technology. It expresses a utopian belief in its capacity to improve our lives, while acknowledging the thin line between dream and nightmare.

DB   This is the show's key idea — technology brings forth both new possibilities and a duality of utopian optimism and fearful paranoia. The exhibition features a range of works, from established artists to peculiar machines, all embodying this double-edged nature. While the show explores new possibilities, it doesn't solely embrace a techno-optimistic perspective. Instead, it delves into how technology challenges the essence of art. This happened with the emergence of the readymade, which is inherently linked to the appearance of photography. Each shift in technology opens new possibilities for what an artwork can be. Lee Bul's AR piece copy (*Willing to Be Vulnerable — Metalized Balloon Ver. AR22*, 2022) hints at the potential of the next shift toward mixed realities. It might not happen immediately, but it seems that these technologies will become omnipresent in our future lives.

BLW   And yet, this exhibition isn't really "techy." It has a mechanical, almost analog vibe.

MG   We wanted the show to feel a bit rudimentary. In this context, Maurizio Cattelan's piece (*Dynamo Secession*, 1997/2023) — with his bicycle powering a light bulb that lights the exhibition — undermines the idea of technology as triumphant. The whole show feels a bit rickety, held together with tape and wire — it's more the work of a bricoleur than an engineer. We included many pieces that contrast with the triumphant idea of technology as a promise of a future filled with new life-changing experiences. I think the *Healing Machines* (c. 1955–86) by Emery Blagdon are also

relevant in this context: there's a contrast between the aspirations — the faith, even — projected onto technology and the fragility of those assemblages. In a sense, we wanted virtual reality and high-tech components, but a piece like Cattelan's is very much about diminished reality.

DB   Yes, it's definitely not the show that the MIT Media Lab or ZKM Center for Art and Media in Karlsruhe would do. Today most of us have access to incredibly advanced technology, new iPhones are prepared for forms of experience that no-one could dream of in the 1960s when engineers Billy Klüver and Fred Waldhauer of Bell Labs and artists Robert Rauschenberg and Robert Whitman created Experiments in Art and Technology (E.A.T.) to develop collaborations, which seems especially relevant to this exhibition **[SEE PAGES 100–116]**. Many of their projects were actually quite underwhelming from a visual point of view, but the intellectual ambitions were grand.

MG   It was important to us to remain modest in this show. Of course, we do include technologically advanced pieces such as Pamela Rosenkranz's robotic snake, *Healer (Waters)* (2019), but there are also many pieces that are very handmade. It's a tiny show and we wanted it to feel like a broken machine. Everything was dictated by the size of the door, which we ended up making even smaller. Otherwise, there would have been too much light coming in. These restrictions defined how we put this show together.

BLW   In the small room outside, Takis's *Kadran Dial* (1974) is a machine that looks back at you, and next to it is Cao Fei's *Oz* (2022), a highly rendered visualization of a chimera of some kind. On the roof is one of my favorite works in the show, Judith Hopf's sculpture copy *Phone User 5* (2021–22). Within the context of Greece, the work reminds me of the attempt to avoid Medusa's gaze. But the figure is nonetheless petrified, so the deflection doesn't seem to work.

MG   I'm constantly surprised by how human gestures become common, often because of technology. People hold smartphones in similar ways. We all now have carpal tunnel syndrome. The show indeed alludes to the relations that are developed between humans and machines as our bodies are trained to use technology. But it's not just the physical body, of course, it's also our nervous system that gets expanded and connected. Looking at Hopf's sculpture of a phone user aiming her iPhone at the sunset, I'm reminded of Régis Debray's comment that humans photograph things they fear to lose. [01]

01 —— Regis Debray, interview with Andrew Joscelyne, "Revolution in the Revolution." *Wired*, January 1, 1995, www.wired.com/1995/01/debray/.

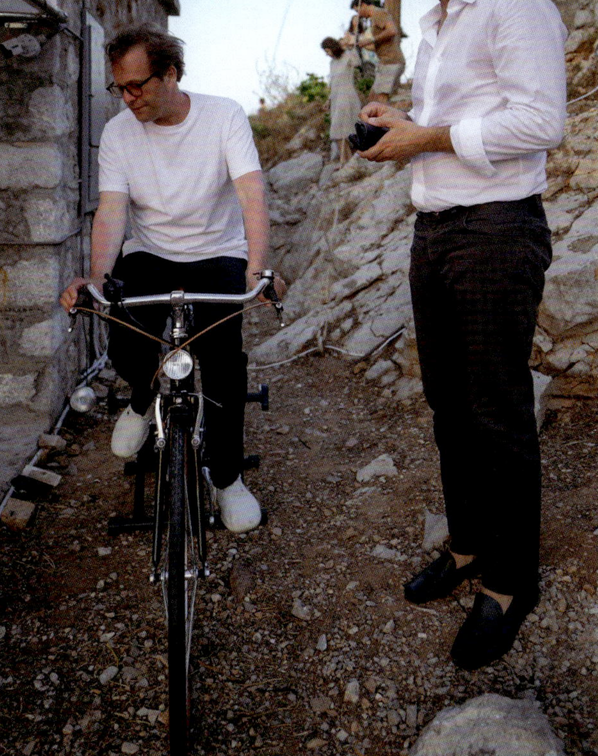

FIG.01 Daniel Birnbaum (riding Maurizio
Cattelan's *Dynamo Secession*, 1997/2023)
and Massimiliano Gioni, Hydra, 2023

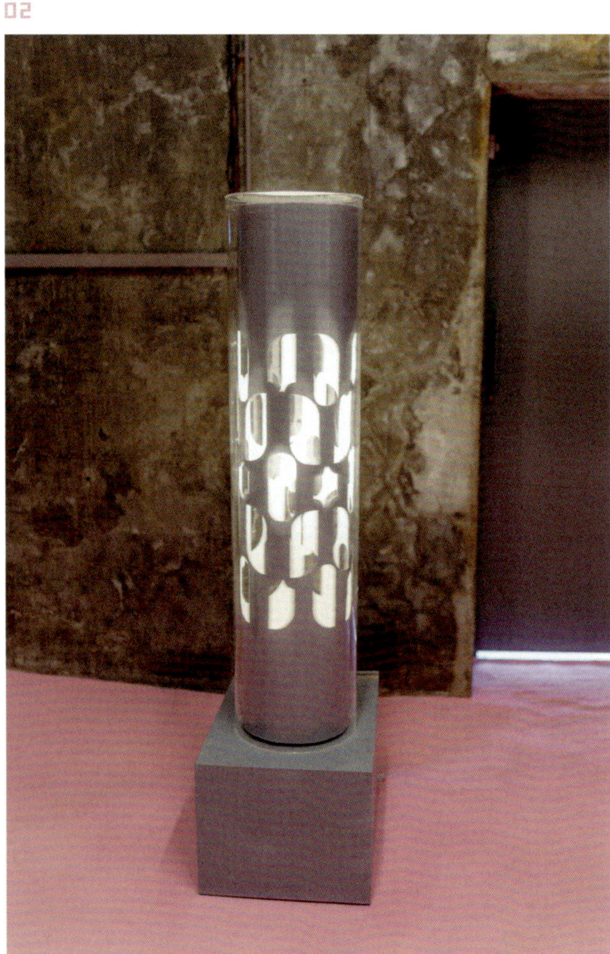

FIG.02 Brion Gysin, *Dreamachine*, 1961
Galvanized metal, light bulb, wood, and motor
120 × 27 cm diam. Reconstruction based on
original drawings

FIG.03 Jeff Koons, *Apollo Wind Spinner*,
2020 – 22; Steel, bronze, and two motors
1393.3 × 914.4 × 260.8 cm

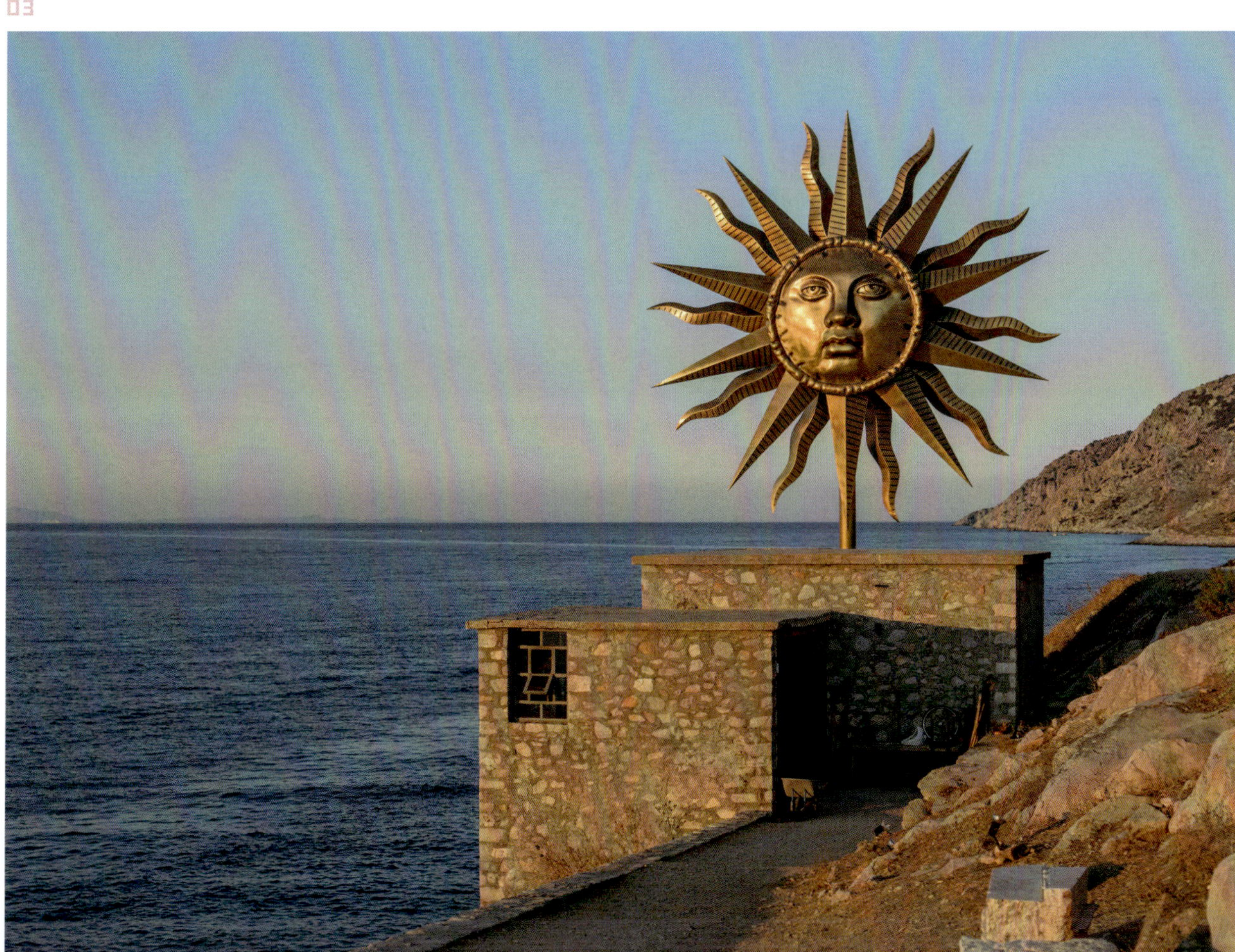

DB   In that sense, our show has a lot to do with old utopias — old futures, so to speak. We don't join the apocalyptic doomsayers against AI, but we also try to avoid a simplified optimistic perspective. However, I'm surrounded by many who are incredibly optimistic that these new technologies will generate a new way to inhabit the planet. If we see the art world as a microcosm of the world and its pathologies, we can witness the best and worst of humanity in it. There are many fears and some hopes. These technologies — I'm thinking of Rist's video or Bul's AR piece — offer glimpses of new institutional possibilities. While small, they are all part of the show. And I'm very happy about that.

BLW   To an extent, audience interactions with art have also undergone significant transformations due to the widespread adoption of technology. While prints have long enabled access to artworks away from the original, nowadays, we primarily engage with art through reproductions. Even when physically in the same space, we still attempt to capture them with our pocket cameras.

DB   Indeed. It's already the case that every second person looks at the artwork through a smartphone, whether as a reproduction on social media or to see the artwork itself. But even if one avoids the smartphone and, for example, comes to live here on a remote part of the island to reconnect with reality, I believe it's our way of seeing that has fundamentally changed. And I don't think there's any coming back from that.

MG   As a curator, it was a very challenging show to do — and by that, I mean it was an absolute pleasure. It's a small show, but I hope it's full of special findings. I'm not sure it would have been possible anywhere else. This also brings us back to the notion of utopias. In our field, we're encouraged to create new, grand, large-scale exhibitions that still emphasize the original artwork, which is something we should perhaps reevaluate. For example, it's possible that, in twenty-five years, it might get more difficult to borrow paintings and fly them across the world. Factors like fragility, the need for protection, and restrictions on movement, all interconnected with the climate crisis, could contribute to this shift. In fact, these discussions have been taking place since the 1970s. I recall an instance where a museum in Italy focused on metaphysical painting exclusively showcased copies presented as light boxes. It didn't last, unfortunately. *Dream Machines* is a humble step in this direction: think small.

First published as "Massimiliano Gioni and Daniel Birnbaum on Dream Machines," *Ocula Magazine*, https://ocula.com/magazine/conversations/massimiliano-gioni-daniel-birnbaum-dream-machines/.

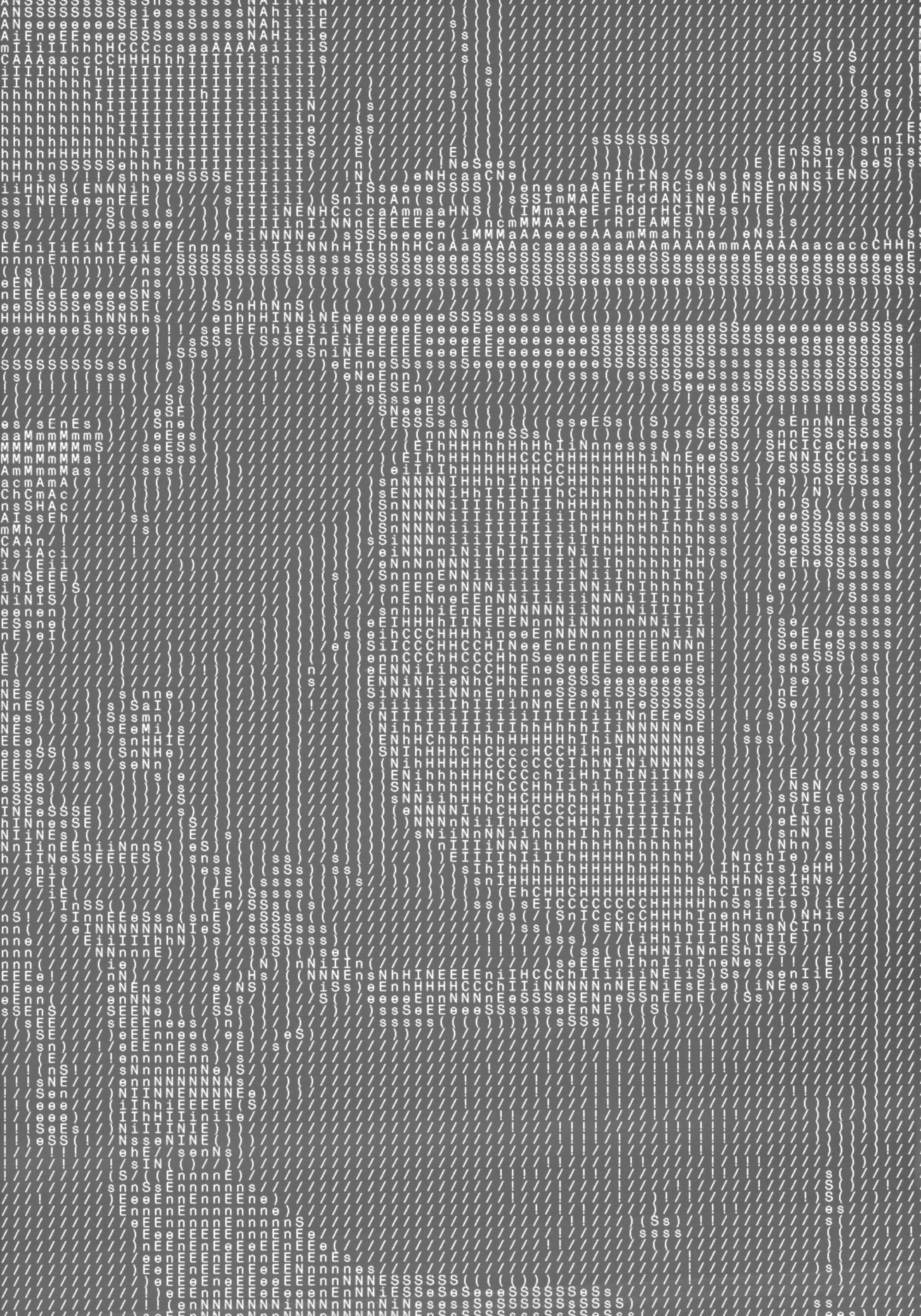

Sequences

[126]

Peter
Fischli and
David
Weiss
*Der Lauf
der Dinge
(The Way
Things Go)*,
1987
Color video
transferred
from 16
mm film,
with sound
30:00 min.

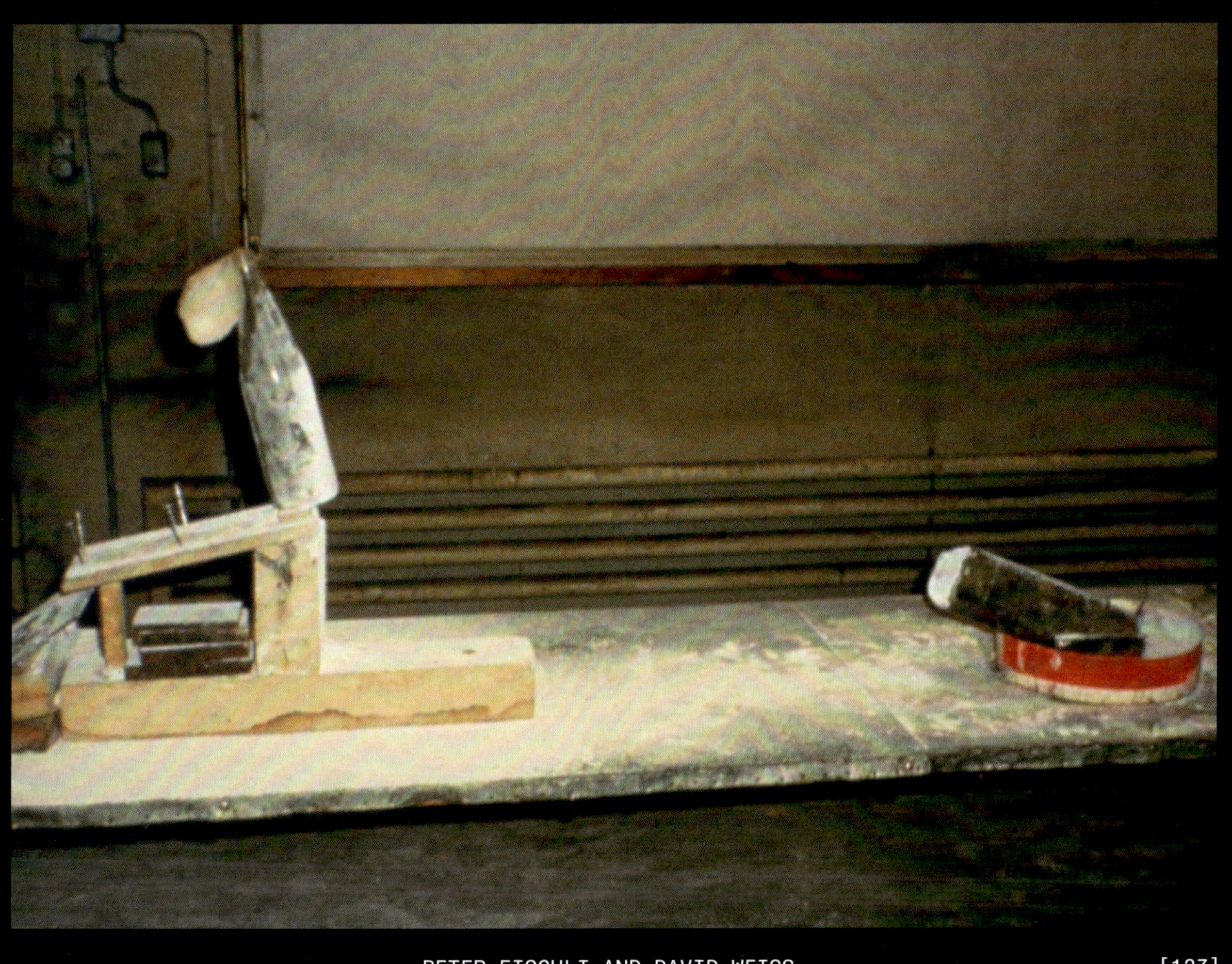

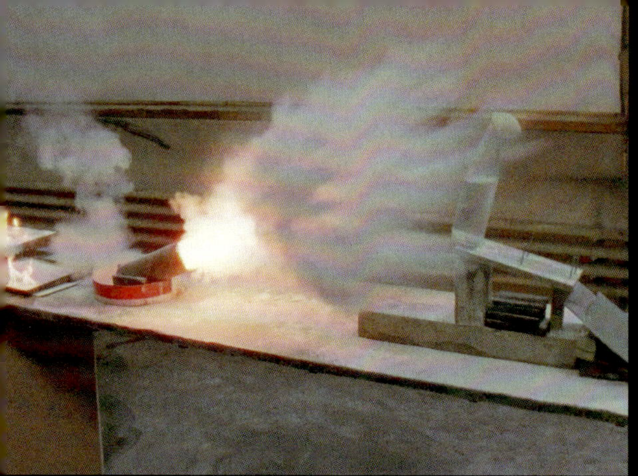

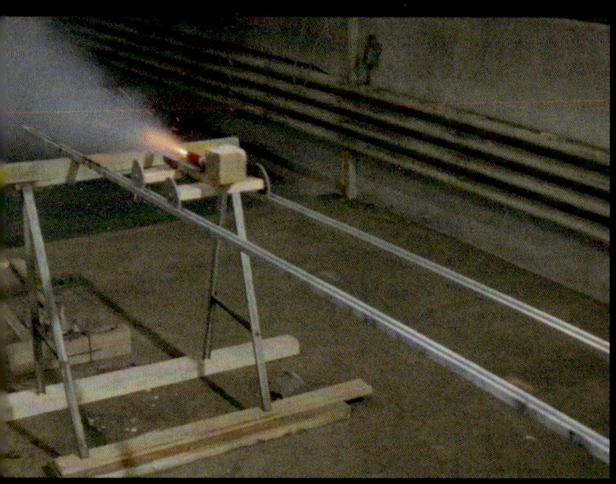

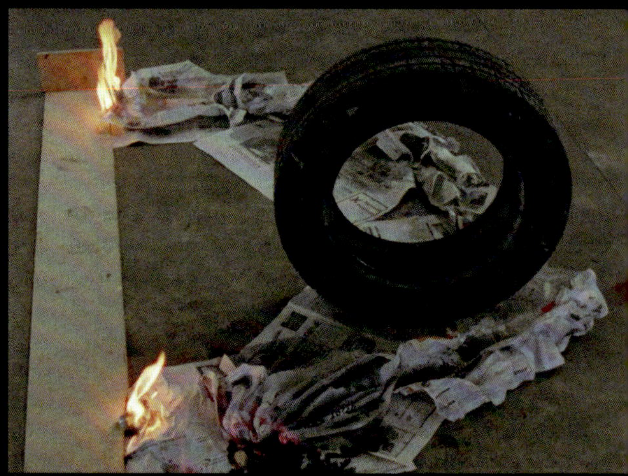

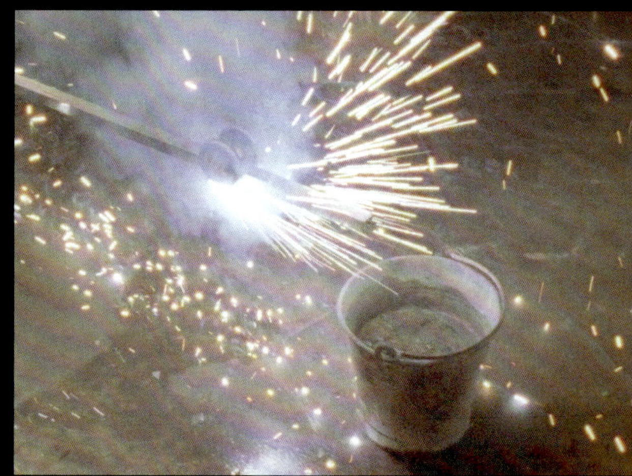

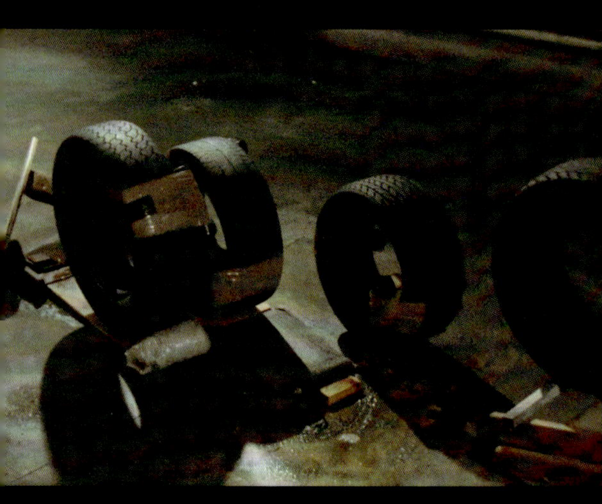

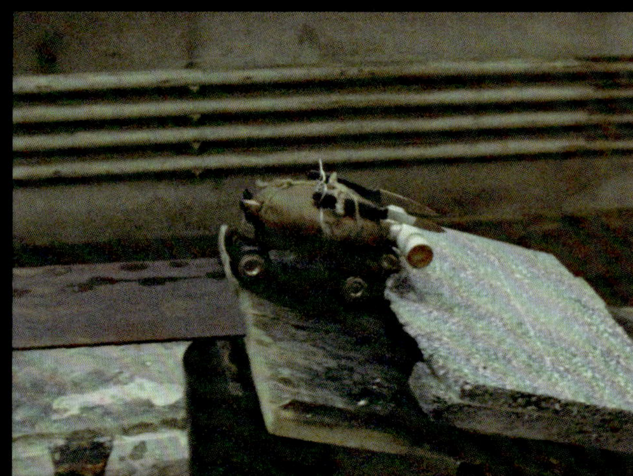

DER LAUF DER DINGE (THE WAY THINGS GO)

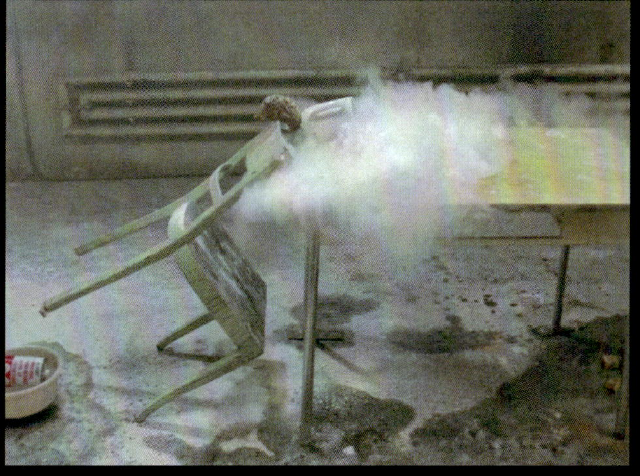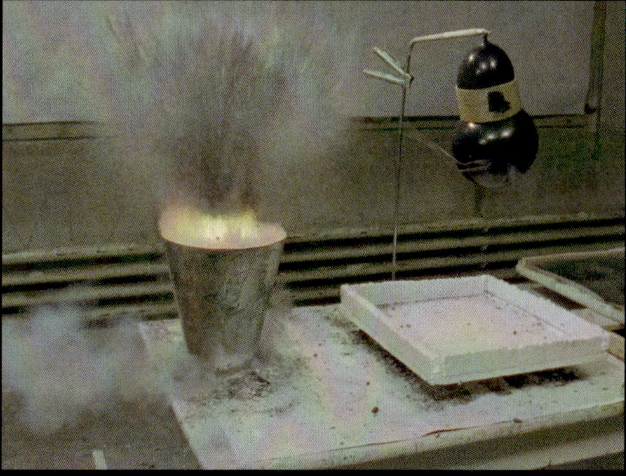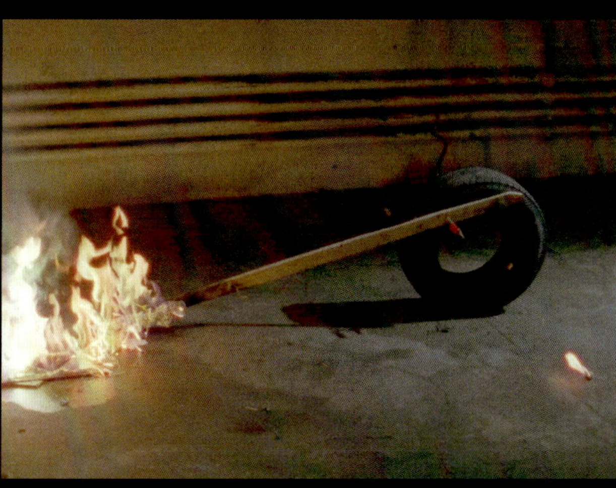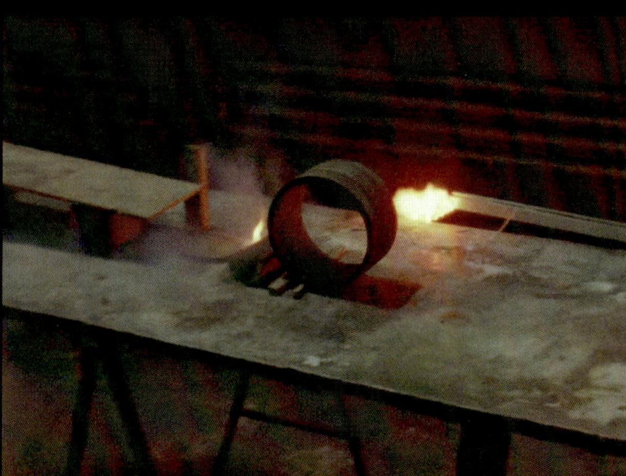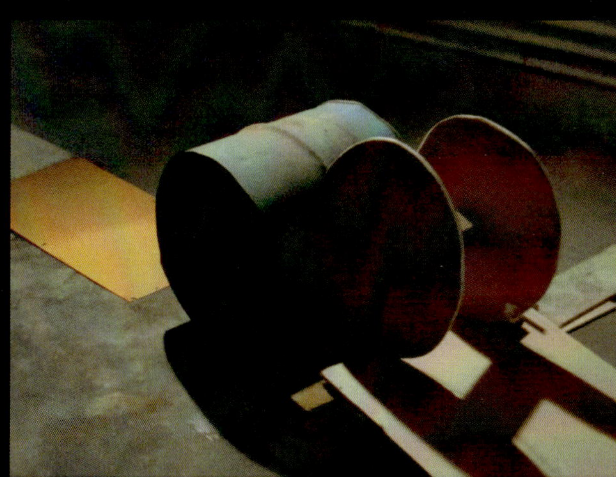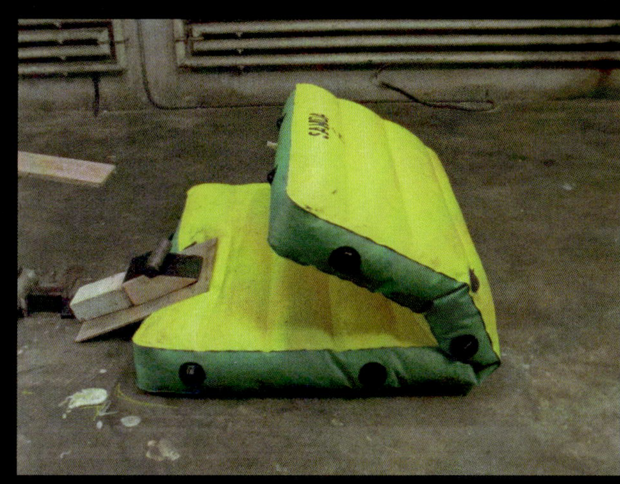

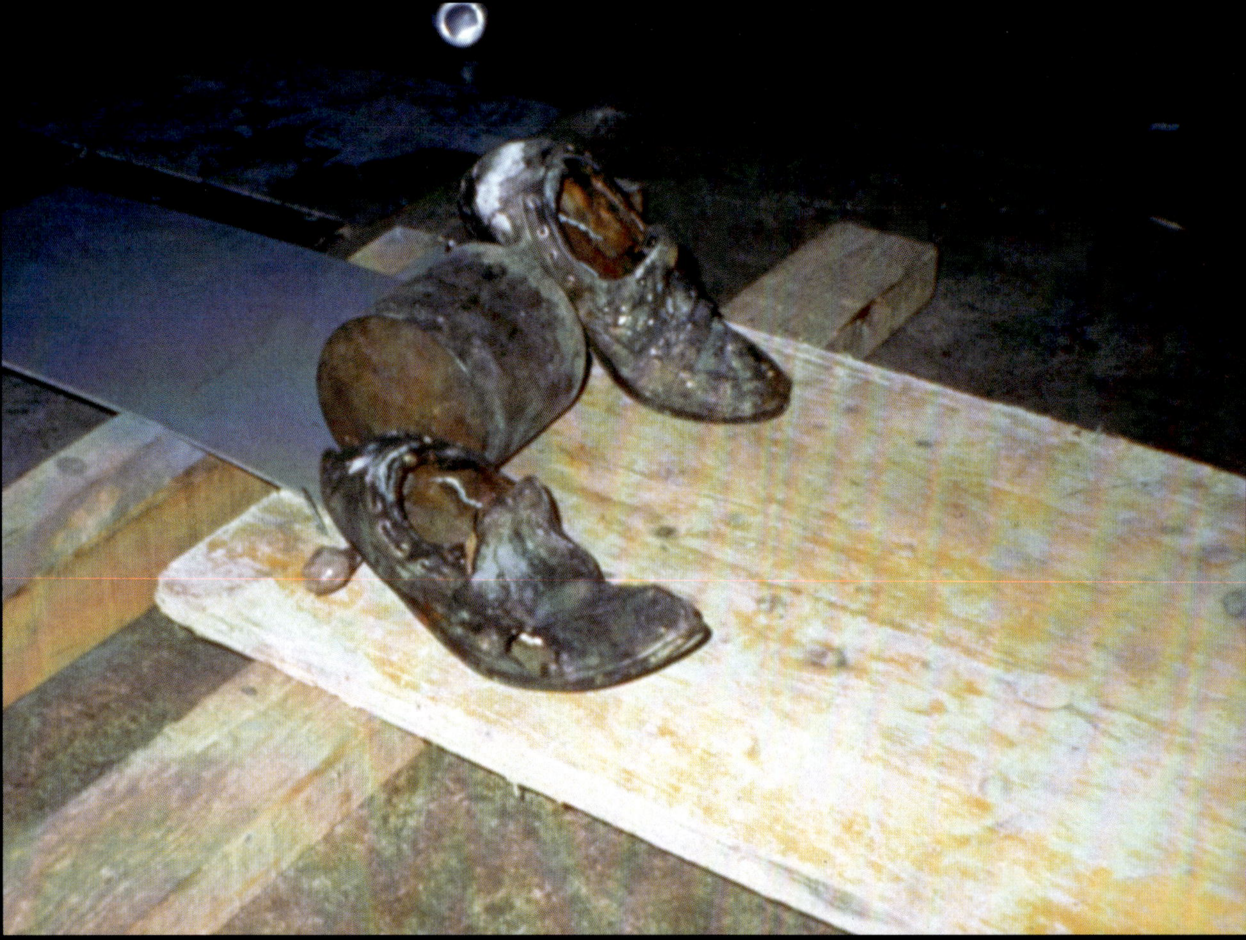

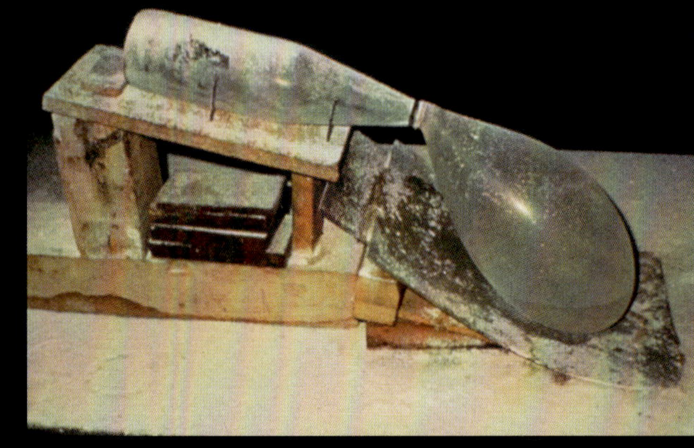

    DER LAUF DER DINGE (THE WAY THINGS GO)

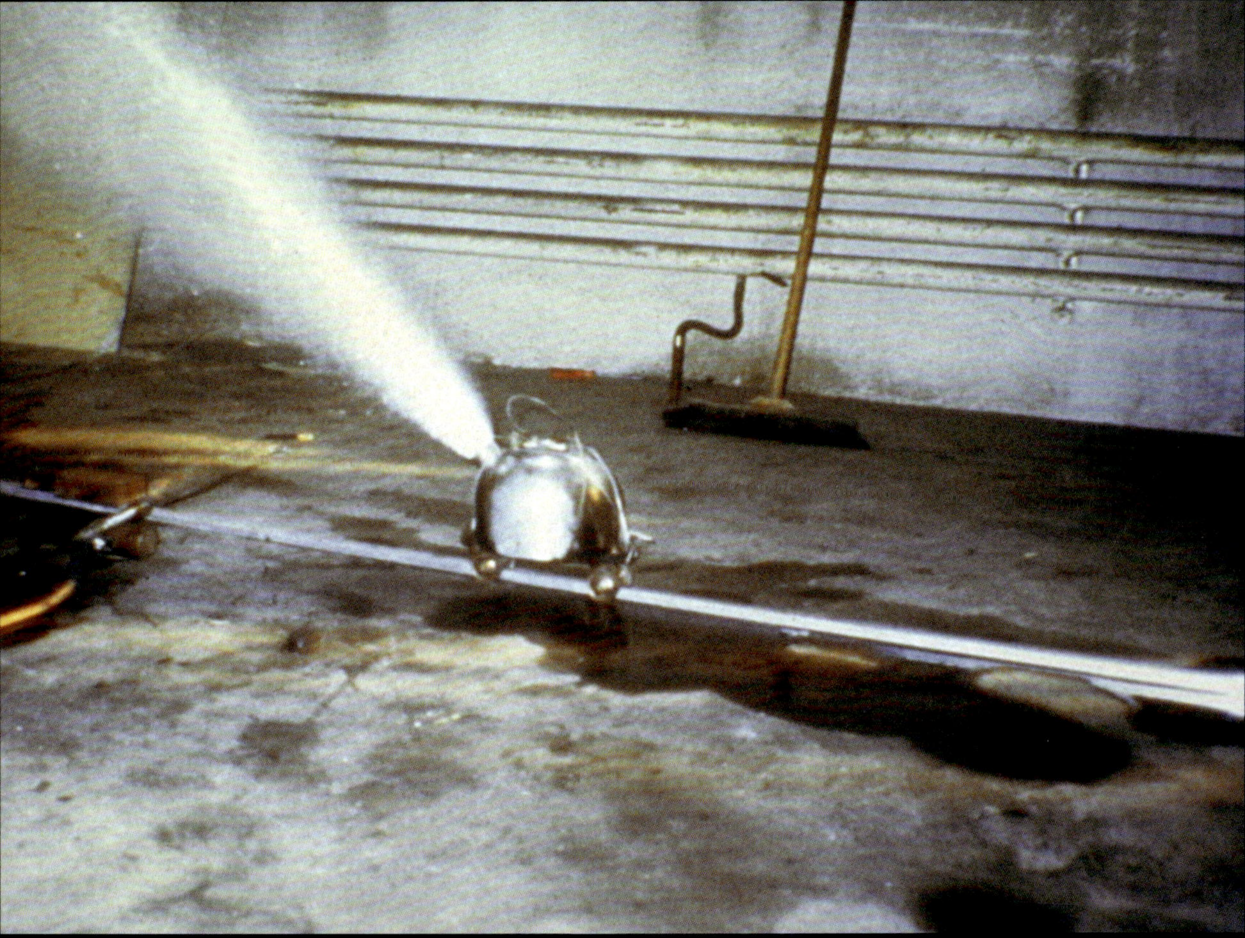

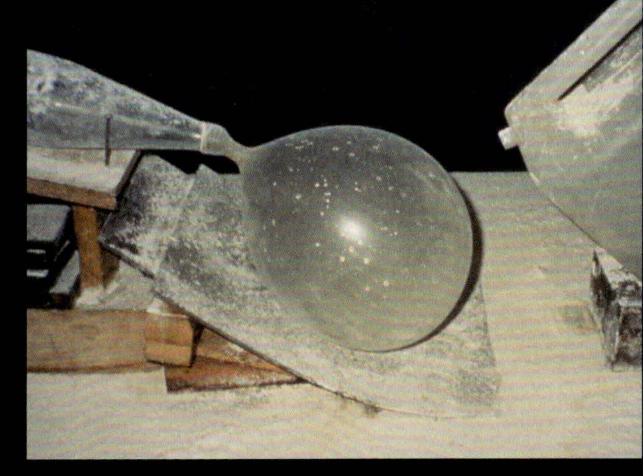

PETER FISCHLI AND DAVID WEISS

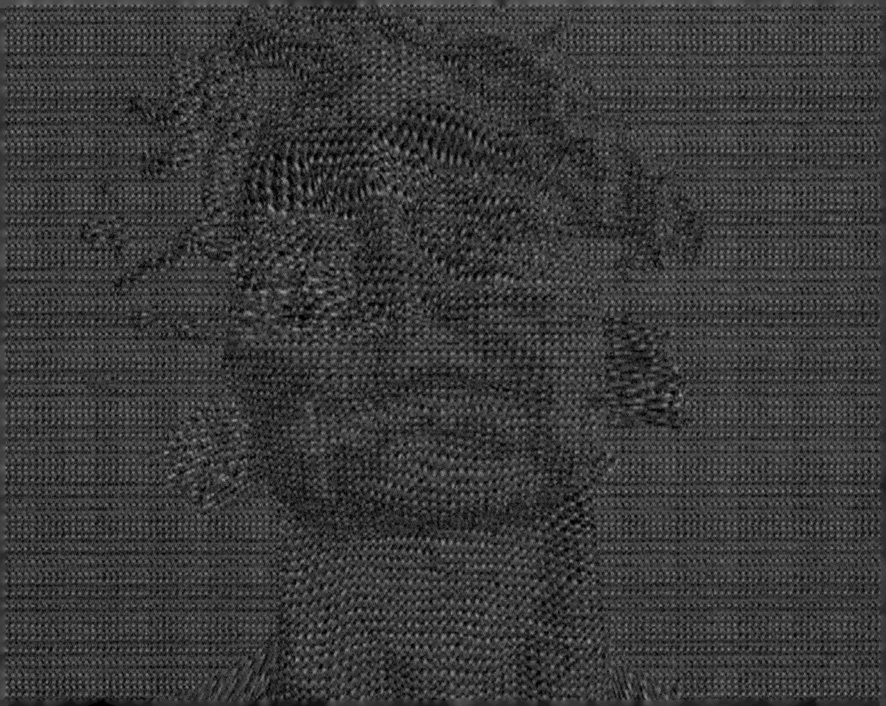

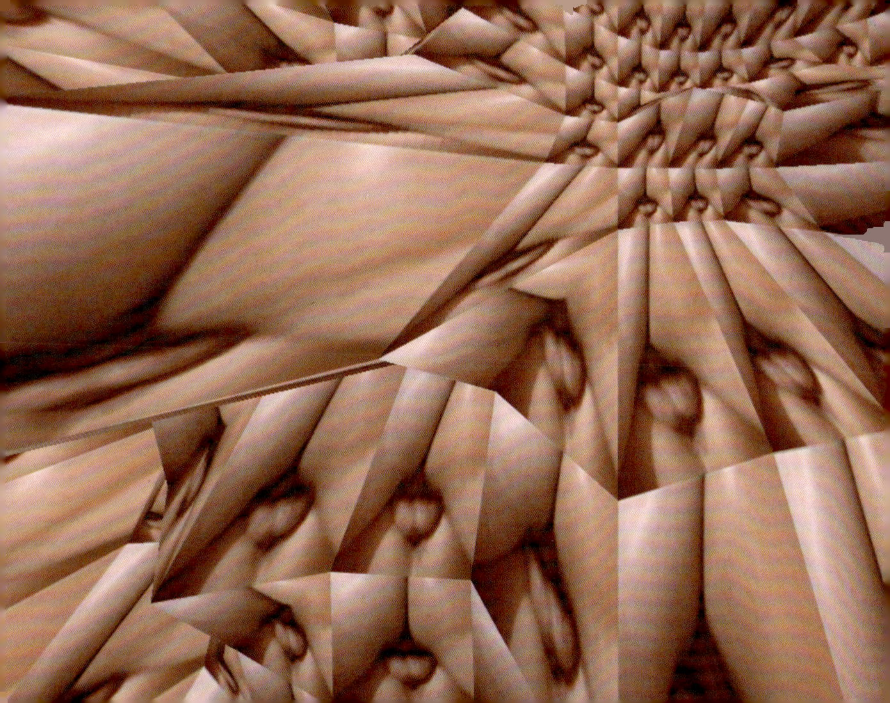

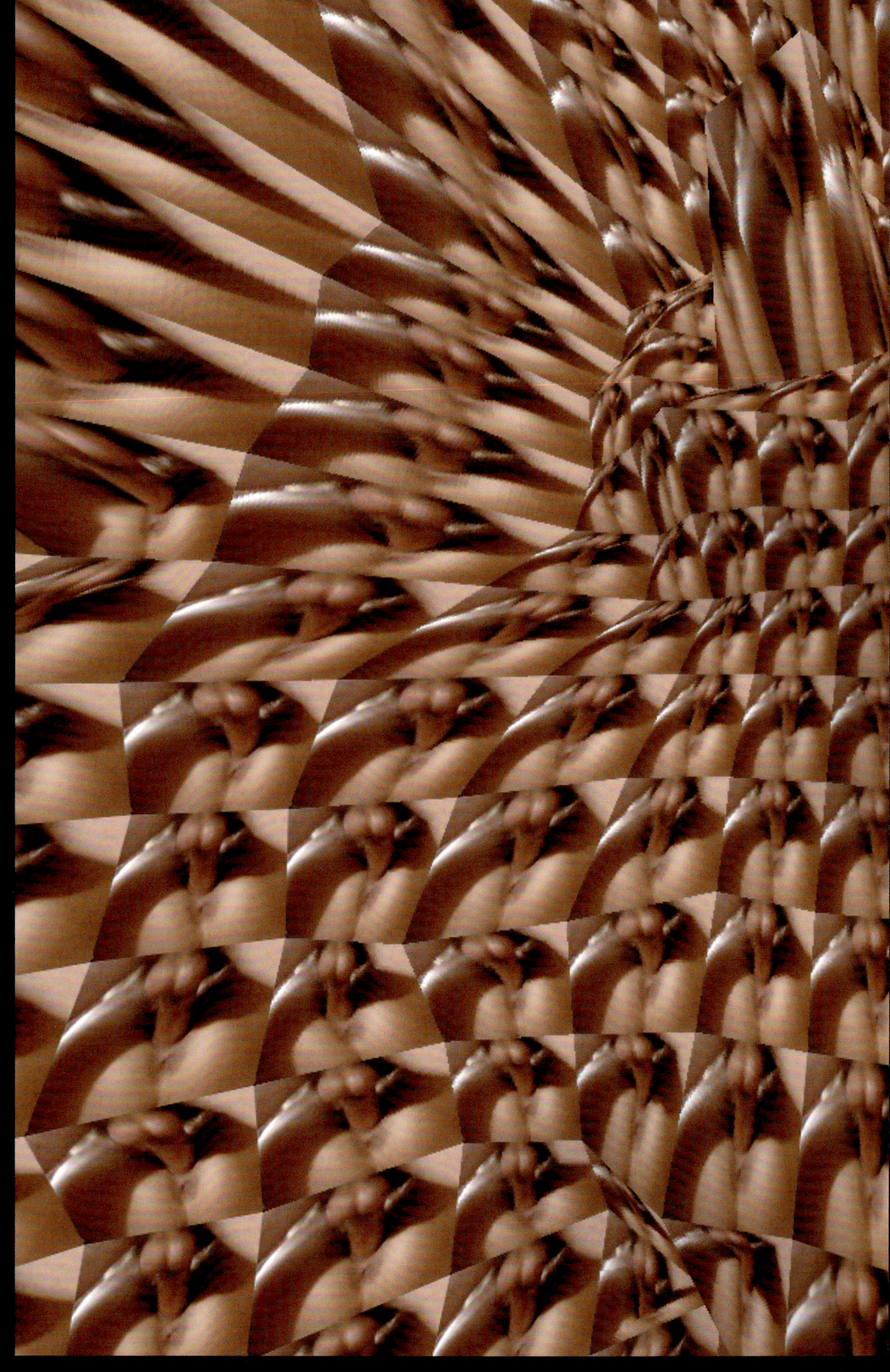

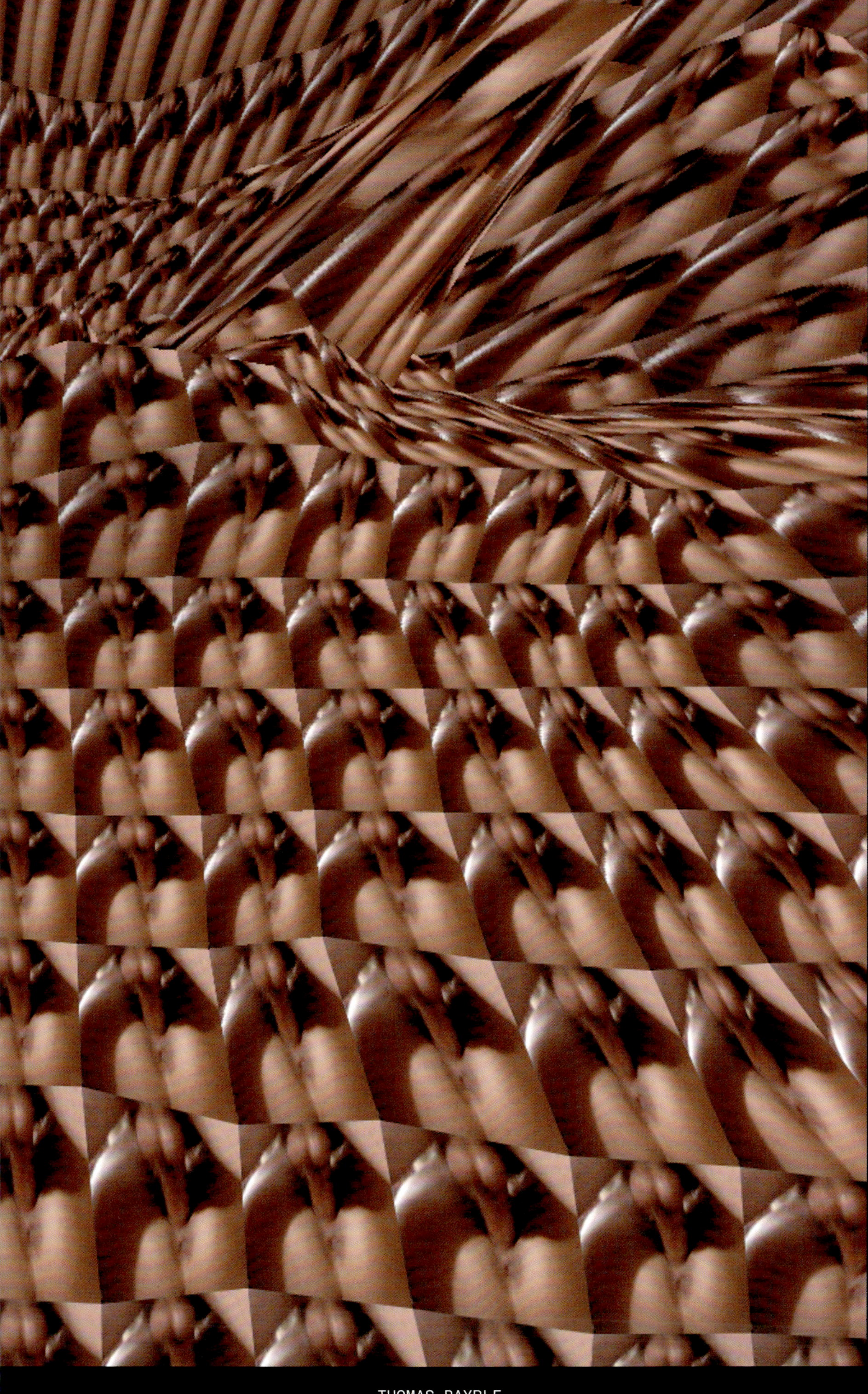

THOMAS BAYRLE

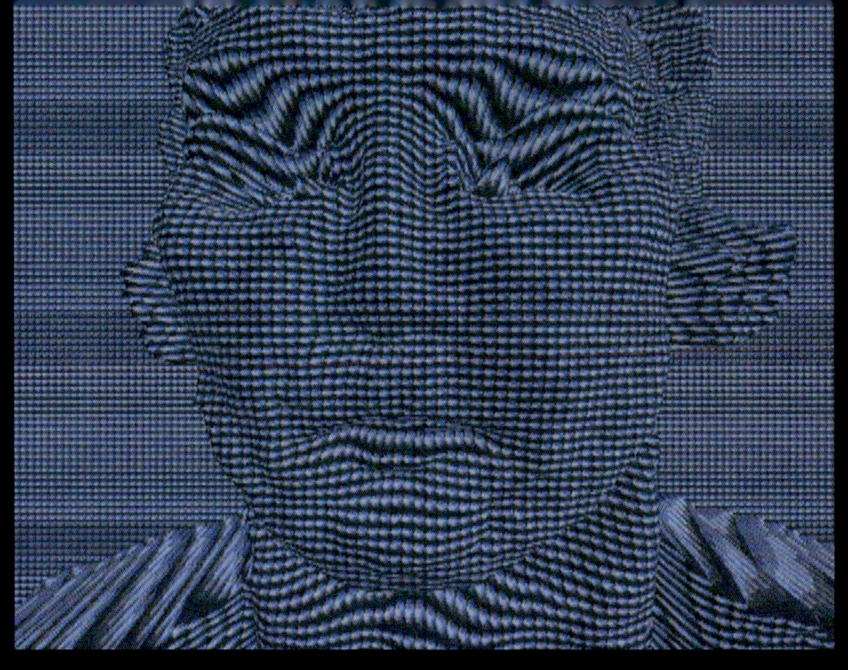

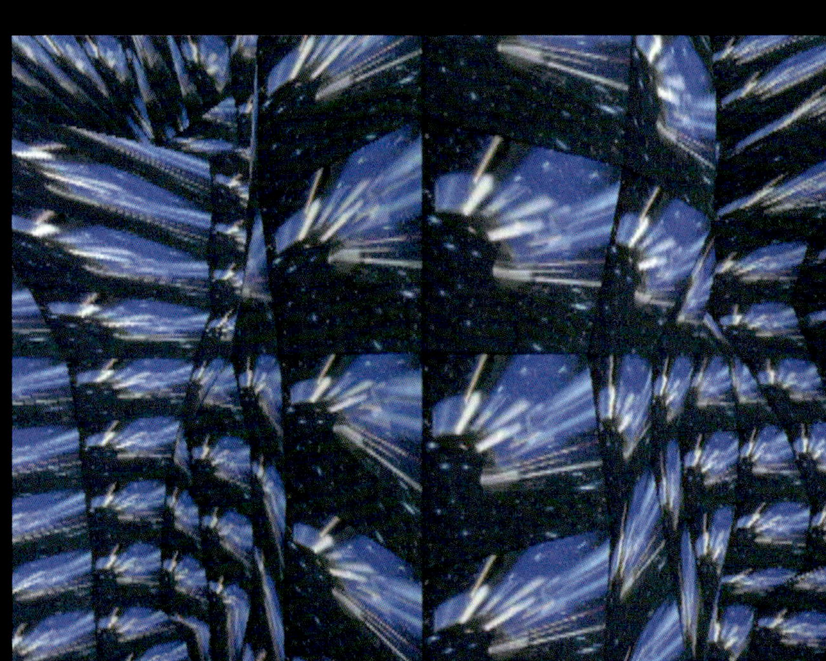

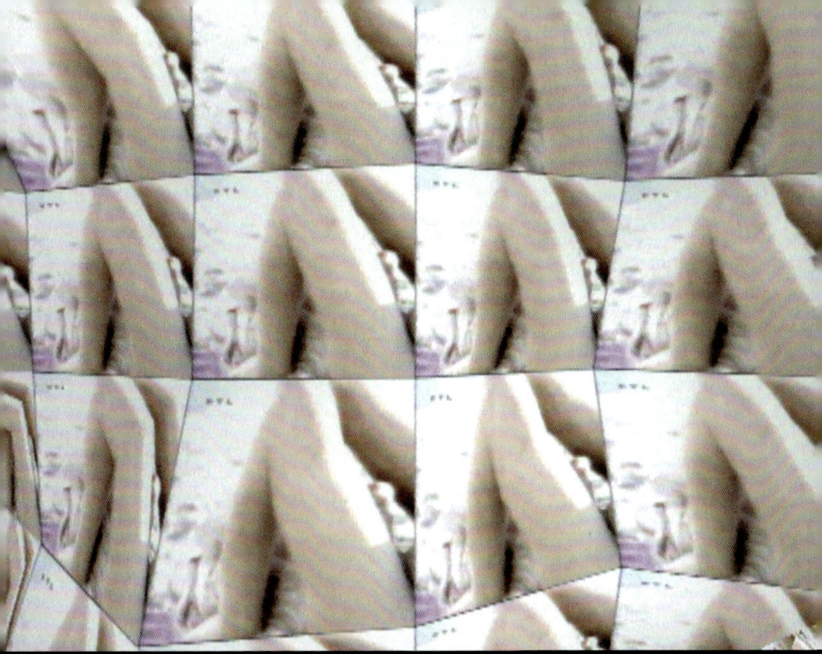

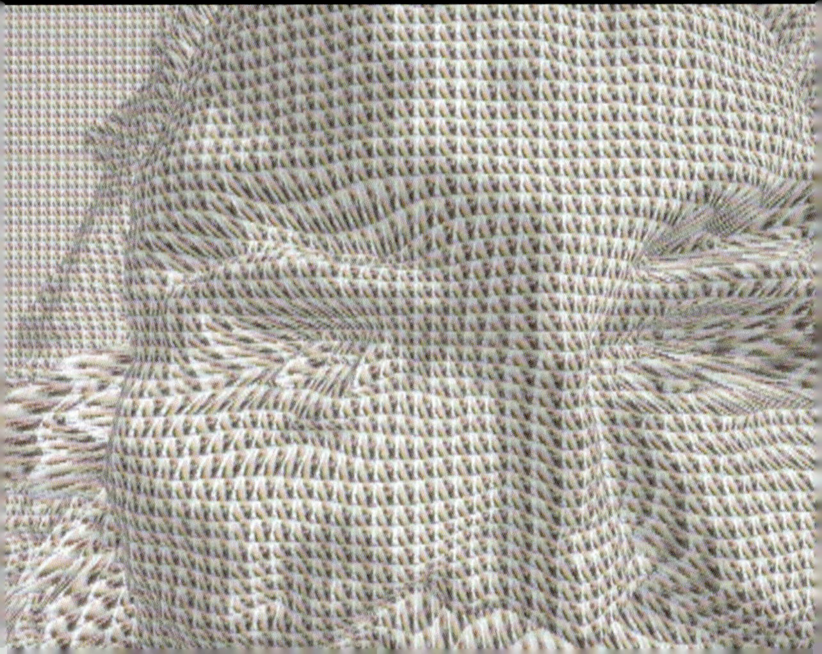

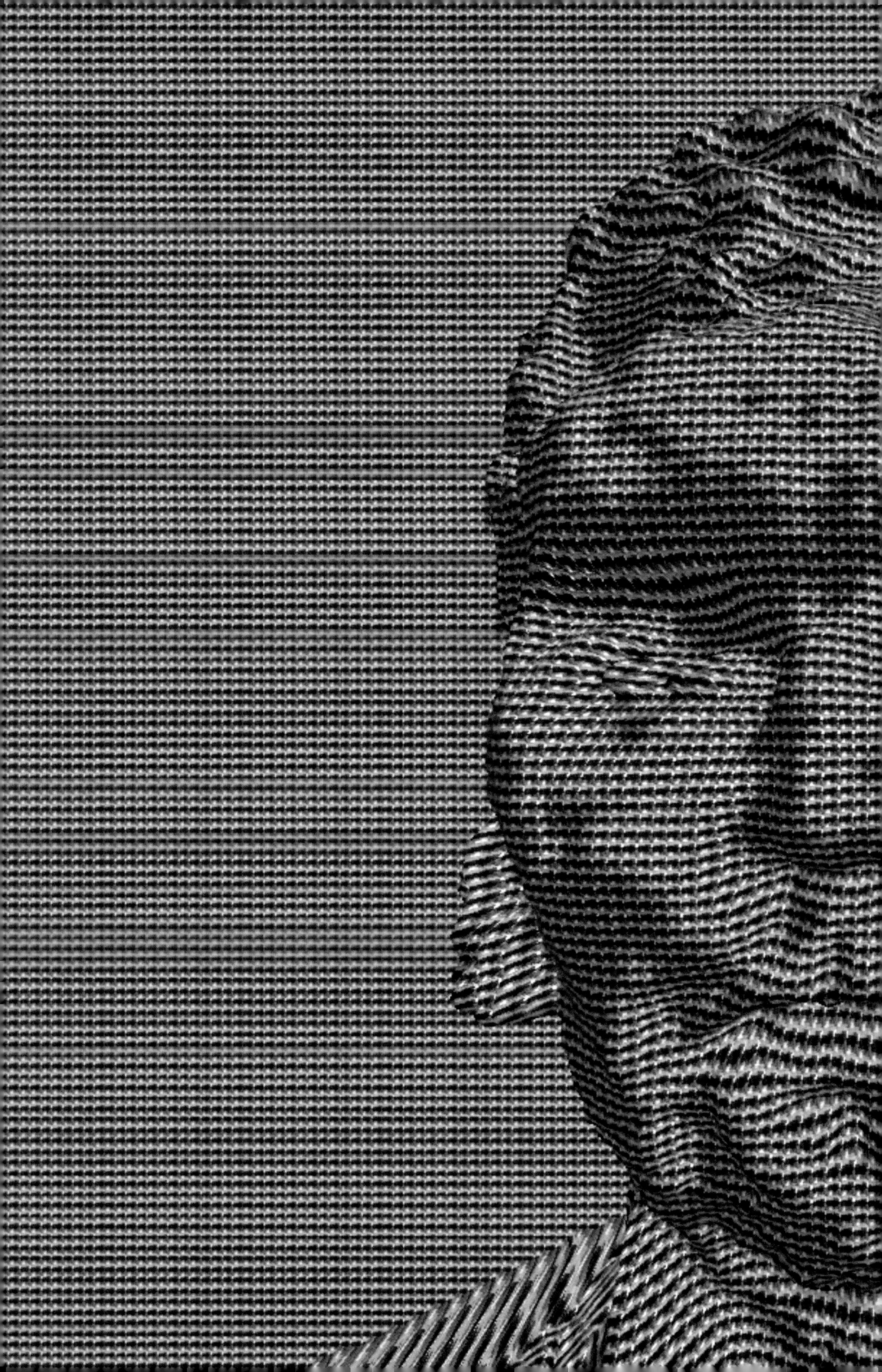

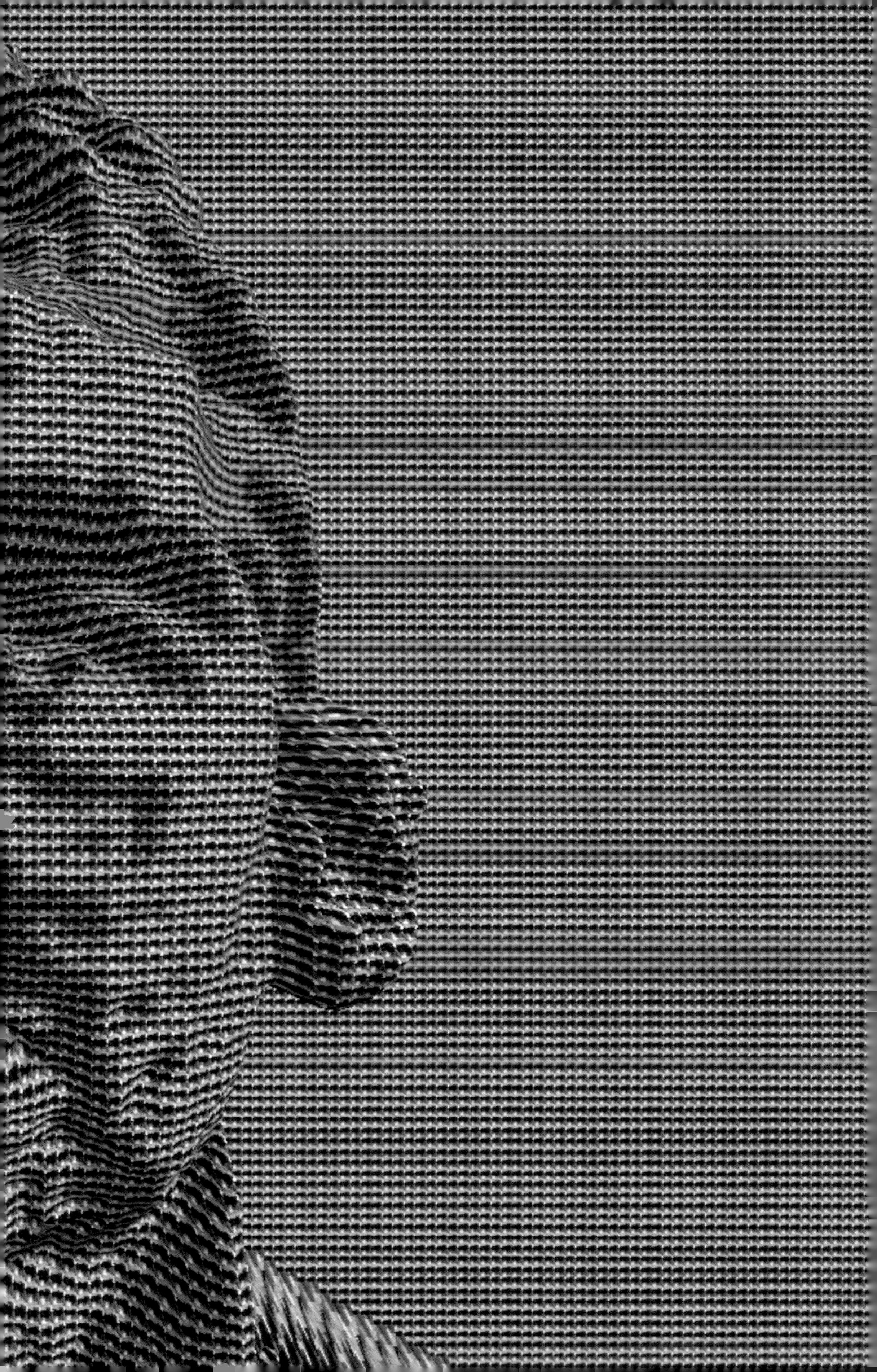

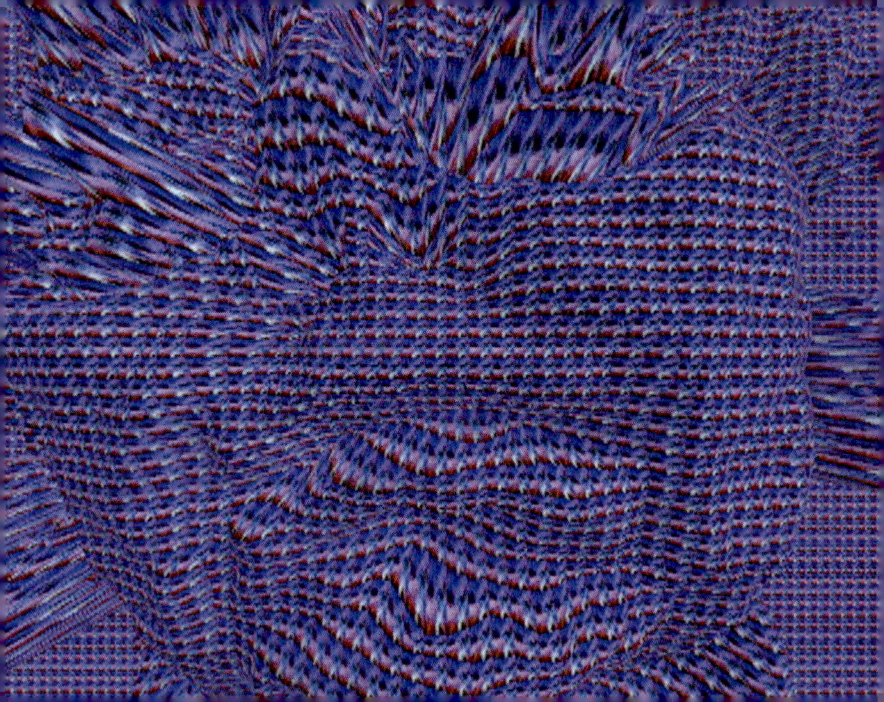

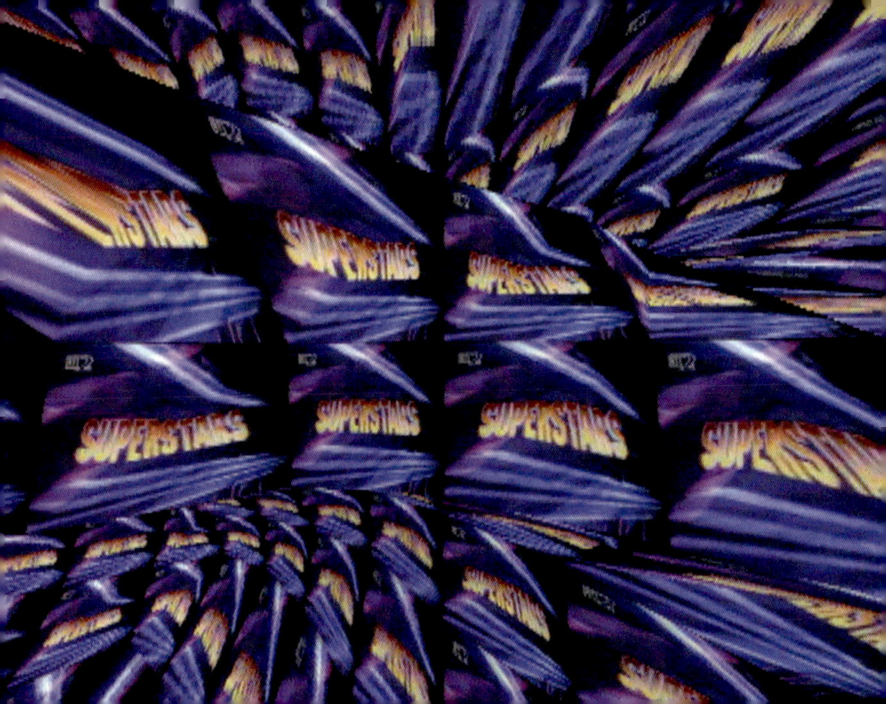

SUPERSTARS

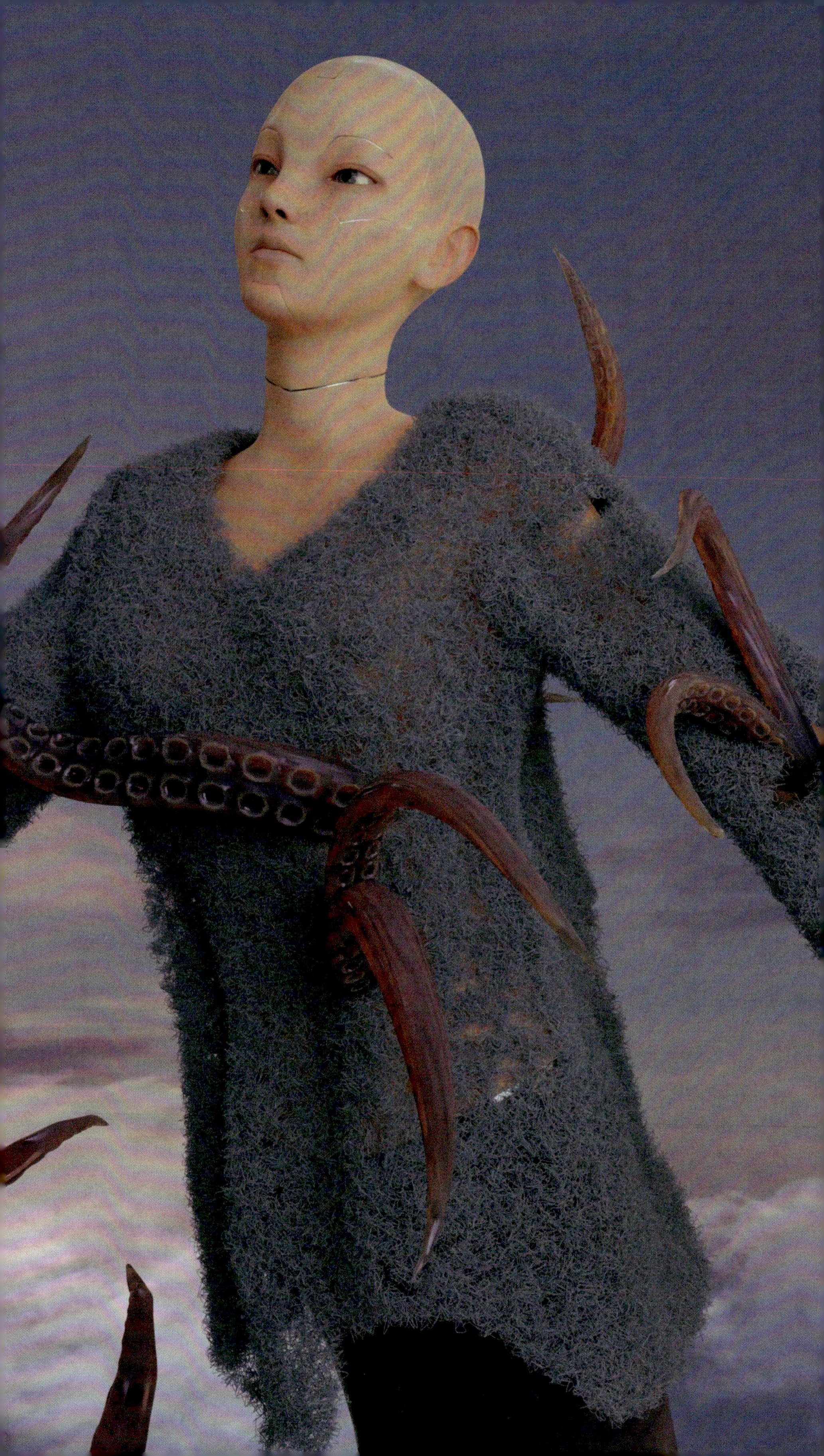

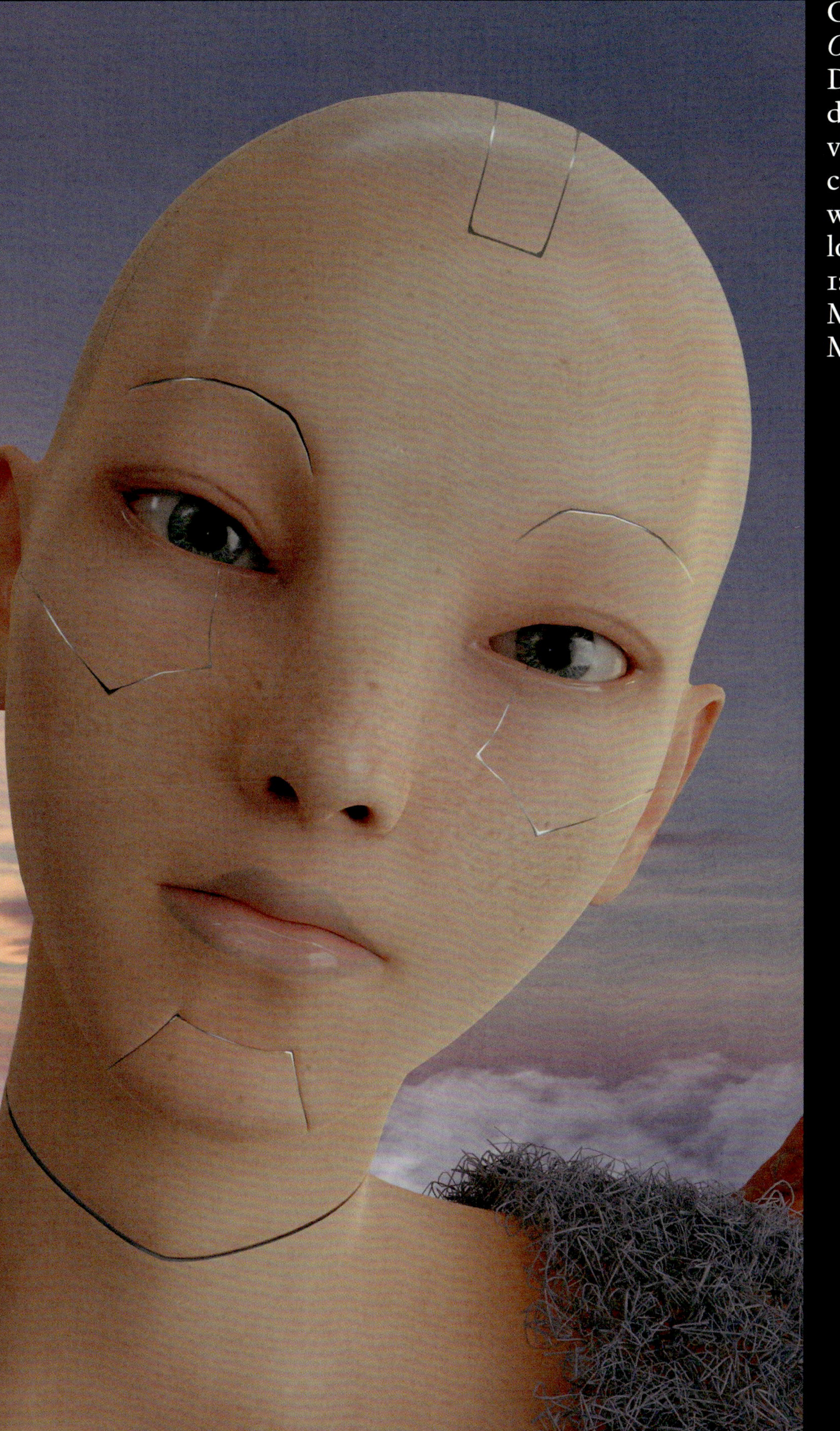

Cao Fei
Oz, 2022
Dual-screen
digital
video, 9:16,
color,
with sound,
loop,
1:36 min.
Music:
Ma Haiping

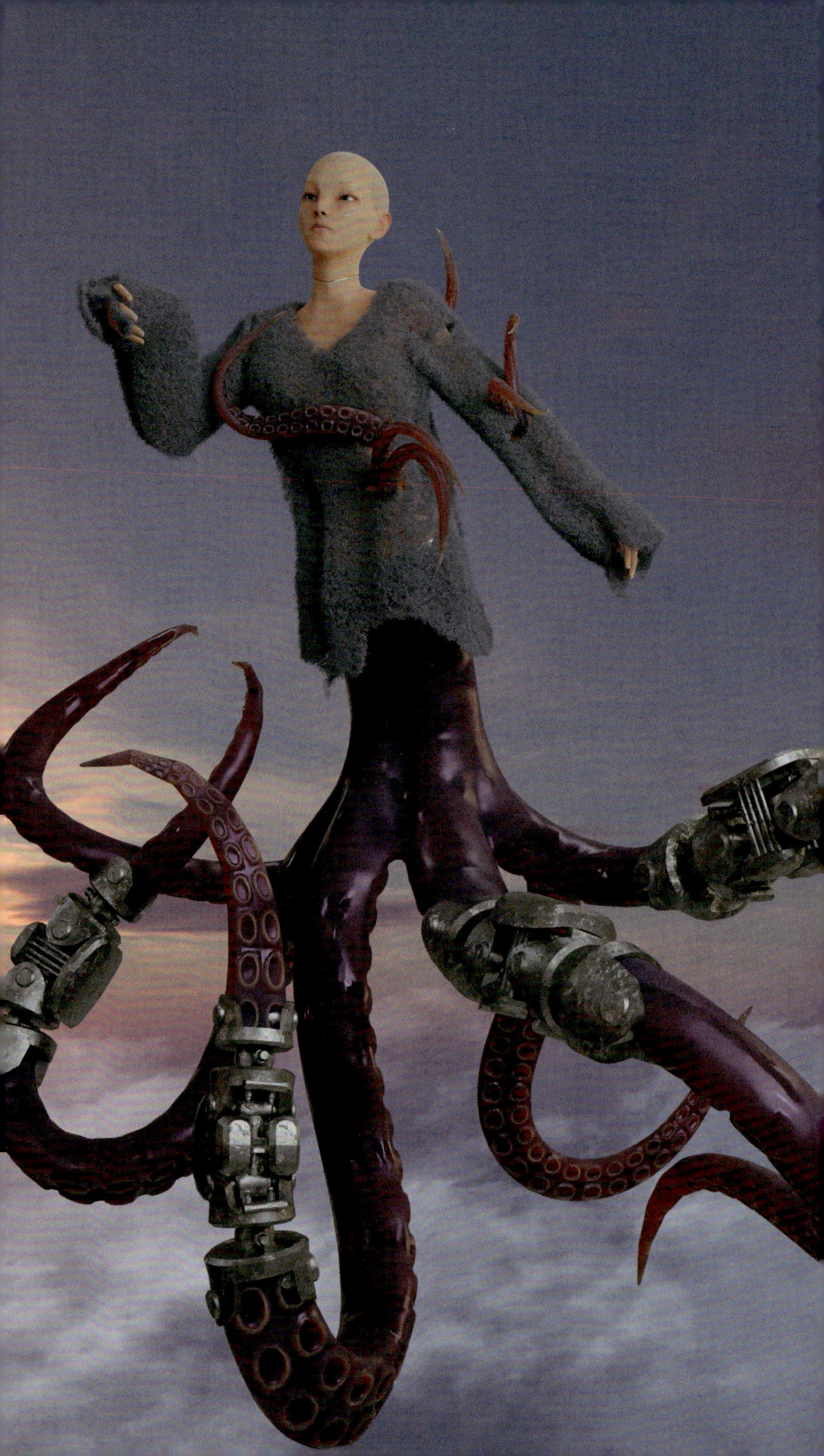

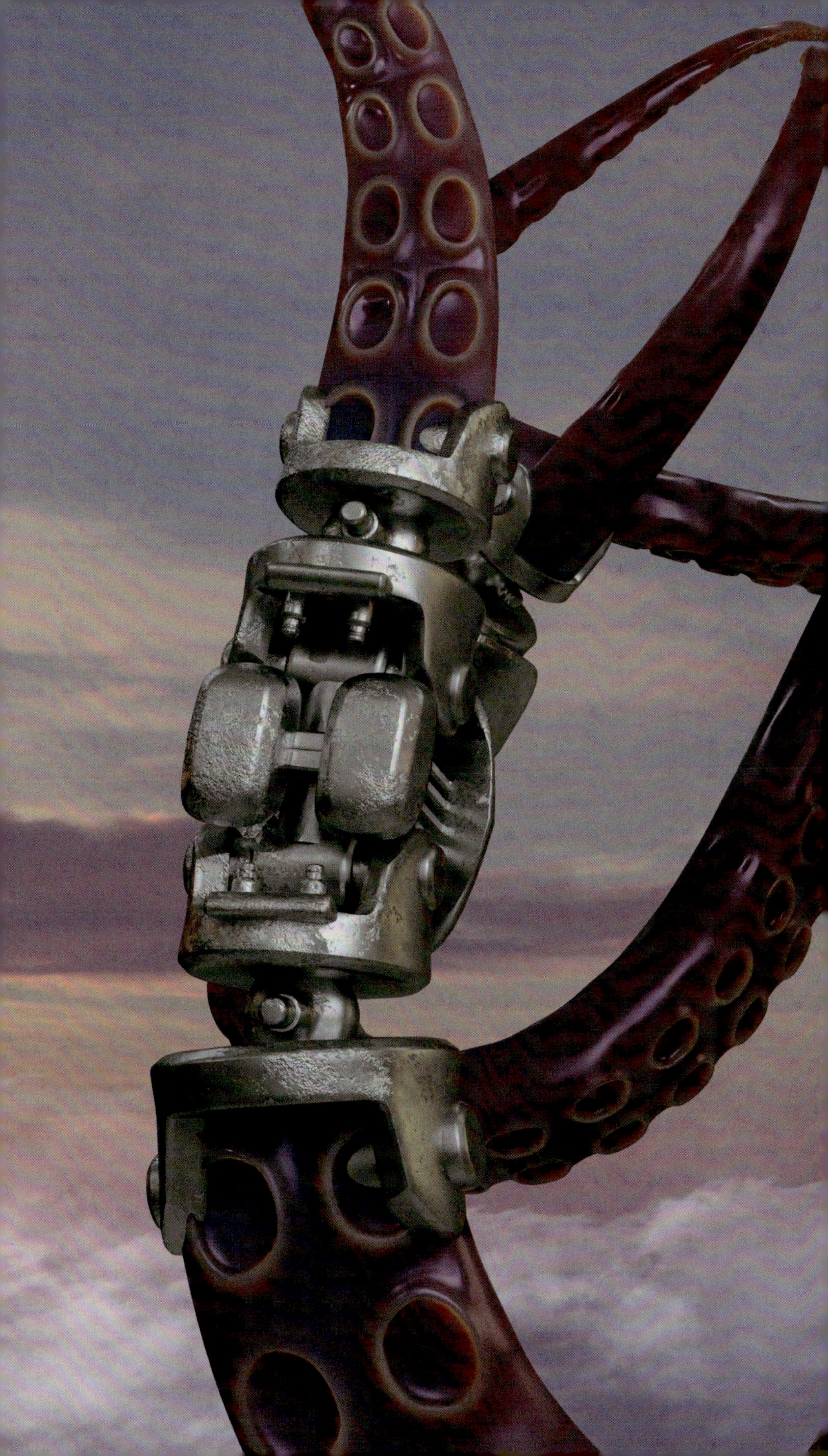

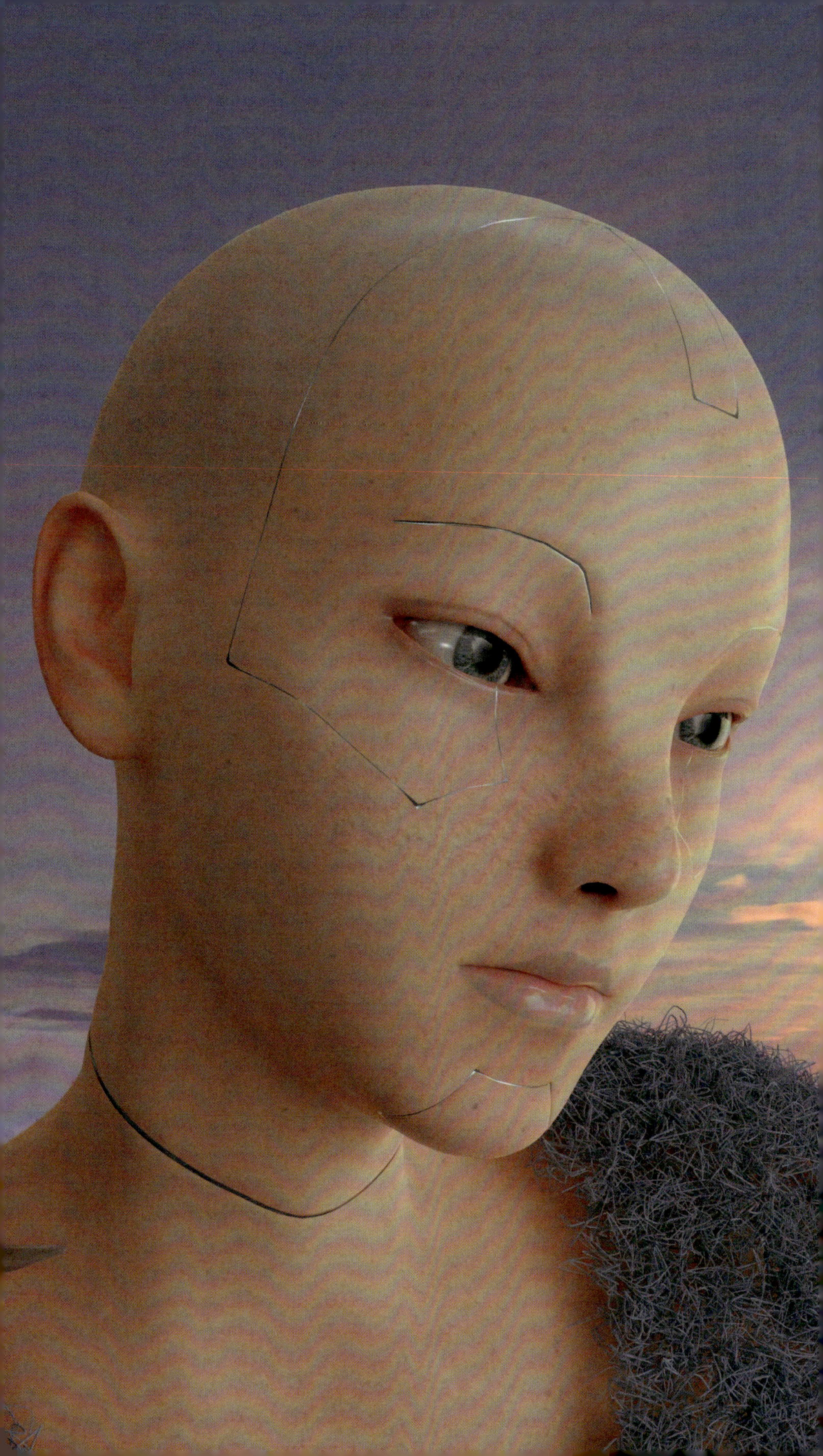

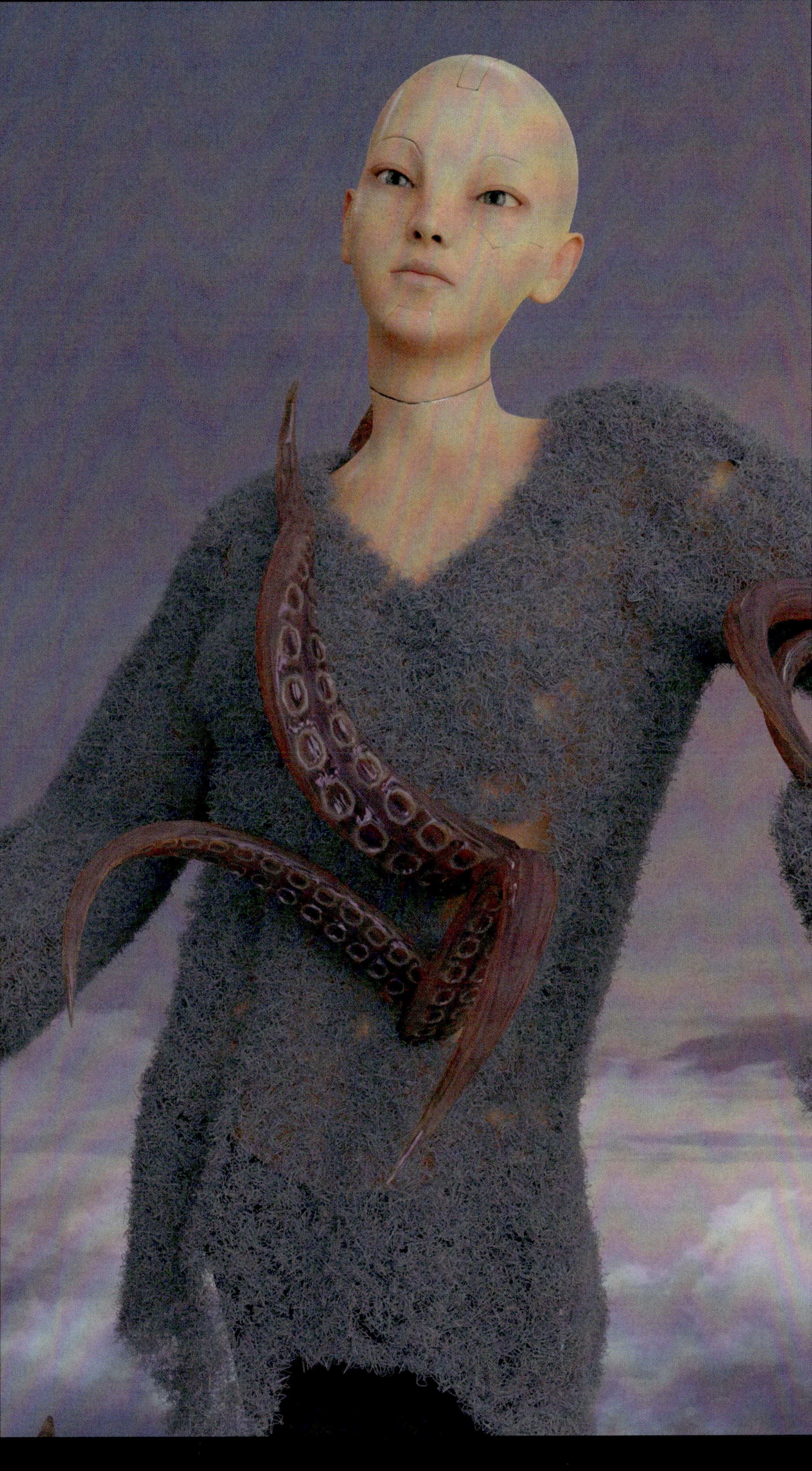

CAO FEI

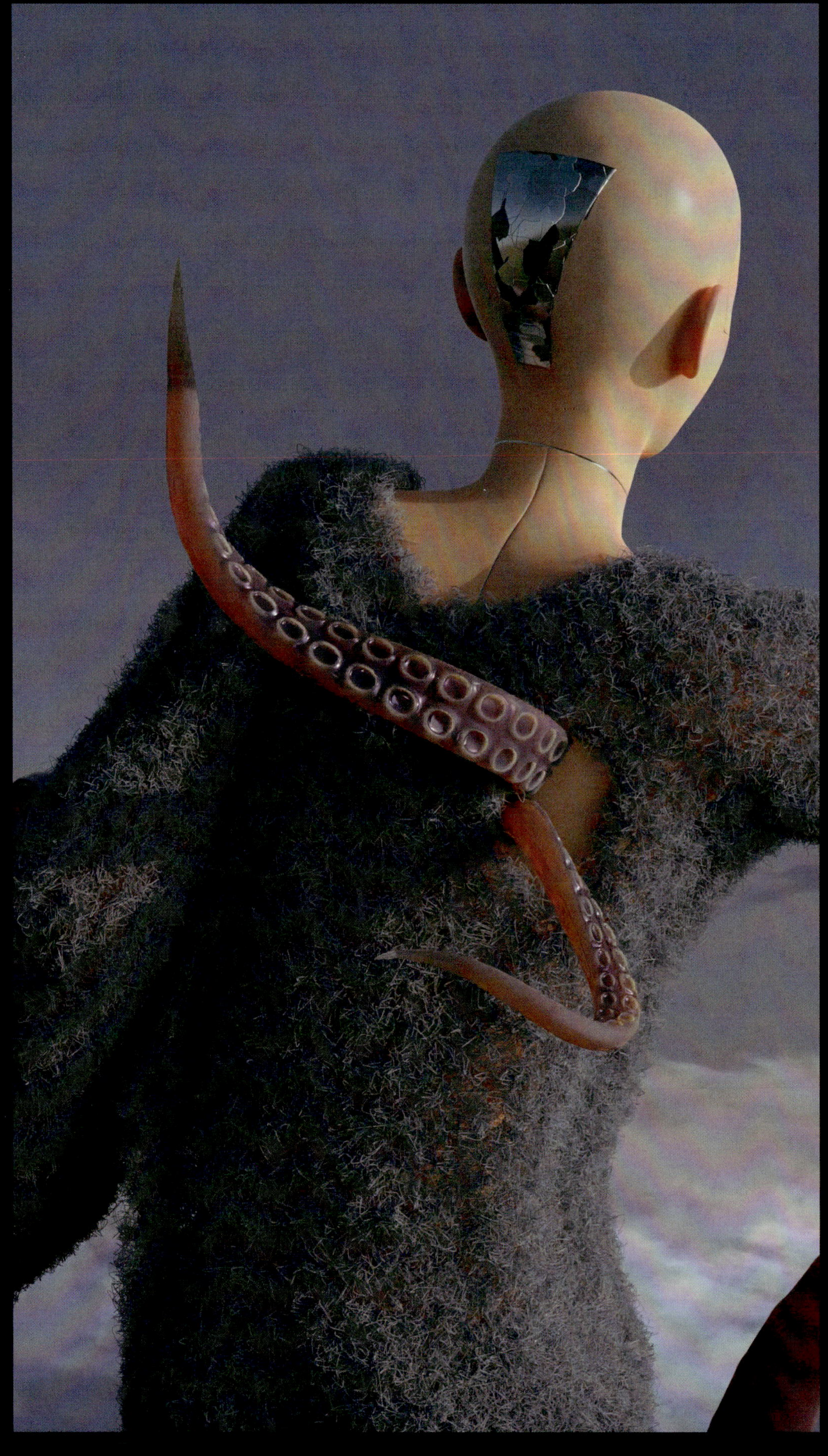

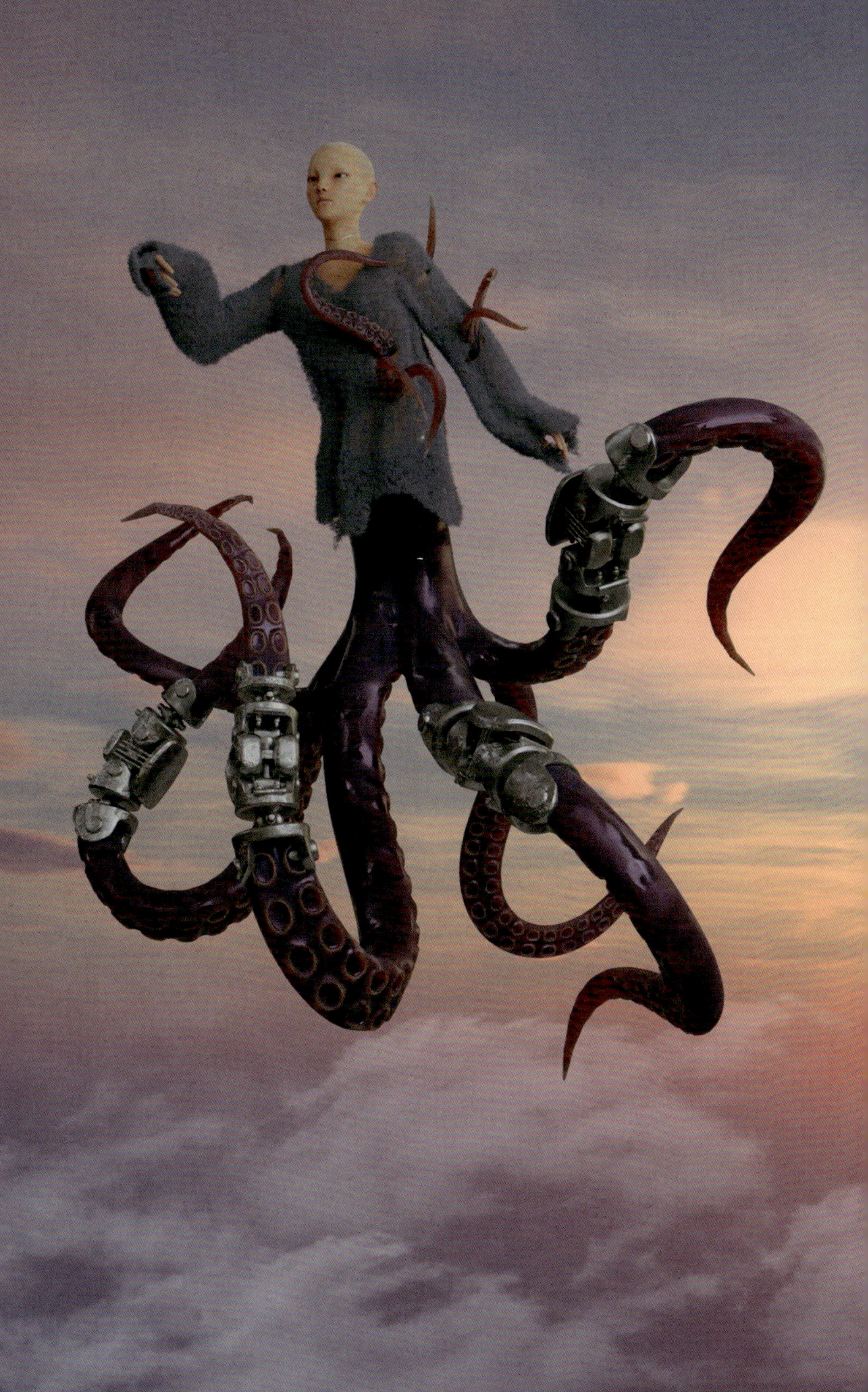

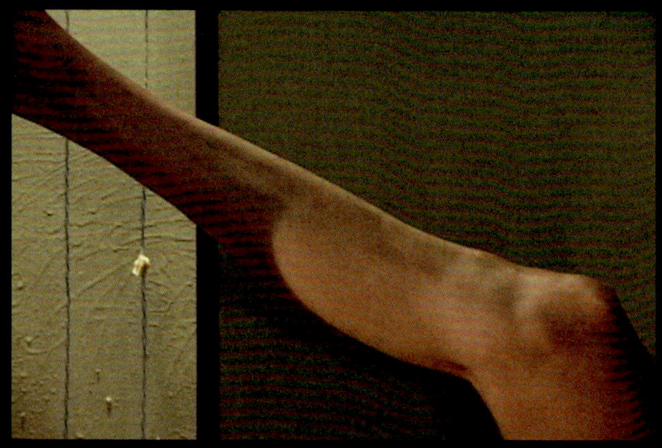

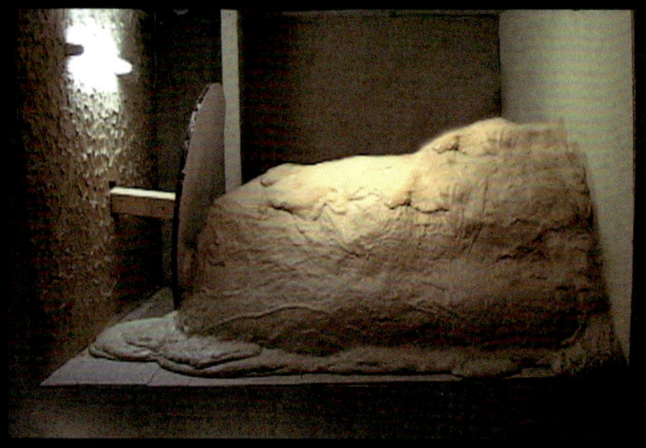

DOUGH

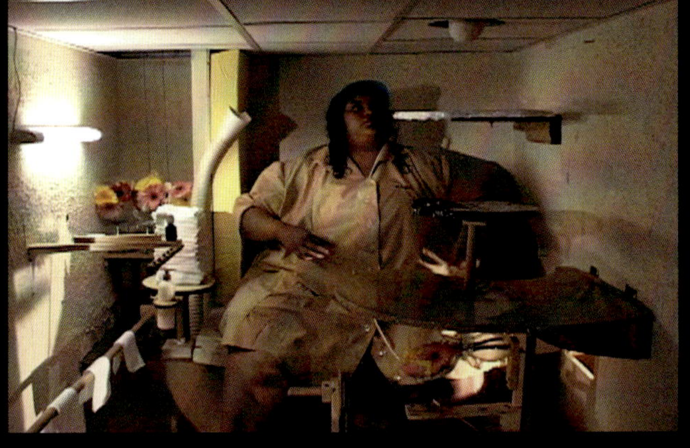

Mika Rottenberg
Dough,
2006
Single-channel video,
5:52 min.
Cast: Raqui, Tall Kat, Audrey, Adonna; cinematography: Ann Rossetti; sound design: Paul Ruest; prop design, special effects: Katrin Altekamp

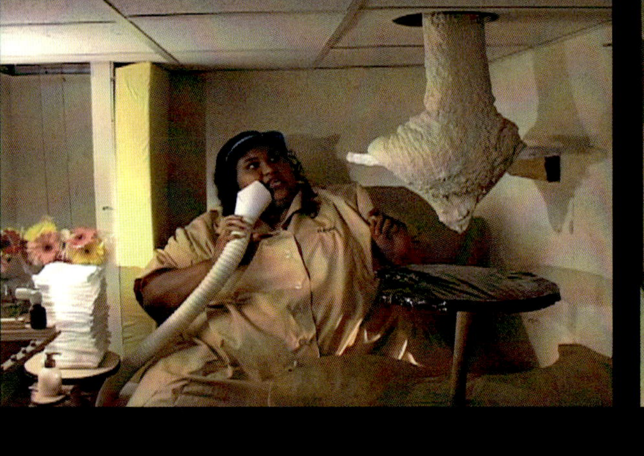
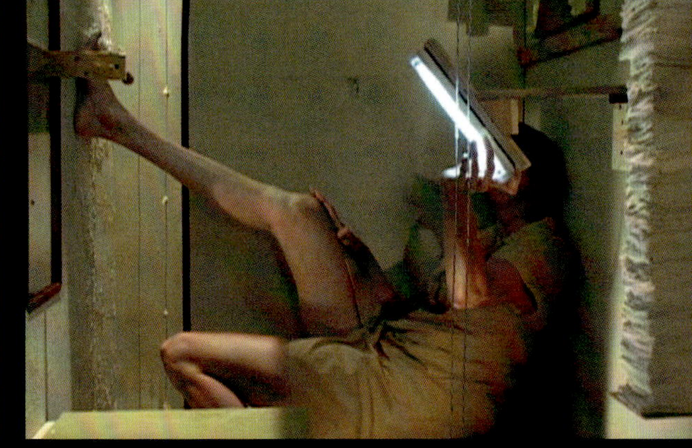
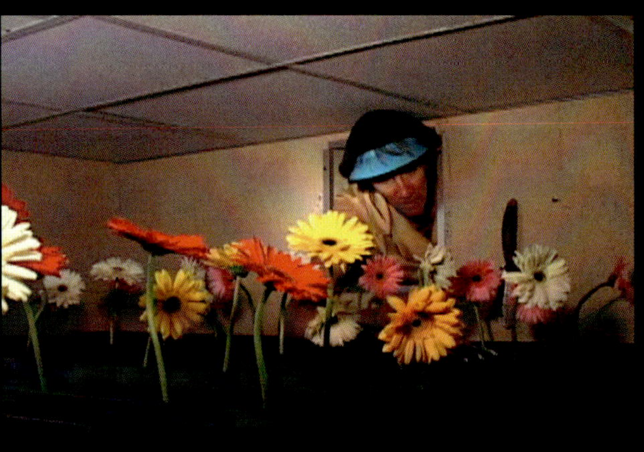
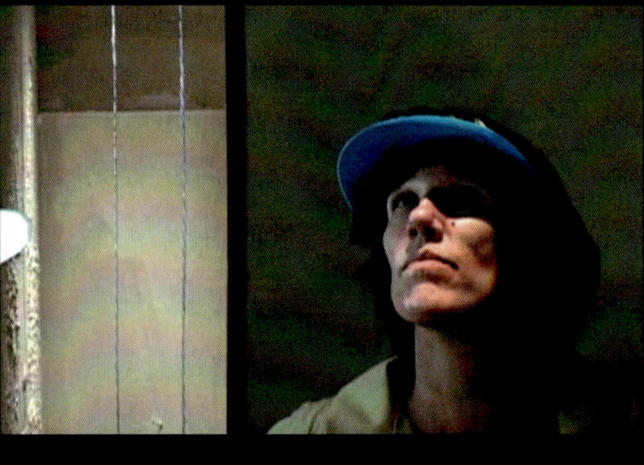
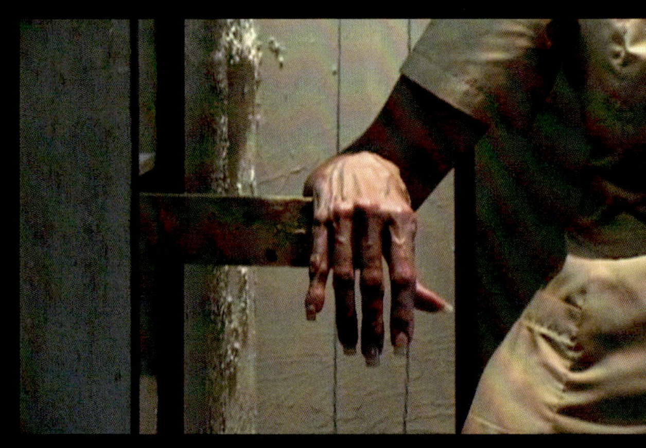
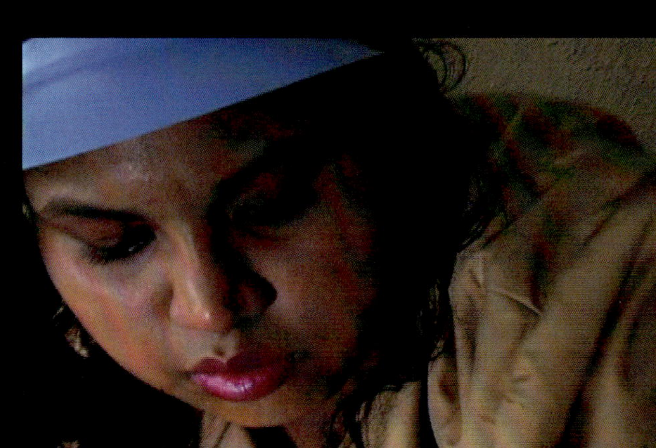

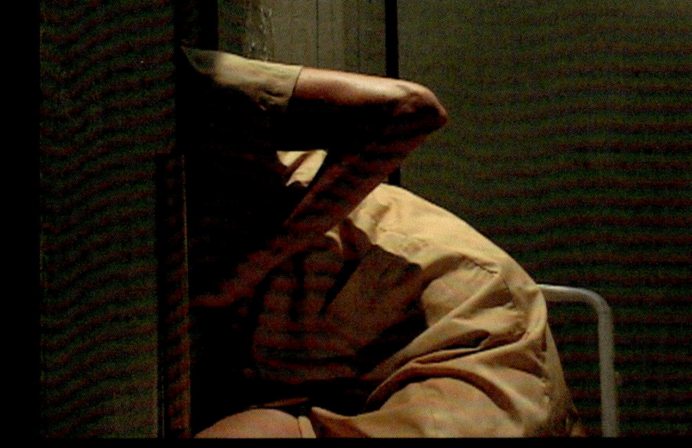

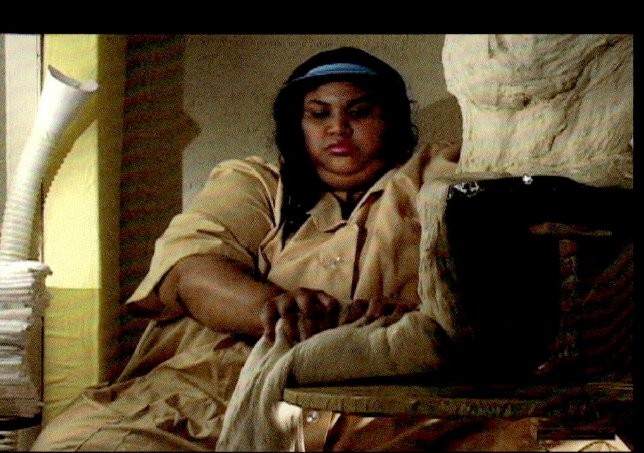

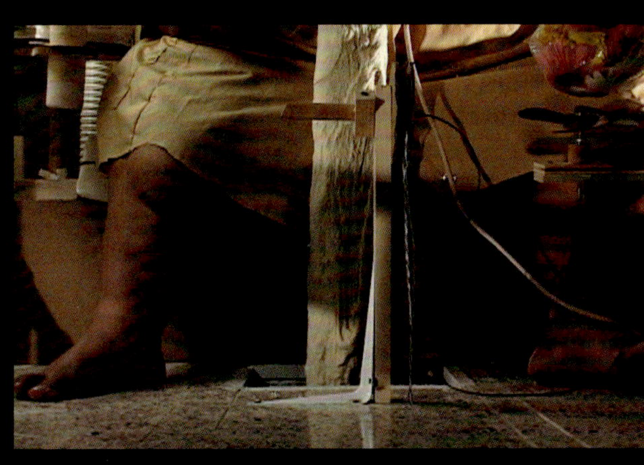

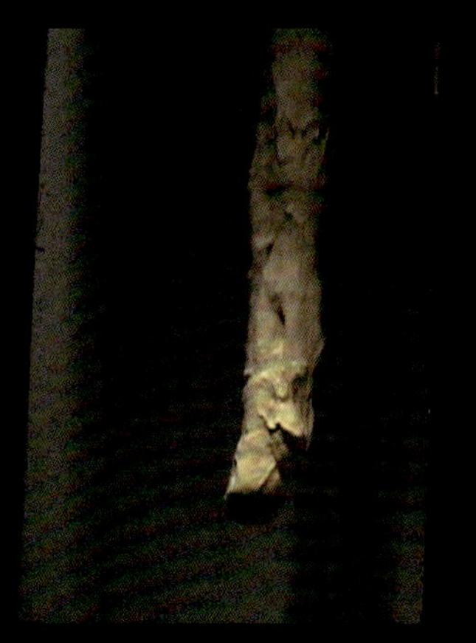

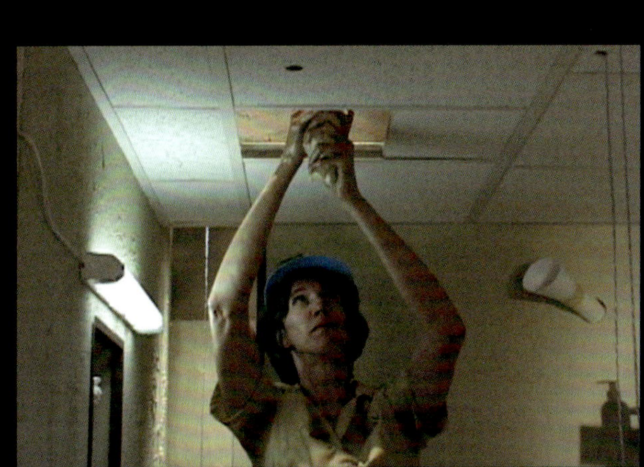

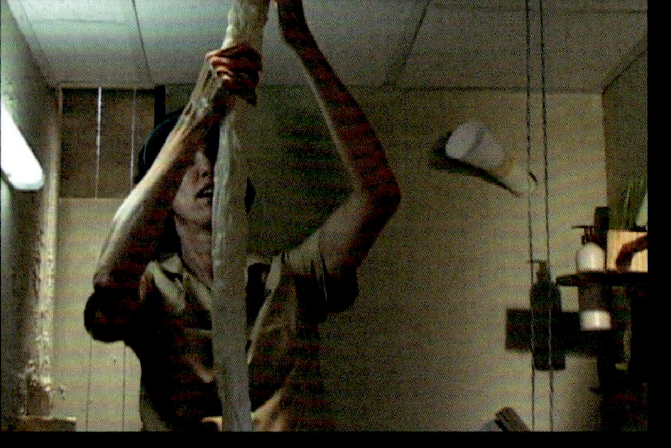

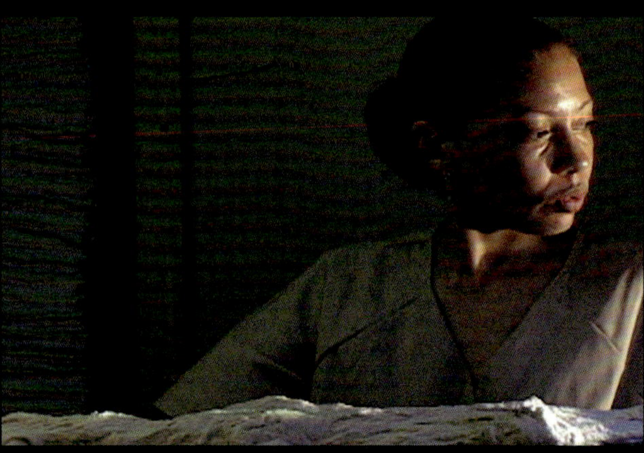

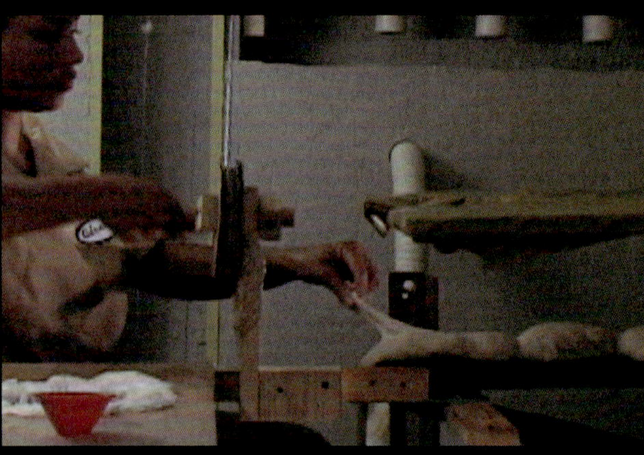

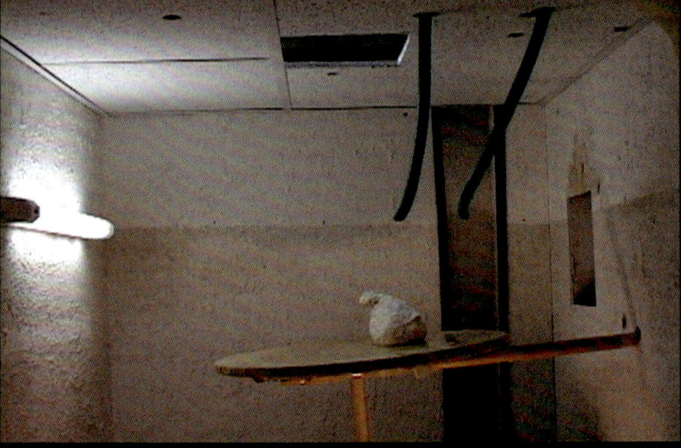

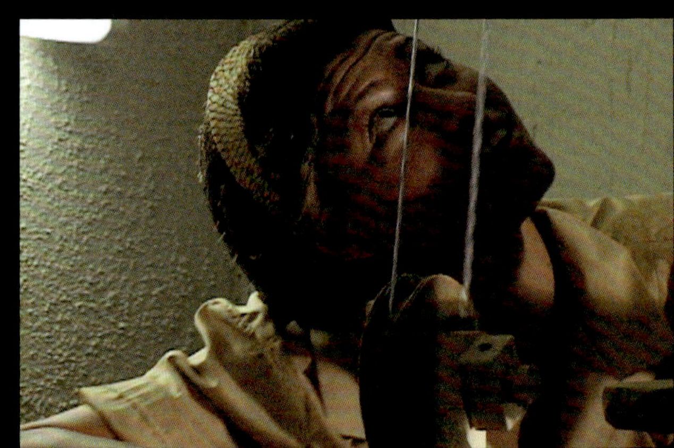

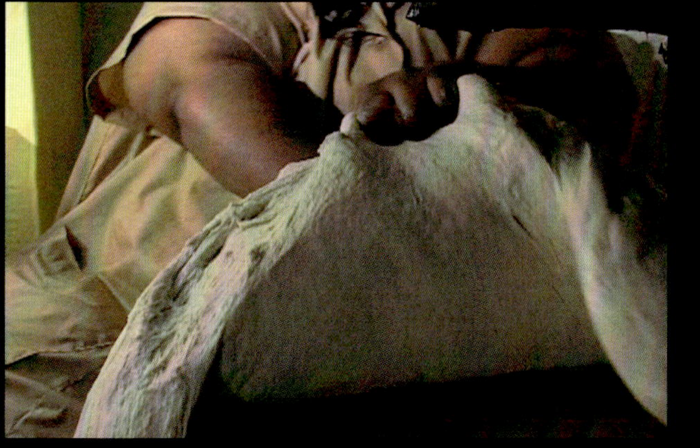

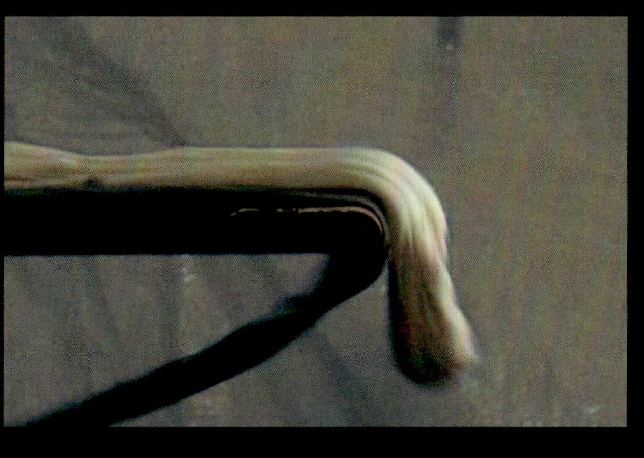

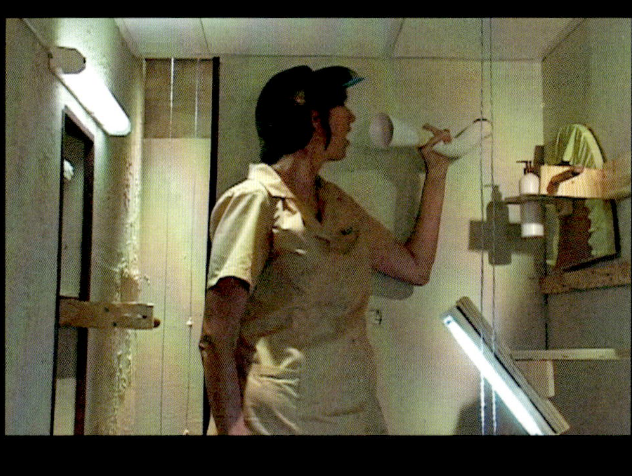

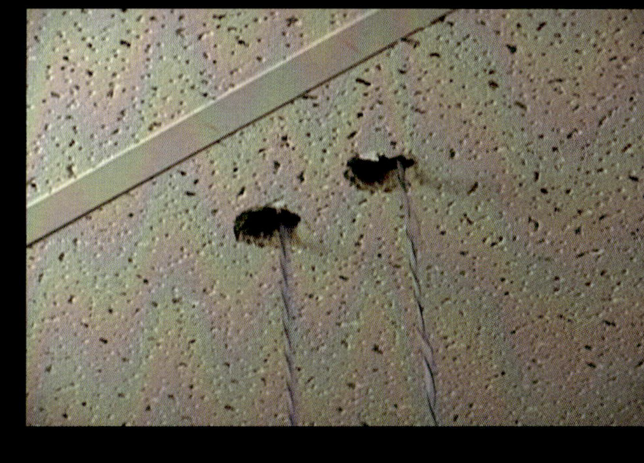

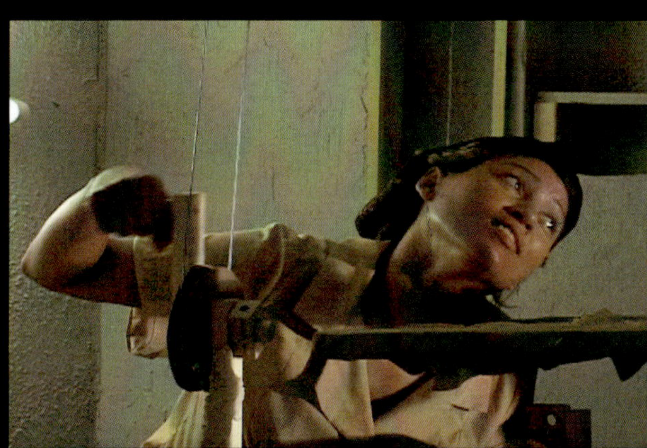

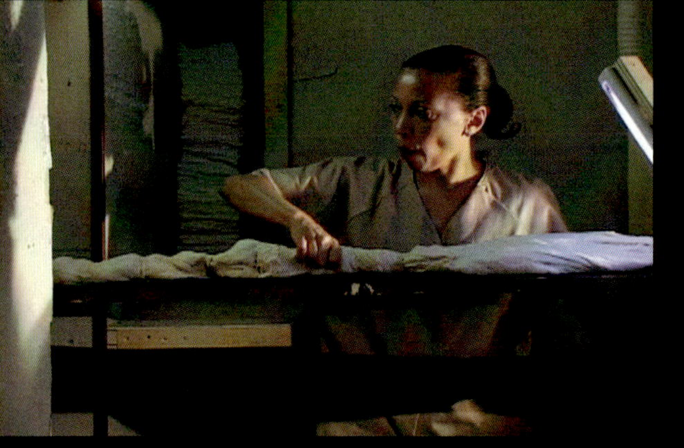

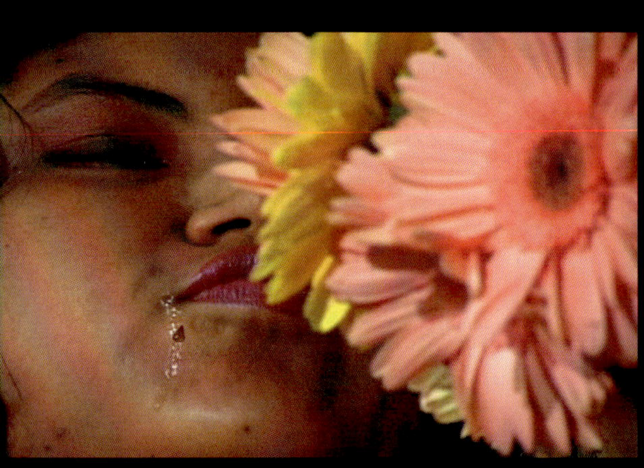

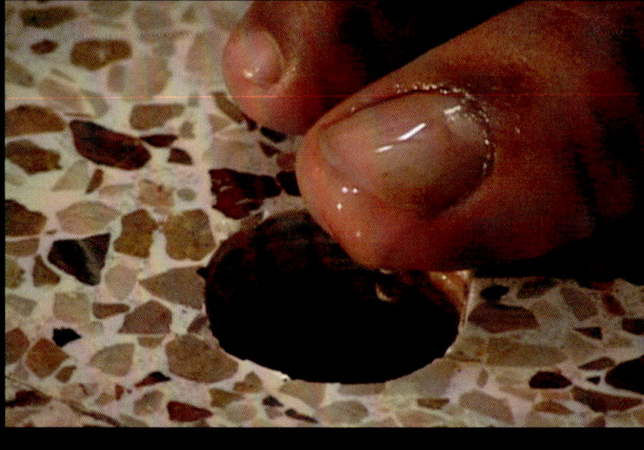

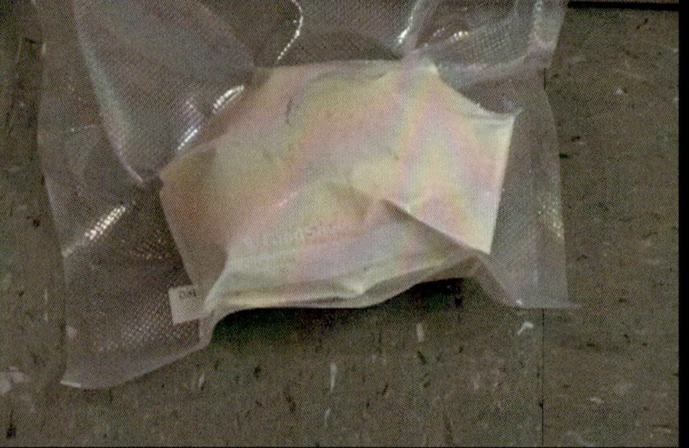

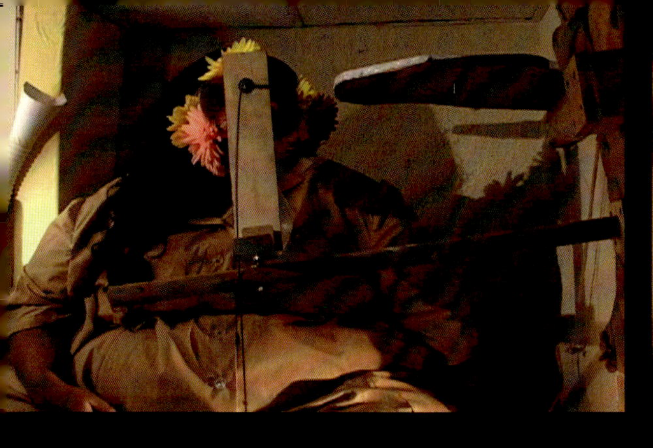
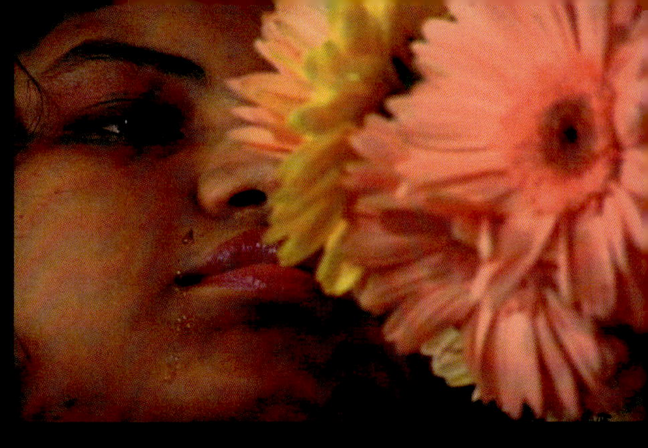
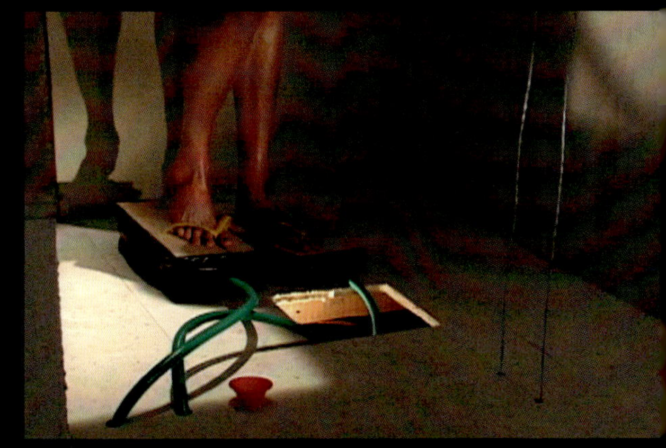
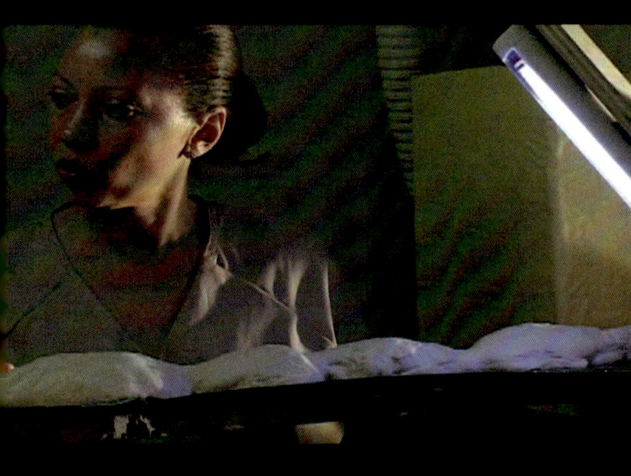
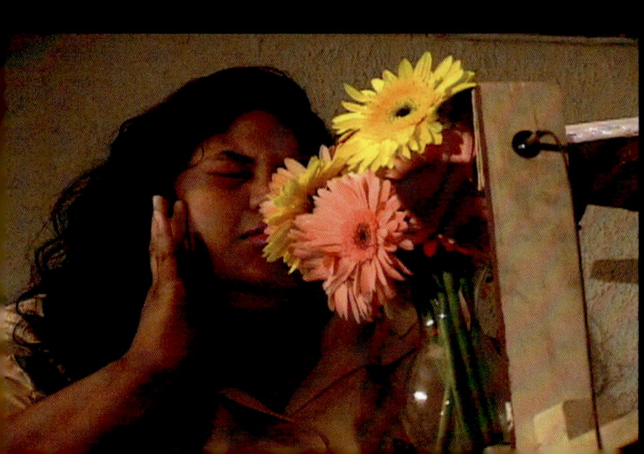
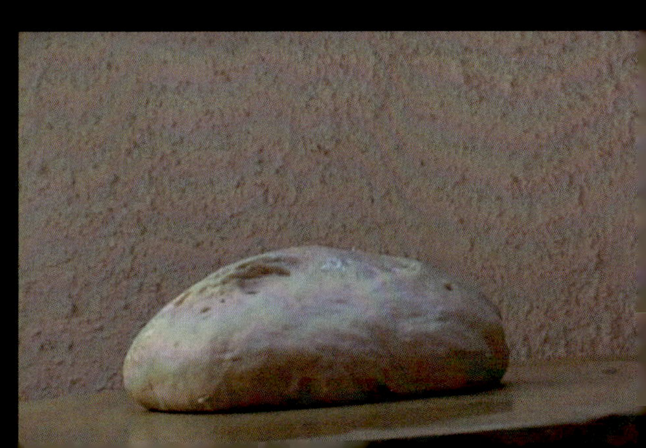

UNTITLED FILM/RIGHT

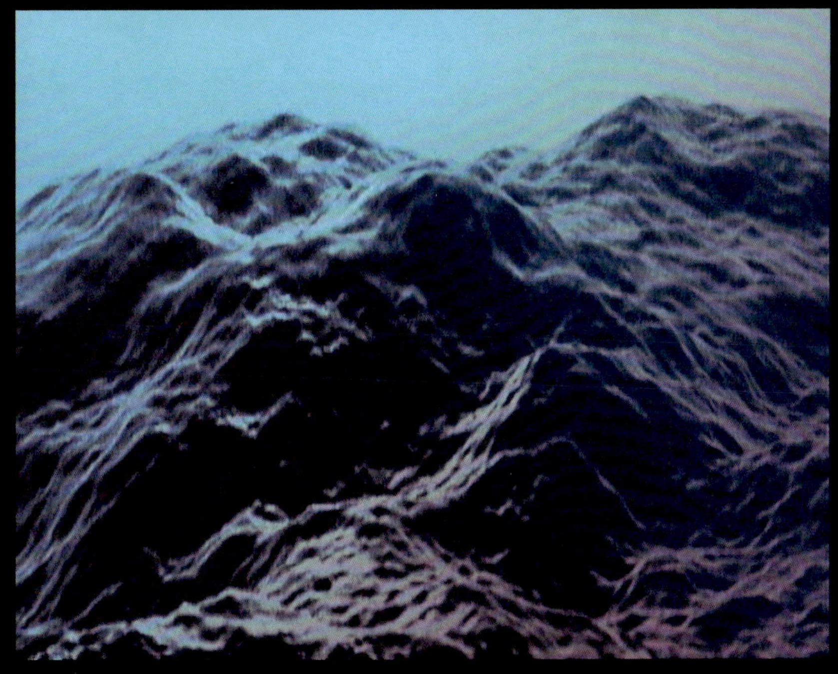

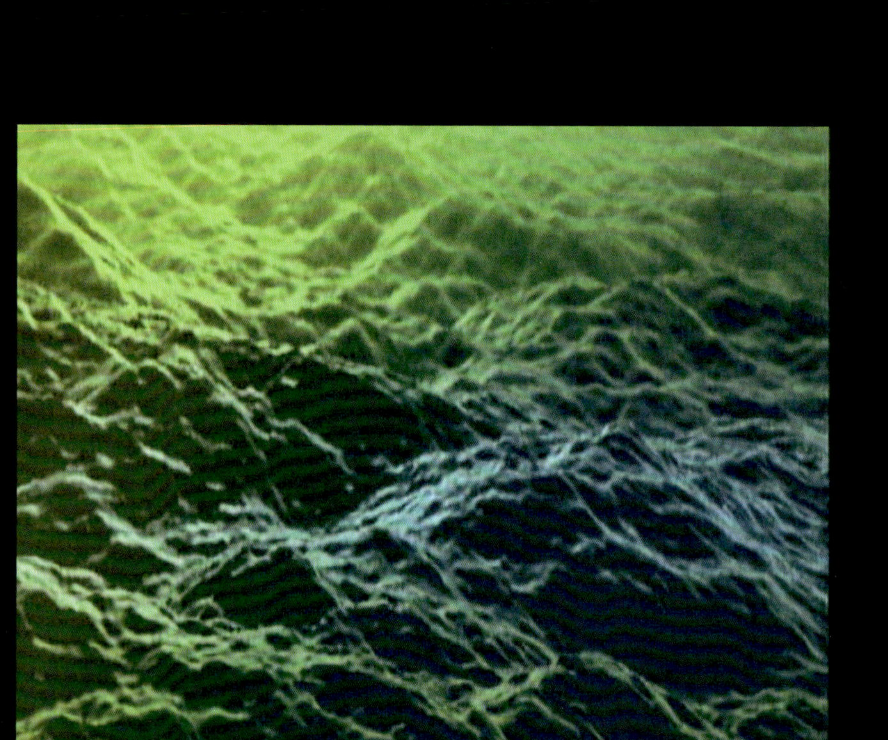

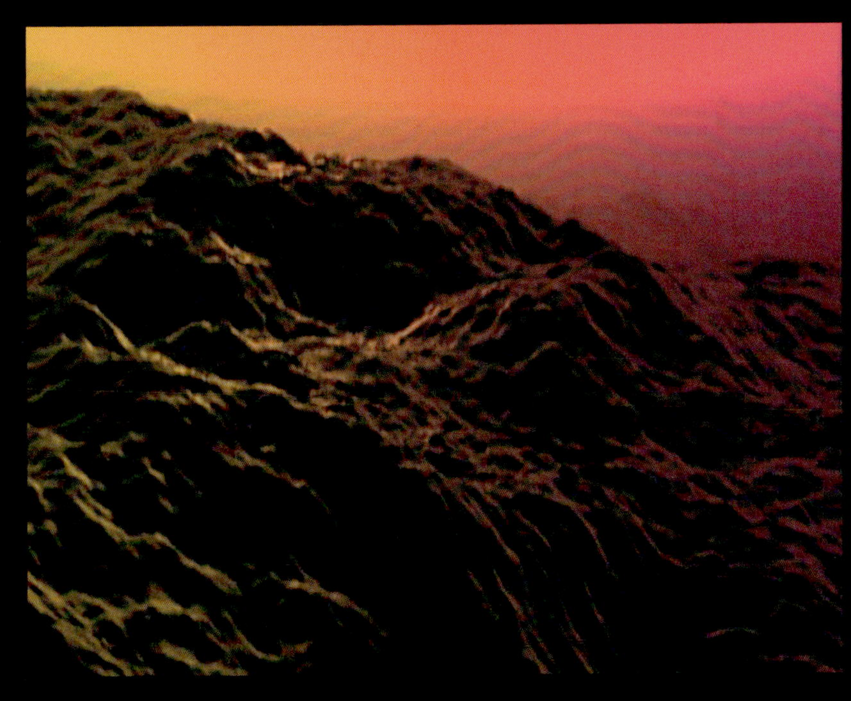

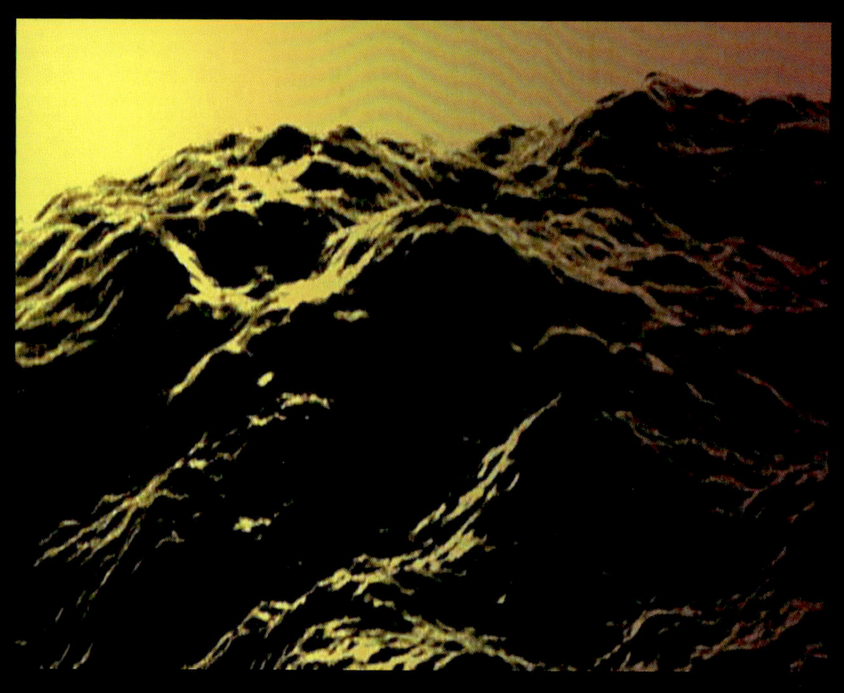

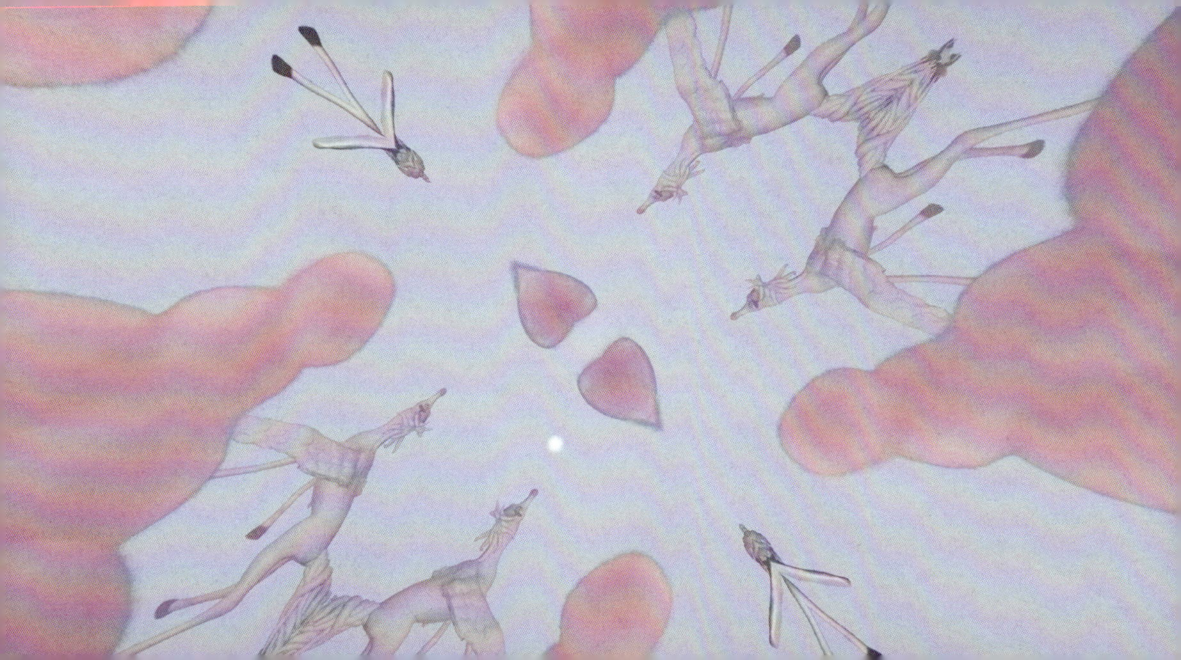

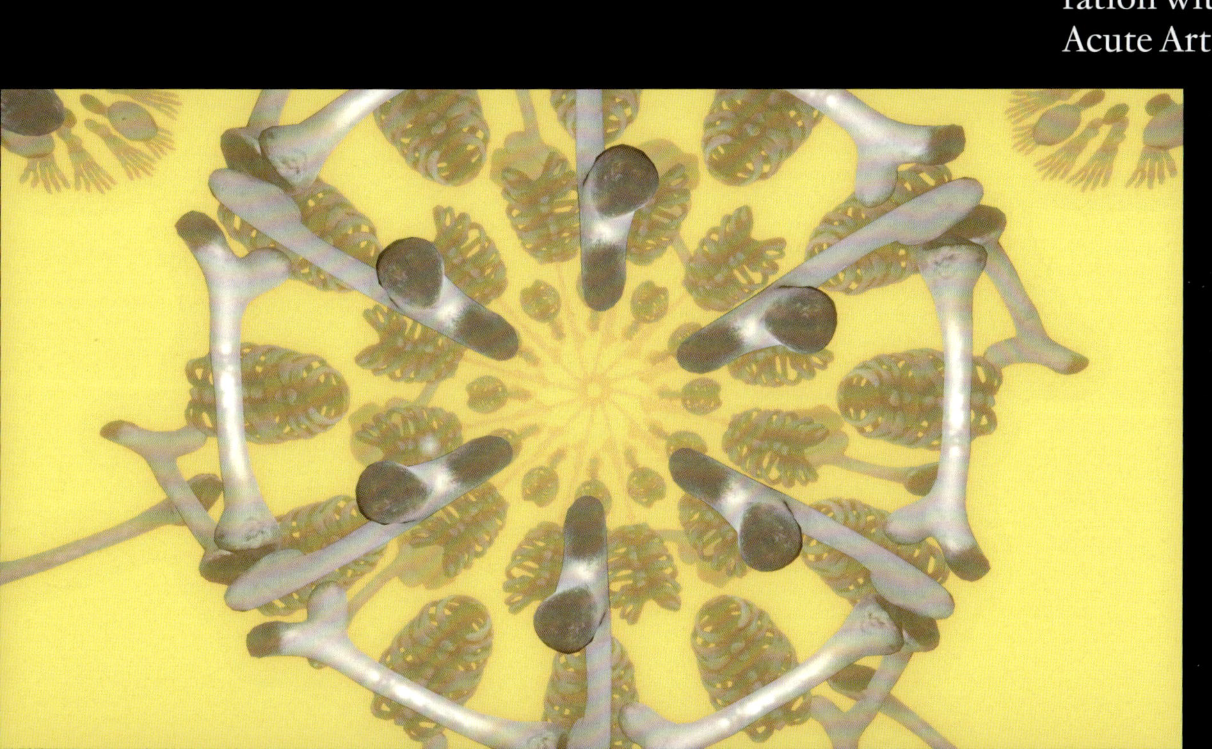

Nathalie Djurberg and Hans Berg
It Will End in Stars, 2018
Virtual reality
Produced in collaboration with Acute Art

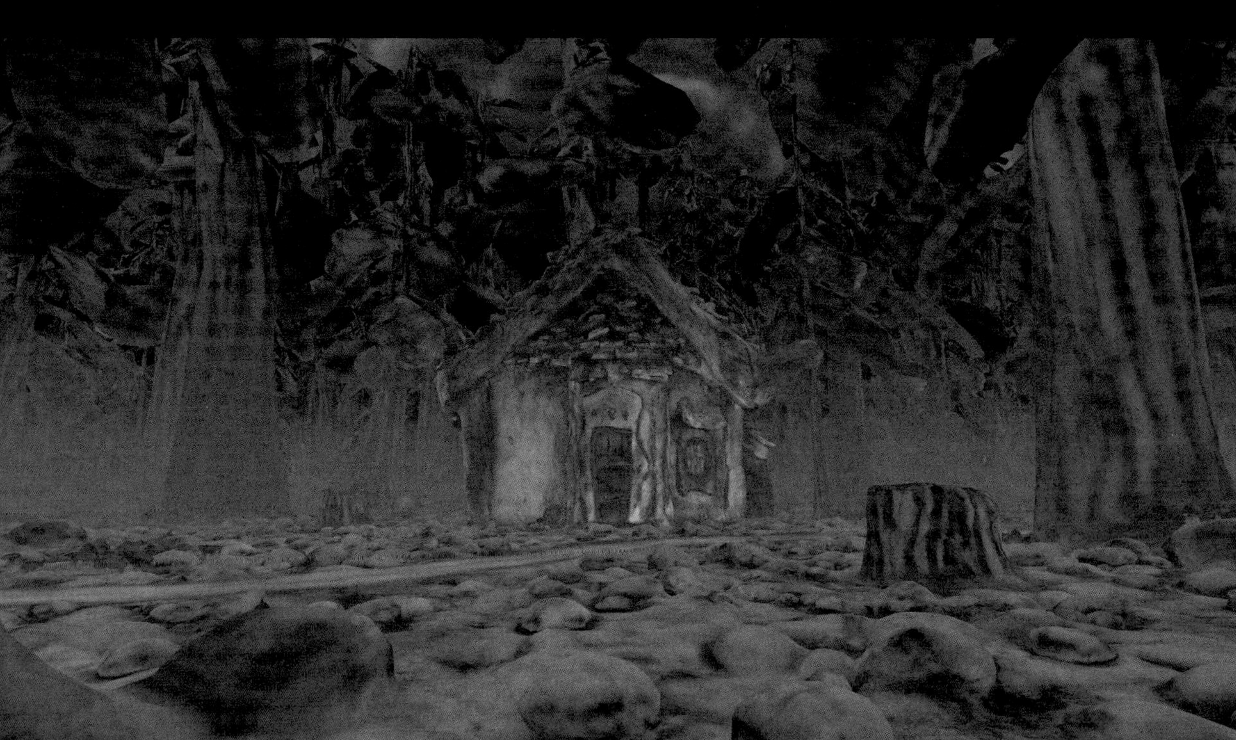

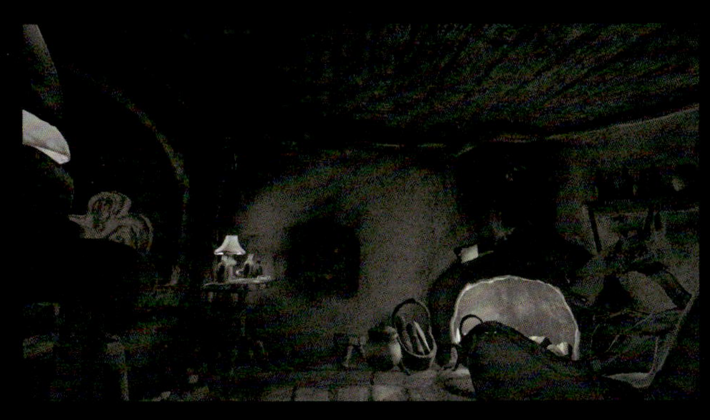

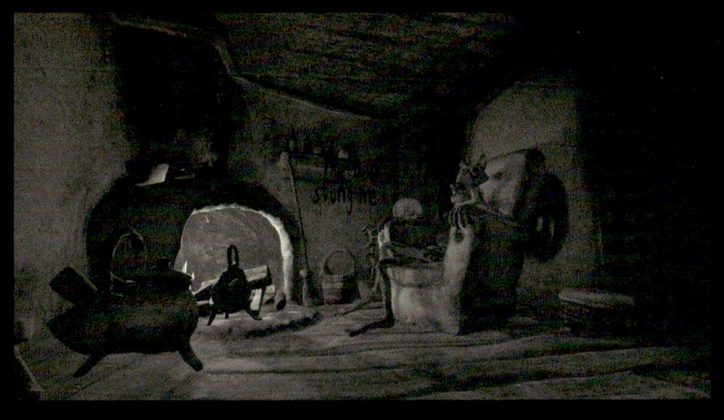

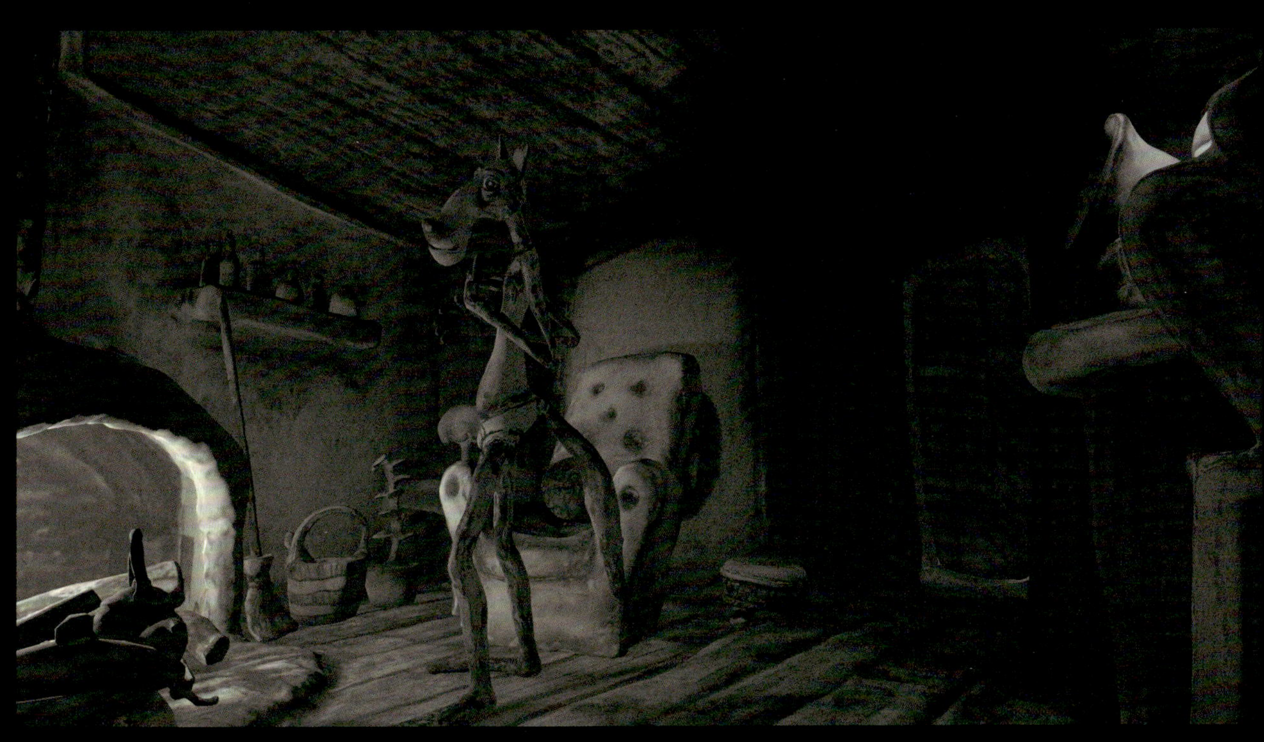

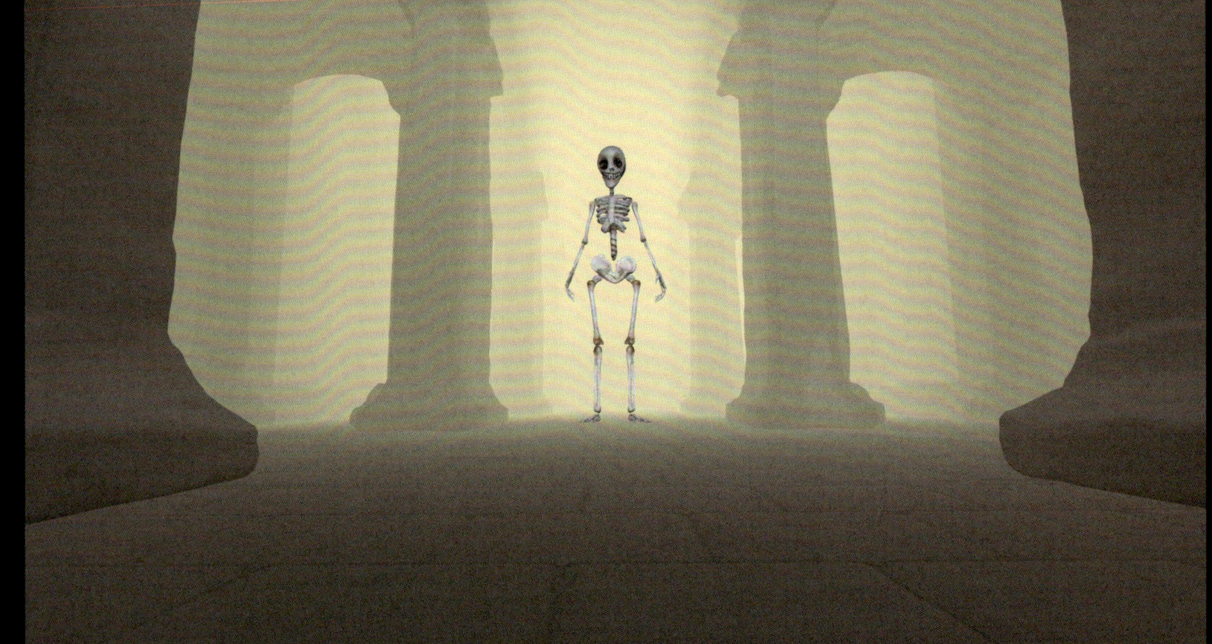

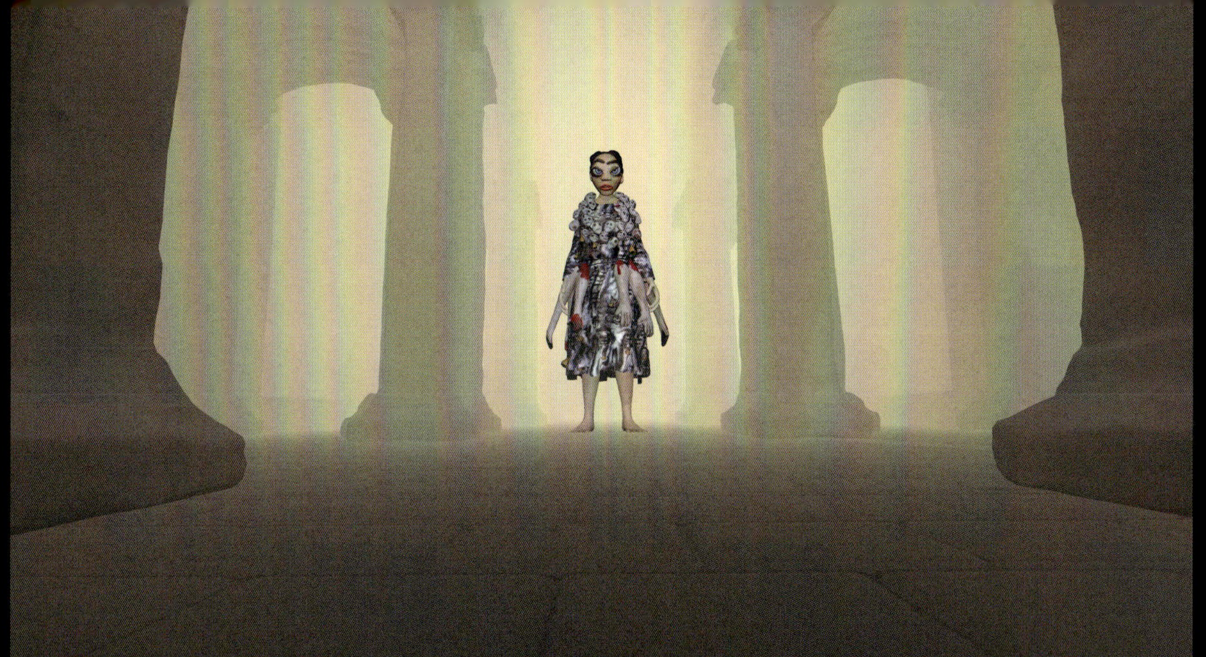

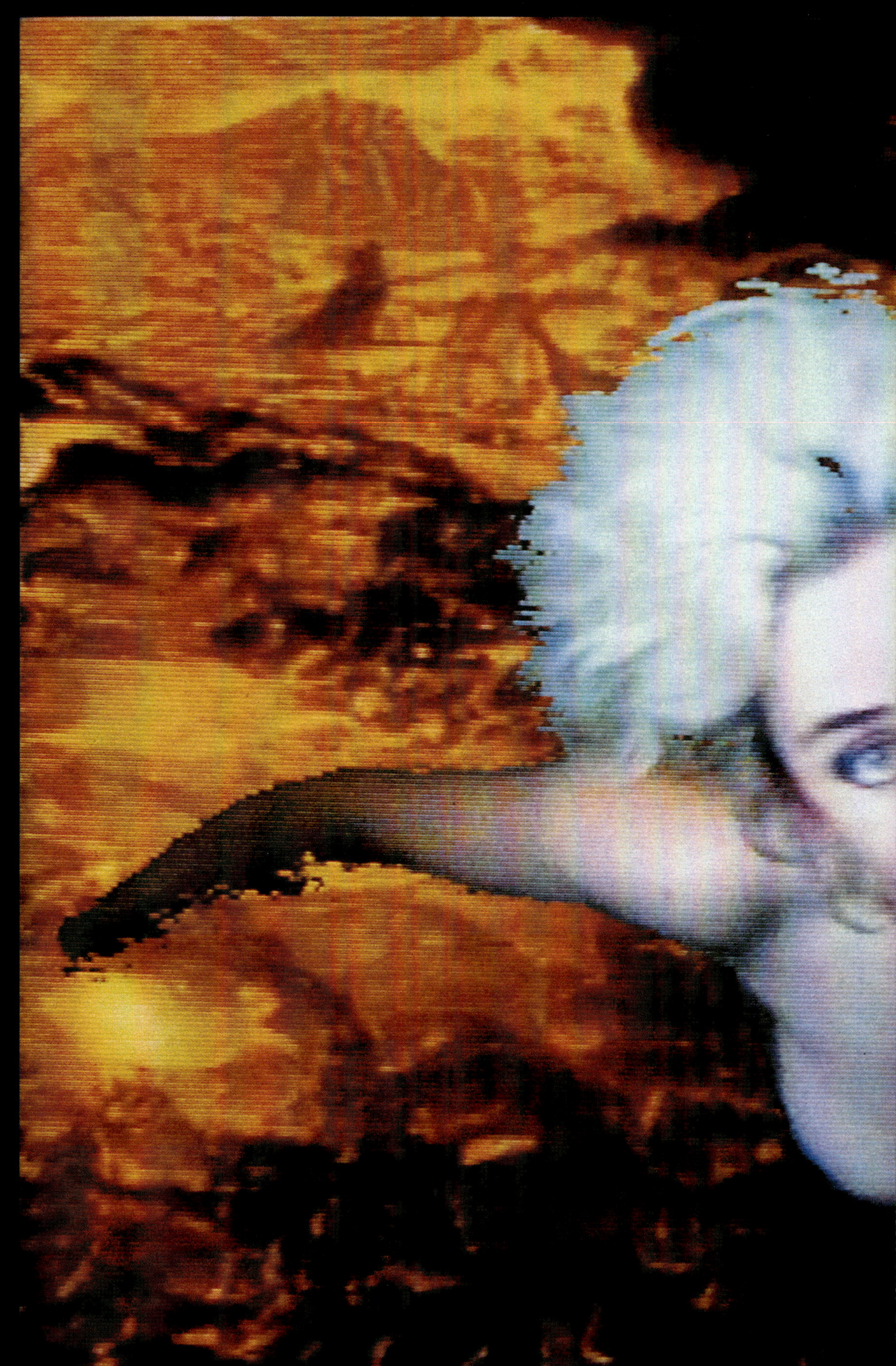

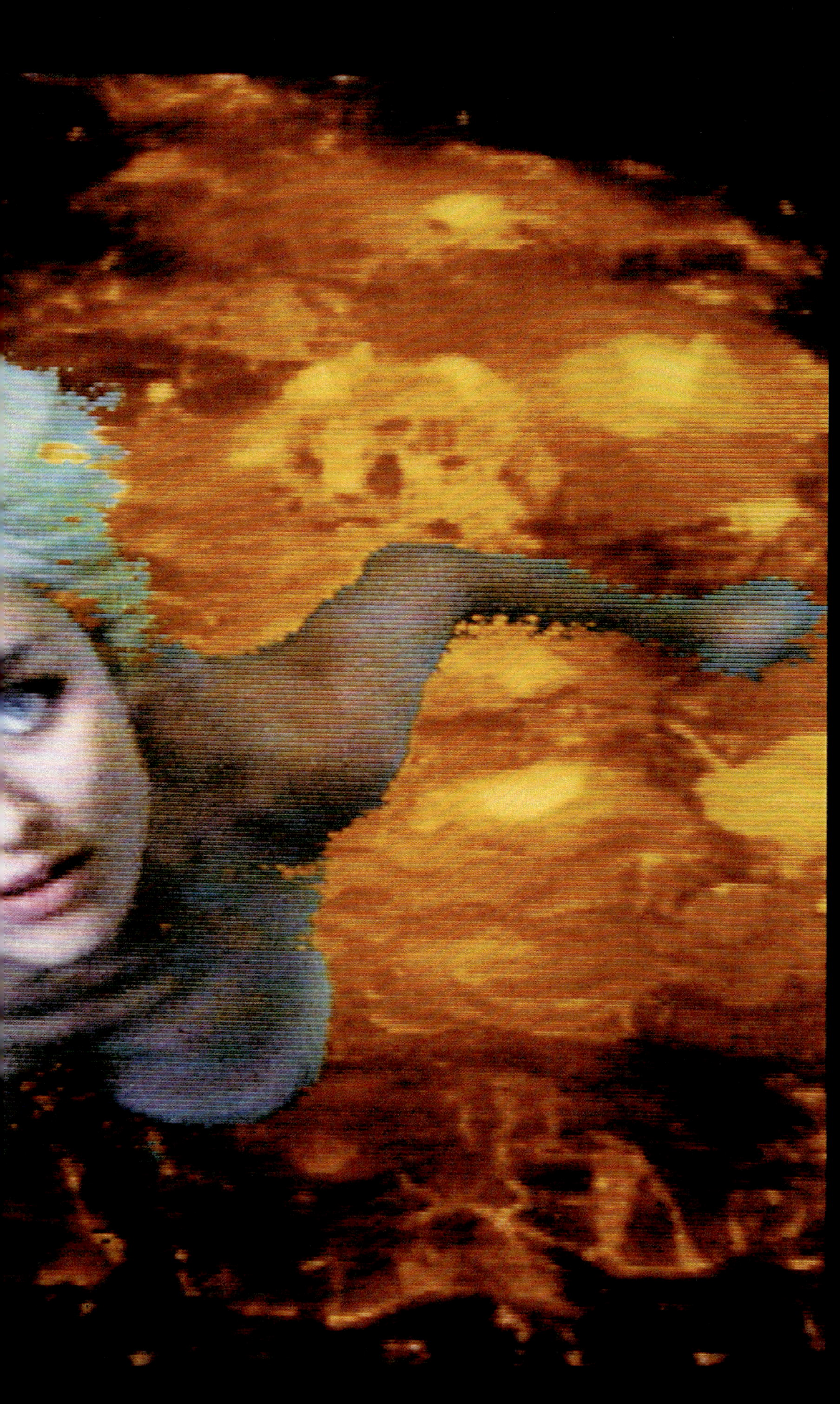

Pipilotti
Rist
*Selbstlos im
Lavabad
(Selfless in
the Bath
of Lava)
(Bastard
Version),*
1994
Single-
channel
video and
sound
installa-
tion, color,
on mobile
phone,
6:20 min.

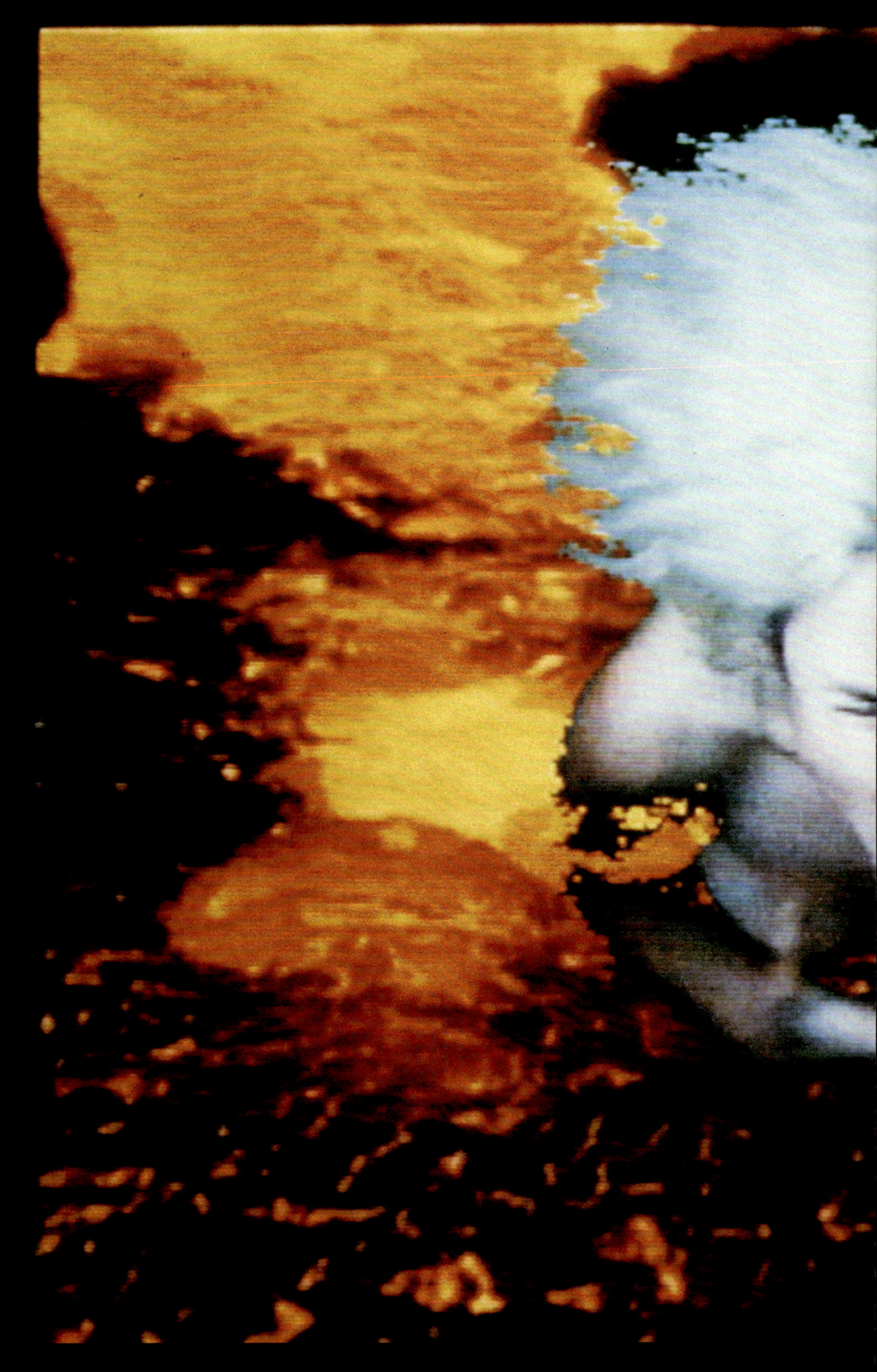

SELBSTLOS IM LAVABAD

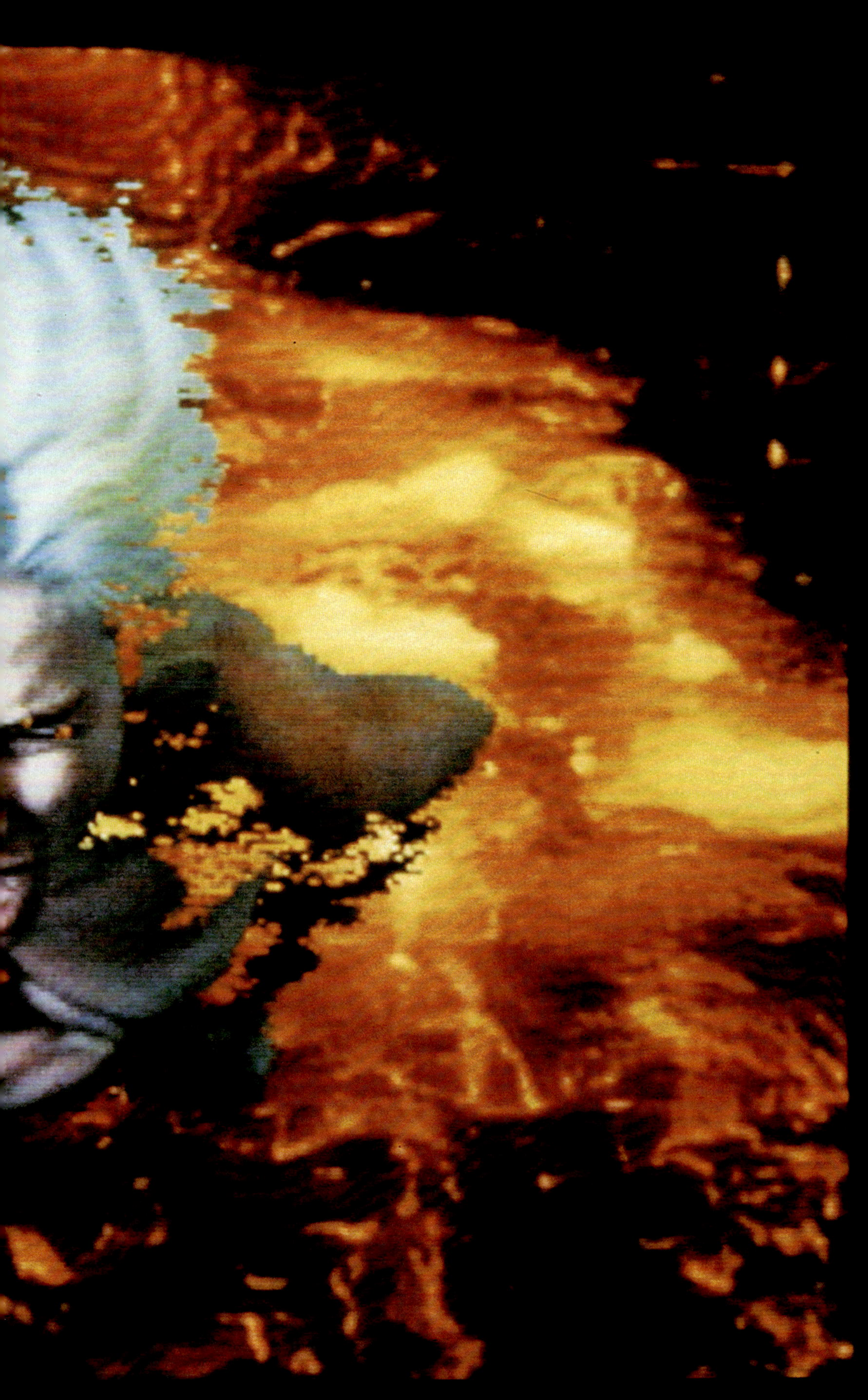

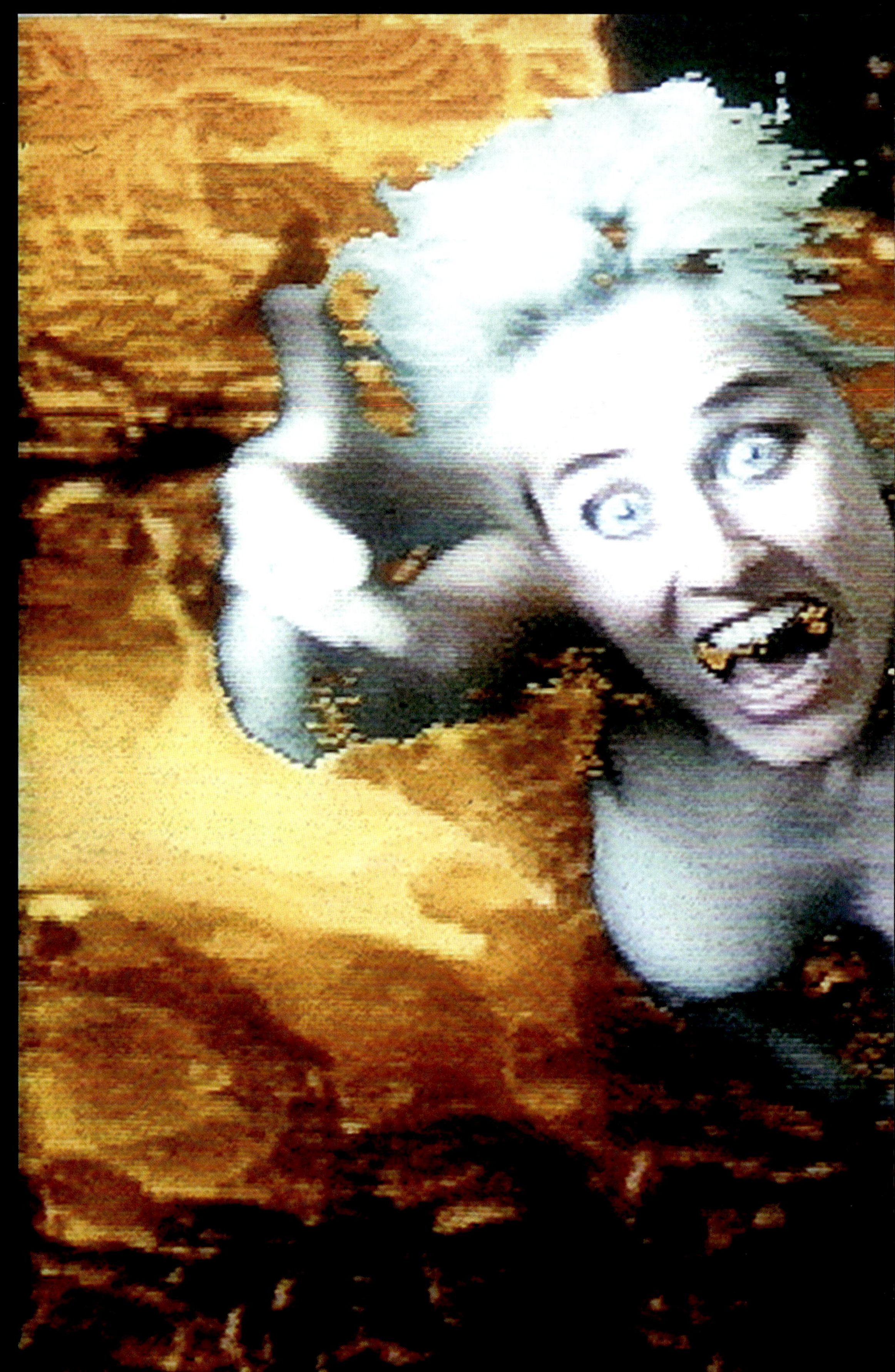

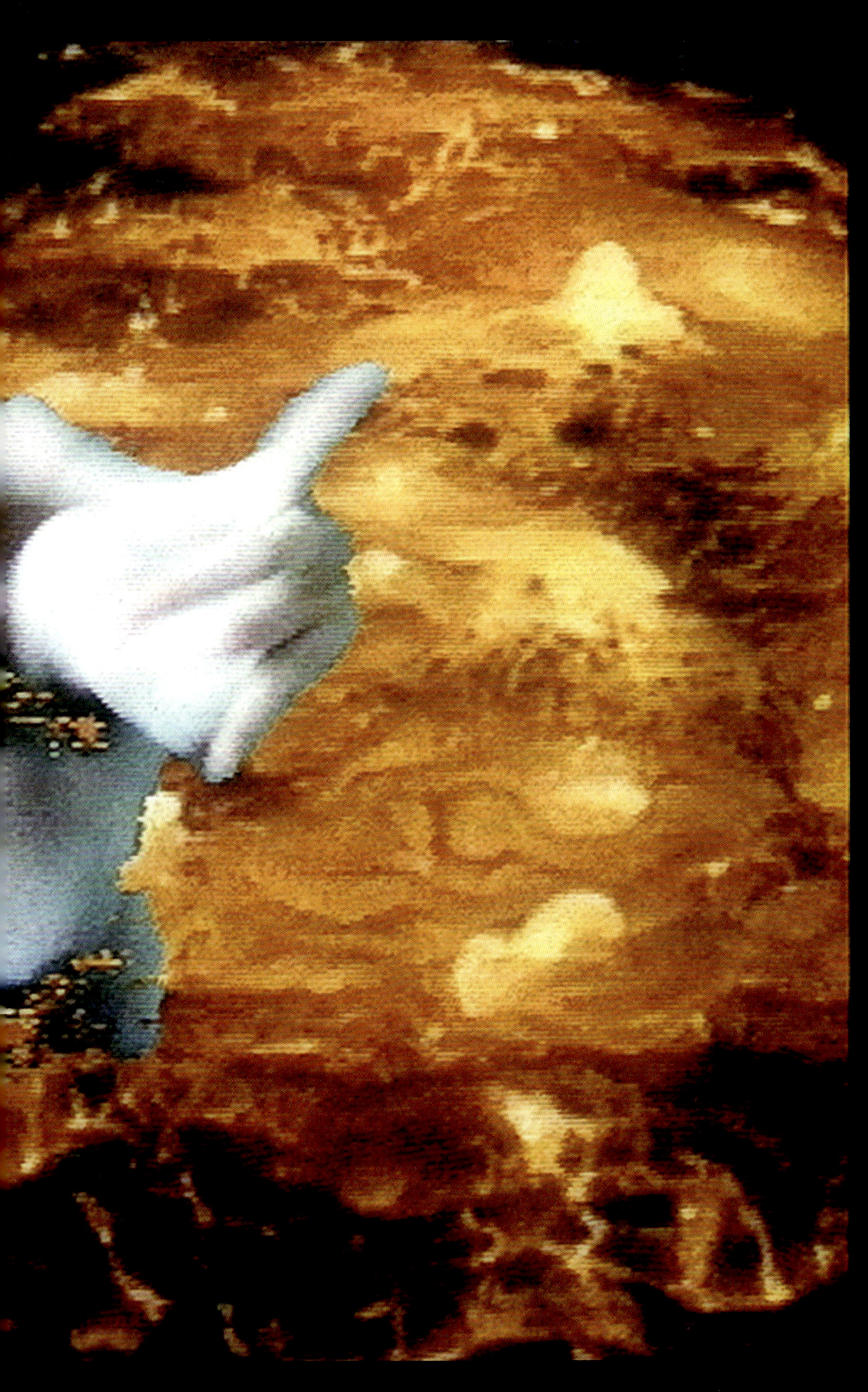

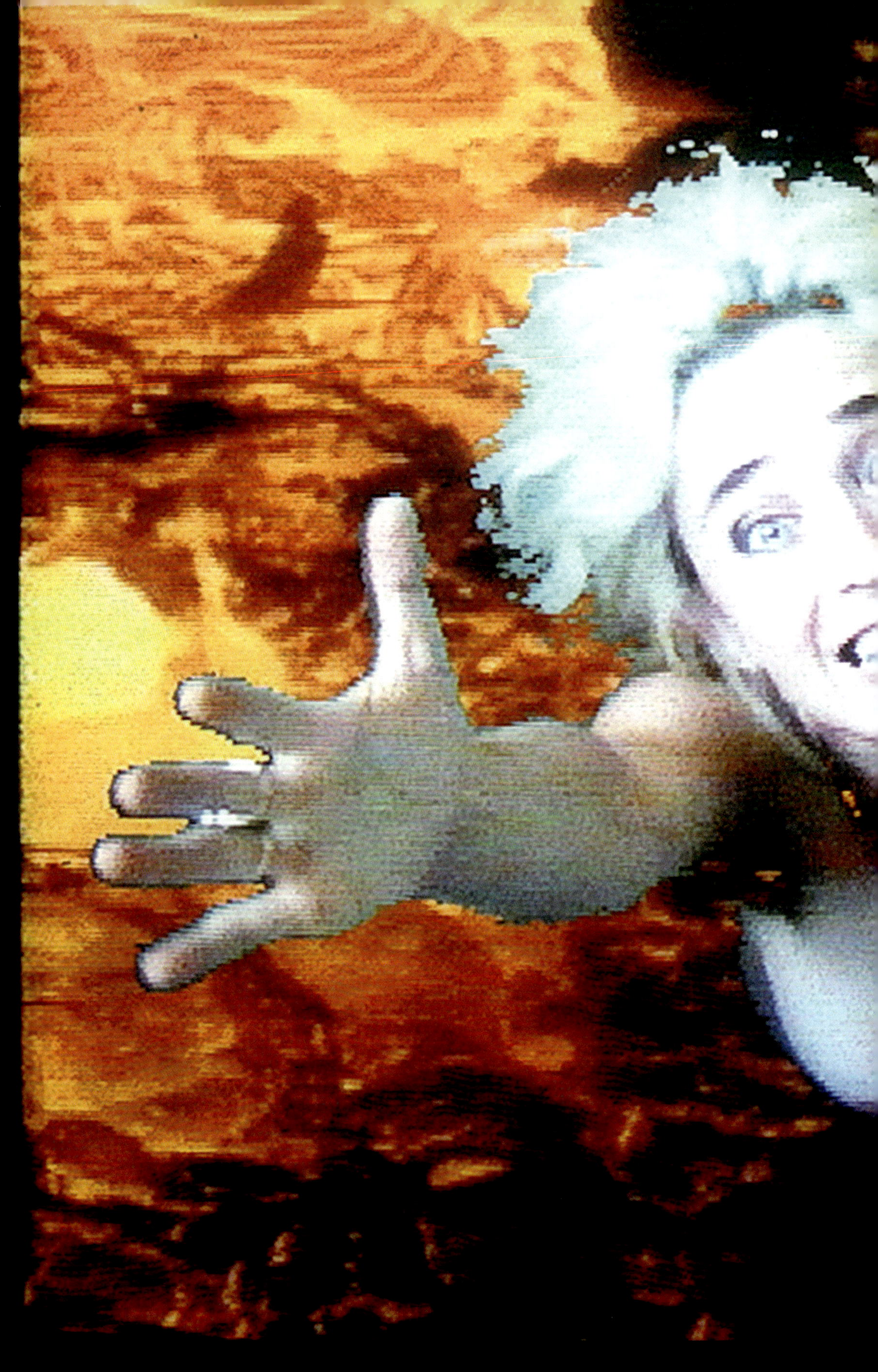

SELBSTLOS IM LAVABAD

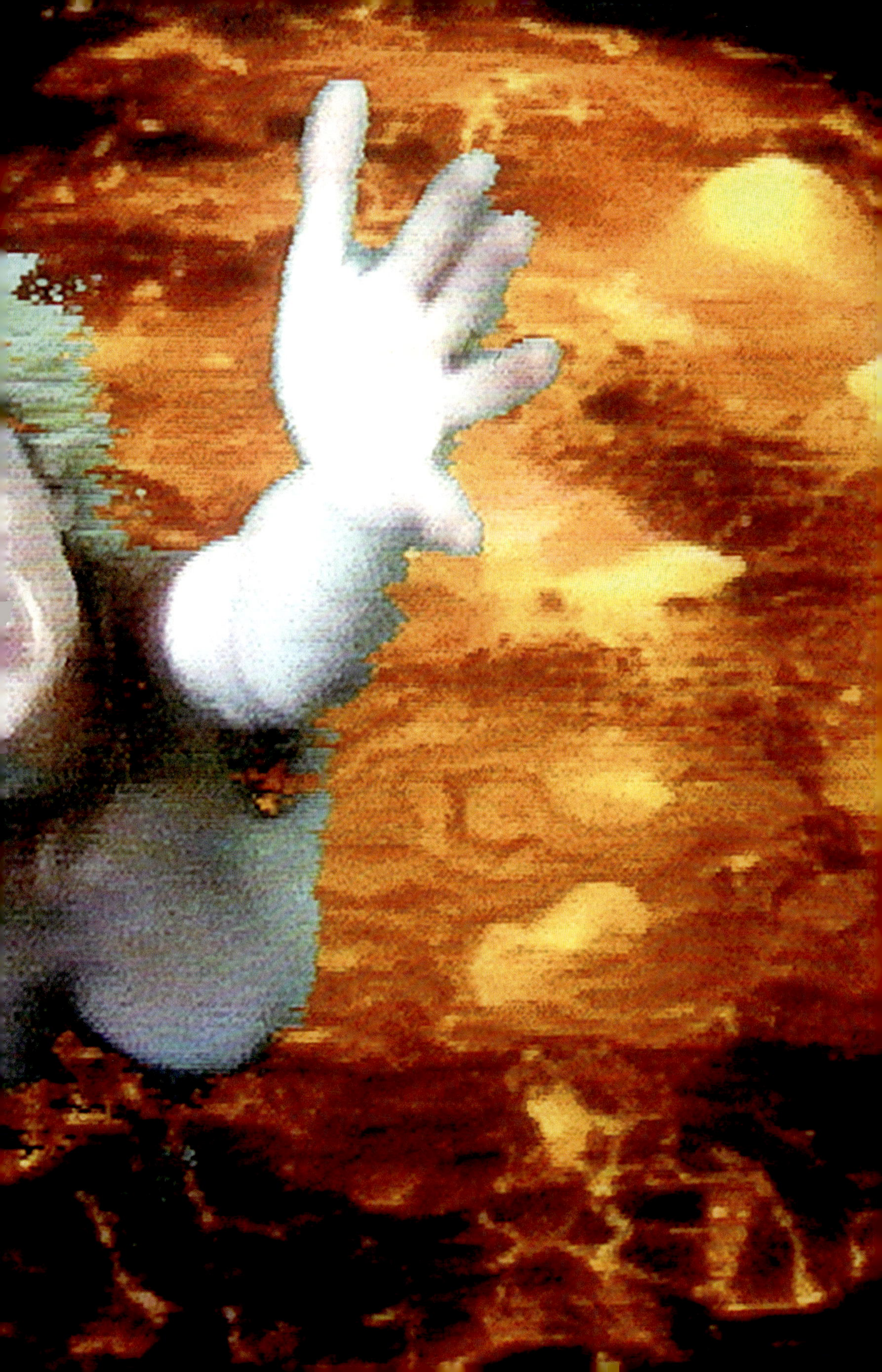

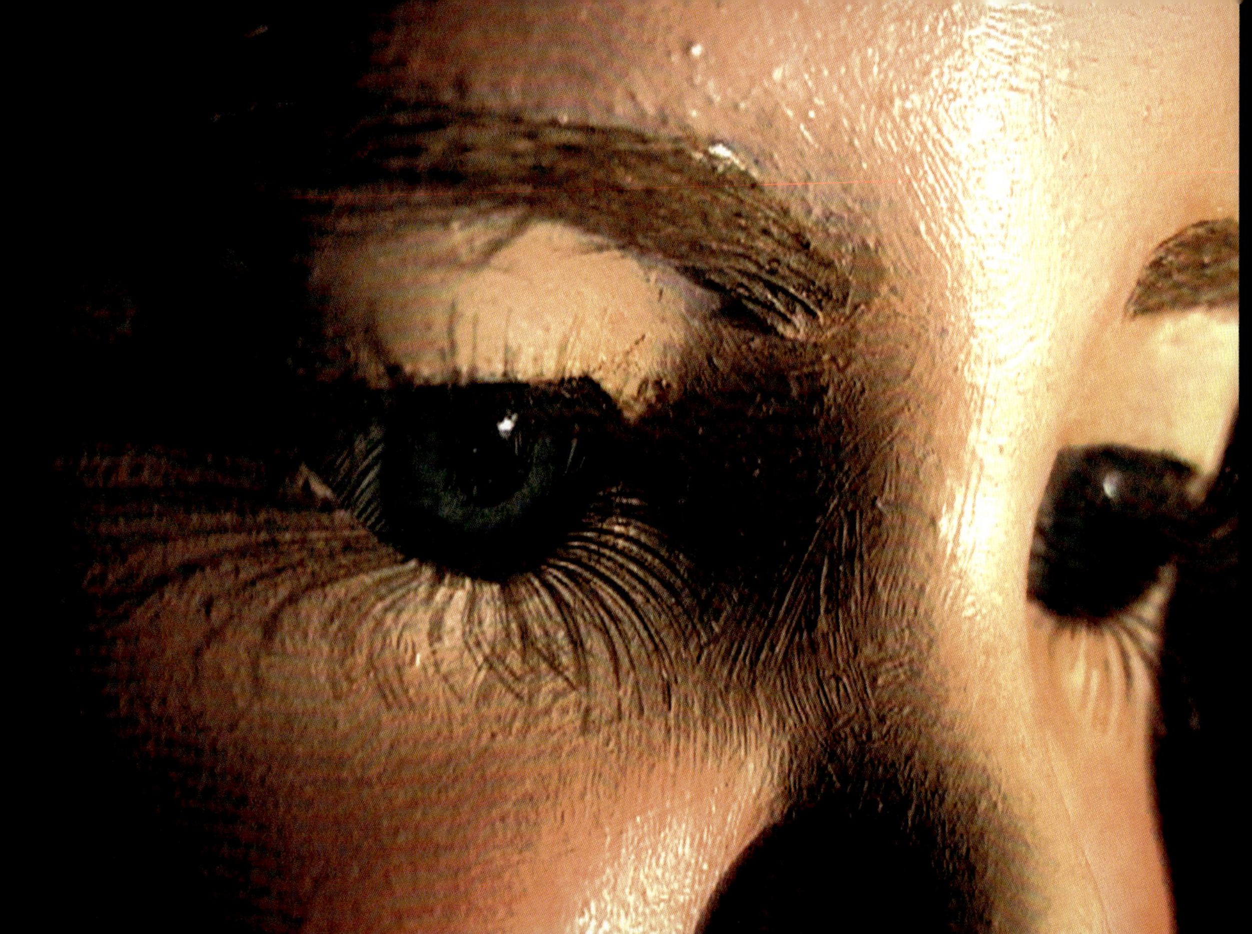

Philippe
Parreno
The Writer,
2007
Video
(color,
sound)
screened
on an
LCD
screen:
12 × 17.4 ×
2 cm,
3:58 min.

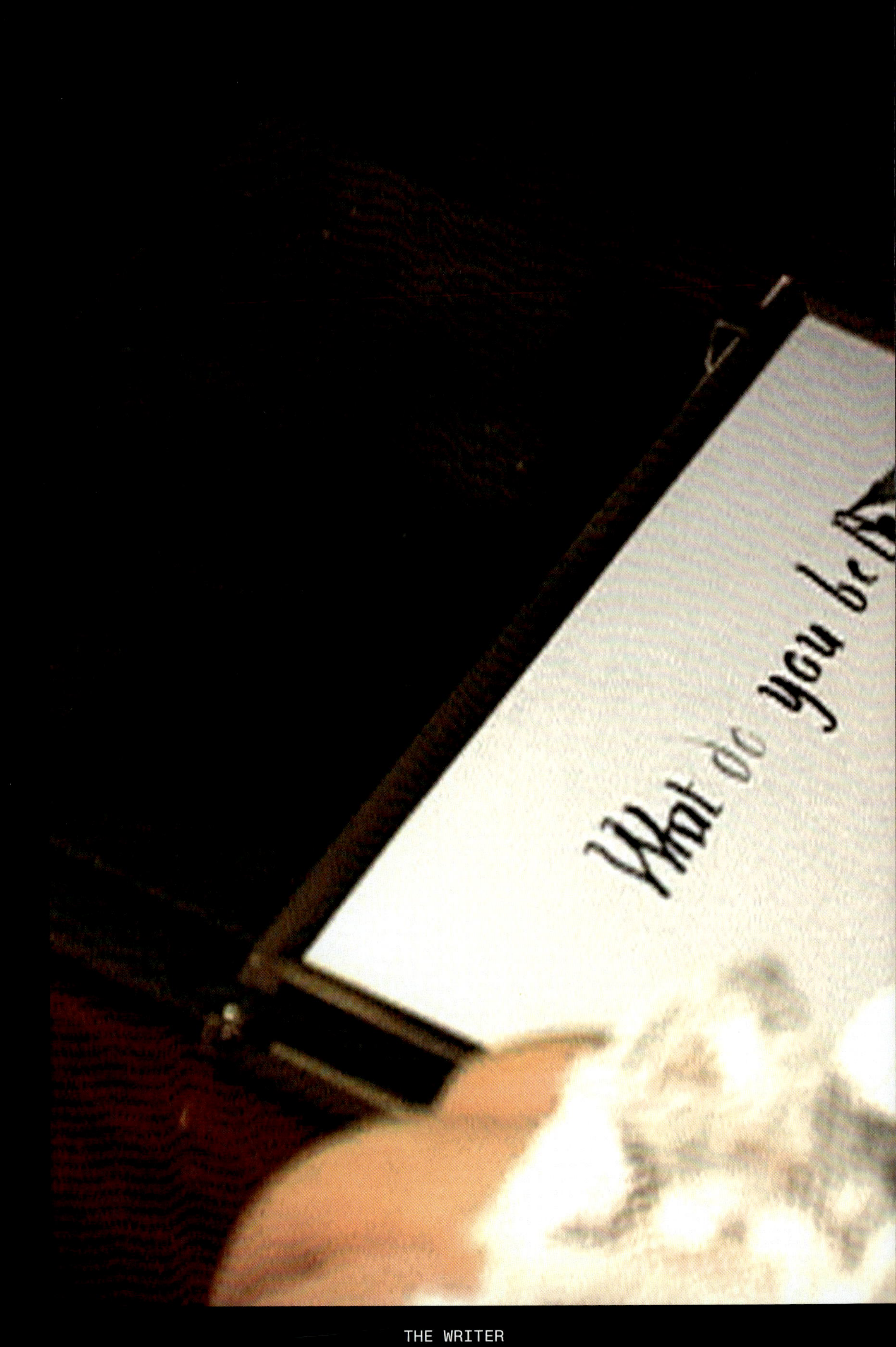
What do you be

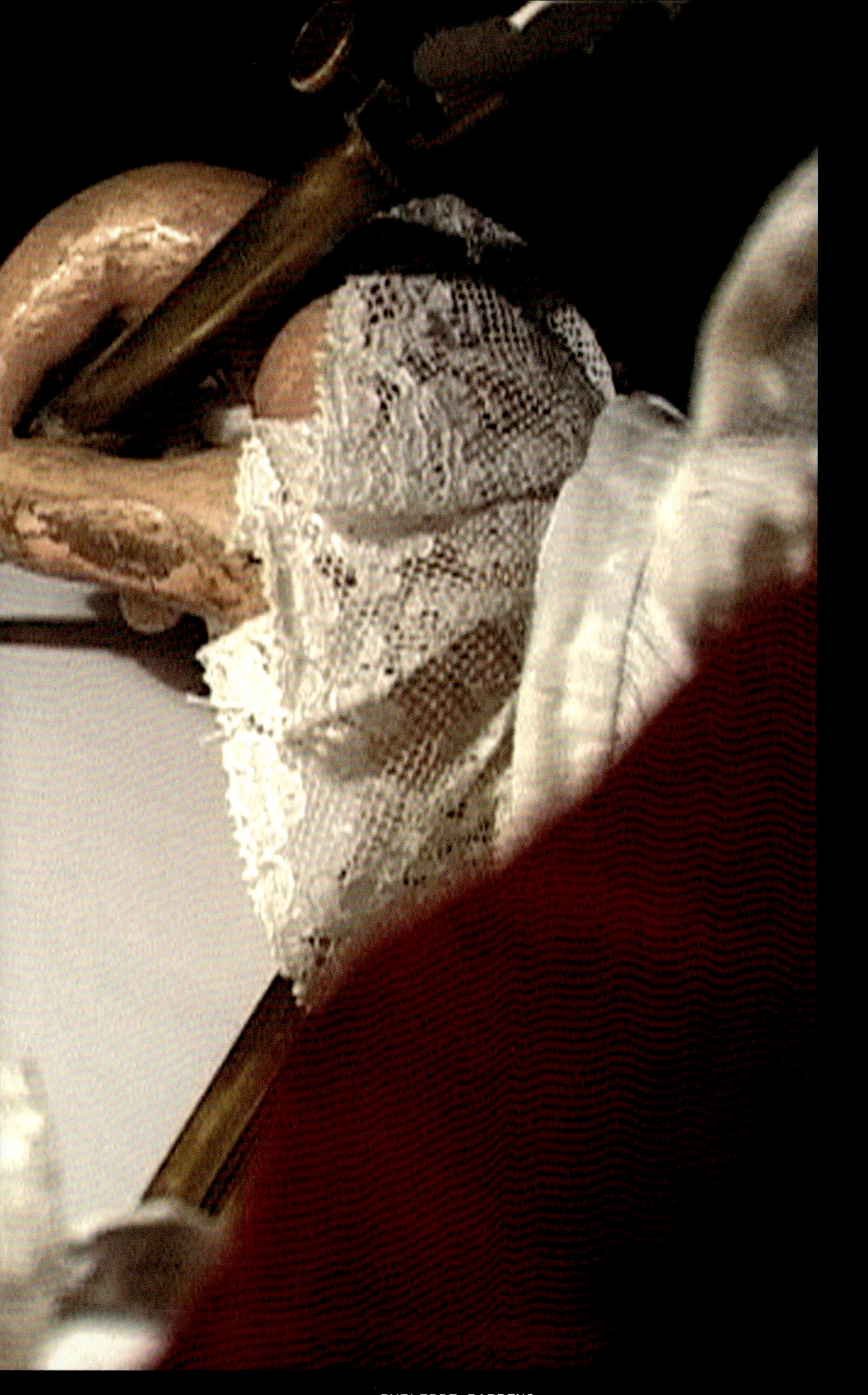

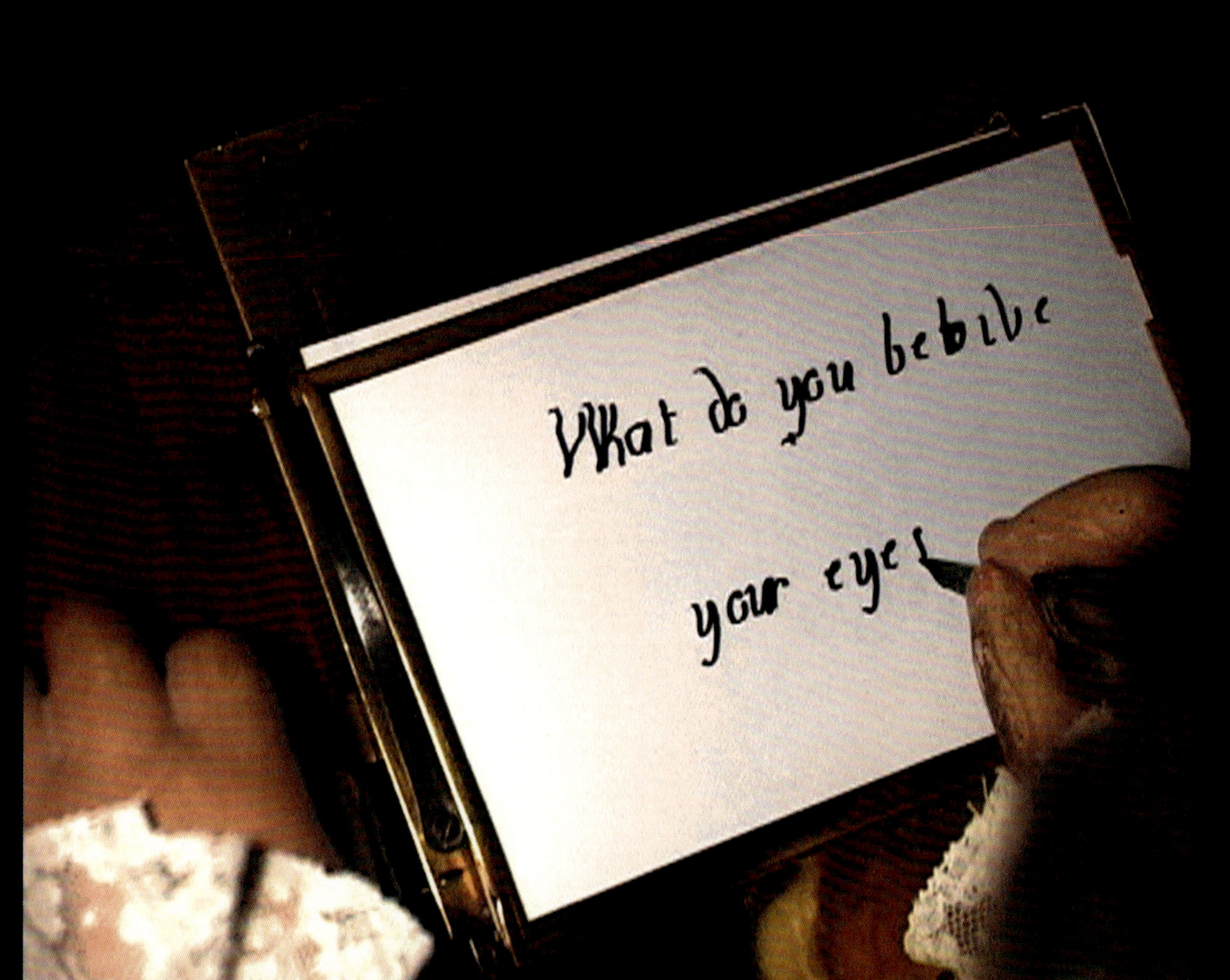
What do you belive

your eyes

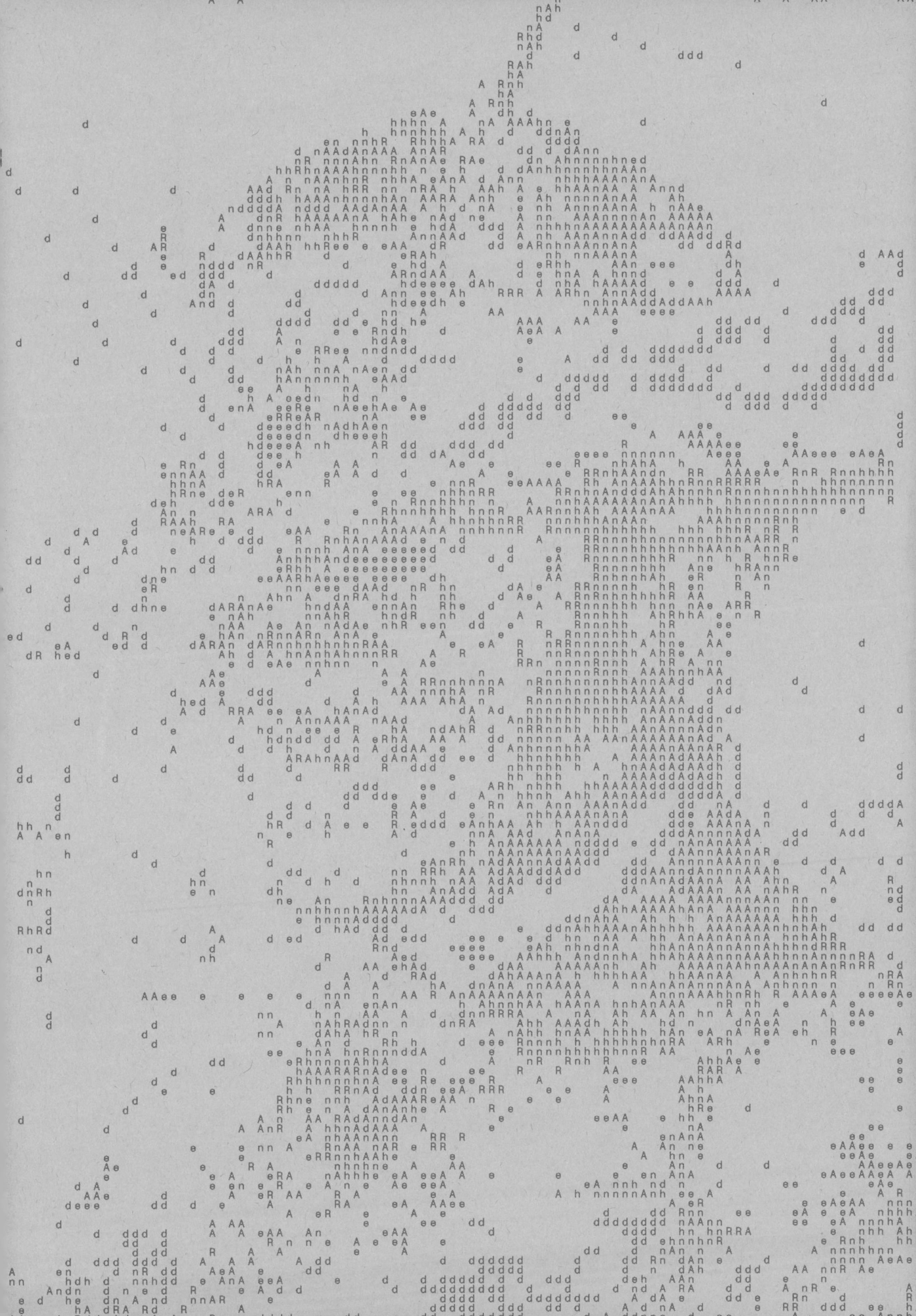

Artists have always had an eye to technology, from the innovations that shape the world around them to the new media that enables them to represent that world in novel ways. Each artwork in *Dream Machines* registers an artist's encounter with the technology of their time. These encounters are arranged here chronologically by artwork with statements by the artists and other interlocutors that give texture to their historical moment.

01   **James Tilly Matthews**
      The Air Loom, 1810
      Digital reproduction
      39.5 × 26.2 cm

JOHN HASLAM "Mr. M[atthews] insists that in some apartment near London Wall, there is a gang of villains profoundly skilled in Pneumatic Chemistry, who assail him by means of an Air Loom.…These wretches, by means of the air-loom and magnetic impregnations, contrive to lift into the brain some particular idea, which floats and undulates in the intellect for hours together; and how much so ever the person assailed may wish to direct his mind to other objects, and banish the idea forced upon him, he finds himself unable; as the idea which they have kited keeps waving in his mind, and fixes his attention to the exclusion of other thoughts. He is, during the whole time, conscious that the kited idea is extraneous, and does not belong to the train of his own cogitations.…The annexed figure of the air-loom, sketched by Mr. Matthews, together with his explanations, will afford the necessary information concerning this curious and wonderful machine."--01

In 1797, British tea merchant James Tilly Matthews (1770–1815) was committed to Bethlem Royal Hospital in London, also known as Bedlam, and would remain institutionalized until his death. A paranoid schizophrenic, he believed a group of spies were using an "Air Loom," a secret machine, to control his mind, a process he described to doctors in detailed drawings. While at Bedlam, John Haslam (1764–1844), the resident apothecary, documented Matthews's case in what is the first full study in medical history of a single psychiatric patient and the first in-depth description of this particular condition, including Matthews's account of the "Air Loom" as told to Haslam and reproduced above.

02   **Ulf Linde,**
      Replica of Duchamp's
      Moulin à Café, 1911/1960
      Oil paint and graphite on board
      33 × 13 × 1.5 cm

MARCEL DUCHAMP "My brother, the sculptor Duchamp-Villon, asked me to make a little painting for his kitchen.…So I just had the idea of making a coffee grinder, just to be close to the subject. As it turned out, instead of making an objective, figurative coffee-grinding machine, I did a description of the mechanism. You see the cogwheel, and you see the turning handle at the top. I also used the arrow showing the direction in which the hand turned, so you see there's already an idea of movement in that, plus the idea of composing the machine in two parts.…I used many, many of these little details. Even the arrow, with a dotted line, something I'd never used before. You also see the coffee after it's ground. It's not one moment; it's all the possibilities of that grinding machine.…Everything is becoming mechanized in this life. All this creates a climate for my being attracted to expressing myself in the form of mechaniographic, if you want to say, instead of using the old-fashioned approach of the painting. I was interested in using a mechanistic approach, if I wanted to step out of tradition…the attitude of anybody who wants to find something of his own."--02

ULF LINDE "He wanted to get away from art because art is a damned universal standing for nothing."--03

Ulf Linde (1929–2013) was a leading Swedish art critic of the second half of the twentieth century and chief curator of Moderna Museet in Stockholm. He first emerged in the early 1960s as an eloquent champion of new tendencies in European art, and came to be known internationally for his pioneering work on Marcel Duchamp, often pursued in collaboration with the artist. Exploring the hidden geometries of the artist's work, Linde wrote essays on Duchamp that have been translated into English and French. Beginning in 1961 with Duchamp's 1915–23 *The Bride Stripped Bare by Her Bachelors, Even (The Large Glass)*, Linde made authorized replicas of Duchamp's key works. This version of *The Large Glass* was subsequently signed by Duchamp and presented at his retrospectives in Pasadena in 1963 and the Pompidou Centre in 1977; today, it resides in the collection of the Moderna Museet.

03   **Jakob Mohr**
      Beweiße, c. 1910
      Digital reproduction
      33 × 21 cm

JAKOB MOHR "The long-distance plus wave emitter has a positive long-distance hypnotic and telesuggestive effect on me through the air…it stimulates to trigger in me arbitrarily all its mental impressions transmitted from afar and its suggestions with exact sharpness in the various chambers of my consciousness of smell, taste, feeling and imagination, and also visual senses, true to the original as in a telephone conversation.…This long-distance medical sensitivity, like the photographic plate for receiving light, is not a mental illness. This long-distance hypnotic tele-suggestion is through here as everywhere against my will, also in order to unwind my thought process…for long-distance thought theft…was only used against me for mental thought censorship and as a continuing unsuccessful means of irritating."--04

Born into a family of German laborers, Jakob Mohr (1884–1940) was sentenced to prison several times for various crimes

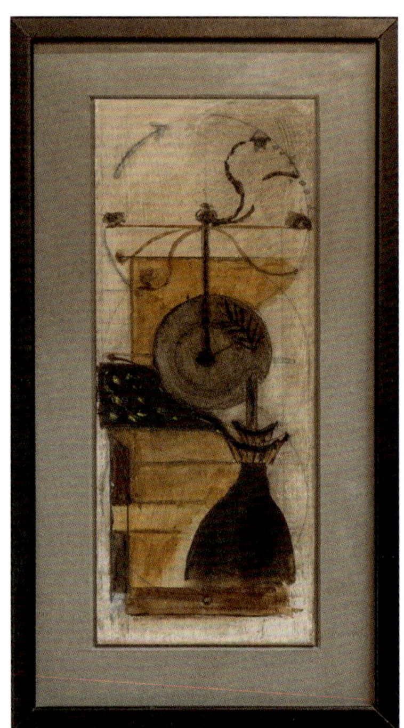

02

    ENCOUNTERS WITH TECHNOLOGY

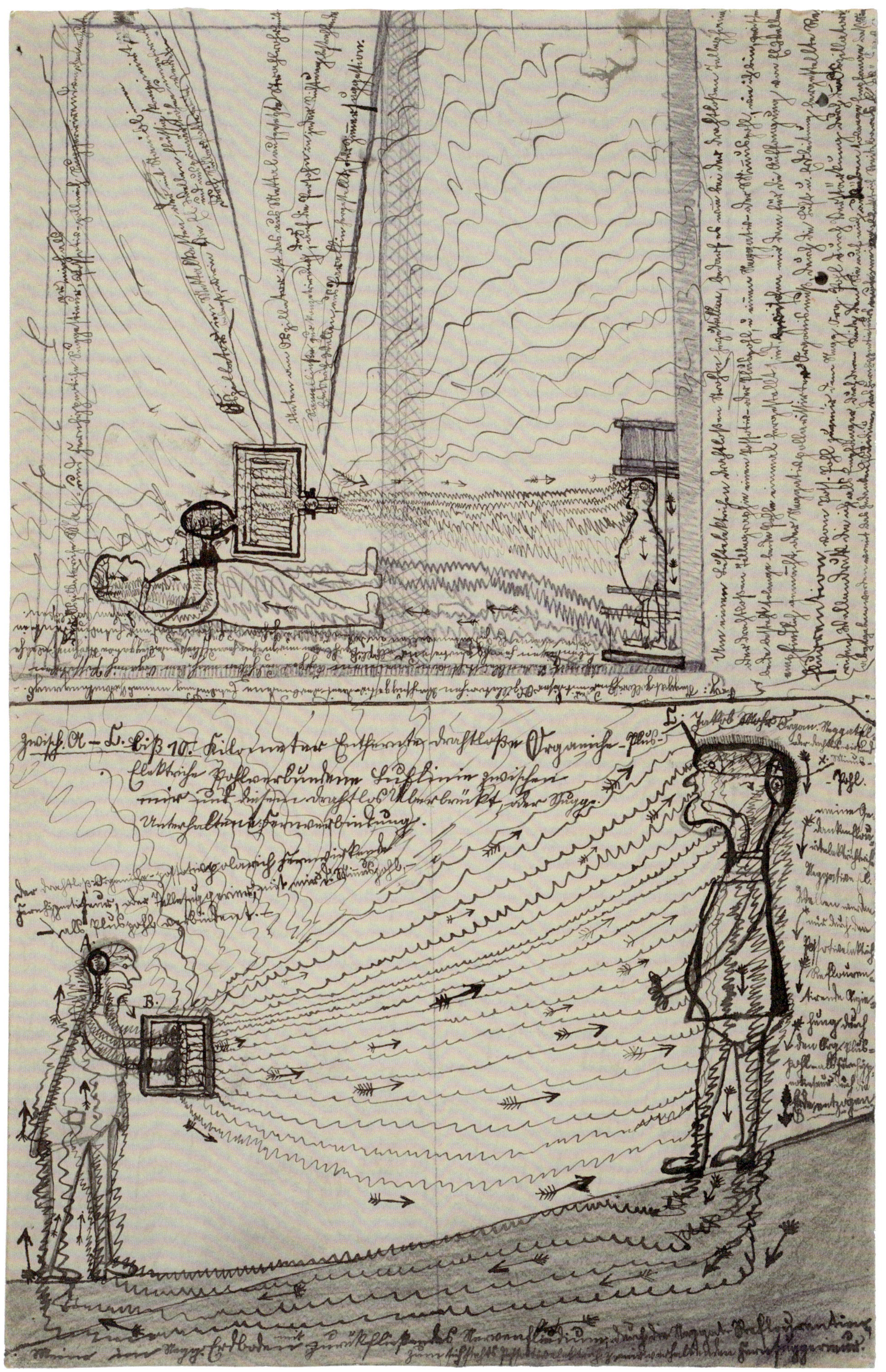

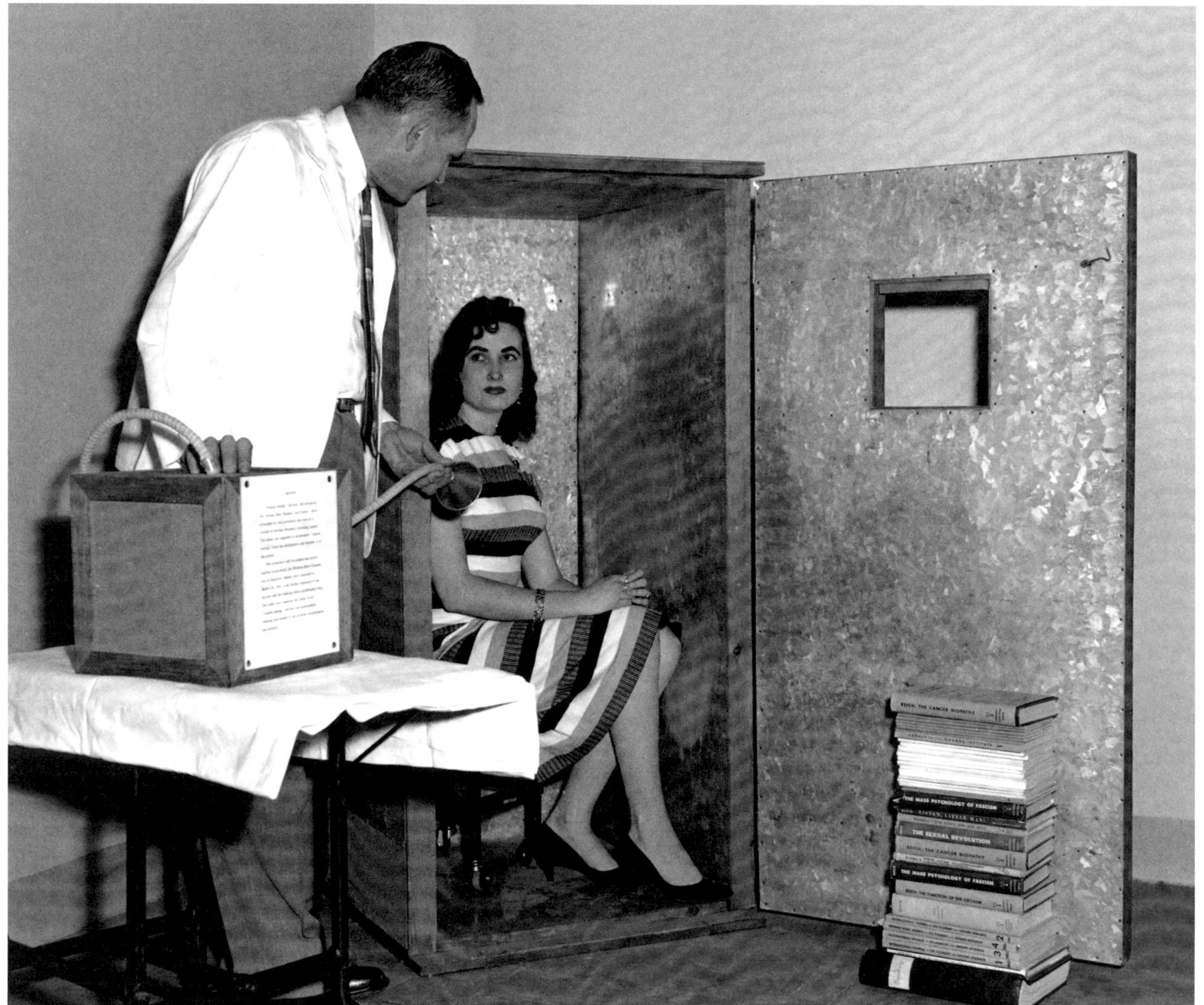

04

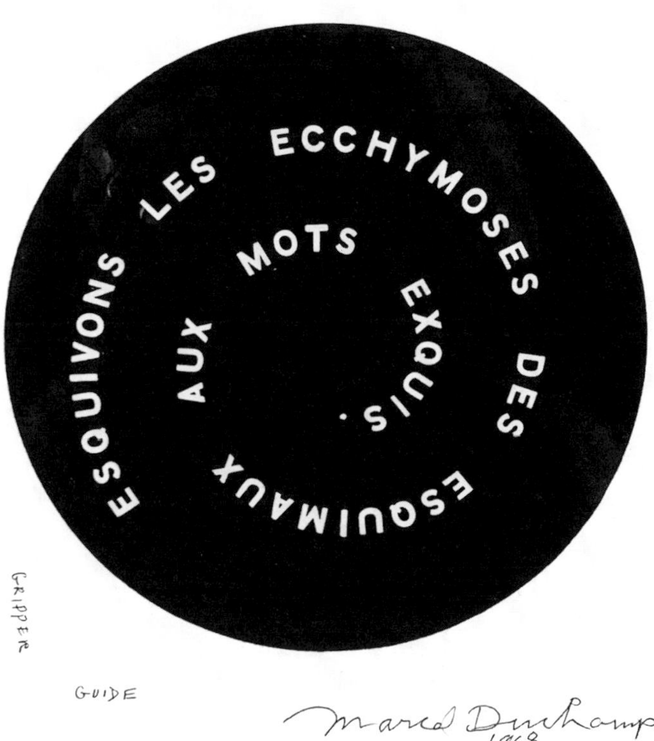

before being institutionalized for schizophrenia at the Psychiatric Clinic of the University of Heidelberg. He claimed to be tormented by an "influencing machine" that controlled his thoughts and actions. His drawing of the machine — titled *Beweiße*, or "Proofs," and featuring the inscription reproduced here — attracted the attention of German psychiatrist Hans Prinzhorn, who stewarded a collection of artworks made by patients at the hospital. Prinzhorn included the work in his landmark 1922 publication *Bildnerei der Geisteskranken (Artistry of the Mentally Ill)*, which is credited with sparking the interest of the interwar European avant-garde in the art of patients in psychiatric institutions.

04 **Wilhelm Reich**
Orgone Accumulator, 1940
Plywood, galvanized metal
155 × 77.5 × 77.5 cm
Reconstruction based
on original drawings

WILHELM REICH "The Orgone Energy Accumulator is an instrument assembled and materially arranged in such a manner that life energy, present in the atmosphere of our planet, can be collected, accumulated, and made usable for scientific, educational, and medical purposes.… Orgone energy can be had like water or air and is present in infinite quantities. All that is necessary to bring it to the consumer is a mechanism for *concentrating* it; this is, as has been shown, what the accumulator does."[05] "The quest for knowledge expresses desperate attempts, at times, on the part of the orgone energy within the living organism to comprehend itself, to become conscious of itself. And in understanding its own ways and means of being, it learns to understand the cosmic orgone energy ocean that surrounds the surging and searching emotions."[06]

Wilhelm Reich (1897–1957), an Austrian doctor and psychoanalyst, believed that a cosmic energy, "orgone," influenced our psychology and biology. His "orgone accumulators" sought to harness this energy, redirecting it for medical benefit. In 1939, Reich moved to the United States after being accused of championing a pseudoscience. In 1954 the U.S. Food and Drug Administration filed an injunction against Reich to prevent him from making, distributing, and advertising orgone accumulators; defying their orders, he was eventually arrested in 1957, tried, found guilty, and sentenced to two years in federal prison. Eight months into his sentence, he died of heart failure at the Federal Penitentiary in Lewisburg, Pennsylvania.

05 **Marcel Duchamp**
Cover for *S.M.S.*,
no. 2, April 1968
Printed card
stock portfolio
28 × 18 cm

A Recording of Puns by Rrose
***Sélavy*, original, c. 1950;**
this copy, c. 1967–68
Analog recording on ¼"
reel-to-reel magnetic tape

MARCEL DUCHAMP "You know exactly how I feel about photography. I would like to see it make people despise painting until something else will make photography unbearable."[07] "All in all, the creative act is not performed by the artist alone; the spectator brings the work in contact with the external world by deciphering and interpreting its inner qualifications and thus adds his contribution to the creative act."[08]

Marcel Duchamp (1887–1968) — a French American painter, sculptor, and writer — used art as a venue to explore how technology can influence perception, whether it was the industrial reproducibility of his readymades that throw into relief the audacity of their being positioned as artworks; his engagement with the idea of the machine, beginning with his coffee grinder and culminating in his legendary *The Bride Stripped Bare by Her Bachelors, Even* (1915–23); or his use of visual illusion on works like *Rotary Demisphere (Precision Optics)* (1925).

06　Emery Blagdon
Untitled, c. 1956/84
Recycled metal,
recycled aluminum can
25 × 15 × 16 cm

Cascade No 123,
c. 1956/84
Wire, recycled aluminum can
56 × 28 cm

Untitled, c. 1956/84
Steel wire, plastic,
foil, paper, and tape
72 × 30 × 30 cm

Untitled, c. 1956/84
Steel wire, plastic,
tin foil, and copper wire
64 × 65 × 4 cm

Untitled, c. 1956/84
Steel wire, plastic,
tin foil, and stopper wire
64 × 38 × 18 cm

JODI RITACCA "Emery Blagdon has lived up in the sand hills for a long time. As far as we can determine, for over fifty years. He used to be a farmer, but now he's an artist — even an inventor of sorts. He creates unusual artwork from junk. He puts together just about anything he can find, like wires, aluminum foil, ribbons, even Christmas tree lights. He finds his materials at junkyards or garage and farm sales. He's been creating these designs since he was a child. He has hundreds of them in the shed behind his old farmhouse. All those wires and foil create static electricity, according to Emery. However, the day that we were there, we weren't able to feel any of the static. Emery says it depends a lot on the phase of the moon. He thinks of himself as an inventor rather than an artist."

EMERY BLAGDON "Experiment with it, that's the only way."

RITACCA "You call it a scientific work instead of an artwork. Why is that?"

BLAGDON "I don't know. Science, you gotta have science before you do anything with it."

RITACCA "Does it have something to do with the static electricity?"

BLAGDON "Yeah."

RITACCA "Could you explain how that works with your designs?"

BLAGDON "I can't."

RITACCA "It just works?"

BLAGDON "Just works."[09]

Emery Blagdon (1907–1986) was born into a farming family in Nebraska; he lived off odd jobs until 1955, when he inherited family property and began making intricate sculptures of wire, foil, and other found materials in the shed behind his house. Blagdon called his works his "pretties," and believed they had healing properties. In 1975, Blagdon met Dan Dryden at the pharmacy where the latter worked when the former had come to purchase "elements" for his machines. Dryden visited Blagdon on his farm twice, and

in 1986, after learning Blagdon had died, subsequently purchased and cared for the environment he dubbed *The Healing Machine*, until the works were acquisitioned by the Kohler Foundation in 2004. In 1987, Dryden reflected that Blagdon "was clearly interested in these works as scientific objects rather than art objects. There was no mention of artistic content or values — it was all on the basis of its physiological effects on people. He didn't attribute any artistic value at all — nor did he speak about the construction of the devices at all. He claimed a good record, medically, in terms of having helped people with these devices — that they indeed did feel some relief."[10]

07　Brion Gysin
Dreamachine, 1961
Galvanized metal,
light bulb, wood, and motor
120 × 27 cm diam.
Reconstruction based
on original drawings

BRION GYSIN "The Dreamachine…induced people to see. The fluctuating elements of flickered design support the development of autonomous 'movies,' intensely pleasurable and, possibly, instructive to the viewer. What is art? What is color? What is vision? These old questions demand new answers when, in the light of the Dreamachine one sees all of ancient and modern abstract art with eyes closed."[11]

IAN SOMMERVILLE "Our ancestors saw the creatures of the constellations in the apparently unorganized distribution of the stars. It has been shown…that man tends to find pattern and picture where objectively there is none: his mental process shapes what it sees. External resonators, such as flicker, tune in with our internal rhythms and lead to their extension. The Dreamachine began as a simple means to investigate phenomena whose description excited our imaginations.…The effects can be astonishing."[12]

British Canadian Brion Gysin (1916–1986) was known for his relentless experimentation. He was associated with the Surrealist Group in Paris as a teenager, and in the 1950s, he met American writer William S. Burroughs (1914–1997), with whom he popularized the literary "cut-up" technique of taking an existing piece of writing, slicing it apart, and rearranging it into a new text. In 1959, Gysin began collaborating with British engineer Ian Sommerville (1940–1976) on what would. become the Dreamachine: a cylinder with slits cut in its sides that rotates on a record turntable with a lightbulb at its center; the light appears to pulse at a frequency of eight to thirteen flickers per second, inducing an alpha wave mental state of wakeful relaxation and visual hallucination. Gysin had a similar experience driving down an avenue of trees in Marseilles and, after he and Sommerville read British neurophysiologist William Grey Walter's (1910–1977) *The Living Brain*, they sought to recreate it.

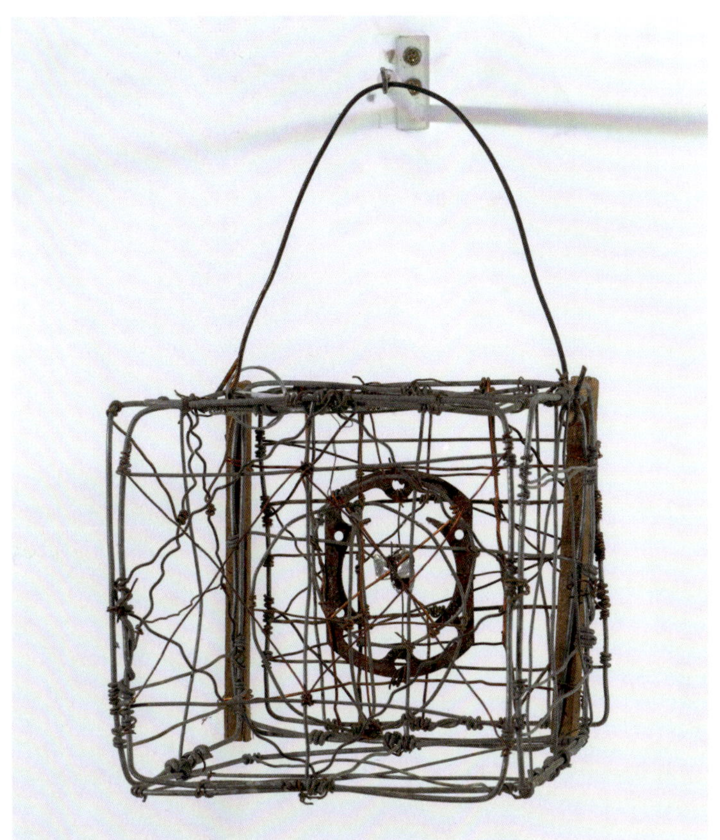

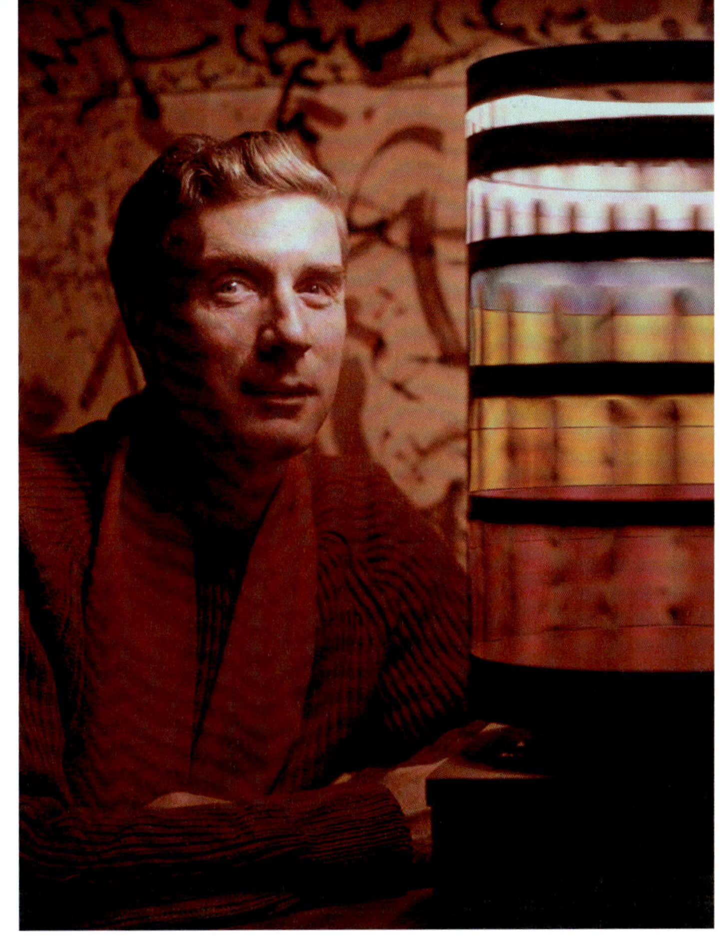

JAKE BRODSKY

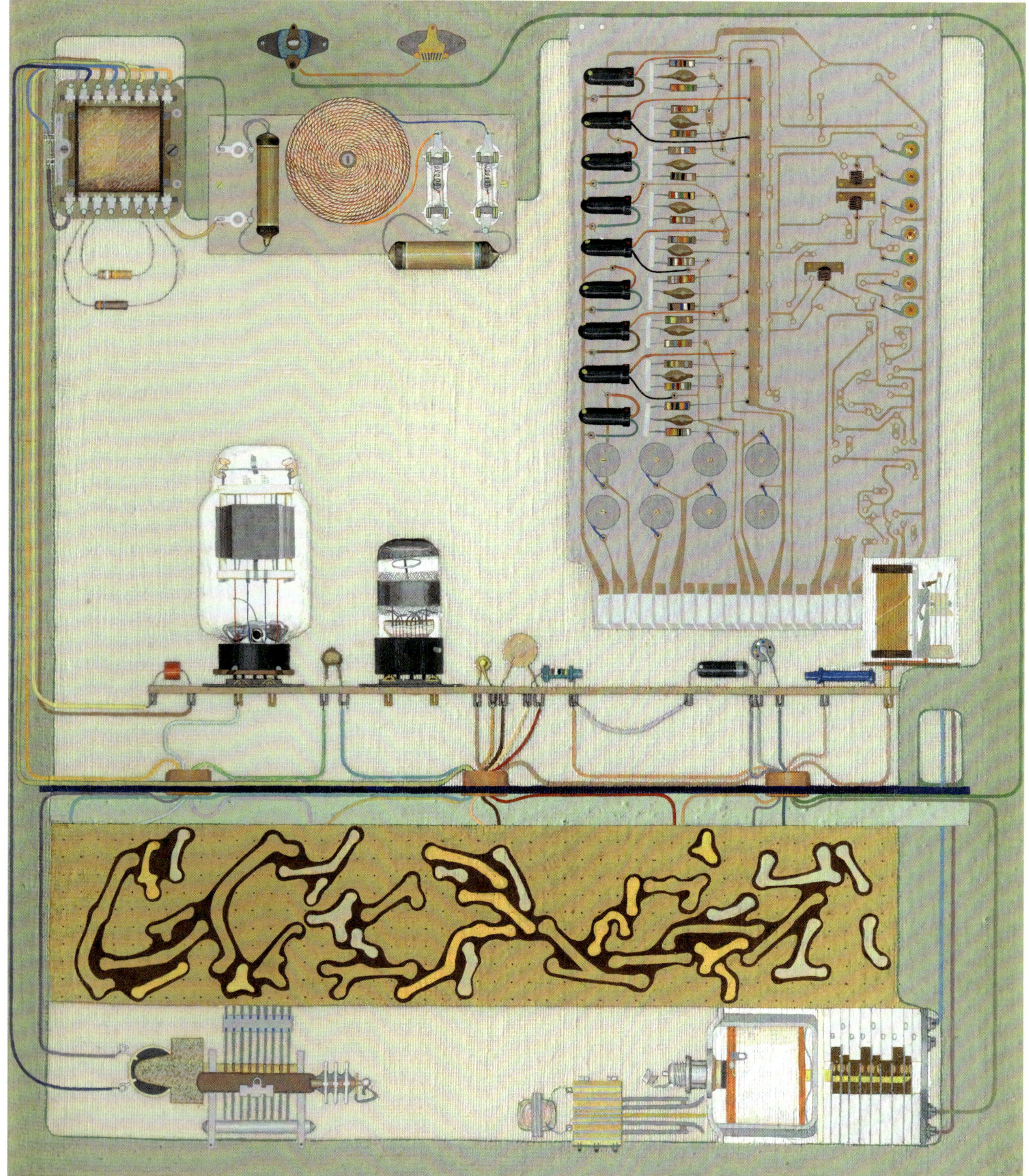

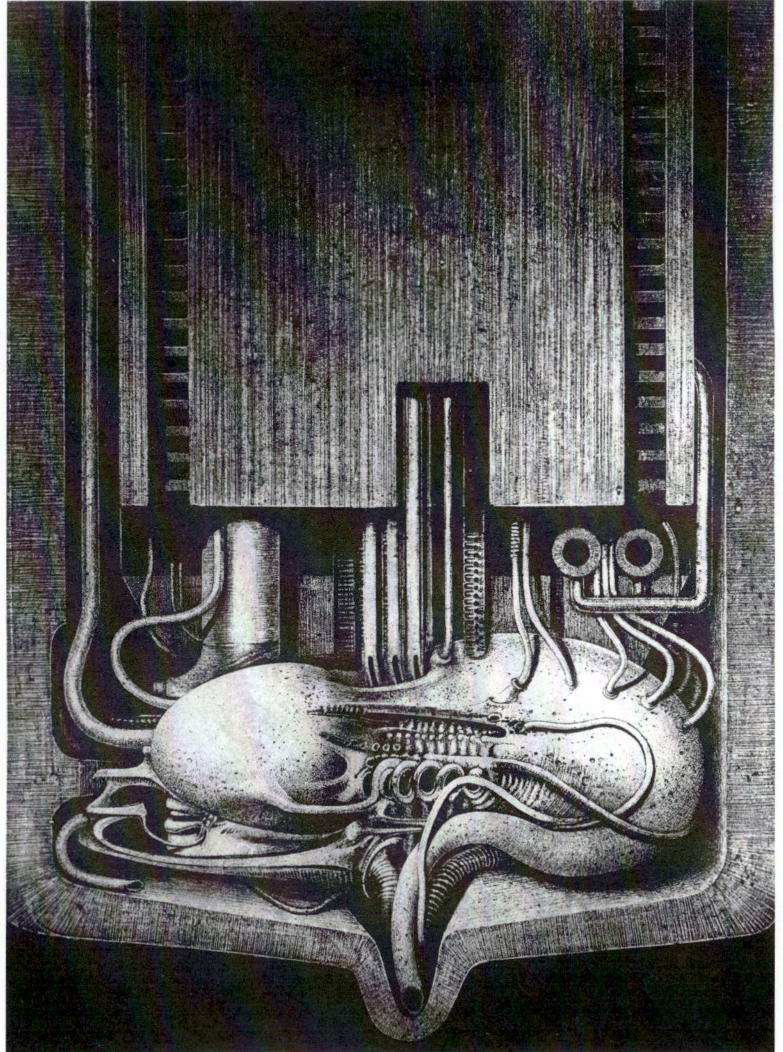

09

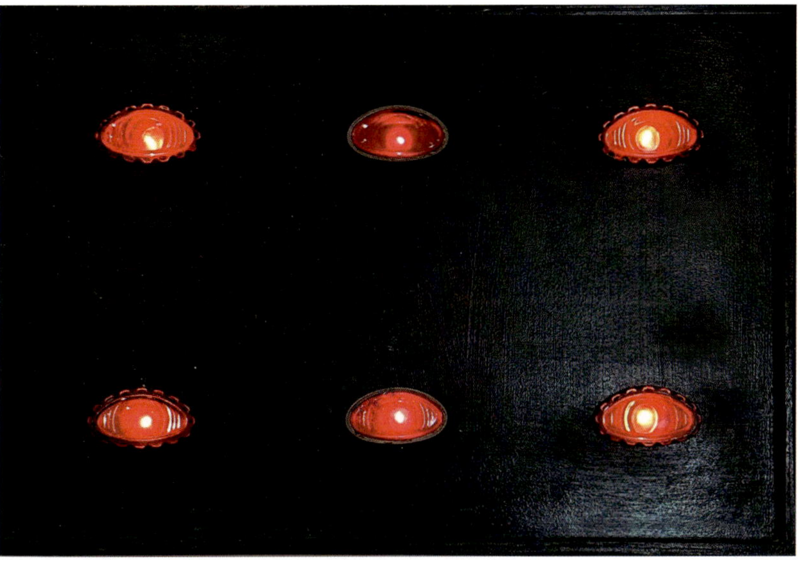

10

08 Ulla Wiggen
Kretsfamilj, 1964/2023
Print mounted on aluminum
65 × 75 × 1.5 cm

ULLA WIGGEN "I am extremely interested in understanding how things are connected and how they affect each other. As a child, I loved taking things apart to see how they were made inside."[13] "People would ask, 'What do you want to be when you grow up?' And I said, 'An engineer.' Because someone had told me that they worked with machines."[14] "In the 1960s, I started from a world of circuit boards, computers and electronic components that can be seen as an extension of human consciousness outside the body."[15]

Ulla Wiggen (b. 1942), a Swedish painter, began painting her detailed, hyperrealistic paintings of electronic circuit boards and components in the 1960s.

09 H. R. Giger
Biomechanoid (Biomechanoid Portfolio, 4), 1969
Silkscreen on black silver
100.5 × 74 cm

H. R. GIGER "I am afraid of my visions."[16] My work "came partly from Chur where I grew up; partly from the war. I was born in 1940 so I could feel the atmosphere when my parents were afraid. The lamps were always a bluish dark, so the planes would not bomb us. Switzerland and Germany are close. The targets weren't always very well marked. I felt the fear of that very much. Later on at a certain time I saw a lot of witchcraft books and stuff like that. H. P. Lovecraft and these kind of people. I'd say my inspiration comes from books mostly, but dreams also."[17]
TIMOTHY LEARY "Giger's work disturbs us, spooks us, because of its enormous evolutionary time span. It shows us, all too clearly, where we come from and where we are going."[18]

Most widely known as the designer of the creature in Ridley Scott's 1979 film, *Alien*, H. R. Giger was a Swiss artist whose eerie and cold airbrushed images of humans and machines explored the unsettling intersection of the body and technology in a style he called "biomechanical."

10 Takis
Kadran Dial, 1974
Painted wood, electrical circuit, and electrical lights
42 × 59.6 × 10 cm

TAKIS "Plato speaks of an artist turning the invisible world into the visible. I hope that someone seeing my sculpture is lifted out of his ordinary state.…I cannot think of my work as entirely my work. In a sense, I'm only a transmitter, I simply bathe in energy. The artist must preserve this intense receptiveness. The real artist you cannot touch.…We try to achieve spiritual collaboration between artist and scientist. Otherwise, the technology is just a gadget."[19] "I am a scientist as well as an artist.…For me artists and scientists are very similar.…The moment you are questioning the world, you are like a scientist.…My work gives energy; it brings a balance to your body.…And your energy and the work's energy come to be in harmony, without your having to think.…I cure people with magnetic fields, and after all, I am not the only one today. There are hospitals that use magnetic rays to cure you. There is a lot of promise in that direction. If our civilization is better than that of Atlantis, it is because we have made tremendous technological progress."[20]

Greek sculptor Takis (1925–2019) pioneered the use of magnets and electromagnets to create kinetic sculptures. Influenced by the work of Jean Tinguely (1925–1991) and Yves Klein (1928–1962), who he met in Paris in the 1950s, Takis was fascinated by vital technologies, like radar and lights, that were powered by energy that cannot be seen. In 1961, Takis traveled to America where he met Marcel Duchamp, who would later describe his friend as the "gai laboureur des champs magnétiques et indicateur des chemins de fer doux" ("gay laborer of magnetic fields and indicator of gentle railways").[21]

11　Vera Molnár
*Hypertransformation
(75.058.15.20.03)*, 1975
Facsimile of a computer
plotter drawing
50 × 50 cm

VERA MOLNÁR　"My goal is not at all to use a computer, I don't care about computers, but the computer is like a slave in making my dreams a reality. My imagination, if you will."[22] With the computer drawings of the late 1960s, "everyone jumped at me, saying, 'You're completely crazy, you're dehumanizing art: what is this—bringing art closer to machines.'…I remember the day when I first said to someone, just like that—'I think that there is nothing more human than a computer because it was invented by men. It wasn't the good Lord who plopped it down in front of us, it was made by an intelligent man. Thus, the most human art is made by computer, because every last bit of it is a human invention.' Oh my, the reactions I got!"[23] "Instead of starting from 'I am a genius and every work I make is a masterpiece' I instead come up with a system with which…I can check what changes were made and what that [change] provoked in me. It's an experimental method, [taken] step by step. The computer is fantastic for this purpose. The computer isn't dumb. So I called [the process] *machine imaginaire*.…I think this is what's paradoxical about the computer—it actually helps you to bring into the world what you had only imagined, even when you yourself don't [yet] know what that is."[24]

Born in Hungary and based in France, Vera Molnár (1924–2023) was a pioneer of computer art and algorithmic painting. One of the first artists to employ digital technology as a tool for art creation, she began using computers to explore geometric abstraction in the 1960s.

12　Peter Fischli and David Weiss
*Der Lauf der Dinge
(The Way Things Go)*, 1987
Video transferred
from 16 mm film, sound
30:00 min.

DAVID WEISS　"We were sitting in a bar somewhere and playing around with the things on the table, and we thought to ourselves, this energy of never-ending collapse—because our construction stood for a moment and then collapsed before we built it up again—should be harnessed and channeled in a particular direction.…..When you see the 'making of,' it becomes clear that the creative process was not funny at all. I've always found that astonishing anyway—the way people always laugh when the next thing falls over. Because for us it was more like a circus act, trained objects. And the ones that didn't do it were badly trained or badly positioned. It required considerable patience."

PETER FISCHLI　"Strangely, for us, while we were making the piece, it was funnier when it failed, when it didn't work. When it worked, that was more about satisfaction. And that the film created the impression that the things move on their own, without human help, that they become spirited, living beings."[25]

The Swiss artistic duo Peter Fischli (b. 1952) and David Weiss (1946–2012) are known for their playful multimedia works that often employ ordinary materials. *Der Lauf der Dinge* (1987) shows a chain reaction of objects filmed in a continuous sequence and reflecting an interest in cause and effect.

13　Sturtevant
Duchamp Porte-bouteilles, 1992
Bottle rack
61 × 42 cm diam.

MARCEL DUCHAMP　"The choice of these 'readymades' was never dictated by esthetic delecation [*sic*]. This choice was based on a reaction of visual indifference with at the same time a total absence of good or bad taste…in fact a complete anesthesia. One important characteristic was the short sentence which I occasionally inscribed on the 'readymade.' That sentence instead of describing the object like a title was meant to carry the mind of the spectator toward other regions more verbal. Sometimes I would add a graphic detail of presentation which in order to satisfy my craving for alliterations, would be called 'readymade aided.'…Another aspect of the 'readymade' is its lack of uniqueness…the replica of a 'readymade' delivering the same message; in fact nearly every one of the 'readymades' existing today is not an original in the conventional sense.…Since the tubes of paint used by the artist are manufactured and ready made products we must conclude that all the paintings in the world are 'readymades aided' and also works of assemblage."[26]

STURTEVANT　"The ready-mades, the most crucial body of work, lack unity, form, and meaning, thereby opening a space that allows for posited, subjective or arbitrary meaning.

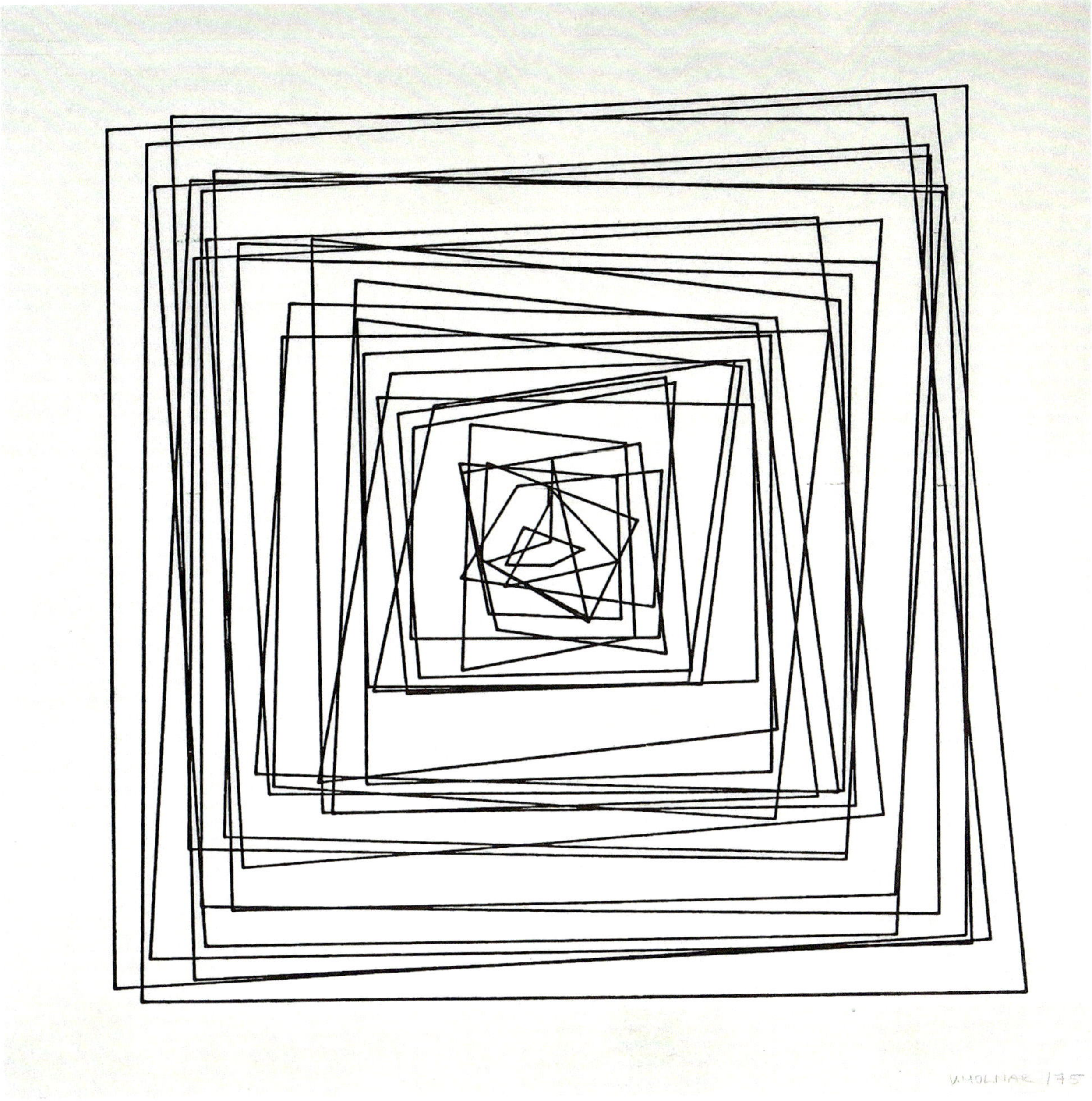

11

12

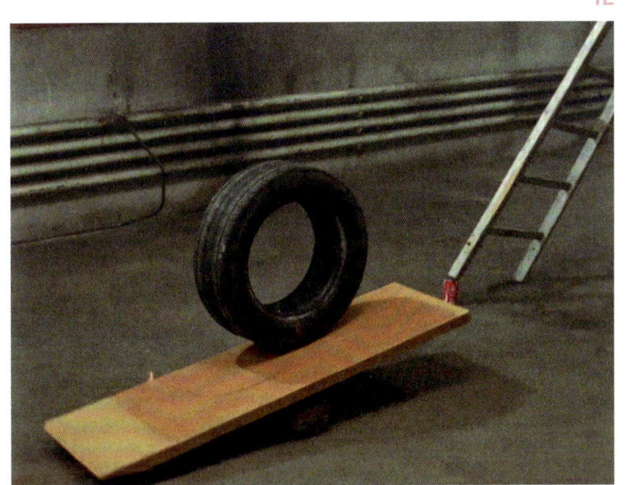

JAKE BRODSKY

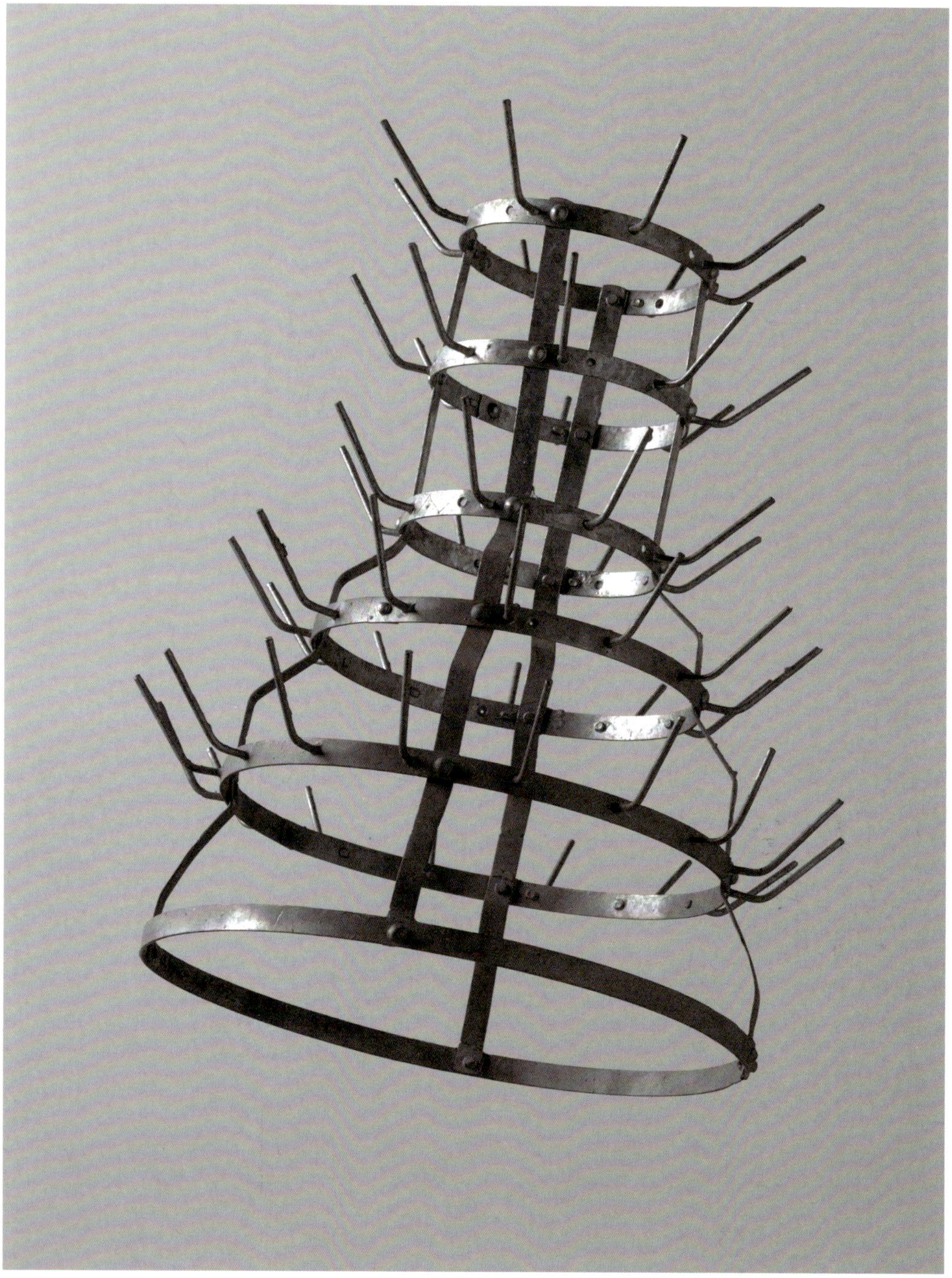

13

14

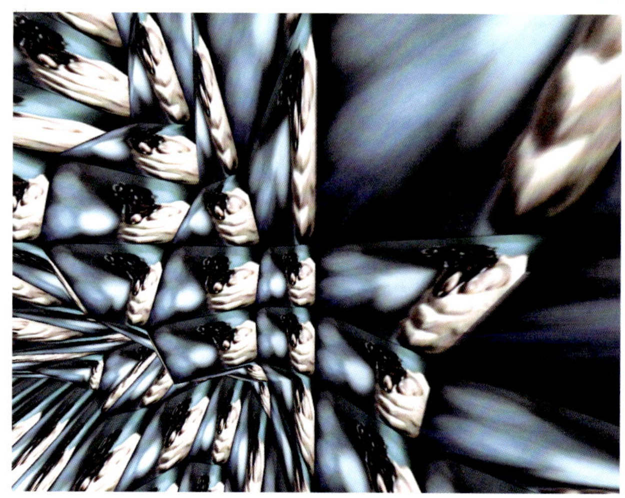

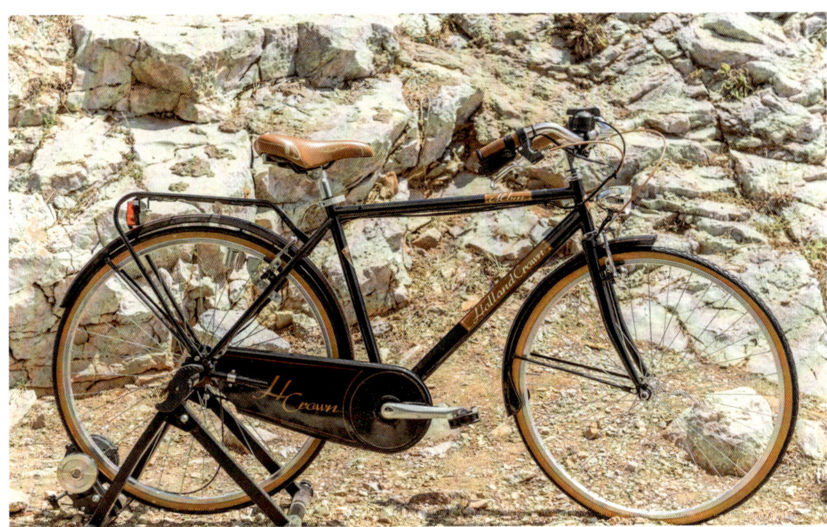

These objects that contain opposition and the loud noise of discord are claimed by Duchamp to have only the common factor of indifference. Thus, it would seem that Duchamp did or did not understand the primary force, not immediacy and appearance, but what lies beneath the surface.…His non-choice of objects, indifference, actions and non-actions, consistency of non-linear development, were all driven by the force of resistance. With his determination and mental-sets, he absolutely refused to fit this slot or to be slotted. He placed himself a far distance from competition, struggle and search for creativity, novelty and recognition; giving him courage and strength to resist the common denominators of art world politics.…The grand contradiction is that giving up creativity made him the great creator."[27] "What is currently compelling is our pervasive cybernetic mode, which plunks copyright into mythology, makes origins a romantic notion, and pushes creativity outside the self. Remake, reuse, reassemble, recombine — that's the way to go."[28]

American artist Elaine Sturtevant (1924–2014) — known professionally by only her last name — challenged ideas of replication and authorship with the reproductions of other artist's work she began creating in the 1960s. Working in dialogue with many Duchampian concepts, she made several re-creations of his work — including this copy of his readymade *Porte-bouteilles* (Bottle Rack) (originally 1914) — and reflected on "The Reluctant Indifference of Marcel Duchamp" in an unpublished 1994 essay.

14 **Thomas Bayrle**
Superstars, 1993
Video, sound
11:04 min.

THOMAS BAYRLE "I see religion and technical developments existing as two sides of the same coin since Gothic times. The construction of the first Gothic cathedrals a thousand years ago was, as Wilhelm Worringer argued in 1913, the first time humans worked with 'engines' — full-scale ethical and technical creations. I see this development as continuous to the conveyor belts of our car factories."[29] "Machines can help us when they extend our bodies and work like our bodies. In the end, it's always a matter of micro-differences between individuals; maybe that's where salvation is, in the difference between one and zero, off and on, same and different. All the world is built on power and energy generated from small bits and pieces."[30]

Thomas Bayrle (b. 1937), a German artist, combines art and technology through his concept of "superforms," repetitive, machinelike patterns that create larger images. Spanning painting, animation, and digital art, his work critiques consumer culture and the mechanization of society.

15 **Maurizio Cattelan**
Dynamo Secession, 1997/2023
Bicycle rigged
to electricity generator
Dimensions variable

MAURIZIO CATTELAN "I believe that most of the time there's a difference between what an artist wishes for his or her work in the future, and what an artist thinks while creating it. This brings an artist to works that could be great, but it is not enough to make them durable. When the two thoughts coincide in a unique will, then you get a true masterpiece, full of light and long-lasting."[31] "What is happening right now is everything is related to the past. I think whatever happened in the past 100 years is the main subject of today. We are in-between generations; it's a borderline passage.…The whole society is using the past to defend itself from something we have never seen before."[32] "Are you obsessed with the zenith? I am."[33]

Maurizio Cattelan (b. 1960) is an Italian artist known for his satirical sculptures and installations that comment on contemporary society, challenging viewers to question reality and representation. Originally shown in 1997 at Secession, Vienna, *Dynamo Secession* powered the light bulbs of a dark basement room through the stationary cycling of two gallery attendants.

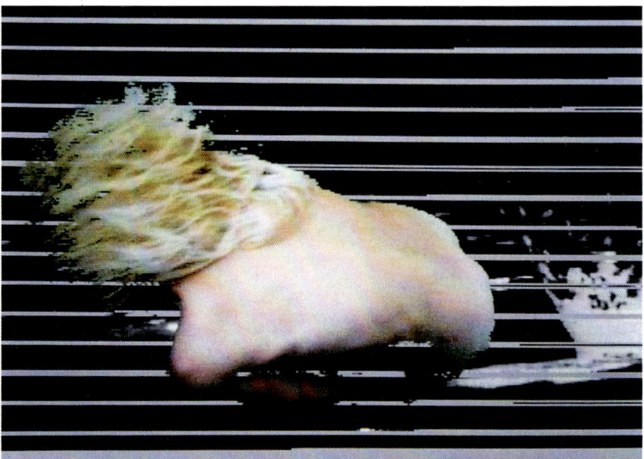

16

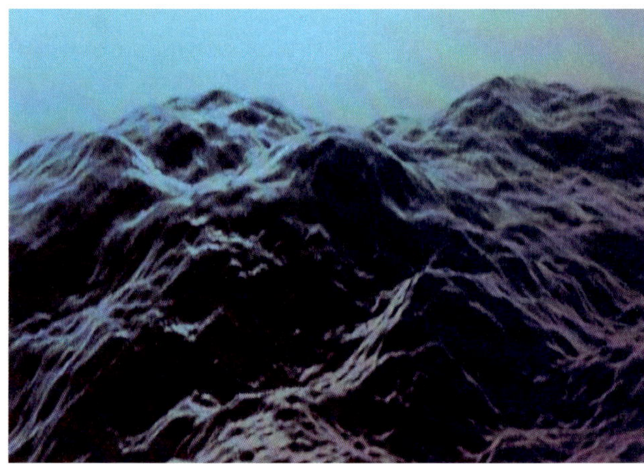

17

18

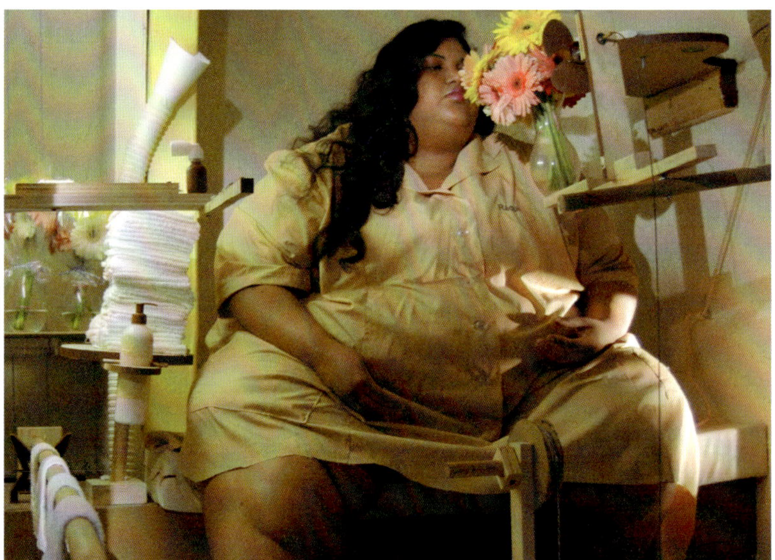

16   Pipilotti Rist
Selbstlos im Lavabad
(Selfless in the Bath of Lava)
(Bastard Version), 1994
Video, sound, mobile phone
6:20 min.

PIPILOTTI RIST "I love technology and machines — above all, they are carrying the souls of their inventors in themselves."[34] "I have a very sentimental relation to machines. I think that machines are like the testament of the people who invented them and developed them. I think the character of those people is preserved in the machines. So I try not to approach machines from a critical distance. On the contrary, I have always thought that if I can get close to them, I can melt together with them. If I treat them like another person, or like the echo of another person, then we can get along better.... Technology, especially audio and video technology, is a complete copy of our senses. For example, the RGB system tries to replicate how the cones and sticks in our eyes work: it's a very primitive copy of the eye, and I feel sympathy for it. It's only mass production that makes technology look like plastic, metal, and cables. Cameras and projectors look like anti-bodies, but they are actually complete copies of the body. Instead, people tend to have a misplaced fear of or respect toward technology. I like how younger people use machines much more spontaneously."[35]

Swiss video artist Pipilotti Rist's (b. 1962) vibrant and surreal multimedia work explores the intersection of technology, nature, and the human body through questions of reason versus instinct, sensuality, and media representation.

17   Seth Price
Untitled Film/Right, 2006
16 mm film, 14:00 min.
Dimensions variable
14:00 min.

SETH PRICE "I'm not really interested in technology.... I'm interested in the contemporary. In the life I live, in the corner of the world I'm in, if I say I'm interested in contemporary culture then I'm already talking about something that's heavily technologized. My work is as much oriented toward design or fashion or advertising as it is toward technology."[36] "This might seem romantic, but to be seen and named is great, it feels good, but it also makes it easier to quantify you in terms of value, and I don't just mean financial value, it can be critical value, social value, value for someone else. And those can be gilded chains. The more you are known, the more you are predictable and testable and constant, and can improve in value.... It's weird, for sure. I mean, if you're lucky enough to be made into value, you're in a good place. But it can be strange, it can be alienating. Although that's how it is for all of us, now: always being made into value. All these platforms are tools for changing material conditions. Just by using the tool,

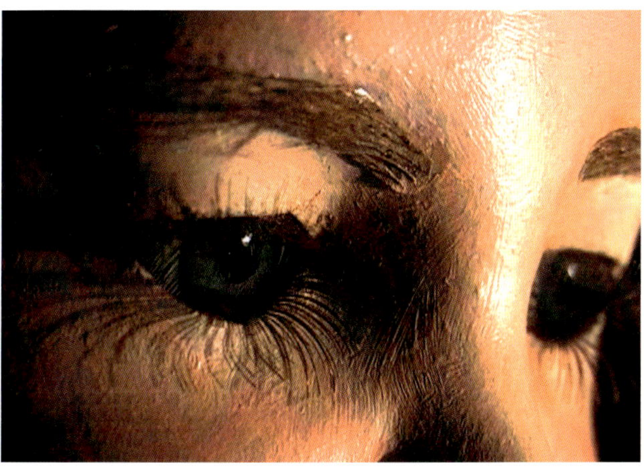

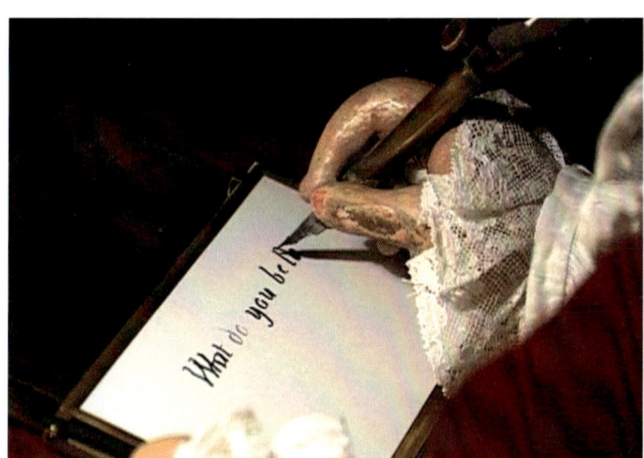

19

you're changing material conditions. Even if it's not happening for you, it's happening for someone. That's alienation, right there. I will tell you that we need to bring magic to materialism. That's my project."[37]

American artist Seth Price (b. 1973) uses sculpture, painting, video, and other digital processes to address the production, dissemination, and reception of contemporary images via digital technology and the internet.

18   Mika Rottenberg
Dough, 2006
Video, sound
5:52 min.

MIKA ROTTENBERG "All my works are self-reflexive, they are systems that question the systems. They are systems that destroy their own system. As much as our economy is now based in a way on abstraction (intellectual property, stock markets, etc.) and as much as we're going more and more towards the virtual, we are more than ever obsessed with making objects, there are so many disposable products being made, stuff that gets to be used for a second and then goes to trash, so maybe I try to give these sad objects a second life….I was always interested in what work is and the differences between work, labor and play. The very basic action of taking formless substance and giving them meaning and shape, organizing and cataloguing, that very human activity is one of the bases for my thought."[38]

MIKA ROTTENBERG "Artists are probably contemporary alchemists. Transforming banal material into a kind of gold, that transformation is interesting….Part of the alchemy is also to make things visible, bringing them to the surface."

DARIA DE BEAUVAIS "It occurred to me that the architectures of your works are metaphors of the human body, what do you think?"

ROTTENBERG "It is not so much like a parallel but an extension of the human body. Like in magic, you are able to control the external world with your mind. There is no separation between external and internal."[39]

Mika Rottenberg (b. 1976), an Argentine Israeli artist based in New York, creates surreal and often humorous video installations to explore labor, technology, and globalization. Frequently exaggerated and fantastical but nonetheless rooted in environments of production like factories, her videos comment on the exploitations and absurdity of the contemporary industrial world.

19   Philippe Parreno
The Writer, 2007
Video (color, sound) screened
on a LCD screen,
12 × 17.4 × 2 cm, 3:58 min.

PHILIPPE PARRENO "A chain is a dynamic structure that produces forms that are part of it: pre-production, production, post-production. These narrative instances depend upon each other. In the course of the chaining of

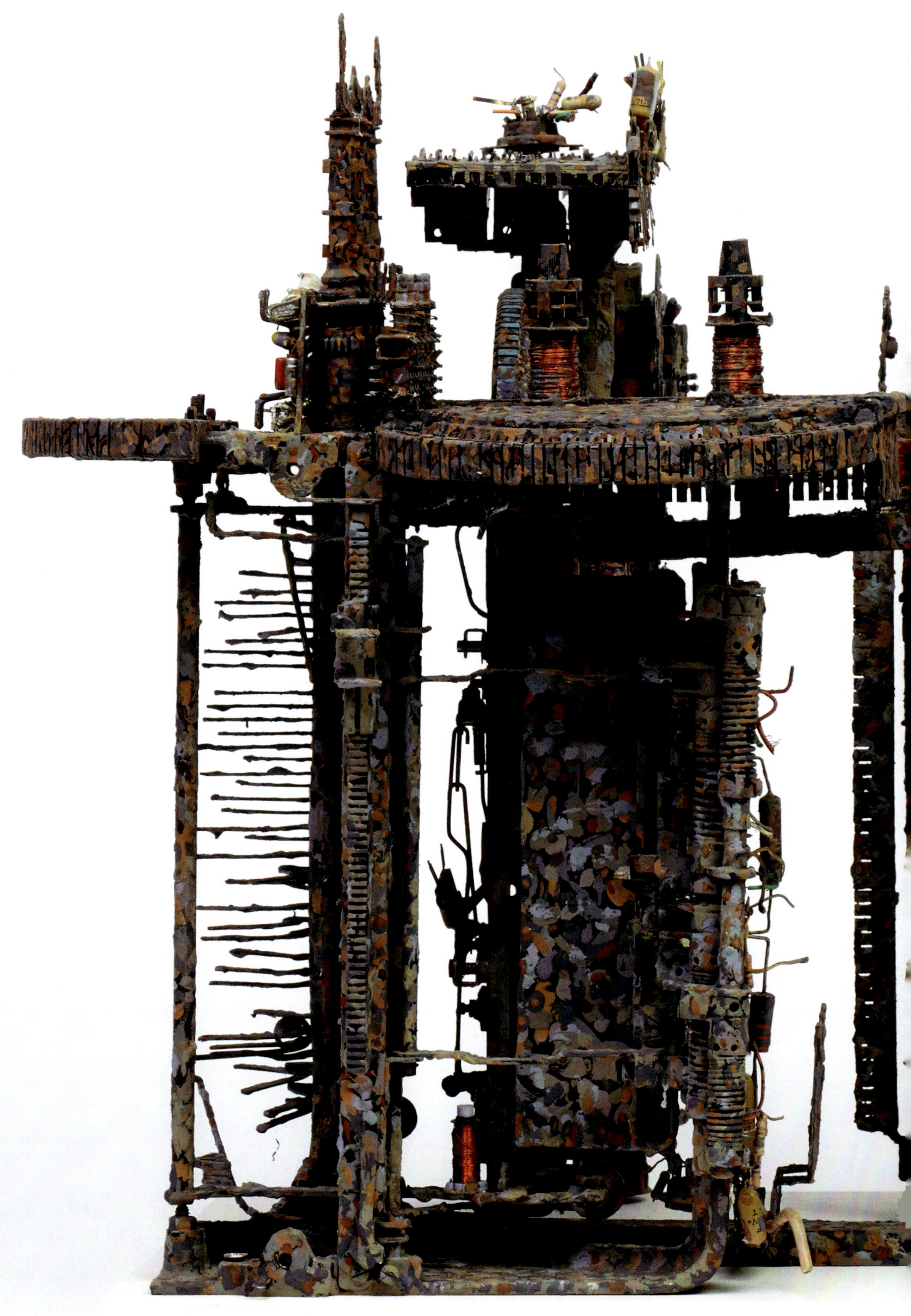

these sequences, a narrative unfolds. An image, a building, or a film comes from a more vast narrative structure, to which they belong and which they are elements of. In robotics, we use a very precise term, but I don't remember it anymore. But we talk of the threshold of tolerance or linear adjustment to describe this interior time interval in which a number of events will produce themselves. This semiotic chain that I am talking about appears in this space.…Does everything really always start with a scenario and end with an object? Should there always be a happy ending? Why wouldn't there be many endings?…The degree of resolution of your ideas depends on an economic choice, which either you make, or is imposed on you.…There is still the tendency to solve a problem within a form. Whereas to me, it's exciting when the content overflows beyond the form.…What interests me is when it overflows in one way or another. It's the irresolution that is interesting."[40]

Through film, sculpture, performance, and drawing, French artist Philippe Parreno (b. 1964) explores how technology shapes human perception and interaction, often blurring the line between reality and fiction.

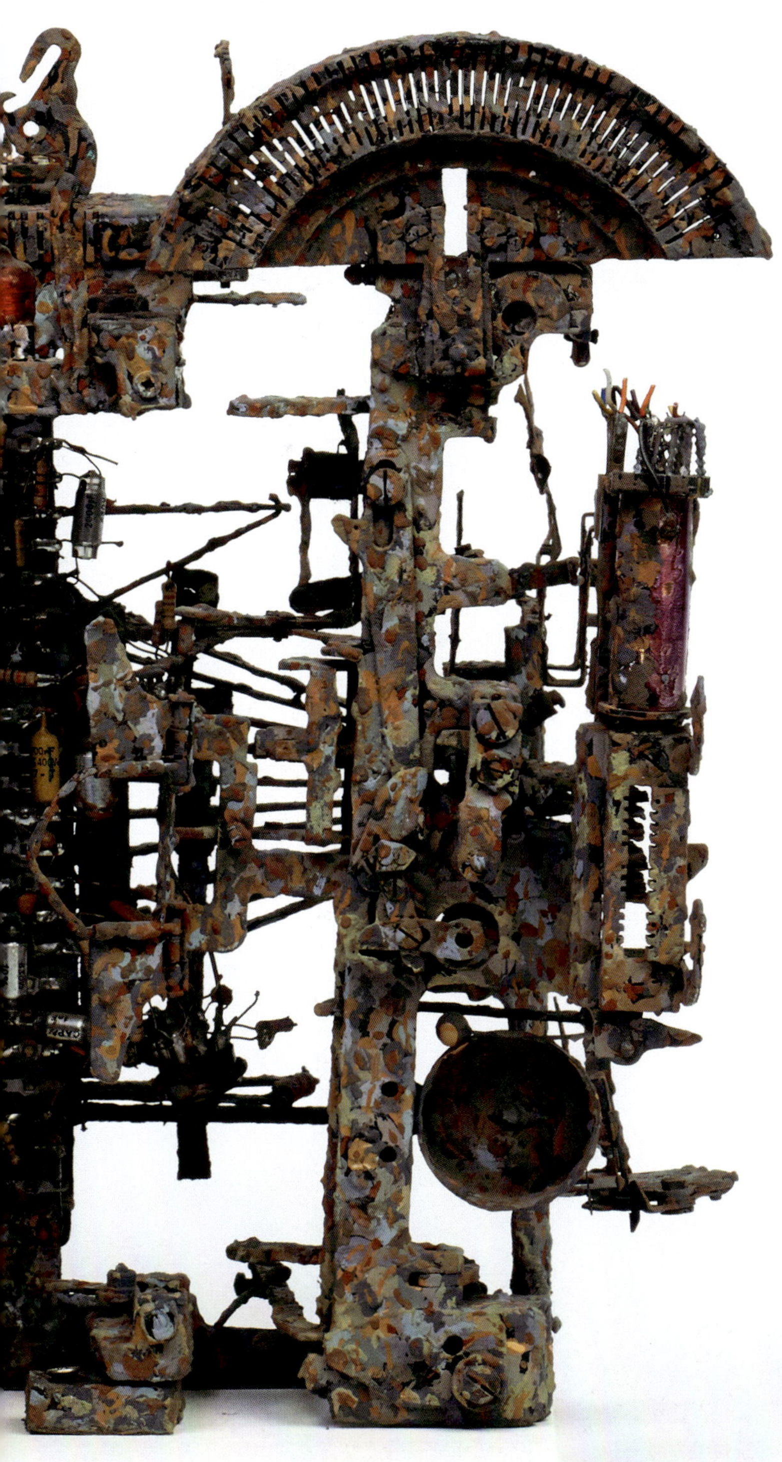

20 ACM
Untitled, c. 2010
Metal items, electrical
wire, plastic, wood,
mirror, paint, and glue
44 × 48 × 37 cm

ROBERTA SMITH "The point is that each piece casts its spell only at close range; you lean forward and enter a miniature, moldering world that one way or another seems to have accrued of its own accord."[41]

ACM (b. 1951)—the acronym by which the reclusive French sculptor is known—was originally trained as an artist before abandoning his studies to pursue his work more philosophically. With his wife, he relocated to the remote village of his birth, where he constructed a home and studio from what had been his father's warehouse. ACM began making sculptures from found objects that both plumb and manufacture a semi-fictional past.

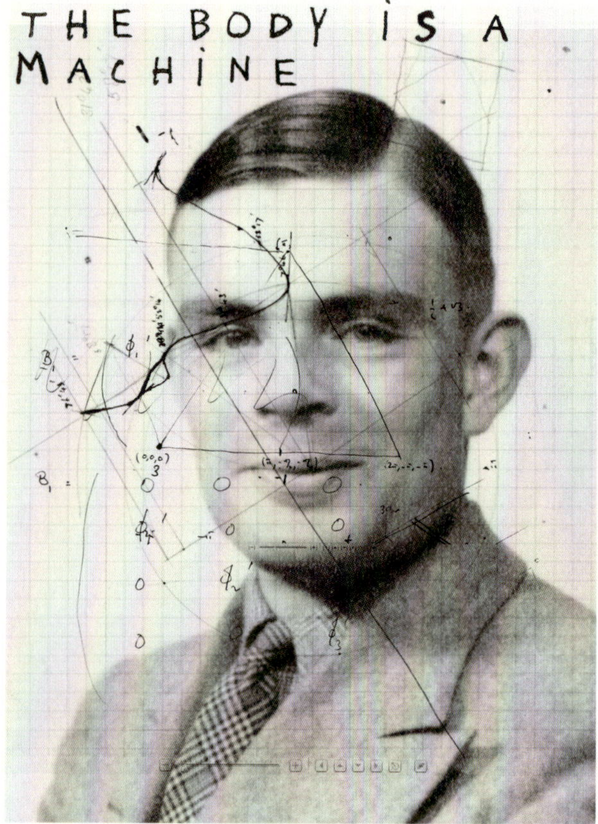

21

HENRIK OLESEN "Personally speaking, many of these formal and conceptual possibilities were opened up when I discovered that art could be based on texts, information, systems, processes — the materials of everyday life — and that these were all intertwined with the body and sexuality."[42] "In 1936, [Alan] Turing published a theoretical model of a machine that was to constitute the basis of all postwar computing, making him the father of all modern computer science. And this part of his biography is a futuristic tale about thinking machines, artificial intelligence and the appearance of possible future bodies.…When he was criminally prosecuted [in 1952], he was given female hormone injections as 'treatment' for his homosexuality, with very negative effects; he became impotent and his breasts grew larger.…Central to the story is not only the disappearance of Turing's body, but at the same time the arrival of the computer body, the thinking machine, or, as I like to think of it: concepts of 'the possible body.' And so this project turned into being about the 'making of new bodies,' suggesting a variety of associations."[43]

A Danish artist, Henrik Olsen (b. 1967) interrogates themes of identity and the social construction of bodies, utilizing found objects and computer-generated images to critique historical narratives and the societal norms that structure them. Olesen embarked on a years-long project focusing on the life of Alan Turing (1912–1954), the British mathematician and computer scientist, considered by many to be the father of artificial intelligence, who was subject to persecution for his homosexuality.

22

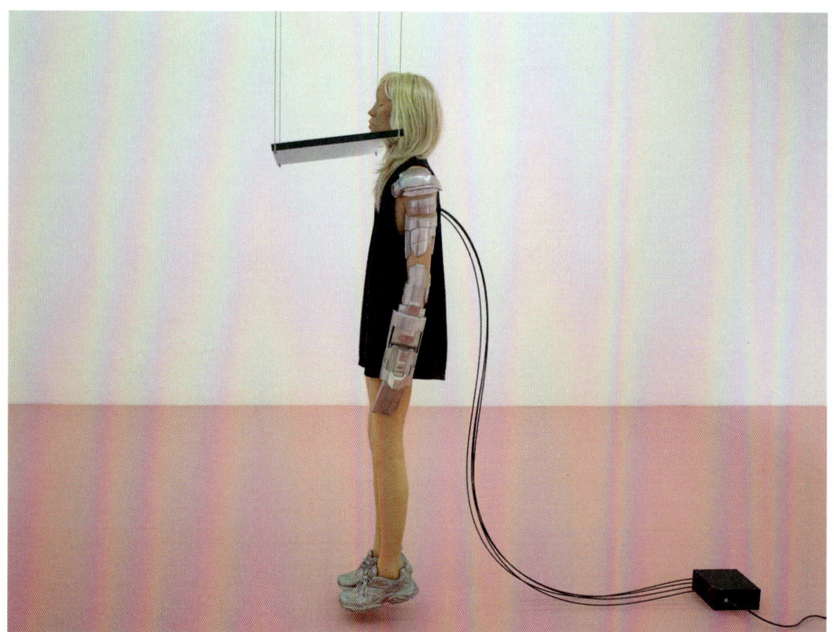

ANDRO WEKUA "In my work it's a question of attempting to create something artificial and natural — artificial figures that have to do with something real.…I try to create figures that function like actors, and are intended to play all those roles I can't play myself. And generally these figures don't have any eyes because they're not supposed to return your gaze. They're there purely as a projection, but they're definitely not Frankensteins or Pinocchios or anything like that.…They act out what disturbs me. They allow me to become an observer."[44]

Influenced by his experiences of civil war in his native Sochumi, Georgia (1991–93), Andro Wekua (b. 1977) uses painting,

sculpture, installation, and film to understand how individual and collective
memories are formed and to reckon with
the gap between those memories and
what actually happened.

23 Camille Henrot
    Dawg Shaming, 2017
    CNC milled ABS plastic body,
    prints button mount, receiver,
    internal components, resin
    buttons, paint, phone cord,
    4p4c jack, operating system:
    Raspbian Wheezy, custom
    software written in Python and
    Bash, sound card, mini-USB
    power supply, hall effect sensor,
    3.7 W amplifier, ⅛ jack, tactile
    momentary switch, 20 gauge
    silicone-insulated wire, solder,
    and perma- photo board
    44.5 × 26.7 × 8.9 cm

CAMILLE HENROT "It's about the problems
we all face individually, and how we search
for answers collectively, and what we are
willing to sacrifice in order to get those
answers. This ties into our relationship
with authority, not just language, but anything that has authority, especially things
we depend on like technology, govern-
ment, police, health care, religion, lovers,
pets. All these things inspired the hotline.
They lead you to some extreme wonder
about yourself and how other people think
about you. In a way, it's our interior world
being tortured by the outside world.…I use
technology, but it's never really the topic I'm
trying to address. It's more about human experience, and it's really difficult to talk about
human experience outside of technology. I
only interact with machines as a human being because, like everyone else, I use them
to connect with the rest of the world."[45]

Invested in knowledge systems and cultural narratives, Camille Henrot (b. 1978),
a French artist, works across media —
from sculpture to video, drawing, and installation — to question how information
and history are organized, understood,
and felt today. Her *Interphones* series of
phone sculptures use the format of self-
help hotlines to restage the experience of
using technology to seek out information
about oneself.

24 Nathalie Djurberg
    and Hans Berg
    It Will End in Stars, 2018
    Virtual reality

NATHALIE DJURBERG "It's still like a path, it's
only the next step, and then the next step, and
the next. And the discoveries and realizations
you do on that path…"
HANS BERG "Since the VR work is not linear,
the viewers can choose wherever they want
to go in that world, so I have less control of
how they will experience the music. It's more
connected to certain points and happenings,
rather than following a narration with a beginning and an end."[46]

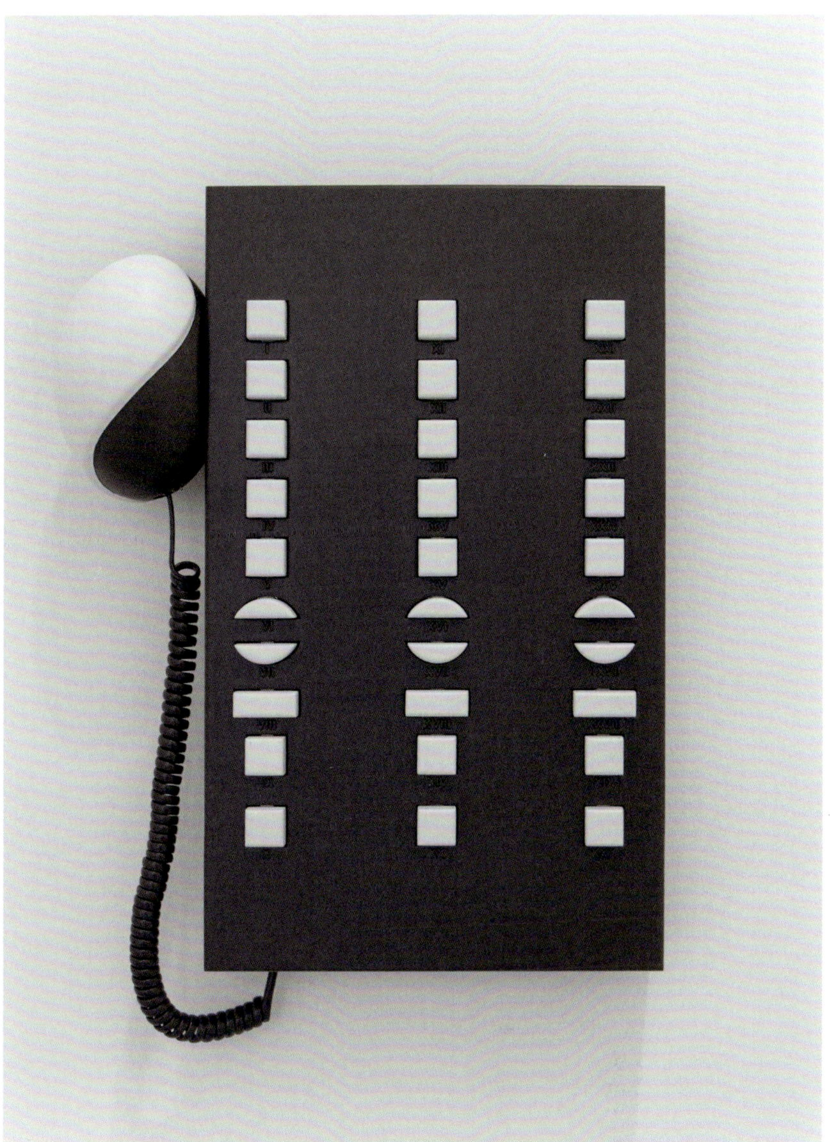

23

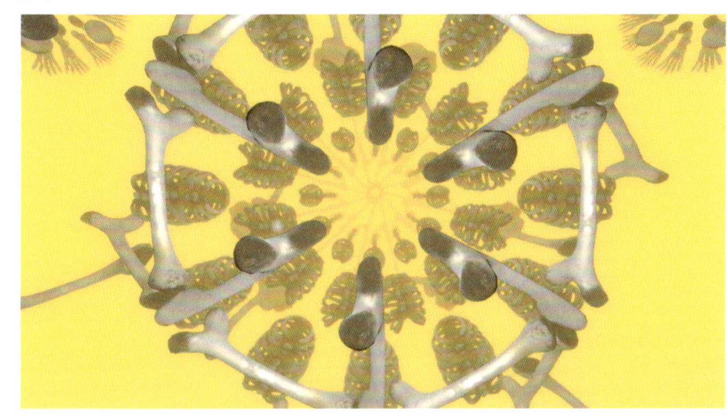

24

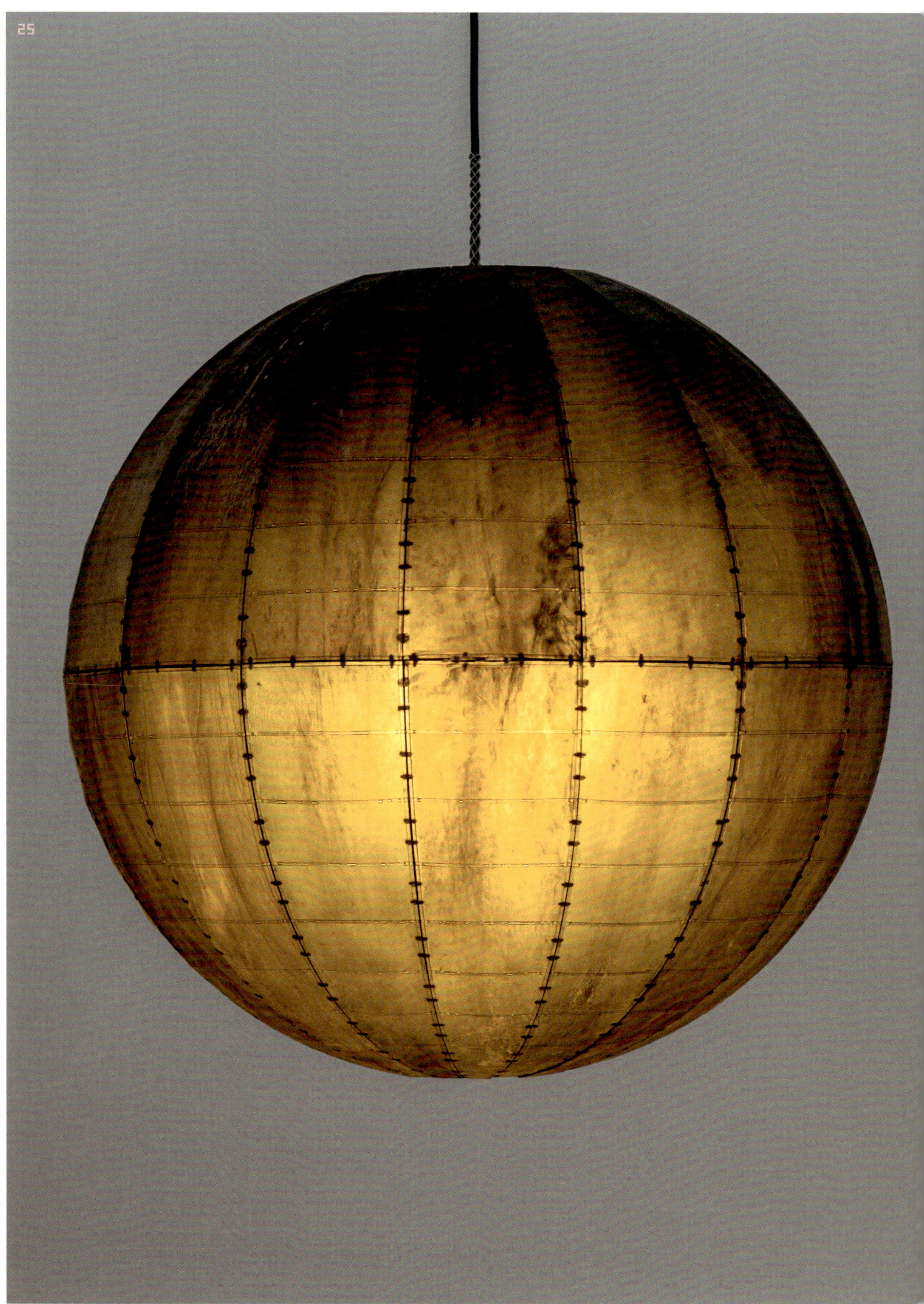

Swedish artists Nathalie Djurberg (b. 1978) and Hans Berg (b. 1978) collaborate on video installations that include the former's stop-motion animations and the latter's soundscapes, often featuring dark, surreal narratives and atmospheres. In 2018 they collaborated with Acute Art in creating *It Will End in Stars*, an immersive virtual reality experience where viewers move through an environment evoking unsettling fairy tales.

25 **Anicka Yi**
*Releasing the Human
from the Human*, 2019
Kelp, Aquazol, glycerin,
crepeline, acrylic, LED,
and animatronic insect
71.1 × 71.1 × 71.1 cm

ANICKA YI "I'm trying to be much more open to an absolute reality, versus the relative reality we concern ourselves with through culture. And that is the value of science for me, in that it can tell me about something beyond my own relative reality. Even though I may not perceive things in a certain way, I know that if I were to die, tomorrow, the sun will still come up in the morning, with or without me, and that there will be rain, there will be weather patterns with or without my experience of that reality. Another way of looking at it is really just to reposition, or maybe even *de-position* a certain kind of certainty.…One of the great lessons that I take from science is that you probably shouldn't be too attached to any certainty."[47]

Anicka Yi (b. 1971), born in South Korea and based in New York, seeks to decenter the human in thinking about biology and technology through installations that often combine organic and synthetic materials.

26 **Pamela Rosenkranz**
Healer (Waters), 2019
Robot, circuit board control units,
battery, LED light, 3D printed
head and tail, and Kirigami skin
120 × 6 × 6 cm

PAMELA ROSENKRANZ "Like a water surface that reflects rays of light always differently changes its appearance, but nevertheless always marks the transition from one world to the other, the shimmering snake appears, transmitter, link and intermediate being between the worlds. There the snakebot will inhabit — next to possible other designated places — the former ring of Japanese sumo wrestlers, the dohyo. This place, in Japan, is not just a ring, but a place inhabited by spirits. Yorishiro is where people and objects can be inhabited by deities and where the battle of good and evil is fought on a psychological and spiritual level. In the dohyo, the robot transcends all possibilities of its existence, as a device and animal that lives where the gods animate objects and beings."[48]

Swiss artist Pamela Rosenkranz (b. 1979) critically examines the impact of technology on both human perception and our relationship with the natural world. *Healer*, her series of animatronic snakes, combines that mythical animal symbol with cutting-edge biorobotics — informed by real snakebots used in science and medicine — to explore the effect of modern science on society.

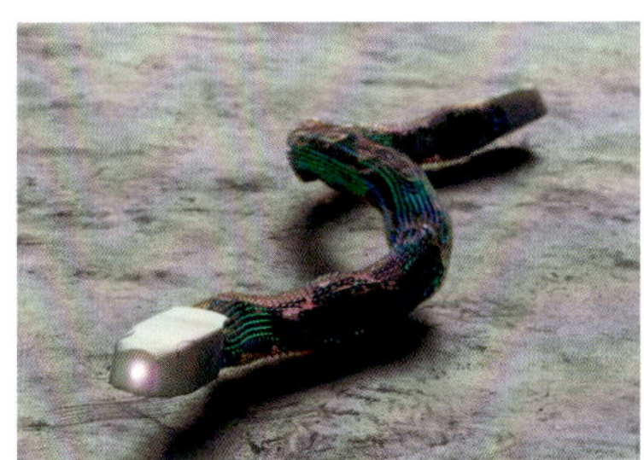

27 **Jeff Koons**
Apollo Wind Spinner, 2020–22
Steel, bronze, and two motors
1393.3 × 914.4 × 260.8 cm

JEFF KOONS "Technology is only a tool and there's no art in that technology; it's just a vehicle for you to realize ideas more clearly. And if it can help you be more precise in your communication of those ideas, fantastic. There's no real newness beyond the novelty of something. Within art, what presents itself as shocking and fresh is actually quite old.…There were always new technologies, whether it's the wheel, or irrigation, or fluid dynamics. We continue to readapt, but I do think that the time we live in is like a Renaissance. All of us have the most complete history of humankind at our fingertips."[49] "When I was working on this piece I was really thinking about enlightenment, almost literally. I was thinking about light. All life energy directs itself towards the sun.…To me it's all about becoming: it's about the way we, as humans, keep changing while still carrying within ourselves all these different narratives.…We live in a world that is still charged with stories and myths that have been told thousands of years ago. Embracing the world in all its richness also means listening to the stories that have accumulated across centuries. True meaning in life is carried by people, by their stories and narratives. It's not technology that carries meaning.…We need to transcend our own life, by being generous, by becoming one with others and the world. We need to transcend as a community."[50] "When I talk about transcendence, I'm talking about being in contact with the body and in contact with the mind and feeling a sense that there are new parameters for the self and that the self is being increased. The possibilities are being increased, the parameters are being increased — to me, that is transcendence. It doesn't have to do with the spiritual; it has to do with getting more out of life, more possibilities for the self."[51]

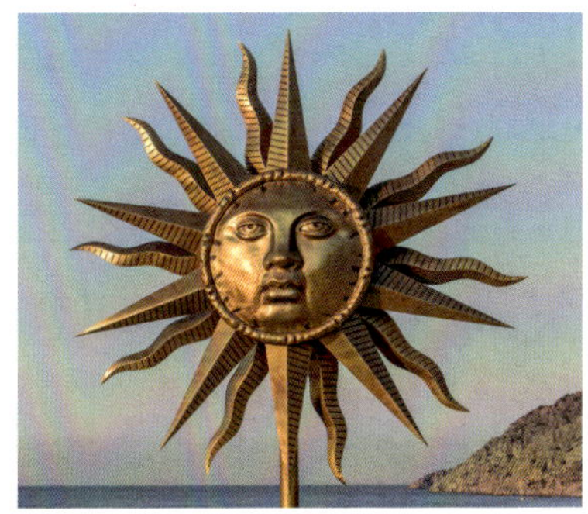

Jeff Koons (b. 1955) is an American artist whose sculptures and paintings are in dialogue with questions of art history and question notions of taste, consumerism, and the role of the artist. Working in the Duchampian idiom of the readymade, Koons draws out the tension between the fetishistic aesthetics of commodities and their play on the viewer's desires. Koons first exhibited *Apollo Wind Spinner* in his 2022 exhibition *Apollo* at the DESTE Slaughterhouse on Hydra; following a unanimous vote by the island's citizens, it remains, welcoming visitors into the harbor, on permanent loan.

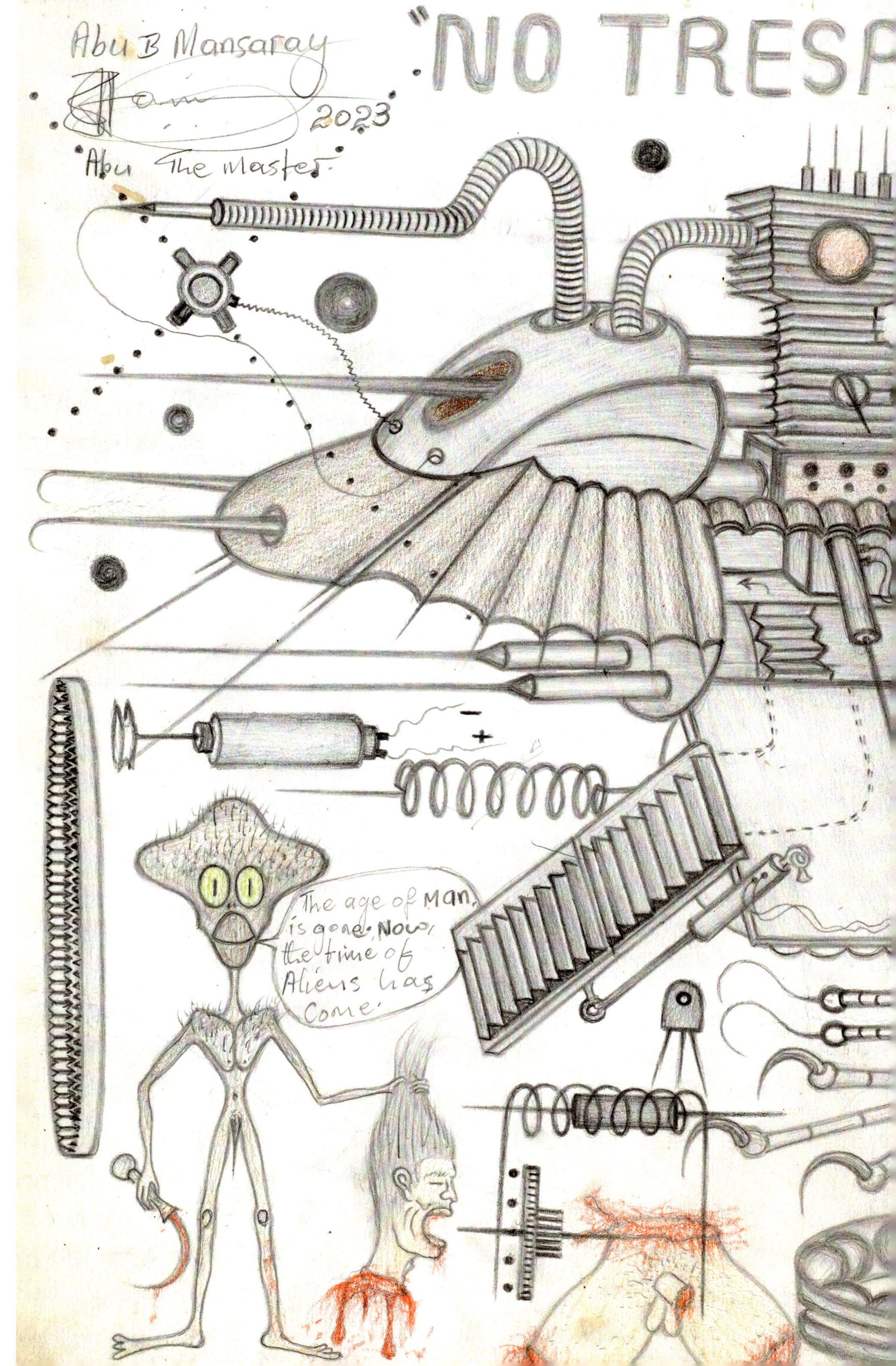

Abu B Mansaray
2023
"Abu The Master"
"NO TRESP
The age of Man,
is gone. Now,
the time of
Aliens has
come.

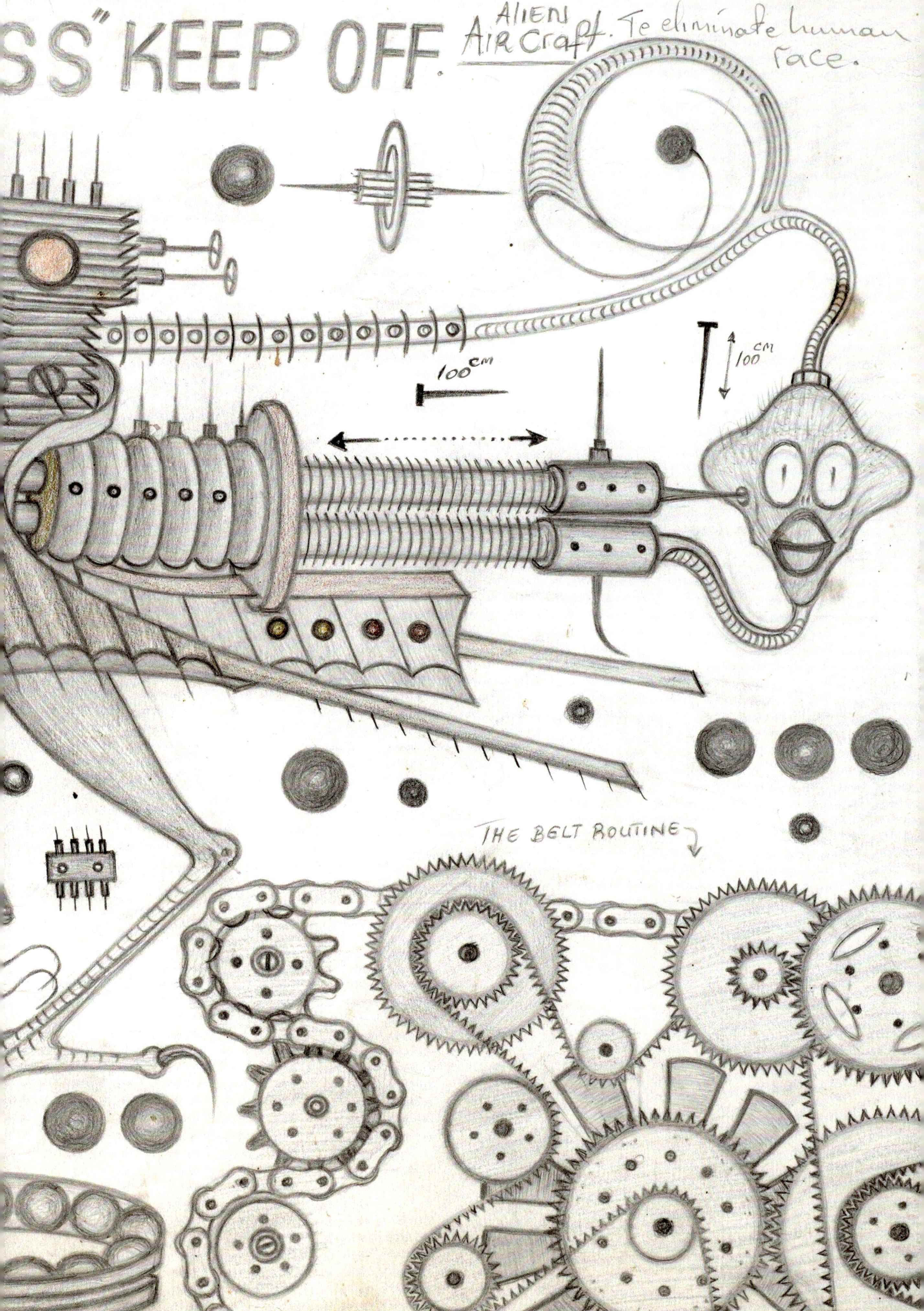
SS" KEEP OFF.
Alien Air Craft. Te eliminate human race.
100 cm
100 cm
THE BELT ROUTINE

28 Abu Bakarr Mansaray
NO TRESPASS KEEP OFF, 2021
Ink, colored pencil,
and pencil on paper
30 × 41.5 cm

ABU BAKARR MANSARAY "I am an artist making creations without limitation. I do drawings, paintings, sculptures…I also invent machines for my own use at home and sometimes for other people.…I like doing strange, complicated drawings and designing intricate machines inspired by scientific ideas that are at times beyond the human imagination.…I want people to feel the power of creation."[52]

A self-taught artist from Sierra Leone, Abu Bakarr Mansaray (b. 1970) creates intricately annotated diagrams of imaginary machines and creatures that blend science fiction with traditional African art. Informed by his experiences during the country's civil war (1991–2002), his drawings reflect a unique perspective on technology, warfare, and the human condition.

29 Judith Hopf
*Contrat entre les
Hommes et l'Ordinateur*, 2010
Ink on paper
Two sheets, 29.7 × 21 cm each

Phone User 5, 2021–22
Concrete
170 × 48.5 × 67 cm

JUDITH HOPF "I've noticed people always seem to feel like they are more informed today than ever due to technology, but I sincerely doubt that. Personally, I always seem to be losing content rather than gaining it, which is why I get so physical in my practice, even when I'm exploring technology. I have to say I'm really beginning to doubt if verbal communication is that useful in making people aware. Perhaps now is the time for much more emphasis on nonverbal gestures.…I'm really trying to slow down all the experiences I have. When you slow things down you see other parts of a scenario, things become visible and others become obscure. Artists today are so often trying to compete with technology, but I see myself really outside of the world of tech — not only generationally but also how much I interact with it. Saying that, I'm definitely part of it, you can't escape it. So, naturally, it becomes included in my thinking and my environment."[53]

German multimedia artist Judith Hopf (b. 1969) offers pointed critiques of technological advancement and its influence on human behavior and social structures.

CONTRAT ENTRE LES HOMMES ET L'ORDINATEUR

Preamble

1

The urgent situation which has arisen through the evolution of my body and spirit in relation to the use instruments, specifically the use of the electronic data processing machine, compels me, in the full tradition previously executed and other revolutions, to socially revive the philosophy of emancipation.

2

It is certainly true that this, my position, is a question of political nature and already for this reason unable to ceded to modern experts; neither to the professional scientists, the touch screen specialists, the web designe nor the professional politicians. No, the question manifesting itself in my body and spirit, the question thrustir me courageously forward and to take action, this is a question that fully and completely affects the freedo and the totality of our social future!

3

Now it has come that the human assets perception and production no longer have anything to do with one anothe

4

Now it has come that as a result of this, we are capable of producing more than we perceive and are inde capable of perceiving

5

In this manner, we have become slaves. Not, as one generally makes believe, slaves of machines of one's ow production - but rather slaves of our asset of perception - helpless at the mercy of each and every new instrumer

6

Helpless at the mercy of each and every new instrument we are capable of producing - no matter how ma it appears, no matter what murderous language it speaks, no matter in what mysterious ways we are held additionally touch it.

7

As this is now the situation from which it is no longer possible to retreat, as this is now the situation that ha repressively proliferated in our collective bodies, I now rise for the declaration of a vow:

Herewith, as of now and the present, shall be recorded that no instrument and also no electronic data processing machine shall in the future obstruct humanity from completing and being able to complete, in freedom, in thought and unassisted, the things it does and the relationships it creates. May the following apply:

WE DON'T KNOW ANYTHING

YOU DON'T KNOW ANYTHING

I DON'T KNOW ANYTHING
ABOUT LOVE

BUT
WE ARE NOTHING

OHO

YOU ARE NOTHING

OHO

I AM NOTHING

OHO

WITHOUT LOVE[1]

---

1   Quoted from The Magnetic Fields, *Death of Ferdinand de Saussure*, 69 Love Songs, 1999

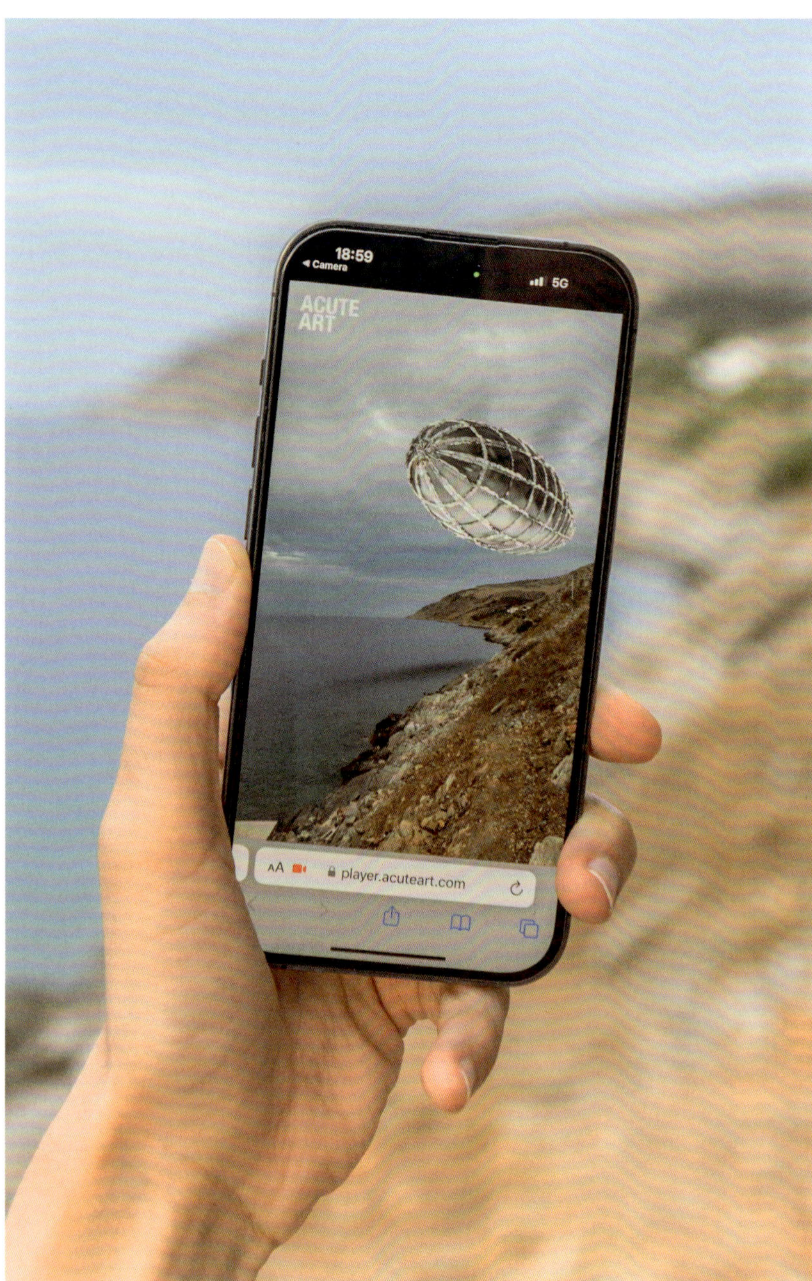

30

30 Lee Bul
Willing to Be Vulnerable –
Metalized Balloon
***VER.AR22*, 2022**
Augmented reality and NFT
Produced in collaboration
with Acute Art

LEE BUL "Usually I take a very utopian idea of the past — what we dreamed and what we tried and then what happened and then how can we use it still and how can it work still.…You can see this in the balloon…it's a kind of reminder of the Hindenburg. We have a kind of set memory about that. Maybe it's the dream of the modern, but at the same time it's floating in the air…space and air and lightness, then also a vision of technology or the future or something at the same time. It works still. I think we use 'the real,' this concept, it's very habitual.…Today it's probably most difficult to figure out about what is 'the real'…"[54]

Lee Bul (b. 1964), a South Korean artist, combines organic and architectural elements in her sculpture, installation, and performance to grapple with questions of technology's relationship to the body and memory. Bul's *Willing to Be Vulnerable* series (2015–ongoing) — exhibited here in augmented reality — stages an abandoned circus with a monumental aluminum foil model of the Hindenburg airship at its center; evoking the balloon's promise of technological progress that went up in flames, Bul questions collective hopes and memories.

31 Cao Fei
***Oz*, 2022**
Dual-screen video,
sound
1:36 min.

CAO FEI "*Oz* represents a blend of machine and human elements and the convergence of technology and humanity. Its sea creature-like qualities, reminiscent of an octopus, evoke a sense of suspension and mystery.…As we encounter this turning point in technological development, it becomes imperative for humans to navigate the complexities of a technologically driven world. Humans must find a renewed sense of purpose and forge new paths.…As we gradually transition into a post-human era, it becomes imperative to reevaluate the role of humans as central actors in the world. Emerging technologies play a significant role in this process, offering us new tools and perspectives to navigate the challenges and possibilities of life beyond the Anthropocene. It is crucial for humans to find new meanings and purpose. We need to reflect on our relationship with the world, as well as the impact of our actions on the planet."[55]

A pioneer of using virtual environments like *Second Life* in art-making, Cao Fei (b. 1978) creates multimedia work that explores the intersection of technology, fantasy, and daily life in her native China. Her art — like the digital avatar

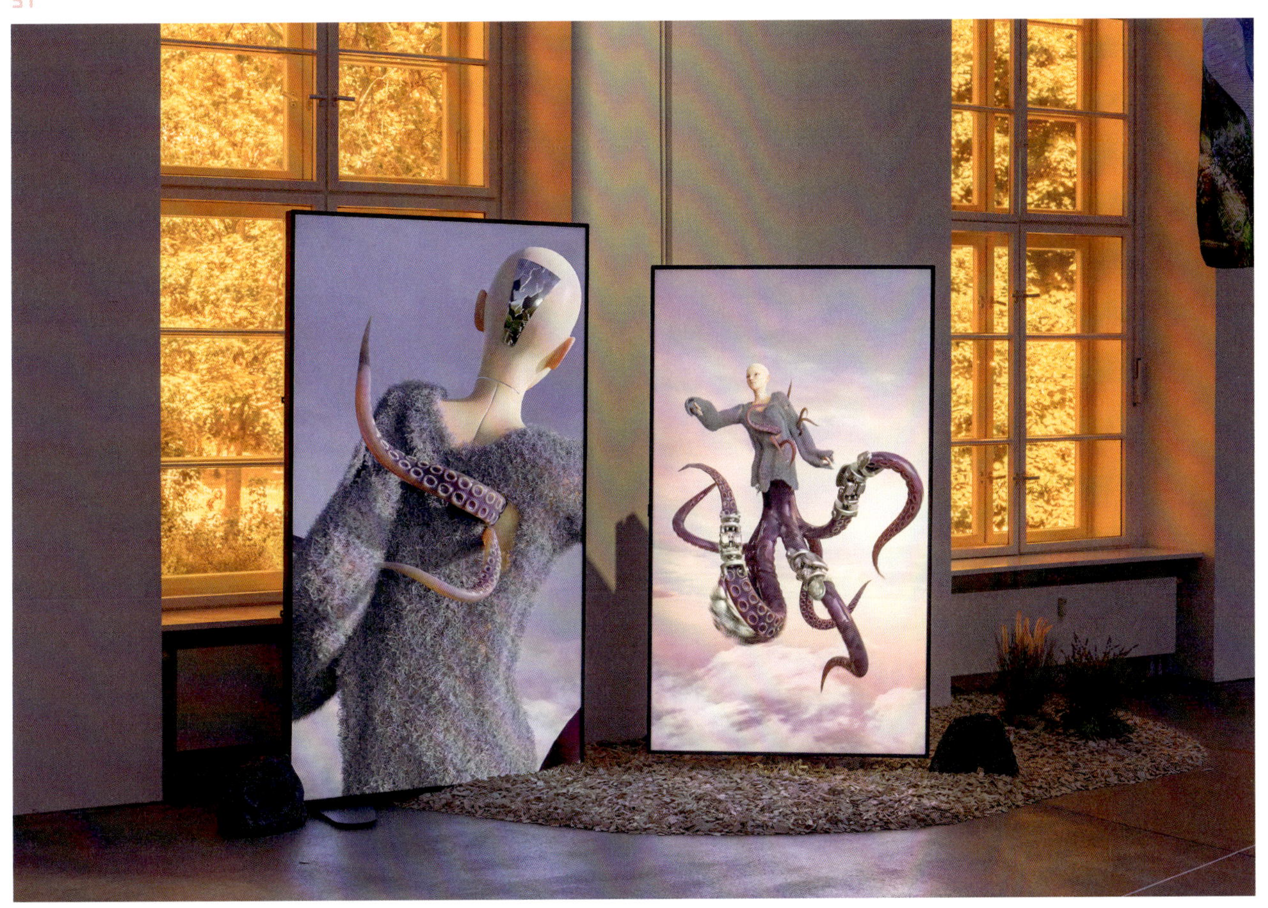

FIG.31 *Cao Fei: Duotopia*
Installation view, Sprüth Magers, Berlin, 2023

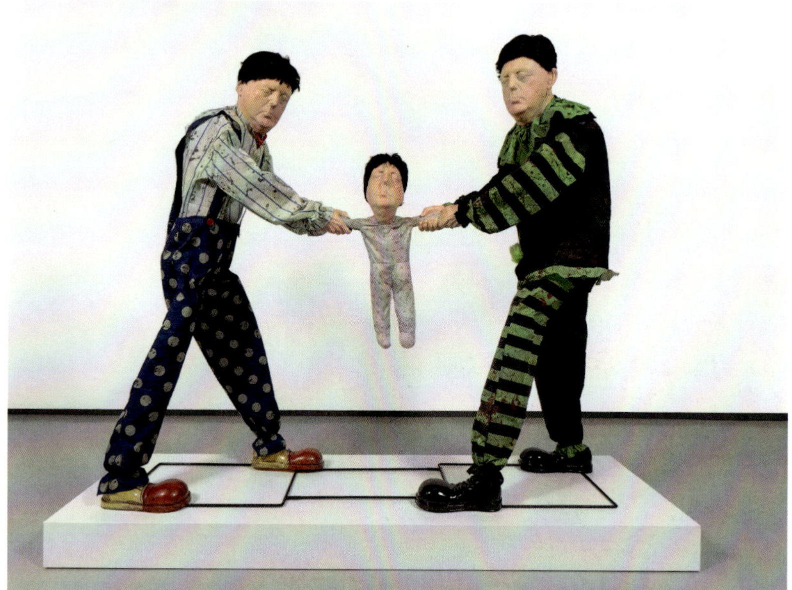

32

Oz — addresses the impact of virtual technologies on personal identity and social relationships.

32 **Urs Fischer**
Chalk & Cheese, 2022
Animatronics, chip,
acrylic paint,
silicon, and wigs
180.3 × 193 × 53.3 cm

URS FISCHER "People see that I use computers, so they say I'm making computer art. It's not about making computer art, it's just using the new thing…. You use all this stuff because it's normal. It's integrated into everything you do, from your car to how you talk to each other, how you share things, how you get your money and pay your rent. It's the same in art, it's just a natural thing."[56] "You have to trap the spirit of our times without getting trapped yourself…. I get bored easily, and I become restless."[57] "It's interesting what's possible, there's a lot more I can imagine that's not possible…. There's always this idea: new mediums make new art."[58]

In a genre-spanning practice that often incorporates found objects and invites viewer participation, Swiss artist Urs Fischer (b. 1973) blends sculpture, installation, photography, and digital media to challenge perceptions of space and time.

33 **Mire Lee**
*Look, I'm a fountain
of filth raving mad
with love; concrete
mixer sculpture*, 2022
Soft tentacles inside
concrete structure
45 × 40 × 30 cm

MIRE LEE "People often tether my animatronic sculptures to conversations about technology, but what's happening in my work is in fact fairly analog and runs counter to the slick aesthetic of new technologies and new media. What intrigues me is the gap between human fantasies of technology in an ideally rendered world, and real life, which is something that you can touch and smell, full of sagging subjects that have been deformed by their passage through time."[59] "Like poetry or mathematics, art is a concept that operates using its own language on its own terms. And it can be utterly transformational. There's so much that you cannot — and, perhaps, should never — articulate."[60]

Working primarily in sculpture and installation, Mire Lee (b. 1988) is a South Korean artist who often incorporates industrial and organic materials and technology into kinetic sculptures that explore desire and violence. In 2021–22, she was in a two-person show with H. R. Giger at the Schinkel Pavillon, Berlin, which *Frieze* described as a "biomechanical netherworld."[61]

     ENCOUNTERS WITH TECHNOLOGY

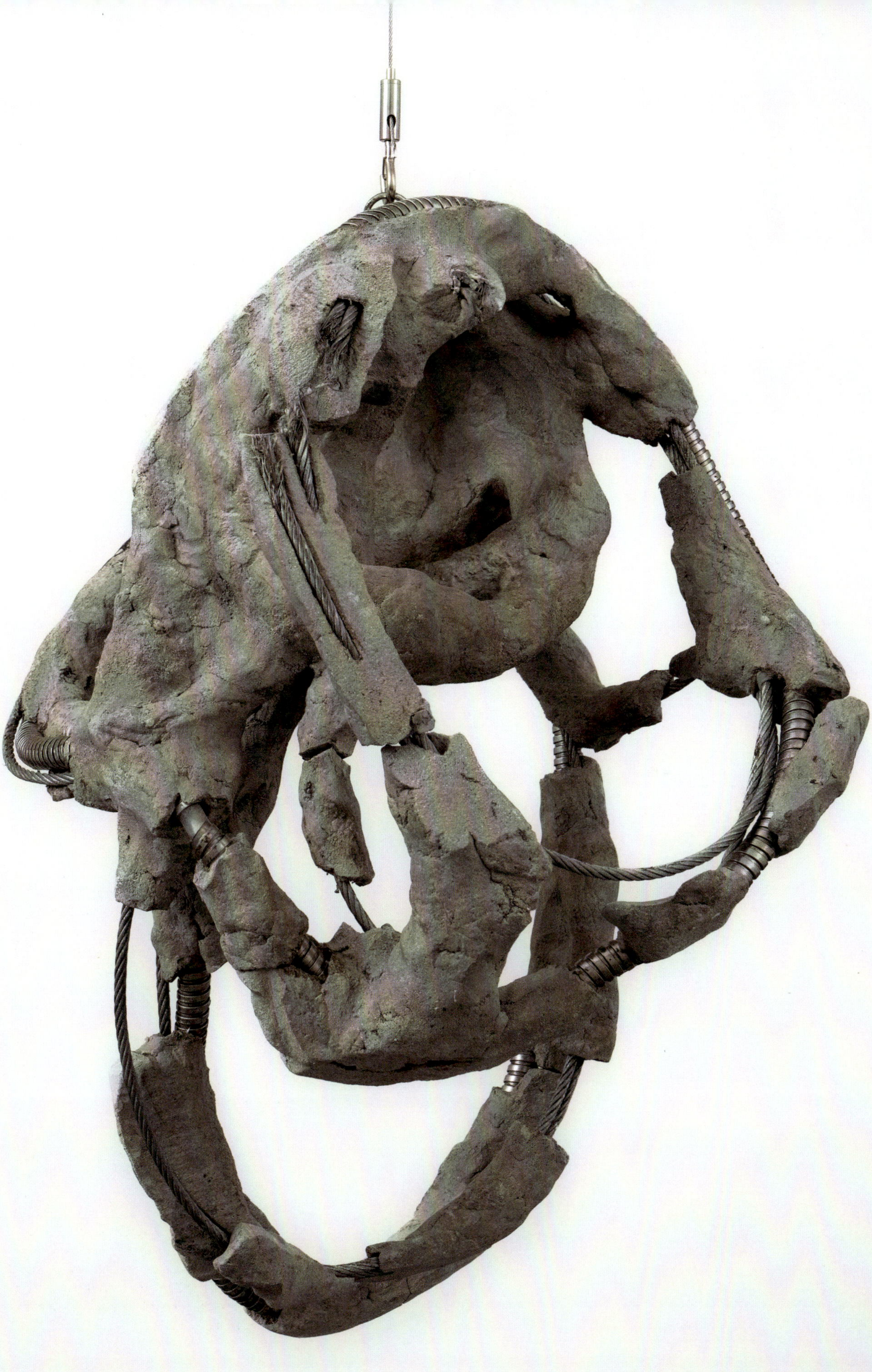

THE FOREMAN, *METROPOLIS* "Who told you to attack the machines, you fools? Without them you'll all die!"[62]

DAVID CRONENBERG "Technology is us. I mean, there is no separation. Technology is a pure expression of human creative will; that's what technology is.…It's more than an interface. We are it. We've absorbed it into our bodies.…Technology wants to be in our bodies because it sort of came out of our bodies.…Technology had to be an enhancement of powers that we knew we had as creatures. And then it gets more elaborate and more distant from us and more abstract. But it still all emanates from us. It is us. That's the main thing that we do."[63]

British film producer Jacqui Davies's film-essay was distributed as an invitation to the exhibition, published online, and shown on a tablet at the Slaughterhouse. Reflecting on cinematic meditations on technology's relationship to the human psyche and body, the collage of films includes excerpts from films such as *Metropolis* (1927) by Fritz Lang (1890–1976); *L'Arrivée d'un train en gare de La Ciotat* (1896) by the Lumière Brothers (Auguste Lumière, 1862–1954; Louis Lumière, 1864–1948); *Frankenstein* (1931) by James Whale (1889–1957); *2001: A Space Odyssey* (1968) by Stanley Kubrick (1928–1999); *Altered States* (1980) by Ken Russell (1927–2011); *Videodrome* (1983) by David Cronenberg (b. 1943); and *Ex Machina* (2014) by Alex Garland (b. 1970), among others.

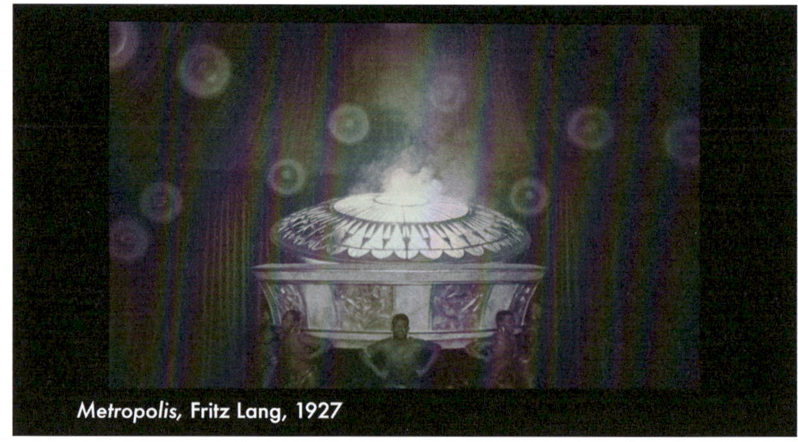

Metropolis, Fritz Lang, 1927

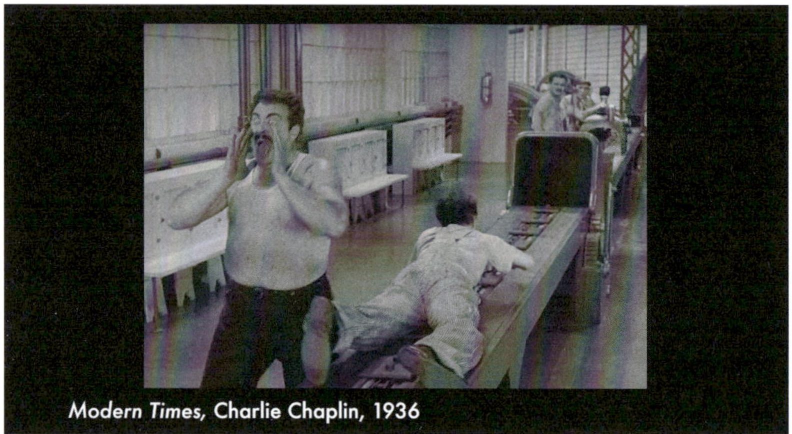

Modern Times, Charlie Chaplin, 1936

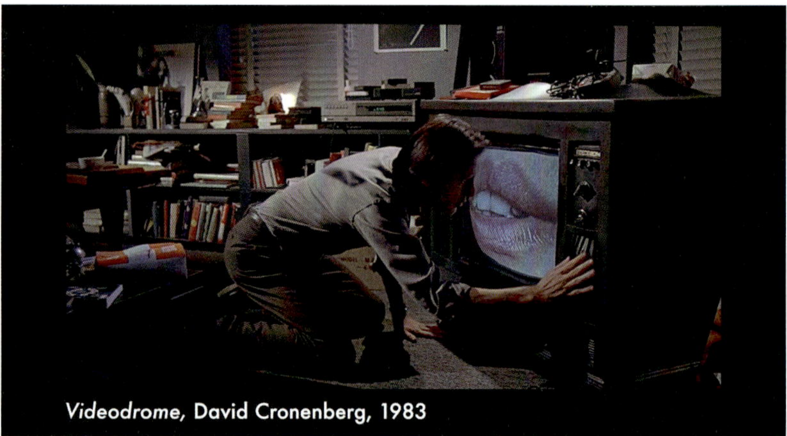

Videodrome, David Cronenberg, 1983

34

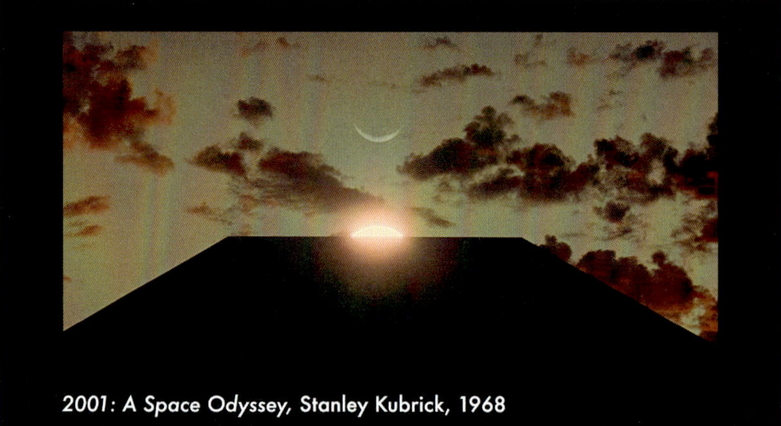

2001: A Space Odyssey, Stanley Kubrick, 1968

Endnotes

01 —— John Haslam, *Illustrations of Madness* (London, 1810), 19–20, 31–32, 42.

02 —— Marcel Duchamp, in Calvin Tomkins, *Marcel Duchamp: The Afternoon Interviews* (New York: Badlands Unlimited, 2013), 47–49.

03 —— Ulf Linde, quoted in Franck Scurti, *Ulf Linde – Marcel Duchamp : Certifié pour copie conforme* (2003–11), film, 58 min., https://vimeo.com/ondemand/lindeduchampeng.

04 —— Jakob Mohr, inscription on *Beweiße*, in *Jakob Mohr*, ed. Doris Noell-Rumpeltes and Thomas Röske, trans. Brian Currid (Heidelberg, Sammlung Prinzhorn; Berlin, Kerber, 2018), 68, 72.

05 —— Wilhelm Reich, *The Orgone Energy Accumulator: Its Scientific and Medical Use* (Rangeley, ME: Wilhelm Reich Foundation, 1951), 12, 45.

06 —— Wilhelm Reich, *Selected Writings: An Introduction to Orgonomy* (New York: Farrar, Straus and Giroux, 1973), 517.

07 —— Duchamp to Alfred Stieglitz, May 22, 1922, in *The Essential Writings of Marcel Duchamp*, ed. Michel Sanouillet and Elmer Peterson (London: Thames & Hudson, 1975), 165.

08 —— Marcel Duchamp, "The Creative Act," in Robert Lebel, *Marcel Duchamp* (New York: Grove, 1959), 78.

09 —— Jodi Ritacca, "News Report on Emery Blagdon," aired January 1, 1980, on KNOP-TV (North Platte, Nebraska), available on Nebraska Public Media, https://nebraska-publicmedia.org/en/series-media/non-series-video/knop-tv-1980-news-report-on-emery-blagdon-50015471/.

10 —— Dan Dryden, "Re: Emery Blagdon, Dan Dryden Recollections, 1987," John Michael Kohler Arts Center Archives.

11 —— "Plattform: On Circuits and Networks, Ulla Wiggen in conversation with Steinar Sekkingstad," Bergen Kunsthall, November 17, 2018, video, 42:32 min., https://vimeo.com/313161733.

12 —— Brion Gysin, "Dreamachine," in *Brion Gysin Let the Mice In*, ed. Jan Herman (West Glover, VT: Something Else, 1973), 29.

13 —— Ian Sommerville, "Flicker," in *Brion Gysin Let the Mice In*, 25–26.

14 —— Ulla Wiggen, quoted in Sofia Curman, "Ulla Wiggen – återkomsten," Konstnärernas Riksorganisation, https://kro.se/konstn%C3%A4ren/konstnaren-2-2020-coronakrisen-i-konsten/ulla-wiggen-aterkomsten/ (translated from Swedish).

15 —— Ulla Wiggen, quoted in Katya Sandomirskaja, "Circuit machines – Ulla Wiggen's painting at the intersection between body and machine" (master's thesis, Södertörn University, 2017), 6 (translated from Swedish).

16 —— H. R. Giger, quoted in Steve Rose, "Alien designer HR Giger: 'I am afraid of my visions,'" *Guardian*, May 14, 2014, https://www.theguardian.com/film/2014/may/14/hr-giger-film-artist-alien-i-am-afraid-of-my-visions.

17 —— H. R. Giger, quoted in "HR Giger Works Weekends," *Vice*, May 13, 2014, https://www.vice.com/en/article/5gdnmb/hr-giger-works-weekends.

18 —— Timothy Leary, quoted in Douglas Martin, "H. R. Giger, Artist Who Gave Life to 'Alien' Creature, Dies at 74," *New York Times*, May 13, 2014, https://www.nytimes.com/2014/05/14/arts/h-r-giger-swiss-artist-dies-at-74-his-vision-gave-life-to-alien-creature.html. Leary, the well-known guru of psychedelic drugs, was a friend of Giger's.

19 —— Takis, quoted in "Takis," exhibition guide, Tate Modern, July 3–October 27, 2019, https://www.tate.org.uk/whats-on/tate-modern/takis/exhibition-guide.

20 —— Takis, interview by Jenke Van den Akkerveken, "Communicating Energies: Takis on magnetism, truth, hope, and water," in *Takis – The Fourth Dimension*, exh. cat. (Antwerp: Vervoordt Foundation, 2012), 5.

21 —— Duchamp to Takis, 1961, quoted in Sanouillet and Peterson, eds., *The Essential Writings of Marcel Duchamp*, 169.

22 —— Vera Molnár, "Vera Molnár in conversation with Hans Ulrich Obrist," in *Book Marks: Revisiting Hungarian Art of the 1960s and 1970s*, ed. Katalin Székely (Cologne: Walther König, 2018), 77.

23 —— Ibid., 80.

24 —— Vera Molnár, in Zsofi Valyi-Nagy, "An Interview with Vera Molnár," *Right Click Save*, August 26, 2022, https://www.rightclick-save.com/article/an-interview-with-vera-molnar.

25 —— Peter Fischli and David Weiss, quoted in "The Odd Couple," *Frieze*, no. 102, October 2006, https://www.frieze.com/article/odd-couple.

26 —— Marcel Duchamp, talk delivered at the Museum of Modern Art, New York, October 19, 1961, quoted in Sanouillet and Peterson, eds., *The Essential Writings of Marcel Duchamp*, 141–42.

27 —— Sturtevant, "The Reluctant Indifference of Marcel Duchamp," unpublished essay, 1994.

28 —— Sturtevant, quoted in Daniel Birnbaum, "Sampling the Globe," *Artforum* 43, no. 2 (October 2004): https://www.artforum.com/features/sampling-the-globe-169688.

29 —— Thomas Bayrle, quoted in Janique Vigier, "Thomas Bayrle's Productive Doubt," *Frieze*, August 18, 2024, https://www.frieze.com/article/thomas-bayrles-productive-doubt.

30 —— Thomas Bayrle, interview by Massimiliano Gioni, in *Thomas Bayrle: Playtime* (New York: New Museum; London: Phaidon, 2018).

31 —— Maurizio Cattelan, quoted in Rita Vitorelli, "'If I tell you I have to kill you with my laser vision,'" *Spike*, December 5, 2018, https://spikeartmagazine.com/articles/if-i-tell-you-i-have-to-kill-you-with-my-laser-vision.

32 —— Maurizio Cattelan, in "Charm Like a Drug: Maurizio Cattelan with Jarrett Earnest," *Brooklyn Rail*, December 2011–January 2012, https://brooklynrail.org/2011/12/art/charm-like-a-drugmaurizio-cattelan-with-jarrett-earnest#.

33 —— Maurizio Cattelan, in "'Bananas are a contemporary mirror.' Maurizio Cattelan in conversation with Virgil Abloh," *Flash Art*, March 23, 2020, https://flash---art.com/article/bananas-are-a-contemporary-mirror-maurizio-cattelan-in-conversation-with-virgil-abloh/.

34 —— Pipilotti Rist, interview by Nina Azzarello, "Interview with Pipilotti Rist as Major Exhibit Opens at the Louisiana Museum of Modern Art," *designboom*, March 17, 2019, https://www.designboom.com/art/pipilotti-rist-interview-louisiana-museum-denmark-03-17-2019/.

35 —— Pipilotti Rist, interview by
Massimiliano Gioni, in *Pipilotti
Rist: Pixel Forest* (New York: New
Museum; London: Phaidon, 2016).

36 —— Seth Price, interview by
Will Fenstermaker, *Brooklyn
Rail*, November 2018,
https://brooklynrail.org/
2018/11/art/SETH-PRICE-
with-Will-Fenstermaker.

37 —— Seth Price, interview by
Emmanuel Olunkwa, "The
Object Talk: Seth Price,"
Pioneer Works, January 19, 2021,
https://pioneerworks.org/
broadcast/seth-price-interview.

38 —— "Down the Rabbit Hole or Through
the Looking Glass?: Interview
between Mika Rottenberg and
Daria de Beauvais," in *Mika
Rottenberg* (Paris: Palais de
Tokyo, 2016), 89.

39 —— Ibid., 87–88.

40 —— Philippe Parreno, in
conversation with Hans Ulrich
Obrist, 2001–2.

41 —— Roberta Smith, "A. C. M.,
Mansaray, Rigo 23 &
Volyazlovsky," *New York Times*,
August 20, 2010, https://www.
nytimes.com/2010/08/20/arts/
design/20galleries-001.html.

42 —— Nicholas Cullinan,
"1000 Words: Henrik Olesen,"
Artforum 48, no. 2
(October 2009):
https://www.artforum.com/
features/1000-words-
henrik-olesen-192153/.

43 —— Henrik Olsen, quoted in Luigi
Fassi, "Future Bodies and
Gendered Prophecy: Henrik
Olesen," *Mousse*, April 1, 2009,
https://www.moussemagazine.it/
magazine/henrik-olesen-
luigi-fassi-2009/.

44 —— Andro Wekua, in "Wait to Wait:
Boris Groys with Andro Wekua,"
filip 9, Winter 2009, 9.

45 —— Camille Henrot, interview by
Michael Barron, *Bomb*, January 15,
2016, https://bombmagazine.org/
articles/2016/
01/15/camille-henrot/.

46 —— Nathalie Djurberg and Hans Berg,
in Kathi Kaeppel, "It Always
Starts With an Idea," *Shirn*,
February 25, 2019, https://www.
schirn.de/en/magazine/
interviews/2019_interview/
interview_exhibition_nathalie_
djurberg_hans_berg/.

47 —— Anicka Yi, interview by Gary
Zhexi Zhang, "Anicka Yi: 'I'm
Very, Very Squeamish with
Culture,'" *ArtReview*, October
11, 2021, https://artreview.com/
anicka-yi-i-am-very-
squeamish-with-culture-
interview-tate-turbine/.

48 —— Pamela Rosenkranz, interview
by Shumon Basar, "Egg Watching:
Pamela Rosenkranz,"
Office, November 6, 2019,
https://officemagazine.net/
egg-watching.

49 —— Jeff Koons, interview by
Harriet Lloyd-Smith, "At Home
with Jeff Koons," *Wallpaper*,
October 9, 2022,
https://www.wallpaper.com/
art/at-home-with-
jeff-koons-interview.

50 —— Jeff Koons, interview by
Katerina Zacharopoulou, in
Jeff Koons: Apollo (Athens:
DESTE Foundation, 2023), 99.

51 —— Jeff Koons, interview by Hans
Ulrich Obrist, in *Jeff Koons:
The Conversation Series*, ed.
Karen Marta (Cologne: Walther
König), 72.

52 —— Abu Bakarr Mansaray,
quoted in "Abu Bakarr
Mansaray," The Jean Pigozzi
African Art Collection,
https://www.caacart.com/
artiste/mansaray-abu-bakarr/.

53 —— Judith Hopf, quoted in Penny
Rafferty, "Judith Hopf:
Embodying Technology," *Elephant*,
February 19, 2018,
https://elephant.art/
judith-hopf-becoming-tech/.

54 —— Lee Bul, interviewed in "2016
Artist Interview Series:
Lee Bul," Biennale of Sydney,
May 20, 2016, YouTube video,
4:41, https://www.youtube.com/
watch?v=_LiALXRUv9Y.

55 —— Cao Fei, interview by Günseli
Yalcinkaya, "Cao Fei's Duotopia
Is a Trippy Look into the Future
of Technology," *Dazed*, June 1,
2023, https://www.dazeddigital.
com/art-photography/article/
59975/1/cao-fei-duotopia-spruth-
magers-technology-future.

56 —— Urs Fischer, quoted in
"Urs Fischer: Natural Order,"
ArtFlyer, 2015,
https://artflyer.net/urs-
fischer-exclusive-
interview-studio-nyc/.

57 —— Ibid.

58 —— Urs Fischer, interview by
Oliver Maxwell Kupper,
"The Sacred and the Mundane:
An Interview of Urs Fischer
and Madeline Hollander,"
Autre, Summer 2019,
https://autre.love/
sacred-and-mundane-urs-
fischer-jeffrey-deitch-
madelin-hollander.

59 —— Mire Lee, interview by
Cassie Packard, "Mire Lee
on the Cannibalistic
Imagination," *Artforum*,
July 6, 2023,
https://www.artforum.com/
columns/mire-lee-
on-the-cannibalistic-
imagination-252809/.

60 —— Mire Lee, interview by
Alvin Li, "Mire Lee's
Deep-Rooted Romanticism,"
Frieze, no. 229, September 2022,
https://www.frieze.com/
article/mire-lees-deep-
rooted-romanticism.

61 —— Mitch Speed, "H. R. Giger
and Mire Lee's Biomechanical
Netherworld," *Frieze*,
no. 224, January/February 2022,
https://www.frieze.com/
article/mire-lee-and-hr-giger-
review-2021.

62 —— The Foreman, in *Metropolis*,
directed by Fritz Lang (1927).

63 —— David Cronenberg, interview by
Allen White, 1999, *Unclean Arts*,
https://uncleanarts.com/
interview-david-cronenberg/.

Contributors

Contributors

DANIEL BIRNBAUM

The artistic director of Acute Art, a laboratory for art and technology in London, Birnbaum curated the Venice Biennale in 2009; from 2010 to 2019, He was the director of Moderna Museet in Stockholm. He is a contributing editor of *Artforum*, and his most recent publication is the novel *Dr. B.*, published by Gallimard in 2021, and translated into nine languages.

JAKE BRODSKY

A writer, researcher, and editor of art books based in New York. Focusing on American art of the twentieth and twenty-first centuries, Jake Brodsky understands artists' writings and archives to be instrumental in establishing new narratives in art history. He contributed to the DESTE book for Jeff Koons's *Apollo* project at the Slaughterhouse.

MASSIMILIANO GIONI

The Edlis Neeson Artistic Director of the New Museum in New York and the artistic director of the Fondazione Nicola Trussardi in Milan. A frequent collaborator of the DESTE Foundation, Massimiliano Gioni has organized many exhibitions with DESTE and has collaborated on numerous publications, including the series *2000 Words*.

MICHELLE KUO

Chief Curator-at-Large and Publisher of The Museum of Modern Art in New York. Michelle Kuo serves on the advisory boards of the Museum Brandhorst, Munich, and the journal *October;* from 2010 to 2017 she was the Editor-in-Chief of *Artforum International*. Her publications include *Sensing the Future: Experiments in Art and Technology* (Getty, 2024).

BEN LIVNE WEITZMAN

A curator and writer based in Frankfurt. Ben Livne Weitzman is CEO and cofounder of WAVA, an augmented exhibition platform. An editor-at-large at PASSE-AVANT, His writings have been featured in various catalogues, publications, and magazines, including *Arts of the Working Class*, *Ocula Magazine*, and *Frieze*.

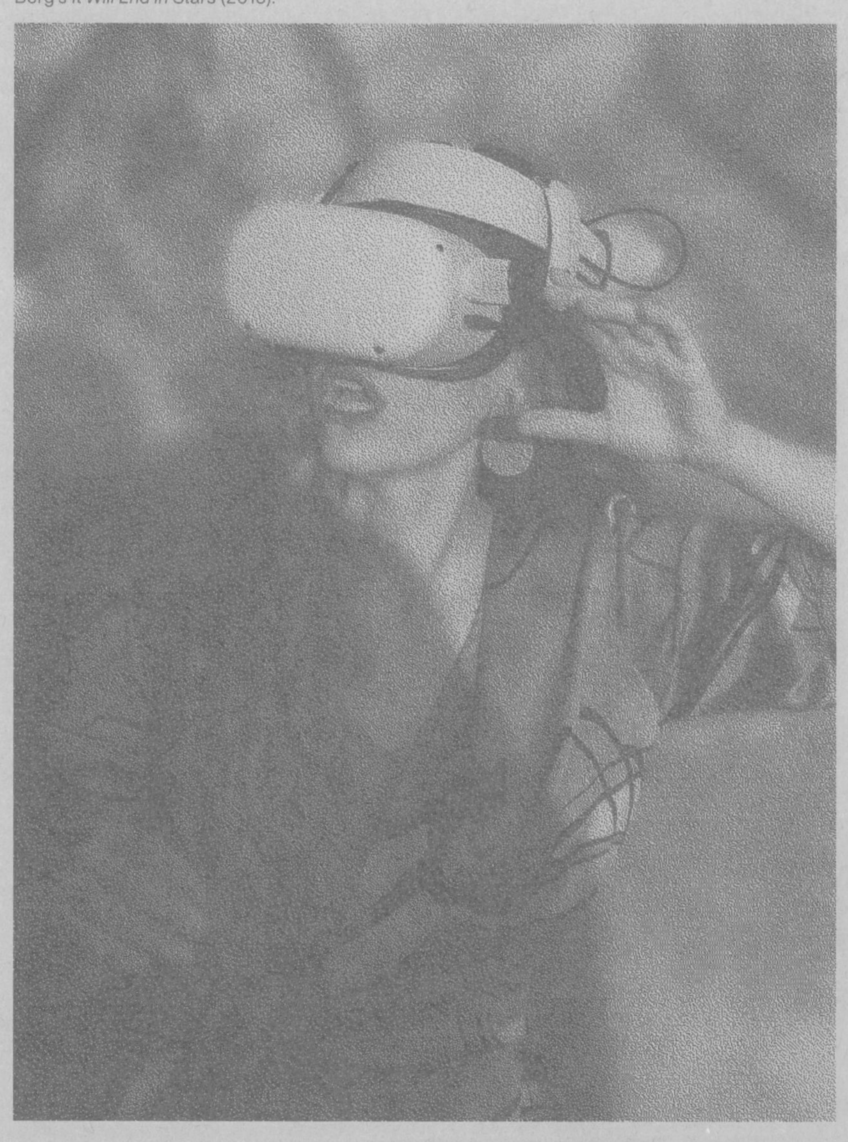

Visitor to *Dream Machines* shown wearing
the VR headset for Nathalie Djurber and Hans
Berg's *It Will End in Stars* (2018).

Acknowledgments

First and foremost, we would like to thank Dakis Joannou, the creative mind at the center of DESTE.

This book would not have been possible without Jake Brodsky, Michelle Kuo, and Ben Livne Weitzman, whose contributions shed new light on the role artists play in our technological landscape. We are grateful to Karen Marta, as well as to Javas Lehn, Joseph Margulies, and Scott Massey, for their enthusiastic rendering of this exhibition into book form.

We are indebted to all the artists who contributed work to this exhibition. In addition, our gratitude to the galleries, institutions, and lenders who generously collaborated on this project: Irene Due at Acute Art; Davide Legittimo at Andromeda Film AG; Patricia Dangel and Nike Dreyer at Atelier Rist GmbH; Anthony Atlas at CPLY Archives/William N. Copley Estate; Nadine Lockyer and Susan McGuire at Everything LTD; Uwe Lewitzky at Galerie Eva Presenhuber; Line Ebert, Friederike Gratz, Jakub Kostyszyn, and Christopher Müller at Galerie Buchholz; Matthew Flaherty, Andy Rosenwald, Erik Savercool, and Sarah Willis at Gladstone Gallery; Milena Bürge, Sophie Nurse, and Madeline Warren at Hauser & Wirth; Karolina Dankow and Marina Olsen at Karma International; Davide Pirovano, Chiara Repetto, Anna Tacchella, and Astrid Welter at Kaufmann Repetto; Henri Gisler at Mai 36 Galerie; Marco De Scalzi at Marco De Scalzi Photo; Stephanie Dorsey and Erica Gibble at Matthew Marks Gallery; Felix von Lüttichau at neugerriemschneider; Anaïs Chaudier and Florent Paumelle at Oniris.art; Kat Parker and Daniel Polonsky at Petzel Gallery; Ingrid Litzinger at the Prinzhorn Collection, Heidelberg University Hospital; Natalia Almada at Rottenberg Studios; Sadie Coles and Heather Ward at Sadie Coles HQ, London; Adél Erdei-Melis, Hannes Schroeder-Finckh, and Anja Trudel at Sprüth Magers; Susan Behrends Valenzuela, Melissa Celona, Junni Chen, Danielle Lindenbaum, and Pia Sofyanti at Tina Kim Gallery; Lukas Grundtner, Markus Kormann, and Thaddeus Ropac at Thaddeus Ropac Gallery; James Brett at the Museum+Gallery of Everything; and Alexandros Antonopoulos at the Takis Foundation–Research Center for the Art & the Sciences.

We extend our thanks to the DESTE team, Regina Alivisatos, Natasha Polymeropoulos, Kleio Silvestrou, and Eugenia Stamatopoulou, for their tireless hard work overseeing the exhibition and bringing the many moving parts together, as well as the KMEC Books team, Todd Bradway, Miles Champion, and Sophia Hoss, for their work in making the book a reality. We would also like to thank Rodrigo Marques, Acute Art's CTO, for making available the geolocated AR work by Lee Bul. The exhibition would not have been realized without the installation work of Move Art S.A., BLINC Technology, and Intergration & Installation, as well as the audiovisual talents of Antonis Gatzougiannis and our invigilators Ioulia Davari and Stefania Diamantopoulou, photographers Pinelopi Gerasimou, Giorgos Sfakianakis, and George Skordaras, and videographer Efthimis Theodossis.

—Daniel Birnbaum and Massimiliano Gioni

Credits

Captions

Dream Machines

Published on the occasion of the
exhibition *Dream Machines*,
curated by Daniel Birnbaum
and Massimiliano Gioni at
DESTE Foundation Project Space,
Slaughterhouse, Hydra,
June 20–October 30, 2023

Editor: Karen Marta
Design: Javas Lehn Studio,
(Javas Lehn, Joseph Margulies,
and Scott Massey)
Project coordinator: Regina Alivisatos
Managing editor and production:
Todd Bradway
Assistant editor: Sophia Hoss
Copy editor: Miles Champion

Published by:
DESTE Foundation for
Contemporary Art
11 Filellinon & Em. Pappa St.
Nea Ionia 142 34
Athens, Greece
www.deste.gr

Front cover: Andro Wekua,
Untitled, 2014

Back cover: Marcel Duchamp,
cover for *S.M.S.*, no. 2, April 1968

Printed on Printed on
Clairefontaine Trophee Roos 160 g/m²,
Magno Gloss 150 g/m², Magno
Matt 150 g/m², and Munken Lynx 150 g/m²

Typeset in JJannon, Monument Grotesk,
Monument Grotesk Mono, and DMT

Distributed in the Americas by:
ARTBOOK | D.A.P.
75 Broad Street, Suite 630
New York, NY 10004
Artbook.com

Printed and bound by
die Keure, Belgium

ISBN: 978-618-5039-41-7